Innovations in Learning
New Environments for Education

Innovations in Learning
New Environments for Education

Edited by

Leona Schauble
University of Wisconsin—Madison

Robert Glaser
University of Pittsburgh

LEA LAWRENCE ERLBAUM ASSOCIATES, PUBLISHERS
1996 Mahwah, New Jersey

Lawrence Erlbaum Associates, Inc., Publishers
10 Industrial Avenue
Mahwah, New Jersey 07430

Cover design by Gail Silverman

Library of Congress Cataloging-in-Publication Data

Innovations in learning : new environments for education /
edited by Leona Schauble and Robert Glaser.
      p. cm.
   Includes bibliographical references and index.
   ISBN 0-8058-2069-8 (alk. paper). — ISBN 0-8058-
2070-1 (pbk : alk. paper)
    1. Instructional systems—Design. 2. Learning, Psychol-
ogy of. 3. Cognitive learning theory. 4. Classroom environment. 5. Non-formal education. 6. Educational
change. I. Schauble, Leona II. Glaser, Robert.
   LB1028.38.I55 1996
   371.3—dc20
                                  95-49701
                                  CIP

Books published by Lawrence Erlbaum Associates are printed
on acid-free paper, and their bindings are chosen for strength
and durability.

Printed in the United States of America
10   9   8   7   6   5   4   3   2   1

CONTENTS

FOREWORD

The present generation of students in the United States can expect to live their adult lives in a very different world from that of previous generations—a rapidly changing and increasingly technology-based world. As citizens and parents, they will be asked to make decisions about complex social and political issues. As workers, they will participate in a global economy in which high-wage jobs will be high-skill jobs that demand complex thinking and reasoning. As a nation, our country's place in the global economy will depend on its citizens' abilities to meet such challenges.

These changes in society and technology, in turn, pose unprecedented challenges for our schools. Although American schools have always offered students a broad choice of courses, including some that make extensive thinking and reasoning demands and others that are less demanding, today it has become critically important that all students learn academically demanding content and skills. This is the challenge at the heart of an education reform movement that has been gaining momentum in this country for the past 20 years.

Recent studies have assessed students' understanding of various topics addressed in the school curriculum with the goal of exploring the impact of instruction on understanding. The findings indicate that most American students emerge from instruction possessing only a fragile understanding of the material. In science, for example, although students can repeat various scientific principles they have been taught, they have difficulty using them outside the classroom to explain everyday scientific phenomena. Similarly, in mathematics, students learn to solve problems by plugging numbers into formulas. When confronted with slightly more difficult versions of these same problems, they often perform poorly. In short, even though our students do acquire sufficient information from classroom instruction to pass school tests, most of them fail to achieve a deep enough level of understanding of the topics studied to result in useable knowledge.

This volume represents one response to the continuing national search for ways of enhancing student learning within both the classroom and society. The chapters in this book were first presented at a conference convened by the U.S. Department of Education's National Research Center on Student Learning at the Learning Research and Development Center, University of Pittsburgh. The conference was organized with advice, encouragement, and support from the Department of Education under grant R117G10003. Planning for the conference involved a wide search for examples of instructional programs that aim to enhance student proficiency in understanding, reasoning, and problem solving.

The chapters that follow introduce the reader to a variety of such programs. They were selected for inclusion in this volume because they represent promising approaches that offer evidence of success. Such programs are presently being used in both school and nonschool settings at various locations throughout the country. Many of them are still in a formative stage, with their developers continuing to work both on further improvements to the underlying approach and on efforts to extend their usage to additional sites.

The volume presents such programs, identifies their key features, explores the mechanisms underlying their operation, and delineates barriers and facilitators to their adoption by others. In the process, it provides many thoughtful perspectives on the nature and design of effective learning environments for elementary and secondary students. In addition to curricular innovations, this volume covers issues such as informal learning environments that occur outside traditional school settings, how teachers adapt to instructional innovations in the classroom and in their philosophies of teaching, and which aspects of school systems must change for lasting improvements to take hold.

As the editors of this volume note, such work reflects a promising new trend in the design of instruction—efforts by diverse interdisciplinary teams of practitioners, researchers, teacher educators, and community members to create fully developed examples of improved learning environments for students. Such complex design tasks pose an interrelated set of challenges that are both practical and theoretical in nature. These include the practical challenge of developing a full-scale model and the theoretical challenge of understanding how it achieves its outcomes.

Team members bring to this enterprise their own unique perspectives, knowledge, and expertise. As these diverse partners work together over time, they have begun to create a shared knowledge base that is vastly richer than the sum of the knowledge each one initially possessed. Collectively, the chapters in this volume document the development of this shared knowledge base. They help us grasp the nature of the advances in scientific understanding of learning, teaching, and the design of learning environments that have emerged to date; they also identify directions for future research arising from such work.

I look forward with great anticipation to the advances in practice and research that this volume promises.

—*Judith W. Segal*[1]
Office of Educational Research and Improvement
United States Department of Education

---

[1]The views expressed in this article are part of ongoing research and analysis at the Office of Educational Research and Improvement and do not necessarily reflect the position of the United States Department of Education.

PREFACE

Innovations in Learning: New Environments for Education documents the growth of a new kind of interdisciplinary teamwork that is evolving among practitioners, researchers, teacher educators, and community partners. The premise of this work is that the design of learning environments and the development of theory must proceed in a mutually supportive fashion. For their part, scientific researchers have learned that a prerequisite to studying the kinds of learning that matter is helping to shoulder the responsibility for ensuring that these forms of learning occur. In many instances, fruitful forms of learning evolve gradually over a long time, and only with sustained practice, teaching, and assistance. Therefore, to support and study learning, researchers are increasingly making major and long-term investment in the design and maintenance of contexts for learning. Practitioners are assuming new roles, as well, reflecting an increasing awareness of the need to move beyond skillful doing. If developing learning contexts are to be protected within and expanded beyond the systems that surround them, it is necessary to foster professional communities that will support reflection about practice, including the generation and evaluation of rich and flexible environments for student thinking. One consequence of recent reforms is that teachers are increasingly regarding such tasks as central to their professional development.

This volume describes coordinated interaction between educational design, on the one hand, and the development of learning theory, on the other, through a series of examples. These examples have been chosen because they are continuing, proven programs with evidence of success. Contributors to the volume are researchers and practitioners who have played a role in inventing these programs and have guided their development over a period of years. The chapter authors were participants in a conference to explore "The Contributions of Instructional Innovation to Understanding Learning," convened by the National Research Center on

Student Learning, at the Learning Research and Development Center, University of Pittsburgh, and sponsored by the Office of Educational Research and Improvement, U.S. Department of Education. Consistent with the theme of the conference, rather than choosing illustrations of a pipeline or "application model of research" from research and then to practice, we have selected interventions in which researchers and practitioners work together persistently to forge common understanding. Thus, although psychologists often mention the desirability of "giving psychology away," our emphasis here is instead on working to retune what we—researchers and practitioners—know together. Such activity is necessarily interdisciplinary, often encompasses long spans of time, and is more akin to engineering in the field than to laboratory science. The common themes that emerge from this activity—for example, the role of tools, talk, and community—belong exclusively neither to theory nor to practice, but to their intersection in commitment to specific contexts of learning and continuing contributions to practice and underlying theory.

The volume is organized into three sections that reflect different levels and kinds of learning contexts. Each of these levels has been the focus of recent cognitive and reform applications to learning and schooling. They are: Education Outside the Classroom, which gives examples of effective learning in informal settings; Learning Inside the Classroom, which introduces innovative approaches to schooling at the classroom level; and Changing Environments for Education, which explains reforms that regard the entire school as the appropriate unit of change.

ACKNOWLEDGMENTS

There are many acknowledgments to be made in producing a work like this, and we would like to express our thanks to all who contributed to the success of the conference and to the production of this book. Leslie Salmon-Cox shouldered the responsibility for the conference arrangements. Elizabeth Rangel handled the technical editing of the volume. The content of the conference was enriched by discussant comments from Howard Gardner, Sam Gibbon, Edward Goldman, Jan Hawkins, Anthony Jackson, and Dennie Palmer Wolf, and the contributions of Diane DeFord.

—*Leona Schauble*
—*Robert Glaser*

Part I

EDUCATION OUTSIDE
THE CLASSROOM

Precisely because the constraints and goals of so-called "informal" learning contexts differ from those in schools, a study of these settings can shake up our assumptions about learners and learning in ways that can inspire new approaches in classrooms. Out-of-school learning environments, for example, provide opportunities to investigate the little-explored question of how children learn while pursuing goals of their own choosing.

It is evident that these out-of-school learning contexts are not simply derivative of school; instead, they have their own purposes, structure, and organizational integrity. For example, the museum environments described by Schauble, Banks Beane, Coates, Martin, and Sterling in chapter 1 and the community literacy center described by Flower in chapter 2 do not exist primarily as satellites to schools. The after-school program described by Pedraza and Ayala in chapter 4 is clearly conceptualized as a learning environment that is *value-added*, that is, something beyond what schooling provides. In many ways, these environments are not very school-like, perhaps making them more welcoming to children who do not regard themselves primarily as students. Importantly, all these contexts emphasize the centrality of joining a working, learning community of peers and supportive adults. In these contexts, children shoulder a great deal of responsibility for the design of their own learning environments to meet their purposes and goals.

Although these contexts clearly are *not* school, it is just as clear that they tend to emphasize and foster their connections with school. Perhaps the clearest case of such a connection is Family Math/Matemática Para La Familia in chapter 1. Programs intended to support children's continued participation in mathematics instruction, Family Math and Matemática Para La Familia explicitly link formal mathematics schooling to the legiti-

1

macy of families' everyday experiences and intuitive knowledge. In these programs, children from diverse ethnic and socioeconomic backgrounds, their parents, and their teachers work together to become more confident and competent learners of mathematics. Similarly, the cross-age tutoring project described in chapter 3 brings university student-athletes, who themselves need help with reading and writing, into a tutoring program for early elementary school children who are having difficulties learning to read. This project, like those discussed in chapter 1, builds school skills on familiar, informal knowledge.

These projects also emphasize a third idea that cuts across the chapters, the importance of interpersonal relationships. The trust and identity that form between the student-athletes and the elementary school children seem essential in the effectiveness of the cross-age tutoring program. In chapter 1, the modeling and consistent values between family, community, and school are central in delivering the message that mathematics is approachable, useful, and fun. The museum environments described in chapter 1 are not just places; they are contexts where caring, competent adults work together with children on projects that matter to both. The after-school leaders described in that chapter are not mere providers of custodial care; they are adults working seriously on the challenge of providing educational enrichment and valuable activity during hours that otherwise might not be used in productive ways.

These relationships are perceived as having personal value, and equally important, as vehicles for enacting personal responsibility between the individual and the community. In Flower's literacy project, teenagers share responsibility for helping their peers communicate by providing clear and critical feedback. Flower and her team of university researchers engaged teenagers in a project in which the teens wrote about issues of special concern to them, such as family conflicts and drugs at school. While drafts of the writing were being prepared, pairs of teenagers worked together to engage in a process of rival hypothesis thinking to anticipate how their peers would react to the writing. An effective "rivaler" helped his or her partner by posing questions such as, "What's your point?" "How do you think your reader will react to this?" "How are you going to deal with that 'rival' idea in your text?" Thus, rather than relying on teachers or other adults, these youngsters were helping each other take responsibility for their own learning. Similarly the science and mathematics projects engaged by the "Young Scientists" in chapter 4 are not disembodied school-skills activities, but projects in which young people assume responsibility for planning and improving their local neighborhood and community. For example, while helping to plan the construction of a city park, students measured, mapped, and marked the land for construction workers to plant flower beds. The children relied on mathematics to do this work, but it was civic and community pride that motivated them to "own" the park project.

Cumulatively, such experiences provide important opportunities for youth. They provide sources of personal and educational support that are widespread throughout communities but too seldom accounted for. In a time when resources for youth are so quickly dwindling, we as a society can hardly afford to overlook them.

Chapter 1

OUTSIDE THE CLASSROOM WALLS: LEARNING IN INFORMAL ENVIRONMENTS

Leona Schauble
University of Wisconsin-Madison

DeAnna Banks Beane
Association of Science-Technology Centers

Grace Davila Coates
EQUALS Project, Lawrence Hall of Science

Laura M. W. Martin
Arizona Museum of Science and Technology

Peter V. Sterling
The Children's Museum of Indianapolis

When we think of learning contexts, we think primarily of families and other environments where adults are present, such as schools. When children are young, their parents take the major role in supporting learning, helping children learn about language, morality, social conventions, attributes and functions of common objects, and other basic information and skills. Consistent with this view of learning in early childhood, much of developmental psychology's research agenda has been concerned with charting and explaining how learning occurs in family contexts. In contrast, once children attain school age, it is usually assumed that schools will take on the major responsibility for guiding learning. Thus, although most would acknowledge that parents and siblings continue to play an important role, studies of children's learning beyond the preschool years focus primarily on learning in school settings or in school-like domains and tasks, such as mathematics, science, or reading. Yet an important "third leg" in the triangle of human development, along with family and school (Comer, 1992), remains largely

ignored and "vastly understudied" (Carnegie Council on Adolescent Development, 1992)—the host of out-of-school institutions and programs that
provide opportunity and support for young people's learning.

Indeed, researchers have begun to turn their attention to out-of-school
learning, especially in apprenticeship situations, learning of traditional
practices and crafts, and workplace environments (e.g., Chaiklin & Lave,
1993; Resnick, 1987; Saxe, 1988; Schliemann & Acioly, 1989). However,
comparatively little analysis has been devoted to the learning that occurs in
the wide range of informal learning environments and programs at the
neighborhood and community level that exist to support children's learning
and development (although for exceptions, see Gelman, Massey, &
McManus, 1991; Heath, 1991; Heath & McLaughlin, 1993; Nicholson,
Weiss, & Campbell, 1994). Youth-serving institutions and programs are
significant because they provide a web of community-based learning resources, including the guidance and companionship of adults and peers,
avenues for learning and practicing new skills, encouragement to pursue
goals and interests that are personally meaningful, and opportunities for
work and community service.

The level of knowledge and skills that children must master for successful
initiation into adult society continues to rise, yet recent changes in the role
and structure of families and schools mean that these institutions may no
longer be able on their own to provide the levels of support necessary to
help children meet the increasing needs (Carnegie Council on Adolescent
Development, 1992). It is thus more important than ever for children to
have available an array of educative contexts that can supply overlapping
and reinforcing opportunities for learning, practicing, and applying skills and
knowledge in supportive and positive surrounds. Yet, the potential of
youth-serving institutions and programs is often overlooked, perhaps because each kind of program serves a different niche, so none of them
command the universal enrollment that schools do. Youth-serving programs
differ widely in organization, intended audience, and function, varying from
national organizations such as Boy Scouts and Girl Scouts to local grassroots
organizations; from 4-H clubs and hobbyist societies to local sports leagues;
from religious organizations to theatre groups; and from club-like activities
organized around specific subject-matters to libraries and museums.

A premise of this chapter is that careful analysis of such out-of-school
contexts can both challenge and expand our notion of what is at stake in
children's learning. Moreover, such an analysis can also inspire reexamina-
tion of our assumptions about the necessary forms and constraints of school
learning by reminding us that typical classrooms are not the only effective
ways of organizing children and adults for the task of learning. In some

instances, out-of-school learning contexts are designed specifically to sideskirt the constraints and connotations of formal, school-based education—for example, to engage children who do not have a strong identity of themselves as learners or to entice children to exploring subject-matter, like science or mathematics, that youngsters often find unappealing in school instruction.

In the remainder of this chapter, we sketch some of the important dimensions of difference between out-of-school and in-school learning. Next, we briefly describe three examples of effective informal learning programs—projects chosen primarily because they are ones in which the authors of this chapter have been directly involved. Finally, we review the implications of these learning contexts for cognitive research and formal education.

LEARNING WITH A DIFFERENCE

Here, we take a closer look at informal learning in contrast to classroom learning. What assumptions about learning underlie out-of-school learning contexts, and how do they differ from assumptions about learning in school? How do these ways of regarding learning both complement and challenge what goes on in classrooms?

First, the goals or purposes of most informal learning contexts tend to be broader than those emphasized in traditional schooling. Strange as it may seem, informal education projects may not regard learning as their first priority. Similarly, they do not by-and-large aim exclusively for improvement on classroom-oriented measures, but instead tend to emphasize wider goals better captured by terms like enculturation, development, attitude, and socialization. The goal of helping young people develop self-identities that are consistent with desired values is often central in informal learning (e.g., Fine, 1988), for example, enhancing the young person's sense of self as contributor to community life, self as valued member of a working team, self as effective learner. Although the development of identity is considered important in school as well, it rarely takes center stage in the planning of administrators or teachers. Such objectives are not usually addressed directly in the curriculum and the success of teachers and classrooms is not evaluated with respect to these broader goals.

In many out-of-school settings, learning is explicitly tied to other agendas. For example, social interaction among peers or among adults and children is often regarded as an important value. Productive organizations for youth offer the "group cohesiveness necessary to frame and sustain social identity in terms of group norms, values, and goals" (McLaughlin & Heath, 1993, p. 220). Moreover, participation in out-of-school programs is usually voluntary, so engagement, fun, or entertainment are often of specific concern in the design of these contexts—whether a child enjoys the experience is likely to determine whether or not participation continues (Mielke & Miller, 1995). The context must first and foremost be engaging, and it is assumed that affective and cognitive learning are intertwined (Leichter, 1979). In many informal learning programs, social interaction, entertainment, or attitudinal agendas may be regarded as primary; learning is regarded as following from these more primary outcomes. In contrast, schools more often take the opposite perspective, treating learning as the primary concern and often regarding motivation as an individual difference or as a secondary concern.

The boundaries between informal learning contexts and the rest of daily life seem more permeable than they are in schools. These boundaries are fluidly crossed by parents, other adults in the community, and children of different ages. As we show later in the example about museums, adult experts—weather forecasters, veterinarians, attorneys, video producers, flamenco dancers—bring their expertise into the museum and work hand-in-hand with children to collect data about the atmosphere, learn about bats, explore the implications of changing laws concerning search of citizens, film claymation movies, and develop choreography for dance performances. In the Family Math Project, a mathematics equity program that we describe later, parents and children work together on mathematics problems that are related to the everyday life of the family. In after-school settings, family needs for quality child care intersect with providers' opportunities to offer activities that enrich children's understanding of school subject matter and skills. Rather than being segregated into same-age peer groups, as they are in schools, children in out-of-school contexts typically accomplish their learning in groups of mixed age, who have different expertise and knowledge about the activity at hand.

Out-of-school learning is much more supportive than schools typically are of individual differences in interests and talents. Because so many informal learning contexts focus on encouraging children's personal interests, it is taken for granted that the path of learning in these contexts will vary substantially from individual to individual. This view stands in contrast to the expectation that in school, every child should master a uniform curriculum. Informal learning also exemplifies a related view of teaching: Instead of relying on a teacher whom children are encouraged to regard as all-knowing, out-of-school contexts more often put learners into contact with an array of teachers, each with knowledge of a particular kind of domain or skill. The implicit message is that nobody knows everything, and different kinds and levels of contributions from different participants are the norm. The emphasis is not on being told the answers by somebody who already knows them, but on finding out together how to get the job done. Accordingly, locating the right information and resources—learning how to learn—is an important part of the game.

Activities in out-of-school contexts are often, although not always, organized around generating a product or a performance rather than acquiring an organized body of subject matter. In general, the emphasis is on what you do, rather than on deriving knowledge and skills. Rather than mastering content knowledge for some unspecified reason that will presumably coalesce in the future, children who participate in informal learning environments are often learning to make progress toward a meaningful goal—for example, to be able to explain a museum exhibit to a younger child. Strong orientation toward achieving recognizable goals has been identified as a crucial element in successful youth organizations (Fine & Mechling, 1993). Evaluation is targeted toward the product or performance and is used to guide the ongoing activity, rather than to rank individuals. Rather than a separate activity, evaluation is an integral component of participation and often takes the form of the development and application of consensually negotiated critical standards. The response of an audience may frequently be taken into account, but it is up to the participating group to decide how well things are going, not the test norms.

Although we have described the foregoing attributes as characteristic of out-of-school learning contexts, they could be applied effectively in school as well. In fact, several chapters in Part II of this volume describe in-school experimental programs that are incorporating some of these principles into classrooms. For example, the Cheche Konnen, QUASAR, and Schools for Thought Projects focus on social interaction, project- or performance-based learning, concern with motivation, explicit attention to students' personal identities of themselves as learners, and establishing closer ties to community and parents. Many classroom researchers have found it instructive to rethink the design of classrooms in light of what works in out-of-school learning environments. Because the constraints of these environments are somewhat different from those that operate in schools, informal learning contexts can serve as laboratories for testing innovative approaches to learning. Many of these approaches are difficult to implement in school settings because they challenge strong expectations held by parents and other citizens about the desirable forms and structures of schooling. Such expectations may be difficult to dislodge because they are based on adults' memories of their own experiences as students. Hence, existence proofs and exemplars that embody new principles of learning in an effective way can serve a valuable role in discussions about school restructuring (Nicholson et al., 1994). It is to such examples of promising informal learning contexts that we turn now.

EXEMPLARS:
INFORMAL LEARNING ENVIRONMENTS

In this section, we briefly describe three different informal learning contexts for children—museums, after-school settings, and family learning programs. We might have used other programs as examples—for instance, the projects described in Part I of this volume—Project ARGUE, the cross-age tutoring project at the University of Virginia, or the Young Scientists' Club. Here we describe informal learning programs that we know well from our own experience. In the final section of this chapter, we draw on these examples to discuss the research issues that emerge in informal learning.

Museums

When people come to a museum, they have an idea of a museum. That is, they have a concept of museum built on personal experience or reputation. This concept involves a set of expectations about who they are in relation to the building, the staff, the collections, and the exhibitions. These initial expectations may be reinforced or challenged when people come to a particular museum and encounter inviters or disinviters that signal whether this place is really there for them.

Perhaps no category of potential invitees has felt more alienated from the idea of museum than adolescents. Attendance at museums by teenagers is extremely low, except for school outings. Yet, museums can be the instrument of change for teens by providing opportunities for meaningful participation that are not available in schools and other institutions. Museums and museum staff, who over the past decades have accomplished a shift from regarding their role primarily as curatorial to one devoted to education and outreach, have access to an impressive array of material and personal resources that can support these opportunities.

For example, YouthALIVE! is an initiative of the DeWitt Wallace-Reader's Digest Fund, administered in partnership with the Association of Science-Technology Centers, to support more than 40 diverse science and children's museums across the U.S. in developing programs that involve young people in museum-based learning and service activities. The

YouthALIVE! initiative provides both financial and technical support to help participating museum staff become more thoughtful and knowledge-able about designing programs consistent with the developmental needs of adolescents. Participating museums make special efforts to identify and target underserved youth groups in their community. Staff receive training to work with adolescents, and community and youth advisors are involved in program planning and implementation. Each participating museum plans for the long-term involvement of a core group of adolescents, and over the longer term, for institutionalization of the programs, which vary from enrichment learning programs, such as science clubs and camps, to service learning programs, in which adolescents serve as volunteers or paid interns.

One notable program participating in the YouthALIVE! initiative is the Eli Lilly Center for Exploration at The Children's Museum of Indianapolis. The Center for Exploration is an example of a museum gallery organized around providing opportunities for adolescents to shape their own museum experience and designed to develop apprenticeship and mentoring relation-ships between youth and skilled adults. The Center was designed by teen-agers, and the activities that take place within it are inspired by conceptual themes selected by the participants. For example, one theme, about the environment, was titled "Waste Not, Want Not"; another was "What's Law Got to Do with Me?" The purpose of the center is to engage young people in examining issues critical to their lives, and to provide them places—dark-rooms, computer workshops, a theater stage, woodshops, video stu-dios—and people with whom to explore those issues. For example, during the environmental issues theme, one group choreographed a "Trash Dance," while another made public service videos for television about recycling. Yet another disassembled old computers and other electronic devices and made jewelry for sale from the components.

Within the Center is a Children's Express news bureau where each week more than 100 young people write and edit a page of *The Indianapolis Star*, Indianapolis' main newspaper, and submit their stories to other Children's Express sites. Four of the Children's Express staff went to Kuwait after the Gulf War to interview Kuwaiti and Palestinian youngsters about the war and its consequences on their lives. More than 25 of these youngsters attended the 1994 Democratic and Republican conventions.

In addition to such specialized programs and projects, young people in the Center also play a role in the museum at large. They conceive, plan, and install exhibits; design videos, training programs, collections management procedures, and programs to help visitors interpret museum exhibits; and build bridges into the surrounding community.

One key to retaining adolescents' interest and involvement in youth-based organizations is opportunities for employment (McLaughlin & Heath, 1993), such as paid internships or positions as "explainers." Because it provides an entry, a museum can bring the invisible adult world of work sharply into focus for teenagers, especially when they serve as part of a team responsible for goal setting, deadlines, rules of engagement, and the resolution of disagreements. In these roles, young people come to understand more about the importance of clear communication, tradeoffs, solid preparation, group decision making, budget compromises, and the reasons for attending to voices within the community.

More than 600 youngsters volunteer at The Children's Museum as interpreters in the galleries, as junior curators, on the Youth Advisor Council, and as program assessors. Each young person has a staff mentor responsible for training, job assignment, and career development. For many youngsters, these responsibilities are of major importance, and the long waiting list for available volunteer spots testifies to the fact that adolescents believe The Children's Museum is a place that invites them into meaningful experiences.

Making these experiences work requires changes in the traditional roles of museum staff, from researcher, exhibition designer, or program planner to collaborator, mentor, guide, and friend. Young people and adults can become fellow explorers on a path to discover what objects, science, history, the arts, and other cultures might reveal, with no textbooks and no simple answers. Yet these changes in roles require careful consideration and training. Many young people have had few positive relationships with adults. Their skills at negotiating the adult–youth world may be minimal, and they may even behave in ways that threaten and challenge adults. Yet it is worth working to overcome this tension, because interaction with peers and adults is one of the major assets that museums have to offer.

Museums need a firm, long-term commitment by trustees and staff to policies and practices that invite adolescents into the full life of the museum. Such a commitment runs counter to good business practice, because activities for adolescents are expensive, staff- intensive, and disruptive of "normal" museum operations. Moreover, the kinds of activities that work best with adolescents are often difficult to explain to visitors, potential donors, volunteers, or other important constituents.

In spite of these difficulties, museums have been enthusiastic about embracing what they perceive as their responsibility to become a vital part of the educative community. Much of the educational promise of museums resides in the resources and programs that they control and can marshal institutionally. Next, we turn to a very different kind of learning context, after-school programs. In contrast to museums, these sites tend to be relatively sparse in learning resources. We consider a program that brings educational resources and materials into after-school sites to help transform them into environments where learning can occur.

After-School Programs

As increasing proportions of parents enter the workforce, increasing numbers of children participate in some form of organized after-school care. There is no way to know for sure the numbers of children who attend after-school programs. States, school districts, national organizations, and community networks do not track how many programs are in place, and enrollment probably varies considerably from day to day. Yet one study estimated that 13 million children under the age of 12 have parents who work, that is, parents who cannot be home when children are not in school (cited in Rogan & Graves, 1989). More and more of these children are spending their afternoons in child care. A child who spends an average of 3 hours per day in after-school care may during the 6 years of elementary school spend more than 3,000 hours, or the equivalent of 3 school years, in an after-school program.

The Children's Television Workshop (CTW), a nonprofit company best known for developing educational television programs such as *Sesame Street*, has been investigating how educational video materials, activity guides and manuals, activity kits, and training for adult caregivers can enhance the educational potential of after-school programs. CTW's work with after-school program leaders and administrators indicates that these programs are shifting from an emphasis on mere custodial care toward a recognition that their mission should include education. In particular, leaders and administrators have begun to recognize that after-school programs have the potential to reach children who may be alienated in school environments, to develop human resources in communities, and to deal with issues that are difficult to cover in schools, such as sex education, self-esteem, and appreciation of diversity (Katz, 1990).

However, interviews with policymakers in the field suggest the wisdom of approaching these objectives with caution (Martin, 1990). In general, these experts fear that too much structure after school may have the potential to stifle creativity and to interfere with the social and emotional issues that children work out in social interaction and in pursuit of their own goals and projects. In particular, policymakers recommend avoiding the temptation to recreate a school-like environment during after-school hours. In spite of these constraints, after-school leaders express a great need for ideas and materials that would help them create positive learning experience for their charges. Because of concerns about heavy-handed education after school, however, the CTW staff concluded that before beginning their own development work for after-school programs, it would be useful to chart the educational opportunities and barriers in these after-school settings. Accordingly, a series of studies investigated the range of activities that typically occur in after-school programs and the preferences of adult leaders and children (Hezel Associates, 1992; Inverness Research Associates, 1991; Katz, 1990; KRC Research & Consulting, 1991).

Not surprisingly, the studies found wide variability in the kinds of activities that typically occur across the spectrum of child-care settings. However, the vast majority of programs provide opportunities that are primarily recreational, partly because youngsters come to the programs having just completed a full school day. Research findings about after-school care leaders' expectations for learning materials and activities are consistent with the general emphasis that informal learning programs place on engagement over education (Hezel Associates, 1992; Inverness Research Associates, 1991; Katz, 1990; KRC Research & Consulting, 1991).

For example, when leaders were asked for their preferred themes for new materials, they chose multicultural relations, health and safety, and conflict resolution rather than school-like topics such as geography or social studies. Both leaders and children rejected activities that have the potential to embarrass children by touching on sensitive topics (such as children's home lives) or by demanding public display of emerging skills that are still shaky. It is evident that these preferences are somewhat inconsistent with the objective of promoting learning in specific school curricular domains. Rather than dividing time by subject matter, after-school leaders tend to divide it by niche, such as sports, arts and crafts, and club time. In the predevelopment research, leaders reported doing very little with school subjects like mathematics or science.

Considering these factors, CTW developed three kits based on popular CTW programs, such as *3-2-1 Contact*, a program that focuses on 8 to 12-year-olds' appreciation of science; *Square One TV*, which targets children's understanding of mathematics and problem solving; and *Ghostwriter*, a program that supports literacy in 7- to 10-year-olds. Kits include videotapes organized around an educational theme, leader guides or tapes, games, hands-on activities, puzzles, and magazines. These materials are distributed on a low-cost or no-cost basis.

Interestingly, when mathematics or science activities could be regarded as games or crafts, the leaders were very willing to try them. They also readily used literacy activities, as long as they were embedded in collaborative, functional frameworks for reading, writing, listening, and speaking, rather than framed as literacy or language arts. Moreover, when they were introduced noncoercively, the CTW researchers saw children happily and readily engage in math games, simple problem solving, and science explorations.

Studies of how children and adults use the CTW after-school materials emphasize that to be successful, materials must be flexible. They need to be appropriate for children with a range of skills and of different ages, preferably without depending on adult guidance. They also need to be adaptable for the variable time slots that are available, typically ranging from 15 minutes to 1 hour. It is desirable to include activities for children in a variety of groupings and settings. For example, the *Square One* math kit provides large group games, small group activities, activities for individuals, puzzles, and hands-on explorations. The materials support multiple use, offering the opportunity for children to extend and deepen their mastery over time. For example, a carefully designed game includes varying levels of difficulty to make entry into the game easy and yet to lure more practiced children into increasingly challenging experiences.

In addition to informing the development of the CTW after-school kits, the studies of after-school projects also raised a number of more general questions concerning how best to support learning in informal environments. For example, it is somewhat ironic that after-school providers asked for activities designed to last from 10 to 30 minutes, given that school reformers are moving away from short time blocks like these so that students can become deeply involved in projects. The implication is that one challenge in after-school settings is to develop curricula that are modular, yet can be cumulative in their effects.

The studies also suggested that after-school settings afford a good opportunity to examine the role of the adult as coach because in these settings, adults adopt roles that are more coach-like than teacher-like. But what are good ways of helping adults become effective coaches? In general, after-school leaders have little or no specific training in domain content, and good coaching usually presumes a solid foundation of knowledge of the game. Thus, it may be desirable for program and materials developers to design activities in which adults can learn along with children, perhaps in adult–child dyad configurations. This possibility raises the question of how best to develop skills in math, science, and literacy at several levels simultaneously. After-school programs are good places for adults to model what it is to be an effective learner and to become effective collaborators with children.

Another challenge is to introduce new information into the after-school system without being school-like. Experts and leaders want help in finding relaxing activities for children after school; children, too, are resistant to school-like activities after school hours. However, relaxing does not mean lying on the couch, it means no serious adult judgment being passed on a child, no obligation to exert oneself in stressful ways, and activities motivated by challenge or curiosity rather than duty. And relaxing does not necessarily mean activities that elicit automatic as opposed to more effortful processing. With the math and science kits, there is clearly a lot of practice, strategizing, and planning that occurs, although children draw the line when things become too tough to think through. In after-school settings, video, television, and other mass media like magazines and records can help introduce information in interesting ways, because in our culture, they are associated with informal learning. As social objects, these media belong more to the voluntary information-intake domain—that is, home. Hence, activities in these formats are more easily tolerated in informal settings. The use of video in after-school programs seems to fill a need to motivate, illustrate, and inspire children's own explorations of the physical and social worlds.

It seems that in after-school programs, the best way of engaging children in learning is to rely on activities and media that are associated with fun, choice, and play, rather than with accountability, coercion, and work. A similar strategy is used in the final informal program that we describe, a program developed especially to address learning of school subject matter—specifically, mathematics. Here the emphasis is on showing how mathematics can be a commonsensical, socially conducted activity that is connected to everyday experience and the familiar worlds of work and family.

Family Learning Programs

Two programs at the Lawrence Hall of Science (University of California at Berkeley) coordinate the efforts of classroom teachers and families to foster mathematics learning of students from diverse ethnic and socioeconomic backgrounds, especially girls. Equals is a mathematics equity program designed to help classroom teachers retain underrepresented students in mathematics. A related program, the Family Math program (and its Spanish-language counterpart, Matemática Para la Familia), helps parents learn how to experience mathematics with their children in a positive and supportive manner. These programs have resulted in improved communication and relationships between children, parents, and instructors.

Although there are links between family involvement and student success, little systematic attention has been given to structural approaches to enhance family involvement in the education process. To address this need, Family Math was developed to help foster understanding, encouragement, and involvement in mathematical learning among parents and other family members. Family Math classes, which are usually taught by grade levels (K–2, 3–5, 6–8), focus on concepts covered throughout the kindergarten through eighth grade mathematics curriculum. An important ingredient of Family Math classes is a nonthreatening atmosphere. This tone is achieved by helping families understand that mathematics includes guessing and estimating, generating suppositions that may prove incorrect, breaking mindsets, and finding alternative solutions.

The program explains how and why content is mathematical, why certain concepts are taught at certain ages, and how concepts are interrelated. These explanations are important, because for many parents, mathematics did not look, sound, or feel like this. For example, before participating in the program, parents expected school mathematics to be a very difficult subject made up of drill, practice, and memorization (Sloane, 1990). A premise of the program is that parents' expectations and attitudes are likely to be shared by students, as well, and that changing students' attitudes toward mathematics is partly a matter of helping the community in general develop a view of mathematics that is more consistent with contemporary goals of mathematics teaching and learning.

In Family Math classes, leaders use a teaching style that parents can profitably adopt with their children as they work on reinforcement activities introduced by the program. This style includes providing experiences that guarantee early success, encouraging students to move at their own pace, and providing invitations to further exploration and understanding. For example, class members might be posed the problem of determining how many small candies there are in a 5-pound bag. Different approaches to this problem are possible and are encouraged. Some students may count the number of candies in a cup, then try to determine how many cups are required to make up larger volumes. Others may determine the number of candies in an ounce, then make inferences about the number of candies in a pound and then in 5 pounds. Invitations for further exploration might involve asking students to determine which of these alternative approaches will result in the greatest measurement variance and why. Students are encouraged to develop strategies for finding patterns, organizing or illustrating information, working with others, and systematically testing and eliminating possibilities. Manipulatives and models are included to help learners and to reinforce the expectations that students should have access to many avenues for learning.

The program also introduces links to careers and the future. Because many adults believe that you are not doing mathematics if you are not computing with numbers and algorithms, parents are reminded that models and concrete materials are used in work situations by most adults. To help make this point, professionals from the community are invited to bring their mathematical tools of the trade to share with the class. For example, a contractor might bring a blueprint and discuss issues of representation and scale, or a delivery person might discuss the mathematics in a customer order form that lists products by cases of different sizes. These discussions help to emphasize that one does not need to be a professional teacher or an expert in mathematics to do Family Math with others.

The purpose of Family Math is to influence how people view mathematics and to help parents help their children to do mathematics. Many of the activities require teamwork and communication between parents and children, generating new understanding not just about mathematics, but about each other as well. Parents recognize abilities and strengths in their children, and children see their parents as colearners and teachers.

Devaney's (1986) interviews with teachers who conducted Family Math courses revealed that parents taking the program are more likely to become advocates for their children by speaking up for change in the mathematics programs at their children's schools. Follow-up surveys (Kreinberg, 1989) found that 90% of parents attending Family Math courses reported regularly playing math games with their children at home. More than 80% talked with teachers about their children's math progress, and 75% said they were better able to help their children with mathematics homework.

Family Math programs have served 400,000 parents and children across the U.S., and the *Family Math* book has been translated into three languages. Over the longer term, the program works for effects that extend beyond local influences on individual students and parents. It is important for parents and students to feel confident about taking a more central role in helping to shape the programs that serve them. As mathematics instruction evolves, parents need to become more active participants in conversations about curriculum, content, and policy. One objective of Family Math is to help parents become interested in and prepared for these conversations.

Hence, among the informal learning contexts we describe in this chapter, Family Math occupies a unique position. Although it is the most closely tied to school, in that its ultimate goals are to enhance students' performance in school subject matter, it accomplishes these objectives by "deschooling" mathematics, that is, lending it some of the advantages of informal learning contexts. These advantages include emphasis on meaningful goals, social interaction across age groups, motivation, personal identity, and ties to community.

The learning contexts we have described—museums, after-school programs, and family learning classes—differ in mission, scope, and locale. They also differ with respect to their orientation toward schools and schooling. Although each of these programs has a clearly articulated stance about its role with respect to schooling, these roles vary considerably, from complement to enhancement to enrichment. Yet equally clearly, each of these programs differs from school in important ways. We discussed how these differences complement what happens in school, and Part II of this volume illustrates how many of these same ideas are now being implemented in school-based instruction. As we describe in the following section, these differences also have implications for the kind of research that is appropriate for studying children's learning in these contexts.

RESEARCH WITH A DIFFERENCE

It can be challenging to study learning in informal environments. In this section, we review both the challenges and some possible strategies for tackling them.

If the primary purpose of the research is assessment of learning outcomes, one concern is how to account for the considerable variability in what gets learned. As suggested earlier, in out-of-school learning contexts, individuals often choose their own path through a menu of resources and opportunities. For example, richness and choice are definitive of experiences in museum. After-school programs offer a variety of activities, some structured and some self-selected. The purpose of Family Math is to help parents become more capable and interested in helping children mathematize their own experience, whatever form that experience takes, suggesting that children's learning about mathematics can be as variable as their experiences. In all these programs, therefore, what gets learned and how much time is spent in learning is far more variable than in school settings; hence, researchers must struggle with the problem of deciding what kinds of learning to look for.

Second, informal educators are more likely to consider their programs to be catalysts of or supplements to learning, rather than having a direct effect on measurement outcomes like standardized achievement tests in science or mathematics (Mielke & Miller, 1995). Thus, standard evaluation procedures that target traditional educational outcomes may very well underestimate the value of informal learning. The broader agenda of informal learning, which often focuses on changes in values, attitudes, and motivation, is difficult to assess because values and attitudes change very slowly, are diffuse and difficult to measure, and are almost certainly contributed to and mediated by many experiences and influences in children's lives. Although it is acknowledged that it may be overly simplistic to expect straightforward cause–effect relations between informal learning experiences and broad outcomes such as values, attitudes, or literacy, there is as yet no consensus about what kinds of assumptions and models would be more appropriate. Learning effects may emerge only over the long term and in circumstances quite different from those where the learning originally occurred. For example, a child who serves as a junior curator in the Natural Science Gallery at the local science museum and becomes fascinated with insects may be developing the origins of a long-term interest that could eventually steer the individual toward later choices in schooling and career. Establishing this chain of influence for a particular individual would be a formidable research task, even though existing research suggests that in general, enduring interests can steer children toward different experiences, which in turn cumulate in different kinds of knowledge (Renninger, 1992).

One way of tackling these research challenges is deliberately to shift attention from studying outcomes of learning as if they were context-free and situation-free products to studying processes of learning in the contexts and situations where they take place. Matusov and Rogoff (1994), for example, suggested that instead of applying a factory metaphor, in which learning contexts are assumed to have value only for the learning that they manufacture, it might be more beneficial to acknowledge these contexts as important parts of children's day-to-day environments, places where valuable forms of interaction are supported and encouraged. Learning is conceived less as an outcome associated with individuals and more as an ongoing activity that occurs in social interaction. From this perspective, it is valuable to study people's changing roles in the learning settings where they are participants (Matusov & Rogoff, 1994). Such a perspective inspires research questions such as, what kinds of support do individuals require to participate flexibly and effectively? Is it possible to track the emergence over time of initiative and leadership within the group? What features of the learning context seem to encourage their appearance? How do participants come to take responsibility for evaluating and revising the ongoing practices within the community and for their own performance and learning (Heath, 1991)? How do children's personal identities change, and how do their conceptions of the learning process evolve? In summary, rather than narrowly focusing on what is acquired at the level of the specific content domain, research in informal learning needs to look broadly enough to account for the mixed agendas of the out-of-school programs, including the support for positive social interaction, the fostering of healthy attitudes and values, and the development of personal identities.

Research also needs to address how informal learning environments are nested within surrounding contexts, and how learning contexts reciprocally influence each other. For example, families play an especially important role in screening and interpreting the meaning of settings of all kinds, including those where learning occurs. Family Math is a good example of a program designed directly to target such interpretations; its objective is to help both parents and their children reinterpret the meaning of mathematics. Even though this agenda is less explicit in museums, there, too, parents help negotiate children's understanding of the materials and exhibits and play an important role in introducing their children to "the specific skills used in reading, interpreting, and learning from objects, visual materials, and print, and the broader skills needed in searching for, selecting from, and attending to museum displays and programs" (Leichter, Hensel, & Larsen, 1989, p. 27). Because there is typically a cyclical flow in which family members physically move from the home to the outside world at the beginning of the day and then back again at the close of the day, the family becomes a critical locale for the discussion and interpretation of experiences that take place elsewhere (Leichter et al., 1989).

How do families and other institutions mediate and interpret learning? One important mechanism is conversation. People in different contexts talk in different ways; for example, the role and form of talk between family participants is likely to be quite different from the functions and structure of talk that occur in schools. Because families share long histories, their conversation may seem terse and elliptical to an observer. Essential background meaning can be presupposed and hence need not be elaborated because conversations build on a foundation of common experiences that can be taken for granted by the participants to the conversation (Leichter et al., 1989). In contrast, detailed explanations and presentational talk may be more characteristic of schools. Minick (1993), for example, discussed how classroom teachers shape children's growing understanding of the distinction between what speakers intend or mean, and what their speech actually represents, a distinction important to school learning but not in everyday communication. Like families and schools, informal learning environments may also encourage forms of talk that have special meaning within the context and that may influence who feels a member of the in-group and who does not. Heath

(1991) traced the role of language in the learning of a Little League baseball team, suggesting that learning to be a baseball player is partly a matter of learning to talk baseball (an account similar to Lemke's 1990 claim that one central task for science students is to learn to "talk science").

In addition to talk, other tools and notations play a central role in learning contexts, whether in-school or out-of-school. Tools, construed broadly, run the gamut from the games and activity kits provided for after-school leaders, to the carpentry materials provided by The Center for Exploration, to the calculators and manipulatives used in the Family Math program. These tools both enable and constrain practices and hence play an important role in shaping learning contexts. Notations, a specialized form of tool, include museum labels, notations for recording choreography, newspaper type fonts, tables for keeping scores for games and activities, Dienes' Blocks, and Arabic numeral systems. Notations play an important role in promoting the fixation, composition, abstraction, and mobility of thought (Latour, 1990). The right notational system can make learning more likely, or in some instances, can even determine whether certain forms of learning are possible at all.[1]

In summary, understanding the nature of out-of-school learning will require research that focuses on the processes of learning that occur in informal learning settings. One potentially fruitful strategy for such research is to track how children enter these environments, become increasingly effective participants, and especially, learn how to learn in them. We have also suggested that it is useful to pay close attention to the mechanisms whereby families, museums, after-school centers, and other institutions mediate children's learning. This mediation often occurs between interacting spheres of influence, such as families, television, museums, neighborhood after-school programs, and schools. Especially important among these mechanisms are conversation, tools, and notations.

Children spend the great majority of their time outside the classroom, so the domain of informal education is vast, not only in the amount of time children potentially spend in it, but also in the variety of activities that it includes (Mielke & Miller, 1995). It is therefore essential to understand more about learning in these settings, not only because of their large, mostly uncharted influence on children, but also because such work may also provide seeds for understanding lifelong learning—conducted mainly outside formal school settings—that will continue to be increasingly important throughout adulthood.

---

[1]The insight that conversation, tools, and notation are central mechanisms for mediating learning is generally consistent with Vygotskian theory, but the discussion here was more directly influenced by Richard Lehrer's (Lehrer & Jacobsen, 1995) analyses of second-grade mathematics classrooms.

REFERENCES

Carnegie Council on Adolescent Development. (1992). *A matter of time: Risk and opportunity in the nonschool hours.* New York: The Carnegie Corporation of New York.

Chaiklin, S., & Lave, J. (Eds.). (1993). *Understanding practice: Perspectives on activity and context.* Cambridge, England: Cambridge University Press.

Comer, J. (1992). A growing crisis in youth development. In Carnegie Council on Adolescent Development, *A matter of time: Risk and opportunity in the nonschool hours* (pp. 18–19). New York: The Carnegie Corporation of New York.

Devaney, K. (1986). *Interviews with nine teachers* (Report of the EQUALS Project). Berkeley, CA: Lawrence Hall of Science.

Fine, G. A. (1988). Good children and dirty play. *Play and Culture, 1,* 43–56.

Fine, G. A., & Mechling, J. (1993). Child saving and children's cultures at century's end. In S. B. Heath & M. W. McLaughlin (Eds.), *Identity and inner-city youth: Beyond ethnicity and gender* (pp. 120–146). New York: Teachers College Press.

Gelman, R., Massey, C. M., & McManus, M. (1991). Characterizing supporting environments for cognitive development: Lessons from children in a museum. In L. B. Resnick, J. M. Levine, & S. D. Teasley (Eds.), *Perspectives on socially shared cognition* (pp. 226–256). Washington, DC: American Psychological Association.

Heath, S. B. (1991). "It's about winning!" The language of knowledge in baseball. In L. B. Resnick, J. M. Levine, & S. D. Teasley (Eds.), *Perspectives on socially shared cognition* (pp. 101–124). Washington, DC: American Psychological Association.

Heath, S. B., & McLaughlin, M. W. (Eds.). (1993). *Identity and inner-city youth: Beyond ethnicity and gender.* New York: Teachers College Press.

Hezel Associates. (1992). *Evaluation of the Ghostwriter leader activity guide.* New York: Children's Television Workshop.

Inverness Research Associates. (1991). *A study of CTW kits in after school settings.* New York: Children's Television Workshop.

Katz, B. M. (1990). *Report on phone interviews among after school program leaders.* New York: Children's Television Workshop.

KRC Research & Consulting. (1991). *Ghostwriter in-home test show study, Volumes I–III.* New York: Children's Television Workshop.

Kreinberg, N. (1989). The practice of equity. *Peabody Journal of Education, 66,* 127–146.

Latour, B. (1990). Drawing things together. In M. Lynch & S. Woolgar (Eds.), *Representation in scientific practice* (pp. 19–68). Cambridge, MA: MIT Press.

Lehrer, R., & Jacobson, C. (1995, April). *Classical and classroom views of the development of spatial thinking.* Paper presented at the annual meeting of the American Educational Research Association, San Francisco, CA.

Leichter, J. J. (1979). Families and communities as educators: Some concepts of relationship. In H. J. Leichter (Ed.), *Families and communities as educators* (pp. 3–94). New York: Teachers College Press.

Leichter, H. J., Hensel, K., & Larsen, E. (1989). Families and museums: Issues and perspectives. *Marriage and Family Review, 13,* 15–50.

Lemke, J. S. (1990). *Talking science: Language, learning, and values.* Norwood, NJ: Ablex.

Martin, L. M. W. (1990, April). *Administrators' and curriculum specialists' meeting.* New York: Children's Television Workshop.

Matusov, E., & Rogoff, B. (1994). *Evidence of development from people's participation in communities of learners.* Unpublished manuscript.

McLaughlin, M. W., & Heath, S. B. (1993). Casting the self: Frames for identity and dilemmas for policy. In S. B. Heath & M. W. McLaughlin (Eds.), *Identity and inner-city youth: Beyond ethnicity and gender* (pp. 210–239). New York: Teachers College Press.

Mielke, K. W., & Miller, J. D. (1995, February). *The influence of informal science education on the development of scientific and mathematical literacy.* Paper presented at the annual conference of the American Association for the Advancement of Science, Atlanta, GA.

Minick, N. (1993). Teacher's directives: The social construction of "literal meanings" and "real worlds" in classroom discourse. In S. Chaiklin & J. Lave (Eds.), *Understanding practice: Perspectives on activity and context* (pp. 343–373). Cambridge, England: Cambridge University Press.

Nicholson, J. N., Weiss, F. L., & Campbell, P. B. (1994). Evaluation in informal science education: Community-based programs. In V. Crane (Ed.), *Informal science learning: What the research says about television, science musems, and community-based projects* (pp. 61–106). Dedham, MA: Research Communications Ltd.

Renninger, K. A. (1992). Individual interest and development: Implications for theory and practice. In K. A. Renninger, S. Hidi, & A. Krapp (Eds.), *The role of interest in learning and development.* (pp. 361–395). Hillsdale, NJ: Lawrence Erlbaum Associates.

Resnick, L. B. (1987). Learning in school and out. *Educational Researcher, 16*(9), 13–20.

Rogan, B., & Graves, S. (1989). *Who's watching the kids?* (Report to the Alabama Department of Education). Birmingham, AL: University of Alabama.

Saxe, G. (1988). Candy selling and math learning. *Educational Researcher, 17*(6), 14–21.

Schliemann, A., & Acioly, N. (1989). Mathematic knowledge developed at work: The contribution of practice versus the contribution of schooling. *Cognition and Instruction, 6,* 185–221.

Sloane, K. W. (1990). *Families in Family Math* (Report to the National Science Foundation). Berkeley, CA: Lawrence Hall of Science.

Chapter 2

COLLABORATIVE PLANNING AND COMMUNITY LITERACY: A WINDOW ON THE LOGIC OF LEARNERS

Linda Flower
Carnegie Mellon University

You are an African American teenager at an inner-city high school where drugs are a fact of life; you pass the pushers on Federal Street every afternoon; someone in your family has a problem with drugs or alcohol. A brochure to help you, written by someone who has apparently not visited your neighborhood, suggests some snappy answers you could make if someone offers you drugs. One is, "I'd rather not. I'm too special." This brings howls of incredulous laughter from your group. Another is "No thanks, I'm all American. I'll stick to milk."

You are reading this drug-education brochure because you have joined a project called ARGUE at the Community Literacy Center, where you and other students have signed on to create a document *by teens, for teens* to talk to a friend about drugs. The first day you learn a strategy called rival hypothesis thinking and start to imagine alternative responses people could have to this brochure and to its "snappy answers" (your group feels that many of these snappy answers would make a person look foolish, if they did not get beaten up first for "having an attitude"). By the second day you are doing collaborative planning with a mentor from the university across town. The mentor encourages you, both in the group and alone, to think out your plan, explain your key points, and imagine how a reader would respond if you said that. You tell her you do not usually plan, you just sit down and write whatever occurs to you, but she is persistent. Moreover, every time ARGUE meets, on Tuesdays and Thursdays, the two of you and a tape recorder spend at least 10 minutes "rivaling" the other voices and positions in this discussion about drugs, which even means speaking for teens who use drugs. With the mentor as a supportive collaborative planning partner, and you as the expert on what a friend might think, you generate as many alternative responses and supporting reasons as you can to the sappy brochure, to the cynical young addict Benjy in an Alice Childress novel, to an ex-addict and to a cop you interview. Eventually you will even rival your own text, imagining ways your readers might disagree with or dismiss you. All the time your collaborative planning partner keeps asking you to think like a writer: "What's your point?" "How might your reader respond?" "How are you going to deal with that 'rival' idea in your text?"

OVERVIEW

This chapter is an account of students in the midst of an instructional experiment—learning to become planners and problem solvers, learning to do rival hypothesis thinking, and coming to see themselves as writers within a community/university context. It begins with a brief introduction to collaborative planning as a theory-based instructional practice and with a description of this unusual instructional program at Pittsburgh's inner-city Community Literacy Center (CLC). However, the focus of this chapter is neither on the practice nor on the program per se. Instead of looking at them, this chapter represents a look through them, at the logic of the learner, and in pursuit of a more contextually sensitive theory of how writers learn. What is interesting about these innovations is not only that they offer students an effective kind of literacy instruction, but that they offer a revealing window on cognition and on the strategic negotiations of the learner.

COLLABORATIVE PLANNING
AND COMMUNITY LITERACY:
BACKGROUND AND RATIONALE

How do you teach literate action? Traditional literacy instruction has focused on either cultural literacy, knowing the great books and ideas of the Western tradition, or on textual literacy, producing a text that meets certain standards for correctness, convention, or style (Brandt, 1990). Textual literacy may define itself in terms of the academic paradigm Olson (1977) called "autonomous text," or in terms of certain venerable modes or genres: argument or description, the essay, or research paper. However, traditional teaching of this sort has come under criticism for two kinds of myopia. One is its focus on individual performance to the exclusion of collaborative problem solving, and the other is its preoccupation with the manipulation of abstract, symbolic information, which ignores the application of contextualized, usable knowledge (Resnick, 1987). "Academic" training with its focus on textual literacy rather than socially embedded literate practice, the argument goes, is giving our students a limited preparation for the workplace or civic life (Erickson, 1988).

The long-standing alternative to such schooling has been apprenticeship which immerses the learner in a social practice and in productive collaborative action (Rogoff, 1990). However, traditional apprenticeship, associated with crafts and the production of goods, is a limited model for general education. Focused on the task rather than on the learner, it offers little direct instruction and does not encourage learners to generalize, question, or reflect. In response, the practice of cognitive apprenticeship has tried to create the best of both worlds by the explicit teaching of intellectual strategies within a social scaffold that models thinking and that supports and shapes the learner's efforts to join in the process (Collins, Brown, & Newman, 1989). Within the study of rhetoric and composition, cognitive rhetoric has argued for a similar change in literacy instruction that would shift from the school-based analysis of textual conventions to the cognitive and social practice of making texts, supported by explicit instruction in the problem-solving strategies a writer brings to a rhetorical situation (Flower, 1993). The educational challenge, then, is to go beyond teaching conventions to teaching literate actions. How do you help students to not merely control important literate practices, such as essay writing, but to embed those practices in literate action—in a planful, social, and cognitive process of using writing to do something?

The instructional practice described here, called *collaborative planning*, is an example of cognitive apprenticeship that takes its design from recent work in cognitive rhetoric. That is, it introduces students to problem-solving strategies for planning based on research that models expert/novice differences and argues for the power of reflective, strategic instruction (Bereiter & Scardamalia, 1987; Brown & Palincsar, 1989; Emig, 1971; Flower & Hayes, 1981; Flower et al., 1990; Hayes, Flower, Schriver, Stratman, & Carey, 1987). At the same time, it takes the strong social perspective of cognitive rhetoric, which envisions writing as a transaction among people, motivated by a rhetorical situation, in which textual conventions and literate practices themselves develop as a response to personal and social problems (Bazerman, 1988; Flower, 1988; Scribner & Cole, 1981; Young, 1978). The claim of collaborative planning is this: One of the best ways to teach literate action is to create a social scaffold for rhetorical thinking, to engage students as writers and planning partners in a process that models literate action, supports strategic cognition, and prompts reflection.

The CLC became a companion in this educational experiment and an innovation in its own right when this collaborative planning approach to literacy instruction was taken out of the classroom and into the context of intercultural collaboration and community problem solving. Students from inner-city high schools, who may not be "school comfortable", join CLC projects to write and publish newsletters on issues that affect their lives and work with community and university mentors who take on the role of collaborative planning partners. At the CLC, these writers learn literate problem-solving strategies, such as rival hypothesis thinking, that let teenagers join the larger community conversation on issues such as drugs, teen pregnancy, and school reform.

Collaborative Planning

If you begin with these goals for rhetorical problem solving in mind, the research on planning in writing suggests an immediate problem: first, students typically do not do it and second, when they do plan they are likely to depend on what Bereiter and Scardamalia (1987) called "knowledge-telling" or on the adult strategies of knowledge-driven or schema-driven planning. Inexperienced writers hang on to these familiar strategies even when the task calls for constructing a rhetorical plan adapted to a particular situation and for facing the conflicts that situation raises (Flower, Schriver, Carey, Haas, & Hayes, 1992). Moreover, this performance may not reflect a lack of effort. "Dorm room" protocols of writers-in-action have shown that student writers, who were struggling with planning problems and in need of in-process help, were unaware of even the options and strategies possessed by other students in their course (Flower et al., 1990).

Collaborative planning tries to change that picture. In a collaborative planning session, the writer as planner holds a loosely structured, collaborative discussion with his or her partner, who takes the role of a supporter and who works to help the writer develop a more elaborated rhetorical plan (for the writer's own paper), to imagine options, and to deal with conflicts.

Collaborative planning creates a social context that tries to lift literacy off the page. It attempts, for the duration of that collaborative session, to transform writing from a textual practice into a rhetorical practice: The writer becomes a rhetor (the Greek root translates to "I speak") and the spotlight shifts from text to cognition and social action. In these sessions, writing is identified with the personal experiences of thinking, feeling, arguing, intending, imagining, and solving problems. At the same time, writing becomes a social interaction, where the gritty immediacy of face-to-face collaboration also leads students to internal conversations with prior texts and remembered voices. In practice, collaborative planning depends on three distinctive features: authority, planning, and reflection.

1. Authority. Collaborative planning differs from peer review, coauthorship, and typical conferences, in that authority and the floor belong to the writer as planner. The writer is responsible for working out a plan. The partner plays a critical role in the process as a supporter, whose prompts and advice help the writer build a more sophisticated and expansive image of a rhetorical problem and its possibilities. Because feedback comes before the writer is committed to a text (which students are always loath to abandon), the process encourages exploration of genuine alternatives.

2. Planning. Collaborative planning builds a scaffold for constructing such a plan. The metaphor of the Planner's Blackboard (Fig. 2.1) represents some of rhetoric's traditional concerns with audience, purpose, and convention as mental blackboards on which writers are generating and posting ideas (cf. Hayes-Roth & Hayes-Roth, 1979). The blackboard's graphic metaphor helps students visualize the distinction we see in our research: inexperienced planners spend their time "posting information" only on the Topic Information Blackboard, whereas experienced writers are generating a more elaborated image of their text as a rhetorical action, posting information for themselves on purposes, audiences, and conventions. Moreover, as the arrows suggest, experienced writers also build links across these imaginary blackboards, envisioning, for example, alternative textual conventions one might use to support a key point or deal with a reader's imagined response.

With the blackboard in mind, supporters will interrupt a rambling discussion with, "Yes, but what's your point?" They ask hard-to-answer questions about "your purpose," and prompt writers to build subgoals by responding, "Yes, I see your intention, but how are you going to do that?" The Audience Blackboard asks students not only to consider the identity and expectations of an audience, a standard rhetorical move, but to simulate a reader's response at key points and plan in accord. Text Conventions prompt writers to consider not only the expectations a genre sets up, but to imagine textual conventions as a large repertoire of available options ("should I merely describe things or build an argument?") and alternative

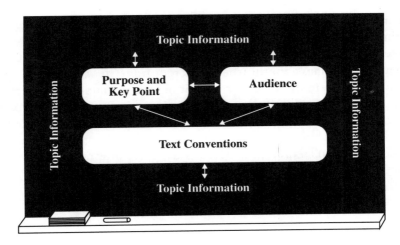

FIG. 2.1. The planner's blackboard: A prompt for collaborative planners
from Flower (1993). Reprinted with permission.

techniques, ranging from standard rhetorical patterns such as cause and effect, to
techniques for formatting and document design. Instead of following a convention,
students consider how they might use conventions to deal with the reader and meet
their own goals.

The Planner's Blackboard then, is both a metaphor for the enlarged problem a
writer needs to consider, and a prompt both partners can use to build a plan and
review their problem solving.

3. Reflection. Collaborative planning also builds a scaffold for reflection—it
helps make thinking visible. Collaboration makes the writer's intellectual and
interpersonal process more articulate and public. The Planner's Blackboard
prompts students to model a repertoire of strategies for each other. Because students
are often asked to tape their sessions, this record creates a basis for reflection on
their own strategic choices.

In theory, collaborative planning translates a social-cognitive theory of
writing into practice. The trouble with collaborative planning is that when
it actually works as a teacher hopes, it becomes a process the teacher cannot
quite predict and can no longer control. Instead of the dutiful, generic
procedure outlined earlier (e.g., setting goals, considering conventions), it
becomes a piece of highly situated cognition, embedded in a rhetorical
problem, constructing an adaptive response to a situation. Planning becomes a strategic act. Therefore, to evaluate this educational practice it
became critical to ask: How are students interpreting this practice; how
are they in fact using collaborative planning? Our formal studies tracing

this collaborative process with college students in freshmen and junior writing classes were encouraging: They profiled a level of student planning not seen when students were alone in the laboratory or dorm rooms. Issues of purpose, key point, and audience rose to prominence in students' thinking. Students were engaging in episodes of sustained reflection, a strong predictor of the quality of the session. They were willing to entertain substantive conflict, the amount of which predicted the quality of the text (Burnett, 1991; Higgins, Flower, & Petraglia, 1992). On the other hand, these studies also showed that merely collaborating—talking with a partner—would not achieve this outcome if students did not also grasp the goals of the process or set goals that required rhetorical planning (Flower, 1994; Wallace, 1991).

As these formal studies were going on, the Making Thinking Visible Project at Carnegie Mellon University (CMU) brought 20 Western Pennsylvania high school and college teachers into a collaborative demonstration project. Given the range of curricular goals in collaborative planning, we wanted to see if and how teachers could adapt the approach to widely differing needs. But the larger goal of the project was to use students' collaborative sessions as the basis for observation and reflection by both teachers and students, which was shared in discovery memos in monthly seminars. Over the 4 years of the Making Thinking Visible project, teachers (including the CMU staff) used collaborative planning not only to teach writing but to carry out individual classroom inquiry projects into the thinking of their own students (Flower, Wallace, Norris, & Burnett, 1994; Norris 1992).

The Community Literacy Center (CLC)

Probably the most unlikely member of this group of educators was Pittsburgh's 75-year-old Community House, a historical and social landmark within the multicultural, inner-city Northside community. The question its director, Dr. Wayne Peck, posed was, could this educational process, bred out of cognitive research, born in a university setting, and developed in school classrooms, make the transition to inner-city, out-of-school literate action? Peck's study on the uses of literacy in this community paved the way. He had demonstrated the value of rhetorically based teaching, and his portrait of community literacy showed how writing had worked as a collaborative enterprise in the neighborhood, not merely to create a text but to compose people for action (Peck, 1991). As the CLC developed, collaborative planning became a hallmark of its attempt to combine strategic thinking, reflection, and collaborative support.

The CLC was launched in 1989 as a community/university collaboration between the Community House and the Center for the Study of Writing and Literacy at Carnegie Mellon University. It argued for a new vision of literacy identified not just with reading, but with writing, where writing is identified with collaboration, problem solving, and power.[1] The CLC was also an experiment in putting research into practice—and to the test—with inner-city students for whom the current educational system often fails. At the CLC, students from inner-city high schools around the city sign on for projects that combine action and reflection on issues that affect their lives—from telling the teenager's side of teen pregnancy to investigating careers, school restructuring, suspension, and drugs. Teenagers, who may have had little success in high school English, find themselves addressed as writers working to produce the two goals of each project: a newsletter that is planned, written, and designed by these writers; and a public "community conversation" that may involve parents, teachers, community, the school board, the media, and the mayor.

This community/university collaboration took new shape when Carnegie Mellon University students enrolled in the Community Literacy Internship in order to make the journey across Pittsburgh as mentors for these teenage writers. The internship starts with an academic introduction to research issues in literacy, discourse, and cognition. College students then join a CLC project, as both the collaborative planning partner of a young writer and as themselves a newcomer to the robust, performative discourse of this intercultural community. When students return to the university, their transition from the familiar practices of academic literacy to those of a multivoiced community literacy becomes the basis for their own observation-based writing on literacy, discourse, mentoring, or education.

Collaborative planning has become the instructional trademark of the CLC. It announces to students that they have signed up to commit a public, literate act that calls on them to develop new problem-solving strategies (from audience analysis to "rivaling") for writing and thinking. It scaffolds this process through group collaboration and one-on-one mentoring, which, unlike traditional literacy tutoring, casts the student as planner/decision-maker and the college mentor as a supporter.

---

[1]Major support for the Community Literacy Center (CLC) has come from the Howard Heinz Endowment and Bingham Foundation. For information about the CLC itself, address correspondence to Dr. Wayne Peck, Executive Director, Community Literacy Center, 801 Union Avenue, Pittsburgh, PA 15212, or Dr. Linda Flower, English Department, Carnegie Mellon University, Pittsburgh, PA 15213.

A Window on Learning

Collaborative planning exemplifies the theme of this volume in several ways; it is an instructional innovation that can change performance, challenge assumptions, and adapt to new settings. Collaborative planning, our work suggests, has a visible effect on how students plan, providing a scaffold and a social occasion for rhetorical thinking and a reflection. As a strategy students control and a cognitive process they also observe, it lets students build more robust working theories of their own writing that challenge old assumptions. It is also an instructional innovation that has shown it can transfer to a variety of classrooms and can support observation-based classroom inquiry by both high school and college teachers. Likewise, the CLC shows how strategic instruction embedded in the goals of community literacy can lead at-risk students to a robust kind of learning, where they approach their writing with some of the expert strategies of rhetorical problem solvers.

This discussion, however, centers on what this instructional practice reveals about learning and how it helps uncover the logic of this constructive process from the learner's point of view.

In the ARGUE drug project sketched at the beginning of this chapter, students were asked to learn a new strategy called *rival hypothesis thinking*, in which writers try to consider multiple, rival viewpoints as they develop their own text. However, in the planning process observed at the CLC, students were not only constructing meaning in the sense of writing their text, they were also constructing their own *interpretations* of what it meant to learn a new strategy for rival hypothesis thinking. Moreover, this constructive process was the site of considerable *conflict*. The voices of the instructor, the partner, peers, and teachers past and present merged and collided with the explicit instruction and the unstated expectations of the assigned task. These voices, in turn, came in contact and conflict with another, often hidden representation—the writer's own goals, interests, and interpretation of all of these voices and expectations. In the midst of this dynamic process of not only writing but learning-to-write, what we observed was often a process of *negotiation*. The text these student writers constructed was a *negotiated meaning* in two senses of the word. First, this meaning represented a balance struck among the power relations of these multiple voices and their conflicting demands—negotiation as arbitration. At the same time, like a canoe negotiating white water, the process of making meaning was an attempt to find a best path among multiple options, constraints, and the valued but incompatible goals the student entertains—negotiation as path finding or navigation (Flower, 1994).

Rivaling at the CLC: A Study in Negotiation

To take the last step in this inquiry, looking through collaborative planning and community literacy at students' thinking, I examine a session with Javon, his mentor, and his friend Scott, discussing Javon's piece for the ARGUE newsletter the group had titled, *Let's Talk About Sex Drugs*. Javon's piece, called "Problems in the Family," tries to talk to other teens by dramatizing a dialogue between Javon and his cousin Donny, who he fears is starting to use drugs. In the study I am drawing from, called "Learning to 'Rival' in School and Out" (Flower, Long, Fleming, & Wojahn, 1993) we compare the way in which Javon and his friends appropriated "rivaling" with the parallel learning experience of students in two college classes that also received instruction in "rival hypothesis thinking."[2] This portrait of learning at the CLC documents a tension that arises when its energetic and explicit strategy teaching is embedded in a situation in which students, not instructors, exercise control over policy, criteria for success, and their texts. At the CLC, mentors work to be supporters rather than evaluators or coaches. On the borderline between "in" school and "out," this situation produced "hybrid texts"—an eclectic mix of literate practices drawn from academic writing, everyday talk, and community discourse. More important, this situation, poised on a border with expanded options and demands, forced student writers into the construction of actively negotiated meanings.

Problems in the Family

The performance we examine, (which includes the plans, the text, and the strategic moves Javon and his two partners make during a 15-minute collaboration) justifies examination for two reasons. First, the learner, Javon, is actively engaged in a decision and attempt to rival; his close friend, Scott, is not only energetically, persistently prompting Javon to do some additional rivaling at a key point in his text but is modeling a realistic option Javon could try. When that does not work, he draws Javon's attention to a checklist of questions the group had generated for being effective with teens. A few

---

[2]This study, conducted by Linda Flower, Elenore Long, David Fleming, and Patricia Wojahn is available as a technical report from the Mellon Literacy in Science Center at Carnegie Mellon University and will appear in Flower, Long, and Higgins (1996), *The Rival Hypothesis Stance: How Students Negotiate a Literate Practice*. Manuscript in preparation.

minutes later the mentor enters the discussion by posing a sort of reality check to Javon's text, modeling the response a skeptical reader might have, and encouraging Javon to acknowledge and answer this rival hypothesis in his text. In short, this is an instance of engaged cognitive apprenticeship: Learning is based on doing, in a process scaffolded by explicit strategy teaching, guided by written prompts and modeling on a real rhetorical task, where the coaching and strong social support from a mentor and a peer prompt the learner to monitor his own intentions while still leaving him in control of his text, making this a significant learning event.

The second reason for our interest stems not from what was being done to Javon, but from what he was doing at the center of this situation. In this episode he is constructing a negotiated meaning, that is, a meaning that arises out of a writer's attempt to balance a network of potentially conflicting goals, constraints, and opportunities. In this case, that network included at least the following elements:

- the rivaling strategy with its various moves and expectations;
- the check list Scott was holding;
- the prompts and modeling from his readers;
- and the social situation with its complicated dynamic for how to "look good" to both a buddy and an adult mentor (Javon and Scott had a well-established and sometimes disruptive pattern of "ripping" on each other).

In addition, the interaction shows the extent to which Javon's personal goals for the text and for finishing the piece, as well as his sense of textual conventions and options, are important voices in this event.

Learning here is more than being swept up in an instructional experience; it is an act of strategic negotiation by the learner. In the face of invitations and options, goals, fears and desires, pressures, and expectations on how to select and connect information, writers embrace, attend, give in, ignore, or resist the voices in this network; they integrate, synthesize, and innovate. Negotiation operates in both senses of the term as writers negotiate and navigate a problem space, seeking a path between Scylla and Charybdis that satisfies as many goals and constraints as possible. They also negotiate and arbitrate the power relations inherent in these multiple demands, choosing whose voices and whose goals dominate this constructive process. Negotiation, in the sense used here, does not refer to the result of tacit accommodations, but to a process of active problem solving in which pressures on meaning-making become the focus of conscious attention.

To model such a negotiation, the metaphor of voices is used to identify some of the expectations, assumptions, goals, constraints, and criteria that appear to have speaking parts in this performance (Flower, 1994). Some of these voices are audibly present: the mentors, friends, readers, the cop, nurse, and addict who visited, all suggesting ideas and modeling ways to think, talk, and respond. Other voices come from the learner's own network of prior knowledge, assumptions, and strategies. To track this process of negotiation—when these voices rise into consciousness and demand problem-solving attention—it is important to try to distinguish voices that could be speaking (e.g., what was taught, what exists somewhere in memory) from the voices that have actively entered the circle of negotiation. We will focus on eight of these shaping "voices": task representation, textual conventions, the draft text itself, assumptions about writing and revision, social pressure of readers, personal goals, perceived conflicts, and the larger discourse community. To identify these categories of negotiable forces, some inferences about Javon's awareness have obviously been made; nevertheless our intent is to illuminate his logic, rather than the educator's intentions.

First, consider some of the elements of this negotiation that a teacher or outside observer might note.

The Student's Representation of the Literate Strategy He Is Using and Learning (i.e., "Rivaling"). Students who are trying to learn a new literate strategy such as rivaling will bring their current interpretation of (and uncertainty about) that strategy to the task. In earlier sessions Javon had vacillated between seeing rivaling as a simple back-and-forth pattern of disagreement (e.g., "you say versus I say") or as a way to generate options and seek agreement (e.g., "I agree with that response, but would it be better to . . . ?"). Javon's shifting representation of what it means to rival shapes the kind of meaning he tries to construct.

Text Conventions. The conventions Javon controls will also shape what seems possible in this fictional conversation with Donny, a cousin experimenting with drugs. Looking at the text in Fig. 2.2, notice the various ways Javon has transformed an oral rivaling strategy into a textual strategy and a set of rhetorical and formatting conventions, built around a dialogue and narrative of clever confrontation.

Problems in the Family
by Javon _____

Drugs today are bad for young and old. They destroy speech and make it hard to play sports, physically and mentally.

I've had a cousin that did drugs. His name was Donny and he started off by watching his dad and friends do drugs. One day I was tired of watching him smoke CRACK and BLUNTS among others, so I walked over and confronted him, I said, Donny today this world is bad and the drugs are much badder, the drugs can seriously mess you up, they make you drop out of school to smoke 'em or either sell 'em. They make you say bad things and make your mother and others sad.

Donny: Drugs can't hurt me. I don't do them all the time and it makes me feel better when I have had a hard day.

Javon: Well, drugs can kill you, you can't get a steady girl friend or have a steady job doing drugs.

Donny: My father does drugs all the time and it hasn't killed him yet, so it won't kill me. The only thing my father has ever done is sell some things in the house and I am not about to do that.

Javon: Well, you will, you just wait and see, I'm not just going to go away that easily. You're going to stop with drugs little by little.

{Inside my mind: I knew he was going to try and shut me out so I tried as hard as I could to try and convince him he was doing wrong, because I knew his mother was behind the curtain on this—she didn't know that he was doing drugs. I thought it up and decided to slip a couple of sentences to his mother and try to get his bad friends away from him and keep him closer to me.}

FIG. 2.2 From: "Problems in the Family" by Javon _____. *Let's Talk About ~~Sex~~ Drugs. A Newspaper for Teens by Teens,* Vol. 1, June 1992. Pittsburgh, PA: Community Literacy Center.

One of the most interesting conventions here is Javon's own invention. As he tried to turn this pattern of back-and-forth rivaling into text, Javon hit on a technique of using the tag line "Inside my mind," a carriage return, and curly brackets to weave his own *private* response into the dialogue. This technique packed in more rivals without disrupting the narrative and allowed Javon, as the writer, to comment on events and Javon, as the character, to anticipate Donny's probable response. However, unlike an essay or exposition on rival positions, the conventions of dialogue tended to create a back-and-forth cycle of comment and response that, as we see, was hard to exit from.

The Draft Text.   A completed draft is always a powerful voice in students' negotiations. As this session begins, Javon is surprised he has already written so much. He has already expanded an earlier draft in response to prompts to use medical information and reasons gleaned from the emergency care nurse. From his point of view as a writer, this text has an ending and appears to be done.

Assumptions About Writing and Revision.   As the literature has amply documented, most students do not revise their writing because they do not see revision as a normal part of the writing process, but they do associate it with criticism and painful correction of errors (Hayes et al., 1987; Sommers, 1980; Wallace & Hayes, 1991). Javon's reluctance to revise at a previous session suggests he was coming to this session with a similar representation. The mentors, on the other hand, had planned this scheduled review session because they valued global revision and assumed that *reseeing* and possibly revising a text at its structured level was normal and necessary. These different expectations probably color how both parties hear Scott's suggestions.

Social Pressure of Readers.   Collaborative planning and rivaling both try to give palpable presence to the reader as a mind to be imagined and a position to which one must respond. In addition, Javon is facing two assertive partners, who not only claim to stand in for skeptical readers, but who agree on their dissatisfaction with the ending. As predicted in the preceeding excerpt, Javon (the character) talks with Mrs. Black. He then returns to "drop a little medical history" on his cousin and reveal to Donny that his working mother really does care about him and his use of drugs. After nearly 20 exchanges between Javon, Donny, and Mrs. Black, the text concludes:

> Donny: Well, I'll go talk to my Mom about it and we'll try to work something out. How would you like to come?

> Javon: That would be good.

> Mrs. Black: I'm sorry that I wasn't there for you at times when you were in trouble, but now I'll try to be a helpful parent instead of a working parent all the time.

In the negotiation over this conclusion, Scott initiates the discussion. He sees a problem with this sudden ending and wants Javon to acknowledge a rival that might be in the mind of the reader. Scott becomes increasingly enthusiastic about his idea, acting out in tone and body language how a skeptical Donny (and, by implication, a reader) might respond to Mrs. Black by replying, "She's just saying that":

Scott: There might another route. Like with his mom. He [Donny] might go to you and say, "Well, my mom's just saying that 'cause you're there. She's just sayin' that . . . She really doesn't mean that." Would that be one [a possible rival]?

Mentor: Sounds like one to me.

Scott: Yeah. Like, "She just saying that. Tonight, she'll come home. . ." Or, no. . . "The next day she'll come home and she won't come home 'til about 10 o'clock and I'll be outside smokin' a little roach."

Javon: That's a whole different story.

Scott is remarkably persistent with this idea, although his voice and level of affect drop whenever he makes a direct suggestion to his friend. Javon, however, becomes increasingly unresponsive. In a school setting we might label his behavior as simple resistance if we had no insight into the other voices he was negotiating:

Scott: It's still the same thing. Like with Donny . . . He'll go outside . . . Like . . . You know . . . how we go outside . . . "Man . . . Nah-hah . . . She's just sayin' that. . . ." That's what happened. I mean, you *could* use that. But . . . [Scott points to a checklist based on goals the writers had generated for talking to other teens.] That's—that's answering this question right here: audience. . . See this writing right here. "Can you predict some rivals teens might have?"

Javon: Oh.

Scott: See that's this . . . Like, if I'm . . .

Javon: Am I gonna' answer this question?

Scott: No. If I'm the audience I might be able to bring that out.

Javon: Oh, yeah . . .I see what you're sayin' . . .

The discussion continues for about 5 minutes until the mentor enters, indicating that she had the same response and asks Javon what he plans to do:

Mentor: I kinda had that response too. Remember, I was jokin' about. . . it sounded too good to be true.

Scott: Oh, yeah.

Mentor: What you've got are some readers doing rivals over here. And you gotta' decide. . . I mean, what you could do is say that . . . You know, "they're just gonna' think that—there's nothing I can do about it." Or, you could try to think about how to respond to us. Do you think there's any way you could respond to us ahead of time. You know, like . . .predicting we're gonna kinda think that?

Scott: Hm . . .

Mentor: See what I mean?

Scott: Yeah. Uh . . . How could you build that into your a [. . . . .] Like Don . . . He's like . . . "Yeah, yeah . . . Okay, Mom." Then you go outside and you wanna know why he said "Yeah, yeah, okay." And then he says, "Well I know she's just saying that and blah-blah . . . blah-blah-blah-blah, blah." I think there's more . . .

At this point the mentor attempts to respond to Javon's rather eloquent silence, trying to articulate what may be on his mind. His return to the conversation is immediate and engaged:

Mentor: You want it to have a happy ending. Is that—is that what you're planning?

Javon: Yeah. I was planning . . . It's a emotional moment—They're cryin' and everything . . .

Scott: [A lugubrious "Ahhhh"]

Javon: So they wouldn't be doin' all that [i.e., rivaling]—it won't be like that.

Personal Goals.   Javon bursts back in the conversation when he sees a way to assert what seems to be a non-negotiable intention: to have a happy ending. Why this way of dealing with the threat of drugs was so important to him is never really clear, but Javon was not alone. In the project, a number of writers shared his intense desire to envision some closure on the problem of drugs (whether in the form of disaster or rescue) and at the same time to exit from this process of "rivaling" where there always seemed to be another rival standing in the wings. Rivaling forced students to confront a good deal of conflict, not only from readers but within the unresolvable dilemma of drugs themselves.

As I hope the tentative nature of these comments makes clear, our knowledge of Javon's goals are at best an interpretation of his comments and actions. What is at stake here is not understanding precisely which voices and goals Javon negotiates, but recognizing that they exist and how the conflicts they create turn his learning into an act of negotiation.

Perceived Conflict.   Javon's personal investment becomes problematic when he begins to see how the voices of readers, the pressure to rival, and Scott's ideas each represent agendas that conflict with his other goals. As the discussion continues, Scott raises the problem of believability: "This ain't no brochure, man" (a reference to the "unbelievable" drug brochures). The mentor prompts Javon to consolidate these ideas into a new plan: "Well, you want a happy ending. And you got some readers who are sounding like they're not sure they're going to believe it" (questioning intonation). When Javon's attempt to do both fails, the voices in this negotiation present a dilemma he cannot resolve and he replies with some exasperation "I wanted a *happy* ending. I wanna be happy. I don't want any doubtin'." His partners remain supportive but unconvinced:

Scott: And they all live happily ever after in the town of merry fairy tales (with friendly irony)?

Mentor: Yes! You got some skeptics over here [Laughter].

Rivaling in general, the instructional agenda of this particular session (to rival and maybe revise), and the pressure of skeptical readers and supporters has come in conflict with the learner's even stronger commitment to another goal. The task of learning to rival in this assignment cannot be separated from the task of negotiating this conflict.

Available Conventions. It is important to realize that up to this point, Javon had been an inventive and persistent rivaler, posing alternatives in his dialogue and his "inside my mind" commentary. In trying to resolve the problem posed by the conclusion, textual convention once again becomes a voice in this negotiation. Different techniques for organizing the text stand as operational, how-to images of how to get out of this dilemma, that is, how to recognize Scott's rival, be believable and still have a happy ending. One solution is simply to add Scott's response, but Javon fears this will just start another cycle of rivaling, which, he dreads, could go on for four to five more pages (This is an unacceptable solution.). At another point, Javon asserts, "I got it!" as he proposes his tried and true move of going "inside his head" but without changing the ending. It just gets another laugh from Scott. As Javon says, "it's kind of hard to put it all together."

The conventions of written text enter into this negotiation in the form of the initial options a writer considers and as ways to resolve conflicting goals in text. For instance, a more experienced writer might have met Scott's objection by crafting a more qualified or conditionalized resolution or adding a commentary, as one student did, on the how hard it is to really convince teens like Donny to change their minds. Yet, it is not clear that knowing such conventions would have let Javon balance all the voices in this negotiation, given the strong emotional tone to which he was committed.

> Javon: That's how I want it to be. I don't want it to be, yeah he goes outside says "yeah, yeah," and then she comes. . . . That's how—you're started all over again, and nothin' really gets settled.
>
> Scott: Yes it does. It'll get settled.
>
> Javon: Yeah but like four or five pages. Somebody gets killed.
>
> Scott: Let's see. I'll save off this and that. . . (He continues to talk under his breath as he shuffles paper. Scott appears to have read the writing on the wall and drops out at this point, but the mentor persists.)
>
> Javon: That's how I'll end it. That's how I'll end it.
>
> Mentor: What? How you gonna end it. How you gonna do it?
>
> Javon: I'm gonna give it a happy ending.

Mentor: But can you give it a happy ending but still recognize. . .

Javon: (Assertively) Everything worked out O. Kayyyy.

Mentor: Can you talk back to us, and recognize what we may be thinkin'
and then . . .

Scott: You could.

Javon: Yeah. Everything worked out okay. They had a—they had
a—they'll have a couple good years.

Mentor: Sounds like they're gettin' married.

Scott: Sounds like this is a soap opera.

Javon: It's kinda hard to put it all together like a happy ending. That's
why I'm just trying a couple different—a couple different
things.

Mentor: Yeah. Yeah. Uh-huh.

The Larger Discourse Community.   The discussion about rivaling and
about this text continues: the mentor asking for a resolution, Scott being
skeptical, and Javon now clinging to his intention. However, with the
references to soap operas and fairy tales, some of the expectations of the
larger discourse community have, it seems fair to infer, also come into this
negotiation, even if Javon cannot accommodate them. As a learner, attempting to rival in the context of this text (which is demanding enough),
Javon is asked to negotiate the voice of this larger community with its
peculiar power to redefine the writer's intentions (a happy ending) into its
own, perhaps unwelcome categories (a soap opera).

Although Javon was ostensibly writing for teens talking to a friend,
the context of rivaling was widened first by the presence of his actual
readers and second by their skeptical allusions, which subject Javon's
imagined world to another, more cynical discourse on drugs. As it turned
out, his partners were justified in drawing such a voice into Javon's
negotiation. After this CLC newsletter was published, a psychiatric
counselor who works with juvenile drug addicts criticized Javon's piece
for not sounding the way addicted teens or heavy users actually talk.
Javon, of course, was neither part of nor talking to that community.

However, the therapist concluded that the writer (Javon) was simply saying what he thought the CLC staff wanted to hear—a pat story in which naive teens abandon drugs and all is well.

I bring in the the therapist's response because it illustrates how easy it is to misread student's negotiations based only on inferences from the text. Although the ARGUE project took a clear antidrug stand, the staff had made repeated efforts to examine drugs from the user's point of view and to get the writers to acknowledge the strong rivals real people, who do choose to use drugs, might mount. An ex-addict talked about the pleasures of the high life, and mentors frequently role-played skeptical readers. Although there was pressure on the teenagers, it was just the opposite of what the therapist assumed. The negotiation that produced this text was far more complicated than the logic of "just say no," and harder to fathom. The drug discourse of the teenagers seemed to inhabit a world that had no middle ground. Drug use of any sort seemed linked in inexplicable ways to scenarios of dead mothers and sons, raped girls, and dead sports stars, balanced in inexplicable ways by happy endings with repentant parents. In ways we can only guess, the social discourse surrounding drugs in this community exerted a strong voice in these negotiations, a voice that was at times in conflict with the style of open, academic inquiry that we brought to rivaling.

Like Javon, I might have found it convenient to wrap up this analysis with a happy ending in which the collaborative session paid off in an impressively revised conclusion. But, in fact, he stuck to his guns and kept the lines in which "everything worked out O. Kayyyy." From an educational perspective, there are different ways to read the logic behind this performance that ends with a scene in which the writer might have (should have?) rivaled and did not. Although the text demonstrates some impressive, persistent rivaling leading up to this point, we could see this as a failure to manage a demanding intellectual strategy or as a stage in Javon's intellectual development. Some readers saw the ending as a quick out to avoid writing. The therapist concluded that the writer was co-opted. However, I would argue that each of these readings fails to understand the more complex logic of the learner. Each reduces a complex negotiation among multiple voices to a unidimensional choice or indication of ability. Each wipes out the conflict and decision making that produced this text. To understand the logic of this learner, we needed to go behind the performance and understand the constructive process that produced it to recognize the logic which constructed a negotiated meaning in the midst of conflicting voices of advice and constraint.

LINKING INSTRUCTION AND RESEARCH

Is Javon's experience, in which learning to rival is learning to carry out a contested performance, unusual? Our research with high school and college students suggests no. Such negotiations among multiple voices and conflicting goals and constraints appear to be a critical but common part of both writing and learning to write.

We are finding that collaborative planning in a setting such as the CLC can play a valuable role in understanding how this process of negotiation works. Because collaboration locates part of the learner's problem-solving process in a social, verbalized event, it gives us an unusual window on the forces that actually enter the circle of negotiation. It helps us see that learning to rival (and Javon's apparent "failure" to consider the skeptical reader) is really a complex negotiation among many voices, among competing goals and available options. Uncovering more of the logic of the learner reveals a writer making difficult and ultimately meaningful choices.

However, if we want to argue that this instructional practice can be a tool for inquiry, we cannot ignore the fact that it also tends to promote new levels of negotiation in the process of learning by making more goals/demands salient to the writer, by inciting conflict among them, and by leading both partners to articulate these goals and conflicts. Indeed, the educational value of collaborative planning is that it does produce such thinking. So is negotiation just an artifact of this collaboration? I would argue that collaborative planning is a lens on this process of negotiation, that instead of creating conflict, it simply makes it more visible, letting us observe more of a process that goes on even when we do not recognize it. As a research tool, then, collaborative planning is implicated in the process it studies; however, it is also more explicit about how it produces that situated cognition than other tools, such as laboratory tasks, which we may assume are less reactive than they really are.

Perhaps the most important link between research and instruction that I see lies in the way an educational practice such as collaborative planning and community literacy can make the process of learning and negotiation open to reflection by teachers and students. Formal research studies, such as the rivaling study described here, can build the case that negotiation exists and alert us to some of the forces to which writers must respond. However, the real payoff for education comes first, when teachers can gain insights into the logic of individual students and into the negotiations that are leading some to confusion or failure and others to satisfaction and success. Second, the even greater payoff comes when students begin to see themselves as thinkers and become aware of their own strategies and choices. This is not to ignore the fact that effective writing depends on having topic knowledge and knowledge of discourse conventions. However, the logic of effective learning is also the logic of negotiation, experimentation, and reflection. The most important thing for Javon to learn out of his six weeks of collaborative sessions at the CLC was not how to find a graceful ending for his text, but how to confront a complex rhetorical problem, how to listen to the rival voices and uncover options within that negotiation, and how to make his own strategic decisions as a writer—and realize that he was making them.

ACKNOWLEDGMENTS

The work reported in this chapter has been supported in part by The Howard Heinz Endowment and the National Center for the Study of Writing and Literacy at The University of California at Berkeley and Carnegie Mellon University. The publication of this chapter was supported under the Educational Research and Development Center Program (grant number R117G10036 for the National Center for the Study of Writing and Literacy) as administered by the Office of Educational Research and Improvement, U.S. Department of Education. The findings and opinions expressed in this chapter do not reflect the position or policies of the Office of Educational Research and Improvement or the U.S. Department of Education.

REFERENCES

Bazerman, C. (1988). *Shaping written knowledge: The genre and activity of the experimental article in science.* Madison, WI: University of Wisconsin Press.

Bereiter, C., & Scardamalia, M. (1987). *The psychology of written communication.* Hillsdale, NJ: Lawrence Erlbaum Associates.

Brandt, D. (1990). *Literacy as involvement: The acts of writers, readers, and texts.* Carbondale, IL: Southern Illinois University Press.

Brown, A. L., & Palincsar, A. M. (1989). Guided, cooperative learning and individual knowledge acquisition. In L. B. Resnick (Ed.), *Knowing, learning, and instruction: Essays in honor of Robert Glaser* (pp. 393–451). Hillsdale, NJ: Lawrence Erlbaum Associates.

Burnett, R. E. (1991). *Conflict in the collaborative planning of coauthors: How substantive conflict, representation of task, and dominance relate to high-quality documents.* Unpublished doctoral dissertation, Carnegie Mellon University, Pittsburgh, PA.

Collins, A., Brown, J. S., & Newman, S. E. (1989). Cognitive apprenticeship: Teaching the craft of reading, writing, and mathematics. In L. B. Resnick (Ed.), *Knowing, learning, and instruction: Essays in honor of Robert Glaser* (pp. 453–494). Hillsdale, NJ: Lawrence Erlbaum Associates.

Emig, J. (1971). *The composing processes of twelfth graders* (NCTE Research Report No. 13). Urbana, IL: National Council of Teachers of English.

Erickson, F. (1988). School literacy, reasoning, and civility: An anthropologist's perspective. In E. R. Kintgen, B. M. Kroll, & M. Rose (Eds.), *Perspectives on literacy* (pp. 205–226). Carbondale, IL: Southern Illinois University Press.

Flower, L. (1988). The construction of purpose in writing and reading. *College English, 50*(5), 528–550.

Flower, L. (1993). Cognitive rhetoric: Inquiry into the art of inquiry. In T. Enos & S. C. Brown (Eds.), *Defining the new rhetorics* (pp. 171–190). Newbury Park, CA: Sage.

Flower, L. (1994). *The construction of negotiated meaning: A social cognitive theory of writing.* Carbondale, IL: Southern Illinois University Press.

Flower, L., & Hayes, J. R. (1981). A cognitive process theory of writing. *College Composition and Communication, 32*(1), 365–387.

Flower, L., Long, E., Fleming, D., & Wojahn, P. (1993). *Learning to "rival" in school and out: A window on the logic of learners* (Tech. Report). Pittsburgh, PA: Mellon Literacy in Science Center, Carnegie Mellon University.

Flower, L., Long, E., & Higgins, L. (1996). *The rival hypothesis stance: How students negotiate a literate practice.* Manuscript in preparation.

Flower, L., Schriver, K. A., Carey, L., Haas, C., & Hayes, J. R. (1992). Planning in writing: The cognition of a constructive process. In S. Witte, N. Nakadate, & R. Cherry (Eds.), *A rhetoric of doing: Essays on written discourse in honor of James L. Kinneavy* (pp. 181–243). Carbondale, IL: Southern Illinois University Press.

Flower, L., Stein, V., Ackerman, J., Kantz, M. J., McCormick, K., & Peck, W. C. (1990). *Reading-to-write: Exploring a cognitive and social process.* New York: Oxford University Press.

Flower, L., Wallace, D. L., Norris, L., & Burnett, R. E. (1994). *Making thinking visible: Writing, collaborative planning, and classroom inquiry.* Urbana, IL: National Council of Teachers of English.

Hayes, J. R., Flower, L., Schriver, K. A., Stratman, J. F., & Carey, L. (1987). Cognitive processes in revision. In S. Rosenberg (Ed.), *Advances in applied psycholinguistics, Volume 2: Reading, writing, and language learning* (pp. 176–240). New York: Cambridge University Press.

Hayes-Roth, B., & Hayes-Roth, F. (1979). A cognitive model of planning. *Cognitive Science, 3*, 275–310.

Higgins, L., Flower, L., & Petraglia, J. (1992). Planning text together: The role of critical reflection in student collaboration. *Written Communication, 9*(1), 48–84.

Norris, L. (1992). *Developing a repertoire for teaching high school English: Case studies of preservice teachers.* Unpublished doctoral dissertation, University of Pittsburgh, Pittsburgh, PA.

Olson, D. R. (1977). From utterance to text: The bias of language in speech and writing. *Harvard Educational Review, 47*, 257–281

Peck, W. C. (1991). *Community advocacy: Composing for action.* Unpublished doctoral dissertation, Carnegie Mellon University, Pittsburgh, PA.

Resnick, L. B. (1987). Learning in school and out. *Educational Researcher, 16*(9), 13–20.

Rogoff, B. (1990). *Apprenticeship in thinking: Cognitive development in social context.* New York: Oxford University Press.

Scribner, S., & Cole, M. (1981). *The psychology of literacy.* Cambridge, MA: Harvard University Press.

Sommers, N. (1980). Revision strategies of student writers and experienced adult writers. *College Composition and Communication, 31*(4), 378–388.

Wallace, D. (1991). *From intention to text: Developing, implementing, & judging intentions for writing.* Unpublished doctoral dissertation, Carnegie Mellon University, Pittsburgh, PA.

Wallace, D. L., & Hayes, J. R. (1991). Redefining revision for freshmen. *Research in the Teaching of English, 25*(1), 54–66.

Young, R. E. (1978). Paradigms and problems: Needed research in rhetorical invention. In C. Cooper & L. Odell (Eds.), *Research on composing: Points of departure* (pp. 29–47). Urbana, IL: National Council of Teachers of English.

Chapter 3

LEARNING TO LEARN FROM EFFECTIVE TUTORS

Connie Juel
University of Virginia

I had a lot of difficulty in school. My parents were told I was learning disabled. I carry this with me to this day. I found early on that I could learn okay, but usually not in the classroom. I learned early on that my best teachers were my peers, the ones who had just been through the same stuff. They could always explain things better to me than anyone else. I even find this to be true in college. (Kevin, fall 1992)

For several years, university students have been writing me about their early school experiences. They reflect on their past experience as they begin to tutor first-grade children who have difficulties learning to read. I tell the students that I am particularly interested in what they recall about learning to read. I find their remembrances clump into two general categories. In the first category are those students who learned to read with relative ease. Most of these students cannot recall how they learned to read; they just seemed to always be able to do so. It is noteworthy that, if these students do recall how they learned to read, they generally link their learning to home experiences:

> . . . the memories that I have of learning to read are fun memories of one-on-one lessons. I learned to read at home with my mother, father, and sister each pulling me to the side at one point or another and trying to give me reading instruction. I guess the most fond of those memories are the ones with my sister, Cora. She was bound and determined, after she had become a very good reader, to teach her little sister the wonders of reading. I spent countless nights with my sister in our room with bedtime storybooks. After she had taught me the sounds to all the alphabet and that the vowels had a

short and long sound, she would take a story and actually go through the entire piece marking short and long vowels. At this time, I must have been about five years old. Believe it or not, I actually caught on to reading and my desire to read took off. (Corinna, spring 1991)

In the second category of students are those who, like Kevin, recall that learning to read, or learning much of anything in school, was difficult and painful. These students usually have very vivid memories of how they felt and they strongly empathize with the children they are tutoring:

> I was the little kid that had trouble reading, the one that use to do anything to get out of reading. I use to tell the teacher that I did not feel well, lost my voice, and use to try to get in trouble just so I wouldn't have to read and instead would be sent to the office or to the corner. Because of these experiences as a child I understand how some of these children are feeling. I have been there. The worst thing that happened to me when I was a child was to be embarrassed. Not knowing how to read can be embarrassing to a child. The other kids in the class laugh at you and make fun. (Norm, fall 1990)

The students who had difficulty in school often report that their self-confidence eroded; some are still struggling to regain it. Others feel they finally began to learn in school only when they overcame their self-doubts and/or rebelled against those who told them (whether subtly or outright) that they were slow. When, as part of the requirements in my university class, students such as Norm tutor young children in reading, they are insistent that their tutoring build-up the child's self-confidence. In the words of one of my students, Greg, who for years had been in special education:

> One bad experience that I think helps me with Michael is when my high-school LD teacher told me that I wasn't smart enough to go to college. She also said that I probably wasn't good enough [at track] to get a scholarship. This made me feel very stupid for about 20 seconds. Then I became MAD! I said to her, "I don't think God put you on this earth to go around and put limitations on people. Furthermore I can do anything I want to do, even do a better job at teaching (or destroying) than you." The point I'm trying to make is that if I didn't have confidence in myself then I would have lived up to what my stupid LD teacher said I was going to be. That's what I draw from that experience, and concentrate on strengthening Michael's confidence in himself. (Greg, spring 1991)

Kevin, Corinna, Greg, and Norm (pseudonyms are used for all students and children) were/are student-athletes at either the University of Texas at

Austin or the University of Virginia. At both universities I have taught classes where students tutor children who are having difficulty learning to read. Some of the university students who enroll in the class, like the three just mentioned, were encouraged to take the class by their respective athletic departments. They needed help with their own reading and writing skill, and that, too, was part of the class. Through exploring their ideas of school and watching them tutor, I have learned a lot about learning.

My first cross-age tutoring class was started at the University of Texas at Austin as a result of two factors. The first was the depressing finding from a recently completed four-year longitudinal study of children learning to read and write in one elementary school in Austin. I had followed the literacy development of children from first grade until they completed fourth grade (Juel, 1994). That study indicated that if a child was a poor reader at the end of first grade, there was a strong (.88) probability the child would still be a poor reader at the end of fourth grade (Juel, 1988). It was likely too, that the poor reader would also become a poor writer. The children in the study appeared victims of the "Matthew Effect" (Stanovich, 1986). According to the Gospel of Matthew: "For unto everyone that hath shall be given, and he shall have abundance, but from him that hath not shall be taken away even that which he hath" (Matthew 25:29). Those first-grade children who learned to read with relative ease liked to read. They read more both in and out of school than their peers who did not get off to a good start. Through reading, they appeared to gain vocabulary, conceptual and world knowledge, and ideas that made them both stronger readers and stronger writers through the years (Juel, 1988, 1994).

The second factor leading to the cross-age tutoring program in Texas was a concern that some student-athletes at the university were unable to handle college-level work due to their relatively weak reading and writing skills. These student-athletes represented the older end of the "Matthew Effect." As children they got off to a poor start in school and they never recovered. Further, by college, they had limited self-confidence in their academic abilities.

The pairing of these two groups came about serendipitously. In a graduate class I was teaching, the students were tutoring elementary-school children who were having difficulty learning to read. One day, one of the graduate students brought to her tutoring session a student-athlete from the university, where she was also tutoring. The student-athlete and the child took to each other, and the student-athlete began to take over the tutoring. The child flourished under the tutelage, and the student-athlete became more responsible as a result of tutoring the child. The idea of a cross-age tutoring match was born.

The graduate student, Joanne Calhoun, tutored several student-athletes at the university. Providing tutors for needy student-athletes, and enrolling these student-athletes in developmental reading and study skill courses, was a way the University of Texas Men's Athletic Department tried to help their students. The courses were not always popular among the student-athletes, however. This may have been caused by the stigma attached to them, as well as to certain aspects of the course content. As a result the instructors of these courses frequently had difficulty with the attendance and behavior of the students. The Men's Athletic Department was therefore quite receptive to Joanne's and my proposal to involve some of the student-athletes in a different plan. In lieu of the developmental reading and study skills courses, some students would be enrolled in a university course where they would tutor children, as well as engage in wide reading and writing about self-selected books. In January of 1990, Joanne and I piloted a program of 20 student-athletes tutoring 20 children. The response to the pilot was extremely positive from the athletic department, the students, and the elementary school, so the program was continued.

In September of 1990, with the cooperation of the University of Texas Men's Athletic Department, I undertook a more formal evaluation of the effects of the tutoring project on both the student-athletes and the children. The Men's Athletic Department placed 15 of their students, those who had scored the lowest on the Nelson-Denny reading test, in my tutoring class for two semesters, in lieu of the two semesters of developmental reading and study skills they otherwise would have taken. Fifteen other male student-athletes, who were the next lowest-scoring students on the Nelson-Denny, served as a control group; these students enrolled in the two developmental reading courses.

Other student-athletes were welcome in the tutoring class. Many, but not all, also needed help with reading and writing. During the fall of 1990 there was a total of 36 student-athletes in the class, including 8 from the Women's Athletic Department. In the spring of 1991 there were 45 tutors. Although the majority of these 45 tutors were student-athletes, word of the class had spread, and other students from around the campus wanted to become involved in the class and did.

The university students were required to complete 4 hours of outside reading for the class each week. The Men's Athletic Department provided funds to buy about 200 paperback books, which were selected by me in consultation with student-athletes and other university students. The books represented a variety of reading levels, with the lowest level at about sixth grade, and a variety of genre (including biographies, fiction, horror stories, romances, westerns, and nonfiction sports stories). The majority of the books were written by African-American authors and were about the lives of this minority group (e.g., Bloods by Terry, 1984; Nigger by Gregory, 1964). The books were placed in the study center used by the student-athletes. The students could read these or any other books and then write about their reading in interactive journals. The journals contained their reading times, pages read, and personal responses to the readings. The students also used these journals to reflect on their own lives, the lives of the children they tutored, and the tutoring itself. The instructor responded in writing to the weekly journal entries. In addition, each student tutored one elementary-school child in reading and writing for 45 minutes, twice a week.

The children were first-grade, second-grade, and special education students who had been designated by their principal and teachers as having fallen considerably behind their peers in reading. The children came from an all-minority elementary school, with a population of about 70% African-American and 30% Hispanic students. The school is located in one of the poorest neighborhoods in Austin, a neighborhood troubled by drugs, crime, and poverty. Because many of the tutors were minorities, came from low-income families, and/or had experienced difficulty in school, they had backgrounds similar to those of the children they tutored.

COMPONENTS OF THE TUTORING PROGRAM

One evening a week all the tutors met at the university for a two and one-half hour class. During this class the tutors and I discussed possible tutoring activities, how literacy develops, books the tutors were reading, and books they had written for the children they tutored. The writing of books was one of seven basic activities that was discussed in the class as a possible activity for tutoring. The tutors were encouraged to select three or four of these seven activities to do in each tutoring session; the activities were chosen based on an analysis of reading and writing samples of their child. Although specific activities were suggested to tutors, the tutors were given considerable discretion as to their delivery. I had learned from the pilot semester of tutoring that instruction was most effective when its implementation was up to the tutor. The seven basic activities are briefly described here.

Writing

Storybook writing was encouraged both by the tutor's written books and by themed-writing centers that were placed around the tutoring room. Each tutor wrote at least two books for his or her child. Ideas and drafts for books were worked on in pairs or small groups during the evening class, and edited by me, other students, or other teaching assistants, before a final copy was made. Illustrations were drawn (by the tutor or with the child) and the book was "published." Publishing meant stitching the pages together and binding them between cardboard covers decorated with wallpaper, contact paper, or drawings. Many of the tutors told me this was the first time they had enjoyed writing. These books were to be read and enjoyed with the children, and to inspire and encourage the children to write books themselves. The tutor also learned how to edit and "publish" the children's books.

The theme-writing centers included books, magazines, and blank writing books that had either construction paper or computer-generated covers with pictures that corresponded to the theme. A typical theme might be "bears," and the themed center would include storybooks and factual texts on bears, and a blank writing book with a cover shaped like a bear. The children and tutors wrote imaginative new versions of stories, retold favorite stories such as "Goldilocks and the Three Bears," or wrote factual texts (e.g., "Bear Facts").

Through story writing, both the tutors and the children could see themselves as authors and as "meaning makers," which helped them understand the reasons for writing (Downing, 1979; Petrosky, 1982). Story writing also increased the children's knowledge of text structures, which can aid reading comprehension (Gordon & Braun, 1982).

Reading Books

There were more than 200 children's books in the tutoring room. These included predictable text, children's favorites, and expository texts. Most tutors read to the children as one of the activities in each tutoring session. Both tutors and children were expected to acquire vocabulary from reading and listening to stories (Elley, 1989; Feitelson, Kita, & Goldstein, 1986) and to increase their imaginations, world knowledge, and motivation for reading and writing.

"My Book"

Reading instruction at the elementary school followed a traditional mode, with the children placed in basal readers and reading groups. The children we tutored were all struggling with the basal vocabulary. One problem with "pull-out remediation" has been the lack of overlap between the reading materials and experiences in the child's classroom and those in the remedial situation (Johnston & Allington, 1991). To link classroom experiences with the tutoring sessions, we created "build-up" readers (Guszak, 1985). These readers slowly introduced both vocabulary from the basal, as well as new words that built on the phonograms used in basal words. The first page of the first build-up reader had one word, "run," repeated many times in different formats (e.g., Run, _____, run. Run, run, run, _____."). There were blanks where the children could either tell the tutors or could write on their own what would "run," with room to draw pictures. These pictures were often labeled by the children with words copied from the build-up pages. Each subsequent page in the build-up added another word.

The build-up readers allowed the children to practice reading the vocabulary from the books they would eventually read in front of their peers in their classrooms. They gained speed, fluency, and self-confidence in reading these common words. The very gradual introduction of vocabulary words, as well as their repetition, ensured success in the build-ups.

"My Journal"

Many of the first-grade children needed to develop "word consciousness" (Morris, 1981). They also needed to understand the communicative function of print, to see their own words written down. The children were encouraged by their tutors to tell them a special word each day. This word was written down by the tutor, copied by the child, and talked about as the child drew a picture based on the word. Finally, the child dictated a short phrase, sentence, or passage using the word. One day, for example, one boy's special word was "vampire." He drew a picture of a vampire wearing a long black cape. He dictated, "I like vampires. They wear big, black capes. They come out at night." The child would read back to the tutor these sentences on subsequent days, as well as read and create other pages in the journal.

Alphabet Book

Many of the children did not know the names of the letters of the alphabet. Alphabet books were computer-generated booklets with each page having one letter and one key picture and word (e.g., M, m, a picture of a moon and the word "moon"). There was room for the child to write down other words that start with "m." Sometimes these words arose from the tutor and child discussions, and at other times, the children used picture dictionaries to generate more words. One boy's "m" words included: Man, music, Martin, mom, mouse, motorcycle, and milk.

Hearing Word Sounds

Many young children who have difficulty learning to read, have difficulty perceiving sounds in words. The children in the tutoring sessions were no different; many lacked phonemic awareness (Clay, 1987; Griffith & Olson, 1992; Juel, 1988; Lundberg, Frost, & Petersen, 1988).

We had several activities to foster phonemic awareness. First, there were numerous books with rhyming words and alliteration, such as nursery rhymes and Dr. Seuss books. The children were encouraged to predict the rhymes, (e.g, "cat, hat,") and play with the alliteration, (e.g., "Peter Piper picked a peck of ...") Second, the tutors played many sound games with the children. They might have the children guess what word they were saying as they slowly said it or they might use a "Marty Moose" puppet, who only likes things that start with /m/, and to name things for Marty. Third, they might sort pictures into piles based on initial consonant sound (e.g., all the pictures that start with /m/ like "moon" in one pile with all the pictures that start with /s/ like "sun" in another pile.) Fourth, a variation of the "Hearing the Sounds" activities described by Clay (1987, p. 65) was made. A few lines were drawn down a sheet of paper, dividing it into columns. At the bottom of each column was a penny. As the tutor slowly pronounced a short word such as "sat," the child pushed a penny up the column as each phoneme in the word was perceived.

Letter-Sound Activities

The major difference between most good and poor beginning readers is the good reader's ability to recognize words (Curtis, 1980; Juel, 1988; Perfetti, 1985; Stanovich, 1980). Poor decoding abilities can keep a child from reading, contributing to the Matthew Effect (Juel, 1988; Stanovich, 1986).

Several activities were available for increasing letter-sound knowledge. First, once a child could do the "Hearing the Sounds" activity described earlier, the child wrote letters into the columns instead of pushing pennies. Second, letter-card boards were used to spell words. Third, children matched the picture cards, sorted into piles based on their initial consonant sounds, to their printed form, with the tutor emphasizing the connection between the initial sound and letter. Fourth, books that contained words with repetitive phonograms were read and discussed (e.g., Wildsmith's Cat on the Mat, 1982).

SUMMARY OF INTERVENTION RESULTS

Children

During the 1990–1991 school year, 27 first-grade at-risk children were identified by their teachers and principal as ones who most needed help. (The balance of the tutored children came from special education and second-grade classrooms.) The mean score of these 27 at-risk children in September on the Metropolitan Readiness Test (MRT; Nurss & McGauvran, 1976) prereading composite was at the 26th percentile. There were 15 other first-grade (lower-risk) children at the school who were considered more likely to succeed at reading in first grade. The mean of these 15 lower-risk children on the MRT was at the 46th percentile.

The 27 at-risk children were tutored twice a week for 45 minutes a session. The 15 lower-risk children each had a student-athlete "mentor." At least once a week they met with a student-athlete, who would talk and read stories to them. In April the school administered the Iowa Tests of Basic Skills (Hieronymous, Lindquist, & Hoover, 1983). The mean score of the 27 at-risk children on the reading comprehension subtest was at the 41st percentile. The mean score of the 15 lower-risk children was at the 16th percentile.

Standardized tests were not meant to be the only measure of the program's success. Throughout the year I met with the teachers and the principal, frequently tape-recording their comments (Juel, 1991). The teachers and the principal were very enthusiastic about the program. They spoke about the increased reading ability of the tutored children, many of whom were moved from low reading groups to higher ones, and about the increased self-confidence in all the children. They stated that this self-confidence spread to subjects other than reading. They reported that parents were also very enthusiastic about both their children's increased reading ability and self-confidence. The following comments of one teacher about a first-grade child are typical of the effect the student-athlete tutors had on the children:

> She is more outgoing than I've ever seen her. She participates in all class discussions. She used to sit there sullenly—wouldn't even participate when called on. I've never had an improvement like that before. She looks forward to his coming now and asks when he is coming. She even drew him a picture of a rainbow. Before, I could never get her to finish anything. Now I wish you could see her papers in math and social studies. I could cry I'm so happy about it. Now she asks if she can stay after school and read to me. I couldn't get her to write her name before and now she is writing cards to her mom and to James [her tutor]. (Excerpt from tape recording, March 28, 1990)

Tutors

The effect of 4 hours of self-selected reading, interactive journal writing, writing of children's books, and engaging in all the tutoring activities on the reading abilities of the 15 target student-athletes was compared to the control group of 15 student-athletes. The Nelson-Denny Reading Test (Brown, Bennett, & Hanna, 1981) was administered by the Men's Athletic Department as a pretest in August and a posttest in May. Scores from the vocabulary and comprehension sections from the Nelson-Denny are combined to form a total score for the test. An analysis of covariance (using the August pretest as the covariate) indicated the tutors had significantly surpassed the control group by May, $F(1, 27) = 21.3, p < .001$. The tutors had a mean grade equivalent of 9.1 in August and a mean grade equivalent of 13.1 in May. In contrast, the control group had a mean grade equivalent of 11.5 in August and a mean grade equivalent of 12.6 in May. In addition, student advisors in the Men's Athletic Department attributed the tutor's increased sense of responsibility, better class attendance, and increased feelings of self-worth to their participation in the tutoring class.

LEARNING ABOUT LEARNING
FROM WATCHING EFFECTIVE TUTORS

Tutoring occurred throughout the day, from 7:45 a.m. to 2:00 p.m. There were seldom more than five tutors in the tutoring room (an empty first-grade classroom) at any given time. This allowed the supervisors (a teaching assistant and me) to more fully focus on particular pairs. The tutors tape-recorded every tutoring session, and many sessions were also videotaped. (The tutors and children quickly adjusted to the frequent presence of camcorders set up on stands.) Videotapes and transcripts of the most effective tutors were independently viewed or read by four people (three graduate students and me). We looked for overlap in techniques and effective interactions. We did not share our observations with one another. Each wrote comments about specific clips in the tapes or spots on the transcripts. There was considerable overlap in the comments, and those features that were commented on by at least three of the four observers informed our understandings.

From observing the tutoring sessions and the videotapes, reading transcripts of the tutoring sessions, and reading the journal entries of the tutors, several macro- and microlevel understandings about learning were made. First, some macrolevel understandings.

Learning in a Positive Social Context and Caring

Noted by all observers was the supportive relationship that developed between tutor and child. One observer said, "You just look at the videos and you see love." Another observer commented, "It looks like family."

In their journals the tutors, who felt their own families had been powerful forces in their learning to read, often remarked that they tried to recreate this "family" feeling with their children. Corinna, who frequently talked and wrote about her sister Cora (see her comments in the introduction), described how she came to understand the type of relationship her child needed:

> When I first began tutoring Yvette, I could instantly see that she was a very rebellious little girl at times. I don't think that she's a bad person, but that she feels she must act in this rebellious way. I noticed that if she isn't talked to in a nurturing way, that rebellious side of her comes out. This was not immediately apparent to me. I began tutoring Yvette last semester; at that time I was under a great deal of stress myself. Towards the end of the semester when I was at my highest stress level, I noticed that she would not cooperate at all. I would ask her questions in a mechanical voice and she would just sit there and refuse to answer. Many times the things that I asked her, I knew that she knew the answer. It didn't hit me until this semester that Yvette's problem could be that she wanted the same type of atmosphere and relationship that I had with my sister when I was learning to read. I think that in her classroom, she can sense that no one really expects her to know anything. What I try to do, when I tutor her, is turn this around and act like there is not a doubt in my mind that she knows the words or the answers. I also try to give her that one-on-one feeling that makes a person feel special. I think by tutoring Yvette with this mentality, I have been able to reach her. (Corinna, spring 1991)

This special "one-on-one feeling" was reflected in the words of another tutor that were spoken to his child on the first tutoring day, "I'm going to come *just to see you.*"

All observers noted the physical affection between the tutors and the children. The pairs sat close together, the tutor often had an arm around the child, and they often held hands. The children frequently asked for, and received, hugs. Not uncommon were sessions ending with scenes such as the following:

Tutor: Did you like the session today?

Child: Yes.

Tutor: That's good. That's good. I'm glad you like it 'cause I like doing
         it too. Are you ready to go back to class?

Child: Could you take me in your lap?

Tutor: Yeah.

The tutors made the children feel special, cared about, and loved. This
was noted by their teachers and parents. One first-grade teacher commented:

> The kids go to tutoring and come back with their chests all puffed out. They
> feel so special that someone cares enough about them to come and work with
> them. All of their reading has improved. Their self-confidence has improved
> (excerpt from tape recording, March, 28, 1990).

Learning Requires Self-Confidence

As was noted earlier, the self-confidence of the children visibly improved
throughout the tutoring sessions. The tutors often wrote about their own
problems with self-confidence. The student-athletes often described how
sports had been a shelter for them, the only place they had felt confident
and proud of themselves. They frequently wrote about their determination
to build their child's self-confidence.

> The most successful thing in my tutoring was when I told Felicity to stop using
> the word "can't." When I first met Felicity she always said "can't." I would
> ask her to read a certain passage or word, "I can't," or I would ask her to read
> a book aloud for me, "I can't." I told her that if I heard her say that she can't
> do anything, I would not talk to her. At first it was hard and it would slip out
> every now and then. Now she is doing really well and her reading has
> improved as a result of it. I think it was successful because she was never told
> that she can do anything that she wants to do. I want her to be conscious of
> what she was doing and saying because she might be failing herself before she
> even tries. (Bettina, spring 1991)

"Can't" was a common word for the children when we began to tutor.
Many of the children routinely said they could not read, could not write,
could not spell, and so forth. The tutors noted this, and their comments
illustrate how they helped the children realize they "could" and "did." Here's
one example (from one tutor and one session) of the type of comments that
many tutors made during the sessions:

Tutor: Do you know what you just did? You just read three pages!

Child: (Laughs.)

Tutor: I think you telling stories, don't ya? I can't read that. You know
           you can.

Later

Tutor: You read the whole page to me! How do you feel about that?
           Okay. Thumbs up! Thumbs up, dude! Way to go, guy!

Later

Tutor: Now you just read five pages and you told me that you can't read.
           Hum! So!

Later

Tutor: You've read six pages! I thought, I thought you couldn't read?

The tutors further tried to build the children's self-confidence by letting
them know they thought they were smart and would achieve. Some comments from various tutors that reflect this are:

I think you're smarter than me!

You smart!

You going to get better, better, and better as the day goes.

I'm proud of you.

You're gonna be a famous writer someday, you got all the pages.

Go for it.

I think you're doing very good. Smack me.

That's a good try.

Tutors often mention that they want their children to be able to appreciate the progress they make. They want them to be aware that although it
does not happen overnight, they are moving in the right direction. Tutors
often pointed out to the children the progress they had made:

Tutor: Hum, so your teacher tells me that you be reading a lot. Is that
          true? Can you tell? Can you see the improvement in yourself?

Child: Yeah.

Tutor: How? How can you see that you've improved? Do you read faster
          now? Can you sound out words a little bit better than you did
          before?

Child: I can sound out words.

Tutor: I mean you just spelled "tape." ... it wasn't up on the board and
          you could spell it. You spelled it in your head. That's the hardest
          way to spell things. So that's improvement right there. You could
          do it without looking. You know all your sounds, now... so, you're
          getting better and better everyday. Have you been practicing?
          (Child nods.) See, that's why you're getting better and faster.
          The more you practice the faster you get.

Learning Is Acquiring the Secrets
of How the System Works

Those tutors who had difficulty in school often describe their feelings as
children as being on the outside, not being privy to the secret of how to read.
I was struck by how often the term secret comes up in their written
reflections, perhaps because in thinking back to my own difficulties in first
grade, that was the word I used. Just like these students, I felt that there was
a secret to reading that my classmates knew, but I did not. This feeling, of
course, leads one to feel like an outsider, to feel alienated, to feel vulnerable.
It also leads one to avoid the task that is perplexing by withdrawing (e.g., "I
can't") or avoiding the task by getting in trouble or getting "sick" (see
Norm's comments in the introduction).

Effective tutors frequently informed their children about how reading
and writing work. They served as informants who were trying to explain
how things work, they acted as if they were letting their children in on the
secrets of how everything fits together. Some verbal examples are:

All you gotta' do is put them [the sounds in words] together.

This is how you are supposed to tell a story . . . (and proceeded to model one).

You can't read a word without looking at it. Look at each word. Read 'em as
you see 'em.

Sound it out. That's your little trick. That's how you figure out these words.

Yvette, Yvette, stop. Listen to what I'm trying to tell you. When you just memorize, that isn't reading what you're doing, do you understand the difference? When you memorize a story then, that's good, too, cause you have it in your head, but then you look, when you read, you look at the word that you're reading and you remember the sounds that each letter makes and you put those sounds together and you make words out of them. So you can look here, and you can look there, and you know that that's an "H" and an "I." The "H" makes the /h/ sound and that makes /i/ so you would know that's "Hi." See, that's how you read. And you look at each word, you just, you don't look at the picture and guess what the words are, you just look here and look at each word and then you read it.

Or this dialogue after the child has misread a word:

Tutor: That doesn't make sense. Could "him" run?

Child: (Laughs.)

Tutor: Does that make sense?

Child: (Laughs.)

Tutor: Okay, what sounds better? The boy "him" run, or The boy "can" run?

Child: The boy can run.

Tutor: There you go. You see you gotta listen to yourself as you read and see if it sounds right.

Learning Occurs Best As a Team Effort

Effective tutors wanted their children to feel like their sessions were a "team" effort. This may reflect their sports backgrounds, but it helped the child feel like one of the "team" of learners, not an outsider. As one tutor wrote, "The reason I keep stressing "we" is because it's a team thing. I let my child know that I am in this as much as they are. It's a learning experience for the both of us." Or as another tutor told his child, "Me and you, we gonna do it."

Learning Occurs Best When It Is at the Right Level

Tutors often reflected on how they reached the child only when they tried to see the world through the child's eyes. Here are some written reflections:

> The response that I got from my child came when I came down to his level and related everything to his world.

> The one thing that I tried to do that didn't work was to imagine him at a higher level. I would try to tutor him with words and things (such as using a dictionary), at a much higher level. I found out that you have to teach them as first graders and not use your own knowledge to tutor. As I went along I stopped tutoring at a higher level (my level) and met him at his level. Whenever he was getting confused, I realized it was because I was seeing things and talking things at my level, not his. I had to really get side by side with him and see words and things like he did, then I knew what to say that might help him.

> In my tutoring I've learned to have more respect for children and their thoughts and actions. I've come to realize that they aren't any less of a person (due to their size) than me. Although they are younger and less experienced, we are similar. They are going to school trying to learn just like I am. They are dealing with difficult subjects, classmates, and teachers, and at times they'll have good days and bad days and would react the same way I would. Through the tutoring sessions I had learned to be considerate of their feelings and their "world."

Learning Is Filtered Through a Cultural Lens

In my first semester teaching the tutoring class, I was telling the students that knowledge of "story structure" could be helpful in both understanding and producing stories. To encourage their own story writing, and to learn a technique that might be helpful with the children, we examined the story structure of The Three Little Pigs. To get at that structure, I asked them questions about who the characters were, what the problem was, and so forth. I had done this for years in my regular undergraduate language arts methods classes. Never had my other undergraduate students answered like this class, however. Who had a problem? What was the problem in The Three Little Pigs? The instantaneous and unanimous answer from the student-athletes: "The wolf. He was hungry and needed food." The answer reflected their own backgrounds of poverty. They viewed the story through the eyes of the hungry wolf, not the well-fed and well-housed eyes of the little pigs.

This shared culture of poverty made the student-athletes especially sensitive to the children's worlds. One illustration of this came when I was observing a child reading a story to her tutor about a birthday party. As the child came to the part about the birthday cake, she stopped reading and put her head down on the table, quietly refusing to go on. Her tutor sensed what was wrong; I hadn't a clue. He said, "I never had a birthday cake either." The little girl looked up and said, "You didn't, either?" She smiled, then continued reading the story.

Sometimes the shared culture of poverty emerged at the most unexpected times. Here's a dialogue as a tutor and his child were spelling words on a letter-card board. The tutor had put up, "bike."

Tutor: And what does that say?

Child: Bike.

Tutor: But what if you have more than one bike? Then what would you put on there? What if you have three or four bikes? Rich kid.

Child: You'll put "S."

Shared culture could mean sharing vernacular language. Here's one illustrative interchange:

Tutor: This word is "don't," and "don't" is an abbreviation for the word do not. So instead of saying, "I do not have any money at all, you say, "Man, I don't have no money."

Learning Is Fostered by Creative Delivery of Content

In the written reflections of one tutor, "Sticking with the basics did not work for us, we had be to creative and free so that we'd enjoy it more. Laville learned best when it was exciting. I probably taught better too when I had to really put effort into making something she needed to learn also enjoyable for her."

Effective tutors often devised games and other creative ways of teaching. My first reaction to some of the games was concern. Were the tutors' games (e.g., alphabet games with homemade game boards, like Hang Man, to practice spelling words) too removed from authentic reading experiences? Then I started to see how much the children learned through the games. Play, after all, is part of the "job-description" of a 6-year-old.

One of the most effective techniques that one tutor devised, which quickly was adopted by other tutors, was role-reversals. The tutors pretended to be the child; the child pretended to be the teacher. Through this role-reversal, the tutor could model thought processes of how to approach an unrecognizable word, and so forth. Here is one example of a tutor pretending to be his child, slowly sounding out words. The tutor calls on his child for assistance:

> Tutor: (slowly reading from My Book) I like to play (he comes to the word "with" and hesitates). What sound does "w" make?
>
> Child: "Wi," and you said it up here (pointing to already read text.)
>
> Tutor: "Wi," I know that.

The role-reversals focused even the most distractable child's attention on the print. The children took particular delight in the role-reversals, perhaps because the pressure to read was lifted off them, and perhaps also because they felt more grown-up. Role-reversals became one of the most effective techniques for helping children with word recognition. This is not too surprising when we recall the saying, "If you wish to learn something well, teach it."

Learning Is Sometimes Fostered Best by Those Who Were the Worst Learners

My experience reading students' recollections of how they learned to read suggest that when learning was achieved early and relatively painlessly, adults were not very aware of the steps and pitfalls in learning to read. This gave them less empathy for the children they tutored, and more difficulty figuring out how to break down the reading process so the children could understand it. Those students who can recall the difficulty and pain involved in learning to read, however, are often better at breaking reading down into understandable pieces for their child. The older poor learner is also more aware of the understandings that they need to help the child develop.

An example of this came about in an evening class at the university, where I was explaining to the students how some methods of teaching reading, such as phonics, require children to connect letters to sounds. We practiced using letter-card boards to sound out and spell words, connecting their letters to sounds. In the middle of this activity one of the student-athletes asked how on earth children could do this if they could not first hear these sounds in spoken words. Using the specific word his group was working on, he continued, "How can a child know what letter makes the /j/ sound in jump if the child cannot hear that sound in jump?" He told us how this had been a real problem for him in school. He said he could not figure out the connection between letters and sounds because for a long time he did not think of words as strings of sounds. This student understood the concept of phonemic awareness in a most personal and concrete way. He told us how frustrating it had been for him when teachers kept telling him to sound words out. He said it was like a light going on when he finally understood about how letters could be attached to the sounds he finally perceived in words. He related how he acquired this understanding: His special reading teacher kept elongating spoken words, sounding them out and helping him experience words as sequences of sounds. His description to the class, and the emphasis he placed on helping the children perceive the "sounds in words" had a much larger impact on the class than all my talk of phonemic awareness. He was also quite effective in helping other tutors devise ways to teach their children this concept (e.g., by elongating the sequence of sounds in spoken words).

Now we look at some of the microlevel understandings about teaching children to read and write that were gained by watching the most effective tutors. These understandings, unlike the macrolevel understandings already described, are specific to learning to read and write.

Personalize Stories.   Effective tutors brought their children into the world of print by making them characters in the stories they read together. It was important to help their children feel a relationship to the stories, as the children did not bring to school a history of hearing stories read at home. (At the beginning of first grade, only a few children recognized any of the 200 children's books in the tutoring room outside of those that had been in their kindergarten classrooms.)

Here are some examples of how effective tutors brought their children to books:

While reading *Curious George*:

> Tutor: Curious George (pointing to "George"). We're going to put Eddie right there. Curious Eddie...

While reading *John Henry*:

> Tutor: So, what is that? Is that John Henry's house?

> Child: Yep.

Tutor: Good. Okay. A hush settled over the hills, the sky swirled
          soundlessly around the moon, the river stopped murmuring, the
          wind stopped whispering, the frogs, owls, crickets held silence.
          Sssshhh. All watching and waiting and listening. Then! The
          river roared (growled). (Laughs.) Have you heard the sound of
          the river ?

Child: Uh huh.

Tutor: The wind whispered, whistled, and sang. The crows croaked, the
          owls hooted, and all the crickets chirped. Welcome, welcome,
          echoed through the hills. And John Henry was born. And just
          down the street Daryl [the child he tutored] was born.

Child: Hu uh. (Laughs.) I wasn't like that. I had a Pamper on when I
          was born.

Tutor: You had a what?

Child: I had a Pamper.

Tutor: Oh, they put a Pamper on you?

Child: Uh huh.

Tutor: John Henry came out smiling and laughing, but Daryl came out
          crying and crying and whining.

Child: (Laughs.) Hunh uh!

Tutor: You did!

Child: When I was a baby, I wasn't crying.

Tutor: You weren't crying? I was crying when I was a baby...

Provide Lots of Visual and Auditory Support While Child Is Reading.   All
observers of the videotapes noted the frequent visual support given by the
tutors, who focused on voice-print matches as children read. This included
having the child or tutor or both point to words, using cards under text lines,
pointing with the eraser end of a pencil, and slow, deliberate reading by the
tutor while pointing to the words. Effective tutors often held and guided the
child's hand as the child pointed to words. Frequently the tutors employed

support reading including choral or echo reading (the child reading a word or sentence or phrase immediately after the tutor) or simple turn-taking. The role-reversals, mentioned earlier, were another way the tutors kept the child's attention focused on the print.

Break Word Recognition and Spelling Down into Small Steps. Often the tutors modeled how to sound out words for the child by talking the child through the process step-by-step. The tutors walked the children through the processes of word recognition and spelling, so that the tasks were clearer, more accessible, and less mysterious. Here is an example of word recognition on the letter-card board.

Tutor: So whenever you see those two letters together, it sounds like "aaaaattt, aaaaaatttt." So what is that?

Child: "Aaaaattt."

Tutor: Right, so what word is that?

Child: At.

Tutor: Right. So you've got the "at." Let's put a sound on the front of it, okay? What's one of your favorite sounds? I know, it's "ssss."

Child: "S."

Tutor: Right. (Puts up the letter "s" in front of "at.") So you go, "ssss"—"at," and put them together. What have you got? You see? You see how that works? "Ssss" plus "at" gives you "sat." What about "M" plus "at"? What does that give you? (Replaces "S" with "M.")

Child: "M."

Tutor: And what is the other part?

Child: "At."

Tutor: Put them together. What do you get? You got the "at." You got the "mmmmm" sound. You put them together and what do you get? "Mmmmmaaaaaaat."

Child: Mat.

Tutor: Good. (Replaces "M" with "F.") So you got "F" and "AT." Gives you what?

Child: (Laughs.) Fat.

Tutor: Right. They come together. You have this word "fffffaaaat." Fat. What do you hear when you say that word—fat?

Child: "Ffff."

Tutor: Right. And the last two?

Child: "At."

Tutor: Right. All we did was change the letters, and you change the sound. (Puts up appropriate letters.) "AT," then "SssAT," then "MmmAT," "FAT." See? What about "B" plus the "AT"?

Child: Buh. Bat.

Tutor: Right. You got it.

An illustration of breaking down words while writing is shown in this dialogue that occurred as the child talked about, drew, and finally spelled his special words for the day for My Journal.

Child: ...I'm gonna make me a bat.

Tutor: You gonna make a bat? Let me see that. Okay?

Child: Does a bat have ears?

Tutor: Uh huh. Do you know how they look?

Child: Does it have a neck?

Tutor: Yep.

Child: They got a nose?

Tutor: Whooee! They got some straight wings.

Child: How you like it?

Tutor: Here's some looong wings! Here's another picture in your book. Some day you can go back and say, "Hey, look at all this that I did...." Why don't you write it? "Baaaat."

Child: (Writes a "B.") Now what?

Tutor: Do you hear the "aaaa" sound?

Child: "A."

Tutor: What about the /t/, /t/, what is that?

Child: "T." (Turns to next journal page.) Now I want to write kid.

Tutor: How you spell it out? What sounds do you hear? (Slowly elongates each sound in kid, repeats kid.) What's the first sound you hear?

Child: (Not sure.)

Tutor: What about the beginning? /kkkkkkkkkk/

Child: "K."

Tutor: K. What next?

Child: I don't know.

Tutor: Kid. Say it slow. "Kiiiiiiiiiiid."

Child: Kid.

Tutor: You have the /k/, but the next one, "kiiiiiiiiiii."

Child: /i/, /i/

Tutor: Hey, good job. So what letter does that?

Child: /i/, /i/

Tutor: Hey, good job. Now we got KI, "kiiiii," what word we trying to
          spell?

Child: Kid.

Tutor: So we got "kiiii." What we need to make it "kiiiiidddd"?

Child: D.

Tutor: That's the way!

CONCLUSION

This chapter illustrates how we can learn about learning from watching those
engaged in it. It illustrates how important the social context that surrounds the
academic task is for successful learning. Shared culture, shared histories of
difficulty with reading, shared insecurities, along with shared mutual respect,
can all support an effective team effort involving the student and tutor.

The chapter illustrates how relatively untrained tutors can effectively
assist children in academic subjects such as reading and writing. This point
is especially important for school personnel to consider when their schools
have large numbers of children who need additional support. While the
benefits of the one-on-one tutoring provided to struggling, first-grade
readers by the popular Reading Recovery program are well documented
(DeFord, Lyons, & Pinnell, 1991), so is its cost both in financial and human
terms. A study by the San Diego Unified School District (1992) found that
the average cost per pupil served by Reading Recovery was $3,250. Reading
Recovery teachers typically are assigned to the program for 50% of the
school day and tutor only four students at a time. The typical Reading
Recovery teacher serves only eight children over the course of a school year.

Schools with large numbers of children who need assistance might find
alternative tutoring programs (e.g., ones that employ older school-age
children as tutors or ones that use volunteers from the child's community
as tutors) to be less costly alternatives. Interventions by nonprofessionals
may not be as effective as those provided by the daily tutoring of a
well-trained professional, as in Reading Recovery. Such interventions may,
however, be good supplements because they can reach children who would
otherwise not receive much individual attention and support. They may be
especially useful in reaching children who need some assistance and individual attention, but who do not need the intensive daily tutoring provided

by programs such as Reading Recovery. Interventions carried out by non-professionals can represent more inclusive models of intervention; privileged knowledge represented by advanced credentials is not required to play an important role in schooling.

In the current intervention, students who themselves had been poor readers proved to be good tutors. Some of these students seemed particularly able to break down reading and writing into manageable steps for their tutees. At times they engaged in explicit cognitive modeling of processes. At other times they appeared implicitly to provide the scaffolding a child needed to accomplish a task in reading or writing. This reciprocal interaction and its individualized, contextual nature is difficult to accomplish within the larger, bustling classroom setting. There is a heightened intensity of engagement of the learner with both the materials and the learning process for more extensive periods of time in the individualized, contextualized setting; this is no doubt one of the reasons behind the success of one-on-one tutoring.

Recall the words of Kevin, a tutor in the study, who was quoted at the beginning of the chapter, "I learned early on that my best teachers were my peers, the ones who had just been through the same stuff. They could always explain things better to me than anyone else." It may be that the difficulty our tutors had with reading had made them more aware of the type of feedback that can help a struggling reader. They may have been more aware of the type of scaffolding implicit in Vygotsky's (1978) idea of the "zone of proximal development," the distance between what the novice can do alone and what can be done in collaboration with a more skilled individual. Vygotsky, in fact, emphasized that this collaboration is highly social and interactive in nature. In the words of one tutor, "The biggest mistake I made was to concentrate on school tutoring alone and not stop to think about what he wanted or how he saw things. Once he knew I was his friend, and not just a tutor, things took off. So my advice to teachers or tutors is know your child, know such things as their favorite storybooks, television cartoons, and their favorite animal. Be a real friend (you will like it). And then see reading and writing from their level to see what you can do to help. They will be more willing to learn when they know you are their friend and they will be more able to learn when you talk to them and work at the child's level."

REFERENCES

Brown, J. I., Bennett, J. M., & Hanna, G. (1981). *The Nelson-Denny Reading Tests*. Chicago, IL: The Riverside Publishing Company.

Clay, M. M. (1987). *The early detection of reading difficulties* (3rd ed.). Hong Kong: Heinemann.

Curtis, M. E. (1980). Development of components of reading skill. *Journal of Educational Psychology, 72,* 656–669.

Deford, D. E., Lyons, C. A., & Pinnell, G. S. (Eds.). (1991). *Bridges to literacy: Learning from Reading Recovery.* Portsmouth, NH: Heinemann.

Downing, J. (1979). *Reading and reasoning.* New York: Springer-Verlag.

Elley, W. B. (1989). Vocabulary acquisition from listening to stories. *Reading Research Quarterly, 24,* 174–214.

Feitelson, D., Kita, B., & Goldstein, Z. (1986). Effects of listening to series stories on first graders' comprehension and use of language. *Research in the Teaching of English, 20,* 339–356.

Gordon, F. J., & Braun, C. (1982). Schemata: Meta-textual aid to reading and writing. In J. A. Niles & L. A. Harris (Eds.), *New inquiries in reading research and instruction* (pp. 262–268). Thirty-first Yearbook of the National Reading Conference. Rochester, NY: National Reading Conference.

Gregory, D. (1964). *Nigger.* New York: Washington Square Press.

Griffith, P. L., & Olson, M. W. (1992). Phonemic awareness helps beginning readers break the code. *The Reading Teacher, 45,* 516–523.

Guszak, F. J. (1985). *Diagnostic reading instruction in the elementary school* (3rd ed.). New York: Harper & Row.

Hieronymous, A. N., Lindquist, E. F., & Hoover, H. D. (1983). *Iowa Test of Basic Skills, Levels 7 & 8.* New York: Houghton Mifflin.

Johnston, P., & Allington, R. (1991). Remediation. In R. Barr, M. L. Kamil, P. B. Mosenthal, & P. D. Pearson (Eds.), *Handbook of reading research* (Vol. 2, pp. 984–1012). New York: Longman.

Juel, C. (1988). Learning to read and write: A longitudinal study of fifty-four children from first through fourth grade. *Journal of Educational Psychology, 80,* 437–447.

Juel, C. (1991). Cross-age tutoring between student athletes and at-risk children. *The Reading Teacher, 45,* 178–186.

Juel, C. (1994). *Learning to read and write in one elementary school.* New York: Springer-Verlag.

Lundberg, I., Frost, J., & Petersen, O. (1988). Effects of an extensive program for stimulating phonological awareness in preschool children. *Reading Research Quarterly, 23,* 263–284.

Morris, D. (1981). Concept of word: A developmental phenomenon in the beginning reading and writing processes. *Language Arts, 58,* 659–668.

Nurss, J. R., & McGauvran, M. (1976). *Metropolitan Readiness Test, Level II.* New York: Harcourt Brace Jovanovich.

Perfetti, C. A. (1985). *Reading ability.* New York: Oxford University Press.

Petrosky, A. (1982). From story to essay: Reading and writing. *College Composition and Communication, 33*(1), 19–35.

San Diego Unified School District. (1992). *Review of data concerning the reading recovery, turning point, and Hispanic reading programs.* San Diego, CA: Author. (Eric Document Reproduction Service No. ED 344 189)

Stanovich, K. E. (1980). Toward an interactive compensatory model of individual differences in the development of reading fluency. *Reading Research Quarterly, 16,* 32–71.

Stanovich, K. E. (1986). Matthew effects in reading: Some consequences of individual in the acquisition of literacy. *Reading Research Quarterly, 21,* 360–406.

Terry, W. (1984). *Bloods.* New York: Ballantine Books.

Vygotsky, L. S. (1978). *Mind in society: The development of higher psychological processes.* Cambridge, MA: Harvard University Press.

Wildsmith, B. (1982). *Cat on the mat.* New York: Oxford University Press.

Chapter 4

MOTIVATION AS AN EMERGENT ISSUE IN AN AFTER-SCHOOL PROGRAM IN EL BARRIO[1]

Pedro Pedraza and Jorge Ayala
Centro de Estudios Puertorriqueños, Hunter College
City University of New York

The Puerto Rican community of New York, the oldest and largest Spanish-speaking community in the city, has remained in a disadvantaged socioeconomic position for more than two generations. The social and life-chance indices of this position within North American society (e.g., housing, health and employment statistics), correlate with the low achievement levels and high dropout rates of Puerto Rican children in the New York City public school system (New York City Department of City Planning, 1994; Rivera-Batiz & Santiago, 1994). Often, motivational reasons are offered by teachers, school authorities, and researchers alike to explain this and other academic achievement phenomena. However, little is known about motivational development and how it might be related to social, cultural, or situational factors in and out of school contexts (Sivan, 1986). In particular, cognitive theories of motivation seem unable to account for observed variations in students' motivational levels as they relate to different social, cultural, and interactional influences in instructional situations (Rueda & Moll, 1994).

This chapter describes an effort by investigators based in a Puerto Rican research institute to address the critical situation of our youth and community through an experimental education project that fosters a community-based and self-determination type of strategy for social change. We approach

---

[1]Barrio is a common Spanish word for neighborhood. However, it is also the usual way of referring to the oldest Puerto Rican community in New York City, East Harlem.

this complex and multidimensional problem at the level of educational practice with a perspective that views the background experiences of the students as a resource to build on and not an obstacle to be overcome, though their needs may be multifaceted. As community members and academic researchers, we approach children as agentive human beings, as opposed to outsiders, a point of view in which lower class children of ethnic or racial minority groups are a priori "disabled" in conceptualizations of their educational potential and needs. We view children as capable and potentially willful masters of their own learning and development though we believe this requires, as an essential component, the development of a socio-historical and cultural understanding of self and community (more so than just decontextualized skills development). The long-term results aimed for are not solely those of upgrading achievement levels in terms of the acquisition of academic skills, but more broadly, individual and social change by way of group study and action on concrete problems of the community.

The institutional mechanism for mediating these goals is an academic/community collaboration focused on an out-of-school science program guided by a socio-historical theoretical approach to pedagogy (Hedegaard, Hakkarainen, & Engestrom, 1984; Moll, 1990; Wertsch, 1985). Initiated in this century by the work of the Russian psychologist, Lev S. Vygotsky, this approach encompasses a general theory of human development at the psychological level that integrates or contextualizes development over time within other social levels of analysis. There are many different emphases, foci, and perspectives within this general approach, as well as lacunae, but Vygotsky established an epistemological foundation, based methodologically on dialectical-historical materialism, which serves as a common ground for adherents.

This approach emphasizes the social and cultural basis of cognitive development and the importance of understanding and using the particular living conditions of the students in the organization of educational activities. As directors of the project, we carefully select activities and themes for their relevance to the children's lives, with a special focus on content and the conceptual development of the children to foster the cognitive processes and skills involved in critical thinking. Only in a general sense has our effort been guided by any particular version or interpretation of Vygotsky's ideas. As a design experiment the project is better described as a naturalistic formative research effort rather than a controlled psychological experiment.

Here we present some ideas that have emerged from our implementation of this pedagogical experiment in a community setting that initiated some rethinking about the relationship between structured learning activities and students' varying levels of engagement with them. We begin with a description of the Young Scientists Club. This leads to a discussion, drawn from our experience in designing and implementing learning activities with the aforementioned goals in mind, that relates to the issue of children's motivation and learning. The research component of the project is briefly described, and some instances of exemplary activity drawn from our observation notes illustrate the issues raised. In conclusion, we suggest some possible implications of these preliminary findings for teaching and learning in relation to the problem of children's motivation and instructional strategies.

PROJECT'S HISTORY, PARTICIPANTS, AND SETTING

The Young Scientists Club (YSC) was started several years ago as an endeavor of a research institute, the Center for Puerto Rican Studies of Hunter College (the "Centro"). The project is now a collaborative effort of the Centro and a community-based organization, the Youth Action Program of East Harlem, New York City. Initially the program was mainly concerned with developing and demonstrating alternative methods of literacy acquisition for children using computer technology. However, the study of the community has become the focus of the learning activities and the understanding of science as a process of investigation a subsequent goal. By community we first mean geographically—the children's immediate neighborhood—and socially—that is, the locus of networks of interactions significant to the children. In a broader sense we define community by reference to groups historically or culturally connected to the children via national/ethnic, racial, and/or social class identities (singly, or in various combinations).

One of our objectives throughout the years in the project has been to promote children's conceptual development by relating their spontaneous ideas and knowledge about important topics such as community and science to more formal or abstract systems of thought (i.e., scientific). The process is one that has involved active engagement through hands-on "scientific" processes of exploration of selected topics that are important to the children, collaboratively building interpretative models of the domains explored, engaging in critical and reflective dialogue and discussions in diverse groups, and participating in transformative actions that somehow contribute to the "neighborhood."[2]

---

[2]We are in the process of exploring more systematically children's developmental understandings of concepts such as neighborhood, community, and so forth.

The project took this turn in emphasis because we view the conceptual and analytical skills developed through scientific investigation as instrumental in building the critical consciousness of the children. By critical consciousness we mean an understanding of community conditions, issues, history, and cultural/linguistic heritage that would offset deficit explanations of community social problems, that is, an approach to the understanding of the problems of the community that does not explain them as the result of cumulative individual failure, or inherited communal deficiencies, or characteristics, whether they be cultural, linguistic, intellectual, or personal/motivational. Rather, our aim is an explanatory approach that explores the social, economic, political, and historical dimensions of poverty, oppression, and exploitation in a manner that treats the consequences of colonialism and racism seriously. The purpose is to set the children on a path, at an early age, of looking for solutions to the everyday problems of the community that goes beyond what they normally encounter in school or through the mass media. The challenge is to consider the child as a whole, attending to both their changing thinking as well as their affect and sense of empowerment. Awareness of macrostructural constraints and of the historical and social nature of the human condition, and their communities in particular, is essential in order for them to make sense of the relative and comparative distribution of power and resources between communities, and to develop an understanding of these social relations that would allow them to see both the structural constraints and the possibilities for social action and human development.

The community served is low income and almost exclusively composed of a Latino and Black population. The participants are elementary school-aged children and the setting is one after-school community center of the Youth Action Program, the Young People's East Harlem Resource Center, in which our Young Scientist Club is one of several programs serving the children of the neighborhood. The first year for the after-school club to be administered by the Youth Action Program was 1992–1993, with the Centro providing curriculum and research support. The setting of the program was a basement space provided free of charge to the Youth Action Program by a local church. The building adjoins some empty lots of land that the community-based organization obtained title to, from the city, as part of a neighborhood improvement project. The property was cleared of garbage and drug dealers, and at the time it was being transformed into a park, with the children of the Young Scientist Club playing a role in its development.

This situation provided us with a unique opportunity to combine empowerment, action, and leadership goals with academic objectives in an after-school program. The opportunity created a setting in which children could engage in activities that had, as an objective, the benefit of the whole community, and in which they could use the academic knowledge they were developing as proactive learners. It was expected that children would then see the usefulness of, for example, math in a domain of their everyday lives, and that this would mediate their motivation to learn such material regarded by them as school topics, not usually of interest to them after leaving school.

From a research perspective the experience created for us a theoretical problem: How to conceptualize the phenomenon of varying levels of engagement in our instructional activities by our participants, and an empirical problem of just what connection these activities really have to the children's real-life experiences. In this chapter we only begin to address the first of these problems; we plan in the future to investigate the second. However, it was our practice that brought us to the issue of motivation as a practical matter. It was transformed into a research problem, theoretically, by a process of reconceptualization that we can attempt to verify, empirically, by utilizing this framework as a guide to reformulating our practice.

RESEARCH COMPONENT

The research component is essential to the functioning of the program, given that we incorporate evaluative processes in planning and modifying future activities on a weekly basis. In these meetings, the staff discusses the transcripts of the observation notes, taken at every session by a researcher through the process of participant observation (i.e., as an actor in the setting.) For the year we focus on in this chapter, the staff consisted of a new science teacher, an art teacher, an assistant to both of them, a community-based organization (CBO) supervisory staff person, and the researchers (only one was consistently present at every session). The focus of the researchers' observations varies but includes changes in children's motivation and attitudes, particular teaching activities, and the acquisition of content material as it is reflected in discussions and in their ability to solve the problems at hand. Another source of information is the material actually produced by the children over time. They have generated work that serves as a basis for an analysis of what they have learned at different points in time. In this chapter, we have used the observation notes to focus on the children's engagement within particular instructional activities. We describe weekly activity components, followed by examples of interactions and dialogues from our observation notes.

Organization of Program Weekly Activities

The program functions three times a week: two days of activities with the children and one day just with the staff. Although such a schedule does not give us very much time with the children, we found the one day for planning and reflection to be critical, particularly given that all adult participants are only part-time staff and are not usually in contact with each other outside of the program. The time spent on evaluation, therefore, also serves staff social and developmental needs. This raises the issue of the process of change adults participating in the project, including the researchers, have had to experience and endure in order to achieve our pedagogical goals. Although it is a topic beyond the scope of this chapter, it is an extremely interesting and important issue.

Instructional Activities

Art Activities—The Mural: Day 1.   Children work with an artist on a project that has the objective of collaboratively designing and painting a mural on a wall of the future park. The children are expected to learn particular technical and conceptual skills, such as the nature of gray values and colors, in the process of drawing and painting about themselves, their families, and the community, which are the themes of the mural. Children work in collaboration and receive assistance from the artist as they reflect upon and provide information about their life histories and particular living conditions.

Math and Science Activities: Day 2.   The young scientists work with a teacher in activities that integrate math and science with the development of other aspects of the park. Some examples of activities are: the selection of playground equipment, marking the land for the construction workers to build the plant beds in the garden section, reading the blueprint, and learning about scales and proportional representation.

Staff Meeting: Day 3.   In these meetings, all staff participate in discussions on what occurred with the children in the immediately preceding sessions or any other session relevant to the topic at hand. Plans, or adjustments to plans, are made and tasks assigned. As mentioned previously, on occasion observation notes are discussed with attention to the voice and perspectives of the nonresearch staff elicited and attended to. Invariably there are multiple perspectives to take into account, which enriches the decision making and the research.

SAMPLE OBSERVATION NOTES
AND INTERPRETATIONS

The YSC has changed over time in response to different circumstances that we have had to face, from year to year, ranging from varying fiscal and spatial limitations, to new personnel, level of material support, and curricular opportunities. Another important variation is the relative contribution that the children make to the formulation of the immediate goals of the program each year. For the year described in this chapter, in particular, the park project being developed by the CBO provided us with an opportunity to involve children in activities basically predefined by adults. In other years we have not had such well-defined project possibilities, and activities have been more wholly co-developed with the children, though in this case, they did decide among potential options for their particular contribution to the park. This process of definition and development of program goals is an essential part of any learning context. Variations in level and form of participation can and do make a difference for children's quality and level of engagement in activities, as these can have different meanings for them as participants. As we argue, differences in meaning are key for understanding motivation and participation in structured learning activities. In our context, to have a "project" for the children, though not completely defined, was not a violation of our principle of incorporating children in the elaboration of activities and goals as an essential ingredient for success. For example, when we actively recruit children to become part of the "club," we try to clearly explain, that the entire staff, with high expectations of everyone, will be working, sharing, exploring, and contributing to the community together. The key is for them to become owners of the project. To some extent, their engagement in program activities reflect whether "ownership" has been achieved at any level, and how this is related to changes in meaning and interpretation of purpose of those activities.

The following sample observation notes[3] from the first session will show how the program begins with a description, in this case by the "teacher" of what this "club" is all about.

---

[3]As indicated, observation notes are taken by a participant observer who assists at every session. The notes presented, for reasons of clarity and brevity, have been transcribed and cleaned. Therefore, they are limited in detail, although the quotes represent literal comments made by the individuals. This was done as much as possible to partially overcome the fact that no tape-recording device was used.

M. T. explains that " ...this is a club for smart kids, like yourselves, who live around the neighborhood... we will develop a project ... through math, science, and artistic activities. ..." She talks about the park (which most children were familiar with) and describes some of the activities they can expect to be doing together, such as "looking through catalogues to choose equipment, painting a mural, and working in designing a garden... We will be asking all of you for ideas because ... the park is for you and the community ... and you really know what you like or don't like about parks and playgrounds. ..." She asks, "What would you really like to have?" The children answer, "monkey bars, slides, swings, baseball and football fields. ..." MT explains that they will be doing things they and their family and neighbors will feel very proud of. "It is a real contribution that you'll be doing because you know how the community needs spaces for different things. ..." There is a discussion of kinds of spaces in the neighborhood and the different individuals who would use the park. Isabel says, "We should write our names in the park!," already showing identification and enthusiasm about the project. The teacher responded with enthusiasm and other children added "no littering to keep it clean." Another says "no dogs," and suggests the need for "security guards." Others add "we should have sprinklers."

From these comments it can be noted that the general goals are explicitly stated by the teacher and that, in this case, children responded positively. However, the meaning of the activities for the children is not taken for granted or believed to have been given by a lecture, but rather negotiated and discussed with the active participation of the children and reinforced at many points in time. Throughout the program, the goals and motives of the activities are re-discussed, given that our challenge was to help the children develop a common understanding and awareness of what we are doing at different levels (e.g., doing math, contributing to the community, learning about ourselves, etc.). The next sample observation note from the following week shows how the concepts of measurement and scales were introduced and related to the children's everyday lives and to a content of interest to them.

The teacher starts explaining that today they are going to deal with something important in their everyday life "...something we use a lot...measurement." Joseph, "Are we going to measure the whole park?" Teacher, "Yeah but not today!" The teacher continues to elicit children's ideas through questioning, asking them about things in their everyday lives for which they think measurement is important. Children mention games, but the teacher continues probing, "Which games?," and "How are measurement and math related to which games?..." Joseph mentions "football and baseball." Children discuss the counting of downs in football, and there is controversy about how many yards there actually are on the field. Children are all speaking at the same time around the topic and are very involved in the discussion.

In this sample, the teacher engages students in a discussion that helped them frame and connect "measurement" and "math" with that of "sports" as a domain of everyday life, therefore appealing to their own interests. Later in the day, the teacher introduced the blueprint of the park made by architects and discussed the kind of work that architects do.

The teacher, as she puts the blueprint over the table, and the children sit close to each other, adds, "The blueprint is a representation of how it is going to be ...it is a plan... and the park is subdivided into different sections." Pedro asks, "Where is the fence?" and children quickly identify it in the blueprint by pointing. "Where is the mural going to be?" Approximately 15 minutes are taken so children can identify areas in the blueprint. Referring to the exact measures of the blueprint, which is full of numbers and symbols, the teacher asks, "Why is it so precise?" After some pause and confusion about the question, Moises answers, "Everything won't fit there!" The teacher, obviously very excited about the answer, continues, "When the workers come, what happens if they don't know exactly where things go?" Jose, who has been withdrawn from the activity, asks, "Why is that so important?" The teacher gives an example of building a house, explaining "you need exact measures in order to build the house in the right way... for example ... the wall in relation to the door...." Children all give ideas about why it is so important to be precise if you want to build something the right way. Manuel and Joseph begin to talk to each other and laugh. Anthony and Jose are running around playing and fighting. Ana asks me if I am always here, as she sees me writing. I say yes, and tell her that I am glad she has been so involved given that this was her first day in the program. She answered, "I like it!" After a pause, the teacher introduces the catalogue from which the equipment would be selected by the children. The teacher explains that "You will have the opportunity to measure the park in order to check if the equipment you'll later choose would fit the space available...." One of the children suggests that we could use "chalk" to mark the land and keep record of what we measure.

An issue that pertains to the nature of the context and of the observation notes themselves, and is evident from the previous excerpt, is the presence of the researchers in the setting and their dominant voice in the notes. At the beginning of the session Pedro Pedraza was mentioned in the activity interacting with the children. This participation from the researchers in what actually goes on in the classroom is very characteristic of our way of operating. This is also evident in the note where the observer in the researcher's own voice states, "Ana asks me if I am always here," and continues to question the nature of the researcher's participation and the purpose of his writing. Throughout the weeks of meetings and program activities, children learn to accept the researchers as part of the setting, though sometimes questioning both individually and collectively the purpose of writing. The researcher in many instances, as new children join in or old-timers seem to "forget," explains what he does in terms of the need to record and investigate issues such as whether they seem to like the activities, that the notes are to be used for staff discussions, presentations, and publications (of course, respecting anonymity). The main point is that the researchers are in fact an intrinsic part of what happens, participating in curriculum development, assisting the teacher in actual practices, and many times in charge of sessions and small groups tasks. They get to know the parents and relate to children as teachers and friends. Of course, this is what is attempted but does not imply that relationships are equal across the board. Sometimes, ethnic, language, and class identities mediate some of the relationships. Our goal is to create a community of practice (Lave & Wenger, 1991) where the researchers are integrated not only in the program, but in the community most immediately served.[4]

The previous excerpt also shows the way dialogue is employed by the teacher to create an atmosphere of sharing and respect. Through dialogue, the teacher also elicits what children's current or possible understandings are in relation to the concepts of measurement and scales and makes connections to what was previously discussed and learned. At the beginning of the excerpt, the teacher introduces the "blueprint" and defines it as a "representation of how it is going to be ... it is a plan. ..." Their knowledge and ability to understand or read two-dimensional representations of the playground was elicited through questioning and demonstrated by them by pointing to landmarks that they recognized from their actual experience with the setting. The need for mathematical precision was discussed and related to their spontaneous ideas about space, construction, measurement, and the needs of the project. At the end of the notes there is reference to a child who is very enthusiastic about "measuring the park," and who even suggests a method for being accurate, to mark the land with "chalk." This idea, brought up from his own experience to bear on the problem at hand, raises again the issue of the kinds of connections that need to be facilitated and mediated. Children's knowledge acquired in other contexts needs to be legitimated.

---

[4]The other issue raised, that of the dominant voice of the researcher in the notes, is also very important methodologically. Our ethnographic approach based primarily over the past several years on participant observation of this kind has responded to a number of needs and demands associated to our context—for example, the need to document what is going on? for immediate feedback in planning and modifying activities although we have limited resources. Certainly, observing sometimes conflicts with the goal of participating, and the observer cannot write down everything that is going on. Therefore, there is certainly a filtering process that is reflected in the researcher's voice throughout the notes, but this is true of any interpretative process used in analysis.

The following excerpt shows an activity very much "school-like" in the sense that it was constructed for learning and for the children to show their understanding of the concept of measurement and scale. Again, this understanding of concepts is conceived as changing as we collaboratively create activities designed to promote development of understanding and of particular skills. The idea is for them to engage in learning because they want to contribute to the park project, which will ultimately motivate them to continue their participation. This motivation is important because in our context most children could and sometimes do decide to withdraw at any time. Our challenge is to sustain levels of motivation in activities that are related to school topics, such as math, writing, reporting, and so on, topics in which the children in our community are usually presumed to be uninterested.

The children have already had their snack and are entering the workshop in apparently good mood, as they converse with each other. The teacher calls for their attention, "OK, guys!," and closes the door as the children sit around the table. She reminds them of what they did last week. She tells them that they worked on and discussed "important and useful things for our everyday life." She asks them who remembers what this was all about. Manuel answers, "Measurement." The teacher asks, "Why is that important?" Manuel raises his hand, but Edwards doesn't wait and says "to measure the park." But the teacher is not satisfied with the answer and asks "Why?" Edward then says, "To know if the stuff fit there." "Very good!," the teacher answers, adding, "What stuff?" The children answer all at once, "The equipment." "That's it!," the teacher says. The teacher explains that today they will work with "proportional representation," and asks, "How many of you know something about scales or have worked with scales at school?" Most children raised their hands enthusiastically. The teacher explains the day's first activity. She divides the children into four groups, giving each group a map of the United States and a ruler. She then explains that in this activity "one inch represents 200 miles." The teacher proceeds to give them two locations or points in the map. The idea is to calculate how many miles there are between one city and the other, measuring first with the ruler in inches and then converting that into miles. She asks them to look for Montgomery, Alabama, and then to calculate how many miles there are from there to the state of North Carolina. Most of the children understood the first part of the task, as they agree that there are three inches between the two points, but couldn't tell how many miles that represents. After some hesitation and confusion, suddenly Jenny answers, "600 miles," the correct response. That was surprising given that she was reluctant to participate in the activity at the beginning of the day, but this showed that she was involved in the task and understood the problem. The teacher proceeds with this activity, using other cities on the map, giving all the children the opportunity to participate.

During this session, the children showed a high level of involvement and enthusiasm during the activity before actually going to the park and taking measurements. The children were introduced to the concept of proportional representation because later activities would include reading and under-standing the blueprint of the park, and assessing the actual dimensions so that the playground equipment purchased would fit the space available. The activity of measuring the distance from two points on a map is artificial. However, the idea of proportion and scales of measurement was introduced in this way. What we wish to highlight is the fact that children were enthusiastic and engaged even though it was a classroom-like activity, similar to those encountered in school. Again, even though the school-like activity described preceded the application of what was being learned and discussed, previous and further discussions and activities framed the con-nections between what we were doing (math) and the ultimate goal or motive for the activities (developing the park to help the community and themselves).

Discussion

Analyzing our experience as we designed learning activities helped us realize the need to develop a comprehensive view of the role of different factors in the children's engagement with those activities. In this case, the context and setting required us to focus on the pivotal influence that motivation has in children's learning. Most important is the reality that, being an after-school program, there is no compulsory attendance, and the children can very effectively vote with their feet. This has put us in a situation over the years of negotiating with the children the content, organization, and pace of activities, thereby forcing the issue of making instruction something of interest to them. However, our theoretical approach allows us to take advantage of this situation by analyzing the process of program development as part of the research integral to understanding how to reach our goals of guided child development, (i.e., formative research.)

Our developmental approach, which treats science and math as cul-tural/conceptual tools, explicitly raises the issues of the relationship that instructional activities might have with issues of self-image, identity, col-laborative work, and levels of social context and analysis developmentally appropriate for the students' engagement. These connections are what mediate children's learning.

In our activities, math is presented to the children as a means to an end, and children need to solve mathematical problems and to be accurate in the process of contributing to the community and themselves. As a consequence, we expect them to understand the usefulness of math in their everyday lives and at the same time develop a sense of social responsibility (citizenship). The motive for learning mathematical concepts and skills is derived from their co-constructed interest in understanding and making a useful contribution to the community improvement project. In that sense, we believe we are making science and math cultural tools useful for mediating the children's lives. Our observation notes show that under these circumstances children have shown excitement and interest in learning and understanding material previously regarded by them as school topics.

The view of motivation that this approach implies is particularly important for refining instructional practice. As succinctly expressed by Sivan (1986), from this perspective, in essence, "the individual no longer acts as the instigator of motivation. Rather, motivation is a socially negotiated process that results in an observable manifestation of interest and cognitive and affective engagement" (p. 210). This framework represents a mediated and activity-centered approach. That is, it "suggests that we examine motivation indirectly through the analysis of the activities within which kids are observed learning or not learning, motivated or otherwise, so that motivation is always a characteristic of the child in an activity of a certain sort" (Rueda & Moll, 1994, p.122).

This view of motivation allows us to interpret the variation we have observed in children's performance, as a function of motivational levels related to both the content and context of instruction. This raises the theoretical issue of how to conceptualize setting and context in relation to learning and motivation in a way that can inform guided-child development. As stated by Rueda and Moll (1994) from a sociocultural and historical perspective:

> motivation must be conceptualized as a "situated" phenomenon: located not solely within individuals, but within "systems" of activities involving other persons, environments, resources, and goals. From this perspective, motivation is accomplished, it is created, socially and culturally relative, it is context-specific. It is not a unitary phenomenon, a general, invariant property of the individual mind, or an abstract property of individuals; it is manifested in activities, involving most prominently, the mediation of other human beings. (p. 132)

We have used the idea of levels of context to signal the possible influences on different participants in learning activities of what we refer to more abstractly as levels of social analysis, that is, economic, cultural (ideological), social (power relations), and so forth. These are all mediated through the discourse forms, participatory structures, and ideologies at participants disposal, as well as the goal of the activity itself and its relationship to past and present social/material conditions of life.

In our experience, in particular at the institutional level of context, (e.g., the social organization of activities), the locus of power for decision making, the purpose and focus of content/instruction, and the ideologies of class, gender, race, and ethnicity, are factors that directly or indirectly affect motivation. For instance, in one particular year at another locale we had a change of institutional context simply with a change in the leadership of the community-based organization. This first manifested itself in ideological organizational changes, such as an authoritarian disciplinarian treatment of the children and a separate and appropriate curriculum for the girls, which had repercussions for the behavior of the children in our after-school program. These changes immediately resulted in the dismissal or desertion from the program of half of our children.

In contrast, in the past year's program, children who had been characterized as problematic at school by teachers, parents, and administrators, showed a higher level of involvement in math activities than the level shown in the school context.[5] We believe that a key contributing factor has been that, in our program, children face the need to solve math problems in order to accomplish practical goals. The motive for learning is helping and understanding. This changes the definition and purpose of the activities for the participants and has an effect on the children's willingness to participate and learn. However, we have to be careful about any claims regarding the long-term effects of these activities, particularly in terms of conceptual development and cross-contextual transfer of skills, although we have instances of qualitatively different forms of engagement. This issue is an important one and it raises concerns related to assessment that we hope to address in future research. Nevertheless, it seems that when learning objectives are contextualized in meaningful ways, these children saw themselves as able to deal with the material.

In summary, we would like to highlight the issue of sustaining the children's motivation in activities that are directed toward the goal of individual and social change through community improvement efforts. The factors involved are multiple and complex. The following seem to be crucial:

- Contextual expectations, resources, participants, and cultural ambiance need to be viewed as a whole system with every aspect affecting the others.

---

[5]In informal conversations with teachers and school administrators they expressed surprise at the fact that a particular group of children were so involved in our program, given that they were "problematic" in their classrooms.

- The teacher as a special participant in the setting must have a deep understanding of the content domain and the children's social world in order to make connections between children's spontaneous ideas and knowledge to the various goals of instruction.
- The quality of social relationships among adults and children is critical.
- Children's communities and experiences should be valued as a resource for instruction, not as obstacles to be overcome.

Conclusions

The lesson for us has been not to ignore or take for granted different aspects of a learning setting or institutional context because of the possible effects on motivation. We have had to pay attention to the connection our micro activity settings have to larger institutional contexts, and these in turn to communities' historical and cultural traditions and to their present conditions. Particularly important is to explore the way motivation is socially and situationally constituted, and how it is affected by relations between the institutional context, the learner's communities and the participants. These relations vary even within what is typically considered homogeneous populations and should not be oversimplified.

In attempting to create learning contexts where children acquire skills and knowledge not taught or successfully taught by schools for our particular population we have been forced to deal with the issue of motivation. Due to the voluntary nature of our project children's desire to participate in the activities we undertake is critical. This forces us to view their motivation as something we negotiate and co-construct with them, rather than viewing it as something given, already formed, such as a defined characteristic of personality or intellectual trait. At best, when schools do treat motivation as something socially construed, it is as a result of processes in contexts outside of school, (e.g., community or family.) Therefore, motivation is still viewed as a predetermined given, even though attention and consideration must be paid to this influence on the children as part of a culturally sensitive pedagogy.

To treat motivation as socially co-constructed is to view it holistically as the result of the interface of institutional and broader contextual factors with those of the immediate setting as played out through the interactions of the actors in that concrete setting, because those larger levels constrain and affect the actual practice in ways not always obvious. In other words, the instructional setting and the socio-historical cultural context within which it is embedded form a system any part of which affects participants' motivation. To us this means that any theory of learning must take these concentric circles of influence on learning outcomes into consideration as does the Vygotskian socio-historical approach already mentioned (see Cole, 1992). We need, however, to develop concepts of the middle range that can make these connections or illuminate these relationships for us (see Rogoff, 1995, as an attempt at this; and Scribner, 1985, and Bronfenbrenner, 1979, for similar discussions on multiple levels of analysis). In terms of school reform policy, this indicates that the proposals aimed at changing curriculum, teaching methods, social organization, school governance, and school-community relations have to be much more organically connected (Tharp & Gallimore, 1988). Restructuring is an apt term for school reform that focuses on the systemic nature of the educational process, although it does not necessarily question the ultimate relationship of these reforms to social goals and values that we believe are imperative. We believe that the educational process should contextualize children's learning in meaningful ways, so that they can deal with academic material in a manner that can affect their community, their position in society, and their own conception of themselves as learners.

REFERENCES

Bronfenbrenner, U. (1979). *The ecology of human development: Experiments by nature and design*. Cambridge, MA: Harvard University Press.

Cole, M. (1995). Socio-cultural-historical psychology: Some general remarks and a proposal for a new kind of cultural-genetic methodology. In A. Alvarez, P. Del Rio, & J. V. Wertsch (Eds.), *Sociocultural studies of mind* (pp. 187–214). Cambridge, England: Cambridge University Press.

Hedegaard, M., Hakkarainen, P., & Engestrom, Y. (1984). *Learning and teaching on a scientific basis: Methodological and epistemological aspects of the activity theory of learning and teaching*. Aarhus Universitet, Psychologisk Institut.

Lave, J., & Wenger, E. (1991). *Situated learning: Legitimate peripheral participation*. Cambridge, UK: Cambridge University Press.

Moll, L. (1990). Introduction. In L. C. Moll (Ed.) *Vygotsky and education: Instructional implications and applications of sociohistorical psychology* (pp. 1–27). Cambridge, MA: Cambridge University Press.

New York City Department of City Planning. (1994). *Puerto Rican Newyorkers in the 90's*. New York: Department of City Planning.

Rivera-Batiz, F., & Santiago, C. (1994). *Puerto Ricans in the U.S.A.: A changing reality*. Washington, DC: National Puerto Rican Coalition.

Rogoff, B. (1995). Observing sociocultural activity on three planes: Participatory appropriation, guided participation, apprenticeship. In A. Alvarez, P. del Rio, & J. V. Wertsch (Eds.), *Sociocultural studies of mind* (pp. 139–164). Cambridge, UK: Cambridge University Press.

Rueda, R., & Moll, L. (1994). A socio-cultural perspective on motivation. In H. O'Neil, Jr. & M. Drillings (Eds.), *Motivation: Theory and research* (pp. 117–137). Hillsdale, NJ: Lawrence Erlbaum Associates.

Scribner, S. (1985). Vygotsky's uses of history. In J. V. Wertsch (Ed.), *Culture, communication and cognition: Vygotskian perspectives* (pp. 119–145). Cambridge, MA: Cambridge University Press.

Sivan, E. (1986). Motivation in social constructivist theory. *Educational Psychologist, 21*(3), 209–233.

Tharp, R. G., & Gallimore, R. (1988). *Rousing minds to life: Teaching, learning, and schooling in social context.* Cambridge, MA: Cambridge University Press.

Wertsch, J. (1985). *Culture, communication & cognition: Vygotskian perspectives.* Cambridge, MA: Cambridge University Press.

Part II

LEARNING INSIDE
THE CLASSROOM

This middle section of the book is the largest, both in terms of number of chapters and number of pages, perhaps reflecting the fact that the classroom is the place where instructional psychology has concentrated most of its effort. By deliberately sandwiching this section between discussions of informal learning and reform at the school level, we hope to encourage thinking about the connections between the classroom and other contexts for learning.

Learning Inside the Classroom features seven chapters that emphasize research-supported strategies for helping both students and teachers engage with and master concepts in school subject matter. Interestingly, these chapters pick up many of the same themes that were introduced in the informal learning contexts in "Education Outside the Classroom." These themes include the value of embedding knowledge development in the service of meaningful goals and activities, the importance of learning how to talk the talk of a discipline, the centrality of personal identity of oneself as a learner, and the advantages of tackling substantial problems together as a community rather than sitting alone at one's desk to memorize isolated bits of information.

Particularly noteworthy in these chapters is that no one grand principle is trumpeted as being the magic lever of reform; instead, it is explicitly acknowledged that these learning principles go from being merely mutually reinforcing to being co-constitutive. Hence, weaving these principles together into design experiments challenges research approaches that implicitly regard reform as the product of independent, additive changes in the classroom, and the role of research as being to identify the effect of each important factor.

Students' personal ownership of learning goals is central to many of these chapters, especially Resnick's "Toward a Practice of Constructional Design." In this chapter, Resnick points out that an important aspect of learning concerns how we adopt and adapt tools to suit our learning goals. How these tools can connect—or fail to connect—with children's personal interests, experiences, and passions is a central issue to whether children learn to work effectively with them. Resnick's approach to this problem has been to design tools that children use to design projects of their own. He aims for construction kits with enough structure so that all users are likely to engage meaningfully with important intellectual ideas, but with enough flexibility so that users' own purposes do not get distorted.

Similar issues are raised in chapter 5, by Warren and Rosebery, "This Question is Just Too, Too Easy!" These authors contrast vignettes from two middle school earth science classrooms, one a traditional classroom where the teacher leads the discussion and one in which students' self-initiated inquiry and debate drive the learning process. The researchers found that self-initiated inquiry foregrounds the concept of dialogism—the interaction of different points of view, voices, meanings, and values—as an important aspect of learning. Unique in this work is that the students' first language is Haitian Creole, and the class is conducted bilingually. Thus, these students are working to acquire two languages: English and science-talk.

In chapter 6, Edward Silver also discusses the importance of communication, this time in the mathematics classroom. "Moving Beyond Learning Alone and in Silence: Observations from the QUASAR Project Concerning Communication in Mathematics Classrooms" is based on Silver's long-term involvement with a mathematics thinking and reasoning project for middle-school students. Many researchers consider an emphasis on the role of communication and social interaction in learning to be integral to effective reform. Students in classrooms where the primary activity is explaining, discussing, and evaluating their own mathematical strategies are understanding mathematics, not just acquiring procedures.

Moreover, student talk serves an additional important function as well: to inform teachers about student thought, so that teaching can be motivated by a view of developing thought, not the objective of completing a textbook sequence. A focus on teaching guided by student understanding is another central theme of this section, one highlighted by Minstrell and Stimpson in chapter 8. In "A Classroom Environment for Learning: Guiding Students' Reconstruction of Understanding and Reasoning," Minstrell and Stimpson tell the story of Mr. Jones, a high-school science teacher who reflects on the kinds of changes he has made in his teaching to ensure student understanding and to provide students with practice in reasoning about the world as physicists do. The authors review some of the underlying principles that have motivated educational reform in this teacher's classroom, including a commitment to attend to student thinking and build from its strengths. The concrete story of Mr. Jones helps readers see beyond the rhetoric of reform to understand what this entails in everyday classroom practice.

In chapter 9, McDiarmid provides further insight into teacher cognition, pointing out that it needs to include not only knowledge about the subject matter, but also knowledge about the epistemology held by practitioners in the field. The author's premise is that beyond understanding the content of history, teachers must come to understand what it means to do history. In "Challenging Prospective Teachers' Understanding of History: An Examination of a Historiography Seminar," McDiarmid examines how a professor can teach history so that students, including prospective teachers, develop an appreciation for the nature of historical knowledge as a contested and interpreted debate, rather than a canon of undisputed facts. By examining the instructional decisions made by the history professor, McDiarmid also provides insight into how a talented teacher can convey knowledge about not only the content of a chosen field, but also its nature.

The final two chapters in this section span subject matter to describe how classroom reform can reshape teaching and learning across the curriculum. Chapter 10, "Schools for Thought: Overview of the Project and Lessons Learned from One of the Sites," by Lamon et al. describes a project that combines the resources of three different research teams led by well-known researchers in an effort to create middle school classrooms that support student achievement and thoughtfulness. The three core programs, the Jasper Woodbury Problem Solving Series, Fostering Communities of Learners (FCL), and Computer Supported Intentional Learning Environments (CSILE), are described and discussed in the context of their integration in two sixth-grade classrooms in Nashville, Tennessee. The authors discuss the achievement attained by students, including subject-matter knowledge and writing ability, as well as performance on standardized tests. The chapter closes with a description of the tools being designed to support the development of classroom communities based on the innovations in curricular structure, instructional environment, and assessment procedures used in the Schools for Thought project.

In chapter 11, "Psychological Theory and the Design of Innovative Learning Environments: On Procedures, Principles, and Systems," Brown and Campione describe the theoretical basis of an instructional program they have been developing for the past decade. Fostering Communities of Learning (FCL, which is also a component of the Schools for Thought Project) is designed to promote the critical thinking and reflection that underlie multiple forms of literacy: reading, writing, argumentation, and technological facility. A major part of the authors' research agenda has been to contribute to a theory of learning that can capture and convey the essential features of the learning environments they have designed for FCL. Brown and Campione describe the system of activities that comprise FCL and discuss the learning principles on which these activities are based, with particular attention to conceptual understanding of the principles and their practical dissemination.

This array of classroom innovations brings a new look to the cognitive science of classroom learning, not only because of the collaborations be-tween researchers and practitioners but also because of the specific focus on relations between teaching and learning. With a few notable exceptions, such as work by James Greeno, Gaea Leinhardt, and Penelope Peterson, early work in education in the cognitive science tradition tended to focus exclusively on learners. Only recently has the field widened its agenda to encompass close analysis of the knowledge and practice of teachers, in response to a growing understanding that changing student cognition is an agenda that is often best pursued by changing teacher cognition.

Chapter 5

"THIS QUESTION IS JUST TOO, TOO EASY!" STUDENTS' PERSPECTIVES ON ACCOUNTABILITY IN SCIENCE

Beth Warren
Ann S. Rosebery
TERC

In his book *Talking Science* (1990), Jay Lemke documents the forms of science talk that predominate in high school. Through his analysis, he shows that science and teaching are social processes dependent on attitudes, values, and social interests, not just on knowledge and skills. He also argues that science education perpetuates a view of science as objective, authoritative, and exclusive in the sense that it is presented in opposition to common sense and as comprehensible only to those possessing special talents. He makes the case that this ideology is maintained, sometimes unwittingly, through particular ways of talking science in the classroom (e.g., Triadic dialogues consisting of teacher question-student response-teacher evaluation sequences) and through the content of the science curriculum.

In this chapter we explore a form of classroom discourse organized around student argumentation that brings into focus an alternative view of science and science education as socially and culturally constituted, meaning-making activities. To elaborate the differences between this emerging discourse practice and conventional practice, we consider two examples—one analyzed by Lemke in *Talking Science* and one drawn from our own work in bilingual classrooms in the Cheche Konnen project—in which students and teachers grapple with the accountability (Bazerman, 1988) of theories, facts, or claims to evidence. A key aspect of our analysis is to examine the implications of Mikhail Bakhtin's core notion of dialogism (Bakhtin, 1981, 1984) for understanding student learning in science. In this way, we intend this chapter to illustrate how our perspective on learning in science is emerging through contact with socioculturally based theoretical perspectives (Bakhtin, 1981; 1984; Brown, Collins, & Duguid, 1989; Lave & Wenger, 1991; Wertsch, 1991) and with the everyday experiences of teachers and students as they work to build sense-making communities in their classrooms.

CONVENTIONAL CLASSROOM PRACTICE IN SCIENCE

We begin with an example from Lemke (1990) in which he shows how an ideology of science as objective, factual truth is enacted through the talk of both teachers and students. In the following, a high school earth science teacher unexpectedly finds himself engaged in a debate about the factual status of the idea that the earth's crust has been uplifted.

1 Teacher: Now let's try and understand this answer that I gave you here. It says,
2   "Marine fossils are found in mountains of high elevations; this suggests that
3   the crust has been uplifted." It means the earth is pushed up, OK? The
4   earth is pushed up. That's what we mean by uplifting.
5 Charley: Couldn't the water go down?
6   Vito: Yeah!
7 Teacher: It's possible that the water level has gone down, but we believe that the earth
8   has been uplifted.
9   Scott: It's just a theory though.
10   Vito: It's always a theory.
11 Teacher: This, this is a fact. This is a fact, OK? This is not a theory.
12   Vito: It's a fact?
13   Scott: Wait a minute, it can't be a fact. There's no proof that the earth was raised
14   up, unless they took measurements.
15 Teacher: They—measurements have been taken.
16   Scott: Measurements have been taken?
17 Teacher: Right now, OK? Now I'm gonna try 'n explain you something else.
18 Robert: How can you prove that that's a fact?
19 Teacher: I'm gonna try and tell you what happens. Just a second, Scott. Just listen
20   carefully. Somebody by the name of James Hutton came out with a theory
21   of Uniformitarianism. Does anyone know what that means?

[IN THE OMITTED LINES TEACHER REJECTS THREE ANSWERS]

22 Teacher: OK. What Monica is trying to say, in one sentence is, what James Hutton
23   tried to prove was: The present is the key to the past. OK? We look at
24   things, things that are happening today, happened exactly the same in the
25   past. [Teacher repeats this.] So the present is the key to the past. So by
26   looking, by looking at geologic formations, we can tell, if things were
27   uplifted, uplifted, or things subsided. OK, just by looking at them. And
28   that's how, that's how there's ways, in which they prove, that things were
29   uplifted, how can they tell they were uplifted. All right, let's go on to our
30   question.
           (Lemke, 1990, p. 141. Reprinted with permission of Ablex Publishing Corpo-
           ration)

Lemke analyzes how the debate over the status of crustal movement as theory or fact unfolds. A student, Charley, challenges the teacher's summary of crustal movement by offering an alternative theory in which, rather than the earth pushing up, the water goes down. The teacher's subsequent defense, couched in a language of possibility and belief rather than certainty, prompts other students, Scott and Vito, to question the scientific status of the teacher's statement as fact or just theory. Scott then links the determination of the statement's status to a notion of proof that derives from measurements. The teacher replies that measurements have been taken and, in response to Robert's request for a proof of crustal movement's facticity, he goes on to invoke Hutton's theory of Uniformitarianism. With that proof, he closes off debate.

Exactly why the teacher closes off debate in the way he does is not easily disentangled in our view. The opening of the episode seems to suggest that he is trying to get through some sort of review. That purpose may very well have conditioned his response to the students' challenges. On the other hand, he may be uncomfortable with the students' challenges; perhaps he is not really in command of the evidence he cites in support of crustal movement. Lastly, the teacher's own relationship to science as a form of knowledge or a way of knowing is not clear; his relationship to science may be no less authoritarian, neither more nor less examined, than that of the students.

Indeed, Lemke argues that in their talk the students and the teacher appear to differentiate theories and facts in similar ways. Theories are arguable, tentative, a matter of belief; facts are certain, not arguable, and objective, backed by measurements. Lemke (1990) noted that in lines 13–15 both Scott and, in his response, the teacher seem to be saying that "a theory is no longer a theory when we have 'measurements,' i.e. data, observations" (p. 142). Theories and facts are thus unproblematically linked to measurements. But what of these measurements? Where do they come from and how, we may ask, is their meaning taken? Directly from nature, it appears, by looking. According to Lemke, this episode makes manifest a particular "ideology of evidence and authority" underlying much of classroom practice in science, namely:

> The rhetoric of "evidence and proof" presumes that evidence itself simply exists, is found simply "by looking." It conveniently ignores that *people* always have to *decide* that something will count as evidence for something else. The notion of *proof* presumes that one particular kind of logic and argument embodies "necessary truths" rather than that such forms of argument are simply specialized genres, used by particular groups for certain purposes. (Lemke, 1990, p. 142)

Evidence, in short, is given, not constructed.

In Bakhtin's terms, the teacher's talk in this episode is authoritative:

> The authoritative word demands that we acknowledge it, that we make it our own; it binds us, quite independent of any power it might have to persuade us internally; we encounter it with its authority already fused to it. (Bakhtin, 1981, p. 342)

The teacher's invocation of Hutton's principle functions in just this way. Whatever the complexities of the teacher's intentions might be, it is clear by the end of the episode that he means to persuade the students that the status of crustal movement as a fact is not modifiable, at least given the purposes operating at that moment. From line 19 to the end, Hutton's principle is delivered with its authority already conferred; the effect of this move is to close off the possibility of argument, of considering either the theoretical or empirical basis for the proof.

Despite the teacher's assertion that crustal movement is a fact, a tension around theory and fact pervades his talk. Lemke points out that the teacher mixes the language of theory and fact ("theory," "prove," "what happens") in his closing monologue. In fact, this tension has been present from the very beginning, both within the teacher's utterances and in the interaction between his utterances and those of the students. Ironically, the teacher underscores the tension when he ends the debate, as Lemke points out, by proving a fact with a theory, contradicting his earlier position. We are left to wonder what might have happened had this tension, which the students brought out with their questions, been confronted. What might the students have come to understand about crustal movement on the one hand, and about the relations among theory, fact, and evidence on the other?

DIALOGISM

In this chapter we are concerned with exploring how an analysis of the dialogism that, according to Bakhtin (1981, 1984), characterizes all discourse can illuminate important aspects of learning. We analyze a genre of classroom talk that we think provides an interesting counterpoint to the earth science lesson. It involves a form of group argumentation that emerged in a Haitian bilingual seventh- and eighth- grade classroom. We are concerned with understanding in what ways this case differs from that of the earth science lesson, specifically, in what ways the group's argument functions dialogically (Bakhtin, 1981, 1984) to *bring into contact* different points of view on what constitutes evidence—how claims are accountable to empirical evidence—and to *open* critical, counter perspectives on what, from the claimant's point of view, is an unproblematic observation or fact. To set the analytic context, we first outline Bakhtin's thinking on dialogism.

Dialogism is a—if not the—core concept in Bakhtin's theory of discourse (1981, 1984). One of the aims of our research is to explore the implications of this idea for learning. For as Bakhtin (see Volosinov, 1973, p. 102) wrote, "any true understanding is dialogic in nature." What does this mean? First, in its most general sense, dialogism defines the relation between words and their objects, and between participants in an interaction:

> any concrete...utterance finds the object at which it was directed already as it were overlain with qualifications, open to dispute, charged with value....It is entangled, shot through with shared thoughts, points of view, alien value judgments and accents. The word, directed toward its object, enters into a dialogically agitated and tension-filled environment, . . . weaves in and out of complex interrelationships, merges with some, recoils from others, intersects with yet a third group ...

> The living utterance, having taken meaning and shape at a particular historical moment in a socially specific environment, cannot fail to brush up against thousands of living dialogic threads, woven by socio-ideological consciousness around the given object of an utterance; it cannot fail to become an active participant in social dialogue. After all, the utterance arises out of this dialogue as a continuation of it and as a rejoinder to it—it does not approach the object from the sidelines. (Bakhtin, 1981, pp. 276–277)

Utterances are thus complexly situated, socially, culturally, and historically. They are populated by intentions, those of the speaker and those of others, both past and present. They participate in an ongoing dialogue; they are responsive to the history of spoken and written words; they are both shaped by it and give shape to it. For Bakhtin, an utterance is also importantly shaped by that which has not yet been said, the "answering word that it anticipates" (Bakhtin, 1981, p. 280). Speakers and listeners are thus oriented toward one another in an attitude of responsive understanding, which may be expressed in complex relations of resistance or support. Such understanding is built on contact, what Bakhtin called "interanimation," between the specific world views, values, expressive accents, ways of speaking, and so forth of different participants in an interaction.

Secondly, in a more specialized sense, the idea of dialogism is tied to a pluralistic view of discourse. In this way, Bakhtin foreshadowed contemporary sociolinguistic perspectives on discourse (Cook-Gumperz, 1986; Gee, 1990; Heath, 1983; Ochs, 1988), what Bakhtin (1981) himself referred to as "social languages (p. 275)." A discourse constitutes a specific point of view on the world. Each discourse is characterized by its own objects, meanings, and values; each has its own ways of conceptualizing and evaluating the world in words, in mathematical symbols, in the lines of a drawing, to name a few. As such, discourses may be juxtaposed with one another in various types of relations, including agreement, opposition, authority, parody, irony, and so on. When brought into contact in these ways, discourses and the world views they embody become subject to evaluation, revision, and refinement (Morson & Emerson, 1990). According to Bakhtin, this "interanimation" among discourses of different points of view, voices, meanings, and values is dialogism; and, as we noted earlier, it creates the ground for understanding, for change, development, and learning.

Viewed from this perspective, the teacher's talk in the earth science lesson was authoritative in that it denied the possibility of sustained, critical interanimation among his viewpoint, his representation of Hutton's viewpoint, and the students' viewpoint(s). Different voices were certainly present in the discussion, even tensions within the same voice. But at various points, no more pointedly than at the end, the teacher closes off the possibility of interaction among the different voices; he does not allow the students to play with his representation of Hutton's view, to argue with it, to test it against their own ideas or other voices (e.g., the writings of Darwin, Gould, or Hutton himself). The teacher, in short, invokes Hutton authoritatively, as the final word. Perhaps more to the point, he speaks through Hutton, merging his own authority with that of the scientist.[1] If the students

---

[1]A stronger reading of this move has been suggested to us by Patrick Gonzales (personal communication, August 1, 1994). Rather than merging with Hutton's authority, the teacher may actually be deferring to it, a shift in responsibility by which he tries to achieve authority he may not feel he has. Read in this way, the teacher's move simultaneously displays a stance toward scientific authority that is uncritical.

wish to continue the argument, they now must challenge the whole edifice of scientific authority, not just their teacher.

In the following section, we explore more fully how a dialogically oriented analysis can open new perspectives on learning and help us make sense of what appear to be marked differences in the talk found in the earth science lesson and that found in our example of student argumentation. We examine how a group of students and their teacher develop particular ways of making and presenting claims by putting into contact different points of view on "accountability" (Bazerman, 1988). By accountability, we mean, following Bazerman (1988), how scientific claims about observed events are made accountable to empirical evidence. We pay particular attention to how norms for evidence are constituted in the dialogic interaction between differing perspectives. The analysis of this group's talk is intended to illuminate a way in which students and teachers may approach the question of accountability to evidence that differs significantly from that enacted in the earth science lesson.

Scott's Claim

The following analysis focuses on a discussion of a claim that one student, Scott, made about a population of snails he had taken home to observe. The discussion is structured as a series of challenges to Scott's initial claim and the subsequent modifications he makes to it. In these disagreement sequences (Lynch, 1985), Scott either deflects the criticism and maintains his claim or modifies it. These modifications in turn prompt additional challenges and modifications. The question of interest to us in analyzing this discussion is how, through these disagreement sequences, the argument functions dialogically to bring into contact differing perspectives on what it means for a claim to be accountable to evidence. Through such interanimation (Bakhtin, 1981), one perspective is evaluated from the point of view of another, creating a space within which new meanings can emerge.

Let us first set the context for the discussion. It took place in a seventh- and eighth-grade Haitian bilingual classroom that participated in the Cheche Konnen (which means "search for knowledge" in Haitian Creole) project during the 1991–1992 school year. In the Cheche Konnen project, teachers—bilingual, ESL, and a science specialist—and researchers are exploring ways to create communities of scientific practice in linguistically and culturally diverse classrooms (Rosebery, Warren, & Conant, 1992; Warren & Rosebery, 1995; Warren, Rosebery, & Conant, 1994). Among the questions we are addressing are the nature of such communities, how to create and sustain them, and the interrelationships among different discourses in relation to students' learning in such communities. By "communities of scientific practice," we mean classrooms in which students construct and refine their scientific understanding by investigating questions they have posed, developing and arguing evidence, negotiating claims, and building and criticizing theories. The curriculum emerges from the students' own scientific activity and is shaped by both teachers and students.

We—teachers, students, and researchers—are working toward the development of classroom communities in which students appropriate the discourse of science: a set of sociohistorically constituted practices for constructing facts, for integrating facts into explanations, for defending and challenging claims, for interpreting evidence, for using and developing models, for transforming observations into findings, and for arguing theories. From this perspective, learning in science cannot be reduced simply to the assimilation of scientific facts, the mastery of scientific process skills, the refinement of a mental model, or the correction of misconceptions. Rather, learning in science is conceptualized as the appropriation of a particular way of making sense of the world, of conceptualizing, evaluating, and representing the world.

The discussion that follows took place in June, at the end of the 1991–1992 school year. Haitian Creole was the first language of the 15 students and their teacher, Mr. S. In addition to other academic subjects, Mr. S. taught science to his students twice a week for an hour starting in the spring term. Like many bilingual teachers, Mr. S.'s experience with science both as a learner and a teacher was limited. As a relative newcomer to teaching, he had in fact never taught science before the 1991–1992 school year. In the context of the Cheche Konnen project, however, he had spent a few months in the fall/early winter of 1991 studying aquatic ecology collaboratively with teachers, a biologist, and other project staff.

In the classroom, the focus of science was also aquatic ecology. The students took field trips to a local pond to collect water and plant samples. Back in their classroom, they set up several aquaria that remained active until June. They spent approximately four months observing plant and animal life in their aquaria and investigating questions at the level of individual species and community interactions that arose from their observations. The students became particularly interested in snails, organisms that reproduced prolifically in their classroom tanks. They studied aspects of snail development, reproduction, anatomy, and ecology.

The class engaged regularly in a routine of sharing and discussing individual students' observations, a routine that was distinctive to science and that drew on the students' evident skill in argumentation (Ballenger, 1994).

Vigorous discussions frequently resulted in which a claimant was asked questions by the other students, sometimes to clarify and other times to challenge points. This routine of sharing observations is one that Mr. S. engaged in with his fellow teachers in the context of a twice-monthly project seminar in which the teachers and project staff collaboratively explored scientific practice based on our own scientific activity and talk, on discussion of readings in science and about science, and on analysis of classroom scientific activity and talk (Warren & Rosebery, 1995).

Prior to the particular discussion with which we are concerned, one student, Murana, confessed that she had not done the observations needed to address her question about whether snails are carnivorous ("Do snails eat meat?"). Scott, who had already reported to the class, replied that he had some data relevant to Murana's question and described an investigation in which he gave meat to snails. In addition, he told the class that he had been keeping a sample of snails at home. When he announced that he had 30 snails in his sample, the class was amazed. The teacher, Mr. S., asked him how many generations of snail he had and Scott answered that he had at least three.[2] Murana then asked him how he knew he had more than one generation and a lively discussion ensued.

"Lively" perhaps does not fully convey the character of the discussion or of the context as captured on videotape. The students were highly animated, frequently interrupting one another. We have tried to show some of the dynamics but decided in the end to trade off accuracy of transcription for clarity and accessibility. Murana was actually milling around the back of the classroom for part of the discussion until she was asked to sit down. There are moments of contagious, perhaps embarrassed, laughter, particularly when the students begin to talk about some mechanics of snail reproduction. The discussion is in short very messy; it does not have the orderliness characteristic of most classroom discussion.

But in its messiness, the discussion perhaps opens up for view some of the ways in which social identity is inextricably a part of a student's learning identity (Eckert, 1990; Lave & Wenger, 1991; McDermott, 1993; Mehan, 1993). We are not going to explore this in any detail in this chapter, although we will comment on it in our concluding remarks. For the moment, we simply want to provide some relevant detail on Scott's history within this class. According to Mr. S. (personal communication, June 3, 1992), prior to

---

[2]The way Scott talks about the number of generations he claims to have is confusing. In line 4 he claims to have two generations of snails whereas in lines 6–7 he says that "the same babies made other babies," which suggests three generations. It seems clear from the conversation that the dispute is over whether the babies of his original snails had babies, that is, whether there are three generations.

this discussion Scott had not participated in any sustained way in science discussion. Usually Scott would take a turn, be challenged, give in, and grow quiet. In this discussion, however, Scott's participation is of a different order altogether, although his credibility, as in previous class discussions, is still very much on the line.

The discussion took place in Haitian Creole. The text has been translated into English; the original transcription is included in the Appendix.[3]

June 1, 1992

1   Scott: OK, I am going to answer Murana's question. This question is just too, too
2   easy.
3   Mr. S: Go ahead.
4   Scott: Murana's question, she asks how do I know there are two generations of snail?
5   Me, I said, when the snails made eggs, the eggs hatched. And when I looked the
6   snails were still there, because I know their colors. And the same baby made another
7   baby and then the little babies laid eggs.
8   James: //Question!]
9   Mr. S: //But how - wait, wait...] - how did you identify them?
10   Scott: Hunh?
11   Mr. S: How did you identify them?
12   Scott: How?
13   Mr. S: Yeah.
14   Scott: I don't understand.
15   Mr. S: No, you say - okay - you have 30 snails.
16   Scott: About 30.
17   Mr. S: About 30. OK. So a mother made babies, right? She laid eggs. But how do
18   you know that the grown babies - right, I don't know, at what size does a snail make
19   babies? I don't know. //Would anyone here] like to know at what size they make
20   babies?
21   Manel: //Yes .]
22   Scott: The babies are small
23   Mr. S: No, talk to the class. [ ] I don't know [ ].
24   Scott: = the little ones are smaller than //an ant.]
25   Mr. S: //Sit down, Murana.] Than what?
26   Scott: Than an ant.
27   Mr. S: OK.

---

[3]The transcription conventions we use are as follows:
//] indicates overlapped speech
- placed at point of self interruption
underline marks stress
[ ] unintelligible speech
(...) omitted segment
= latched utterance, utterances with no time gap between them

28 Manel: And they made babies?
29 Scott: No, they grew and made babies.

At the point we enter the discussion, Scott has just asserted that in addition to his original snails he has two new generations of snails. Murana challenges him to explain how he knows that, and Scott eagerly takes up her challenge. In fact, he is so confident in this move that he treats her question dismissively (lines 1–2: "This question is just too, too easy."). Scott then proceeds in lines 4–7 to recount what he claims to have observed, that the babies born to the snails made other babies.

Scott's account is one of discovery, of "observations made upon undisturbed or unmanipulated nature" (Bazerman, 1988, p. 66). For Scott, its meaning is simply, straightforwardly what he observed; the reported events—the snails made eggs/the eggs hatched/the same baby made another baby/the little babies laid eggs—constitute the "evidence" on which he rests his claim. To lend his account credibility, he uses two strategies. In one, he invokes his own authority as an observer (lines 5–6: "when I looked..."), and in the other he establishes his knowledgeability in this domain (line 6: "because I know their colors").

Scott's account is immediately met with interest. James attempts to take the floor but is pre-empted by Mr. S. who asks Scott to specify his identification procedures. This marks the first, but not the last, call for specification of Scott's methods. Although Mr. S. initiates this line of questioning, he subsequently allows the conversation to unfold along lines the students themselves develop. When Scott says he does not understand the question, Mr. S. enlarges its scope from what Scott observed or knows (lines 17–18: "But how do you know that the grown babies...") to a fundamental aspect of the biology of individual organisms, specifically, the reproductive cycle of snails (lines 18–19: "...at what size does a snail make babies?"). He is in effect asking: "When are snails mature enough to reproduce?"

Thus in this first sequence Mr. S. places Scott's claim into motion around a central concern, namely, how Scott knows he has multiple generations, by what method did he identify the different generations of babies? At the same time, he is indicating his own interest in the question and his appreciation for its authenticity; it is a question to which he, the teacher, does not have the answer. By inviting the students to express their own interest in the question, he establishes it as a genuine ground for inquiry rather than as an occasion for displaying known facts.

Scott deals with Mr. S.'s question by resituating it within the context of his own observations (line 22: "The babies are small..."). His response, however, proves problematic in light of Mr. S.'s reframing, as Manel (line 28) shows: If the babies are so small, how could they reproduce? In the face of Manel's challenge, Scott modifies his claim: (line 29: "No, they grew and made babies."). With this modification, Scott unwittingly introduces a tension into his account, one which will later turn out to be pivotal in dismantling his claim. When he says "they grew and made babies," it is unclear whether this is something Scott has observed and can describe or something he has improvised in the moment by way of explanation. As we see, this modified account, although apparently effective in the immediate moment in disarming Manel's challenge, causes Scott irremediable difficulties later on.

In the next disagreement sequence James raises a question about the basis of Scott's claim.

```
(...)
30   Mr. S: Joel, um, James?
31   James: Yeah, here's what I say, Scott. What if the babies made babies with the
32         mother?
33   Scott: I can't say that. I can't talk about that. I said there are two generations. That's
34         what I said. That's what I said. I didn't say anything about babies having sex with
35         their mothers.
           [Some commotion follows.]
```

At this point in the argument, Scott is able to deflect James' challenge by arguing not with its content but with its relevance or accuracy. James, of course, never pretended to be quoting Scott. Rather he was making a point, somewhat sensationally, about the need to know exactly who mated with whom, if Scott's claim is to be believed. In turning James' question into an instance of reported speech (Volosinov, 1973)—"I didn't say anything about babies having sex with their mothers"—Scott at one and the same time evaluates its content as well as its author. Suddenly it is James' reliability that is in question. James has in effect left himself open to this kind of move by not linking his challenge directly to Scott's account, and Scott takes advantage. For the moment at least, Scott wins the round. But he will hear this line of questioning again, when it is recast in terms of a more articulated biological perspective and tied directly to his own words.

In lines 36–75, Manel launches an interrogation into the material basis of Scott's assertion, that is, what exactly Scott did, how many snails he had originally, how many babies the snails made each day, and other questions.

```
36   Mr. S: Manel?
37   Manel: I have a lot of questions for Scott.
38   Scott: Yes?
39 Claudie: Give two.
```

40 Manel: I ask you, when you took them, how many did you go home with in the first
41   place?
42 Scott: Oh, I took a big - I could have taken about 10 or 5 like that.
43 Mireille: //[ ] Scott who went and [ ]?]
44 Manel: //Can you say how many] babies they made each day?
45 Scott: How many babies they make each day? How would I know? They make them
46   in egg masses.
47 Manel: And you say //that you have 30?]
48 Murana / Mirelle:
          //How did you count them?] How did you count them?
49 Claudie: No, when snails lay eggs there are lots of masses, don't you know that?
51 Manel: No-
52 Claudie: There are many masses.
53 Manel: No-
54 Mireille: Let Scott defend himself!
55 Claudie: No, if it's something I've seen, it's normal for me to say something.
56 Manel: No, Scott should tell me //how many they made] because you had 10
57 Mirielle: //Scott is supposed to defend himself.]
58 Scott: You know why I said there were 30? Because the babies of the babies, the
59   ones that were just born, I counted them. That's it I counted them because, because I
60   used to see them stick to the sides of the container.
61 Manel: OK, Mr. S - Scott, I believe Scott is lying.
62 Mr. S: //Why?]
63 Scott: //No I'm not.]
64 Manel: Because, listen! You have 10 - //listen, listen, listen, listen]
65 Scott: //OK, OK, OK, OK.] I'll bring them tomorrow
66   if you want, [ ] all the snails [ ].
      [Commotion]

67 Mr. S: Listen, let him speak [ ]. Go ahead.
68 Manel: You have 10 snails. When you look into what you put them in you have 30.
69   What about the rest of them, the rest didn't make babies?
70 Scott: I said about 30. Isn't that what I said?
71 Manel: No, I ask you, did the rest make babies?
72 Scott: Yes, they made babies.
73 Manel: [ ] made babies?
74 Scott: Some made babies.
75 Manel: What about the rest of them?
76 Scott: The rest of them? I don't know.
77 Manel: [ ]
      [Some students giggling]

In this sequence Manel seeks to establish how many snails Scott started
with and how many babies they made each day. Manel does not believe that

Scott, who says he started with five or ten snails, can now have 30. It seems
that Manel is concerned with figuring out whether 30 snails is enough, given
the initial conditions. By the end of this sequence, Manel leads Scott into
what turns out to be a crucial modification of his original assertion. Let's
look at how this sequence unfolds.

Scott answers Manel's challenge about the number of babies the snails made
each day with a rhetorically framed assertion of fact (lines 45–46). In this case
Scott's assertion is supported by another student, Claudie, who in lines 49–50
aligns himself with Scott by challenging Manel's knowledgeability (Goodwin,
1990). In this sequence, we also see Claudie arguing for a norm that allows
students other than the "defendant" to bring forth evidence (line 55). Manel
rejects Claudie's argument because for him the argument rests precisely on what
Scott has seen and on *how* he accounts for his observations.

In his challenge, Manel demands specific details from Scott about his
work. In lines 58–60 Scott provides the basis for his conclusion that "there
were about 30" snails. He describes the method he used to collect those data
and why he believes it was effective. Manel remains unconvinced and
accuses Scott of lying. Scott denies the accusation and offers to bring in the
snails to demonstrate the truth of his claim. It is as if Scott is saying that
once the other students see the snails they will agree that they see what he
claims to have seen. Paraphrasing Bazerman (1988, p. 5), Scott's offer
betrays a belief that the scientific claim merely points to a self-revealing
nature, that seeing is believing. The proof, in short, is in the showing.

Scott seems to realize at this point that he needs to produce something
beyond his own account, that his word alone cannot establish his credibility.
But Manel is not satisfied by Scott's offer. He persists in trying to make the
numbers, as he sees them, come out right. In fact, he takes Scott's own
justification and builds the beginning of a new argument (lines 64–75),
namely, that what needs to be specified here is not how *many* snails there
are (perhaps he is conceding this point to Scott) but *which* snails actually
made babies. In response, Scott modifies his assertion a second time to "*some*
made babies," an example of equivocation in Scott's discovery account. Is
this modification based on observation or is it improvised?

Scott's modification provokes a challenge from Mireille. Her question
(line 78) crystallizes the central issue on which both Scott's original and
modified assertions rest:

78 Mireille: How do you know which made babies and which didn't make babies?

In order to establish that he in fact has three generations of snails, Scott
must be able to answer Mireille's question. The debate all along has been

over whether what Scott has reported actually happened. Within the context of this argument, Mireille demands a new level of accountability. She is not just asking Scott to identify which made babies and which did not; rather she is asking him to provide the evidential basis for his statement. Her question makes it clear that *how* Scott knows is essential to her assessment of *what* Scott knows.

After a sidetrack during which another student tries to answer Mireille's question by explaining that snails are hermaphroditic (which we omit here for brevity's sake), Darlene returns the discussion to the main line of argument (lines 79–98). She anchors her question in Scott's claim to have 30 snails and, building on Mireille's challenge, initiates a related disagreement sequence. This line of questioning echoes the one first suggested by Mr. S. at the beginning of the discussion: "At what size does a snail make babies?"

(...)
79 Darlene: But like if you say you have 30 snails
80   Scott: Uh hunh.
81 Darlene: = in how much time did each snail make babies? //Like] if a snail is born
82   today, tomorrow can it have a baby?
83   Asline: //Yes Scott.]
84   Mr. S: //Good question.]   //Good question.]

[Commotion, students cry out, some hoot]
85   Scott: I said that! I said when they grew up. I said when they grew up they made
86   babies.
87   Mr. S: OK, kids, can I say something? That's something I would like to know
88   because we are doing research on that question (in the teachers' group). I would like
89   to know - good question - respond Scott [ ]

[Renewed commotion]
90   Scott: OK, me, here's what I said, when [ ] asked me this, when [ ] asked
91   when the snails are born can they just turn around and make babies right then?
92   I said no. I said it's when they grew up that they made babies because, because
93   I used to put-
94 Darlene: //Let me ask you a question before you finish answering.]
95   Scott: //Won't you let me finish?]
96 Darlene: Before you answer it like that, let me ask you something while you're saying
97   that. Like if you say they made babies, that's what you said, how much time does it
98   take a snail to grow up?
99   Scott: How could I know?
100 Darlene: Well, then, //Scott]
101   Scott: //Snails are always small.]

Darlene reaccents Mr. S.'s earlier question, which he framed in terms of size, in terms of the time it takes for a snail to reach sexual maturity. She asks both about Scott's snails specifically and, to clarify her point, about snails in general. Echoing Mr. S.'s line of inquiry, Darlene situates the proof of Scott's claim in relation to the biology of snail reproduction (lines 81–82); in effect, she is asking what *model* of snail development underlies Scott's claim. In response, Scott repeatedly insists on the letter of his prior statements, that "when (the snails) grew up they made babies." In his denial, Scott is asking to be held accountable for only those things he actually said; he is attempting to reject the relevance of Darlene's question.

Mr. S., however, intercedes at this point (lines 87–89) to support emphatically the relevance of Darlene's question. Why? We suggest that, by reformulating Mr. S.'s earlier challenge, Darlene refocuses the conversation onto a point he considers to be critical in establishing the credibility of Scott's claim. Mr. S. links her question to his own work, marking it as something of interest, outside his own knowledge. Mr. S.'s allusion to his research group, the group of teachers with whom he works in the Cheche Konnen project, may also be taken to suggest that Scott's work does not exist in a vacuum but in relation to the work of others and to a developing body of knowledge. Thus, by taking the floor in this way, Mr. S. lends Darlene's question scientific, pedagogical, and personal authority; it underscores the crucial place her call for a model of snail development has in deciding the credibility of Scott's claim. Mr. S. is, in short, letting Scott know that Darlene's question is one with which he must contend.

Scott recognizes the need to respond (line 90: "OK, me, here's what I said."). He then proceeds to replay in his own words Darlene's question and his reply. He attempts to further explain his thinking but is interrupted by Darlene who in lines 96–98 repeats her question, presumably because Scott has not yet clarified what it means for a snail to "grow up." Interestingly, she invokes Scott's own strategy of owning or disowning particular statements ("I didn't say that!" "Here's what I said-") to redirect the point of the discussion to the question of growth (Goodwin, 1990; Volosinov, 1973): "Like if you say they made babies, that's what you said, how much time does it take for a snail to grow up?" Unless Scott can address this question either with some form of convincing evidence or with an elaborated model of snail development, he will not be able to escape the circularity of his own account. It appears from Scott's subsequent reply (lines 99 and 101) that Darlene has made her point. Scott admits that this is something beyond his ability to know since "snails are always small." But the question of identification is precisely what has been at issue throughout this discussion. In order to elevate his claim that he has multiple generations of snails to the status of fact, he needs to be able to distinguish "which snails made babies and which didn't make babies." This he apparently cannot do given the "data" he has at hand.

In this final sequence, Darlene is in effect holding Scott accountable to his words while at the same time reaccenting them to serve her own argumentative purpose (Volosinov, 1973). Ironically, this has been Scott's defensive strategy all along, one by which he disarmed his earlier critics. Darlene turns the table on Scott by directly taking up his account (as Manel had done earlier, forcing a modification). She challenges his use of the term growth to explain the change in population. On both sides of the argument, then, the students are taking the unfolding discourse as a form of public record (a factual record) that can be used at any point to argue for or against a given claim or challenge.

How does Darlene make her point? Throughout the discussion Scott repeatedly invokes the notion of growth in a general sense, perhaps by analogy to human beings, to support his claim. The requirements of the logic of general biology as he understands it argue that snails, like any living organism, grow, and when they grow up they make babies. When Darlene invokes the same notion, she does so within a different referential perspective (Wertsch, 1991); she is asking Scott to specify what growth means in relation to a snail's reproductive life. Her referential perspective is that of snail biology; Scott's is more general, having to do with a logic of reproduction applicable to living organisms in general. Darlene's use of Scott's words functions analytically to place them in relation to the meaning of growth in the context of snail biology. Darlene does not quarrel with the idea of growth per se, but with its particular meaning in the case under discussion. When at the end Scott wonders aloud *how* he could know how much time it takes for a snail to grow up since snails are always small, he brings into sharp relief the point of Darlene's probing. What, then, does it mean to say that snails "grow up" and, importantly, how can one tell? Scott wants to argue his claim logically, but the students are demanding that, if he is to persuade them of its facticity, he must argue it empirically in relation to the biology of snail reproduction. In short, the students' challenges emphasize the centrality of models, methods, and data in establishing and evaluating claims about their scientific activity.

Discussion

In *Laboratory Life* (1986), Latour and Woolgar argued that scientists transform their observations into findings through argumentation and persuasion, not through measurement and discovery. They portray the activity of scientists within a laboratory as a constant struggle for the generation and acceptance of fact-like statements. Their account details how in laboratories the facticity of a statement is constructed or deconstructed through the "superimposition of several statements or documents in such a way that all the statements are seen to relate to something outside of, or beyond, the reader's or author's subjectivity." These documents (e.g., histograms, spectra, peaks, recorded numbers, etc.) are obtained from what they call "inscription devices" (e.g., bioassays, spectrometers, etc.) generated within the laboratory or from papers written by investigators outside the laboratory; they are, in short, the means by which scientists convince others within their community to take up their claims, to pass them along, to make them more or less of a fact. In this culture, the showing of things that are not present or not visible is inseparable from the telling (Latour, 1986).

The problem of inscription seems to describe at least part of Scott's predicament. In the discussion around his claim, we see that beyond a certain point, Scott's only recourse in the face of continued challenges is to refer back to his own prior account or to modify it according to a logic outside his own experience of discovery. The vague, general language in which he couches many of his responses leaves him vulnerable to criticism. The difficulty he faces is to figure out what would constitute a persuasive account, what methods, model, and data he needs to establish his claim as relating to something outside his own experience or subjective evaluation, and how he can present his claim (e.g., forms of stating evidence). The problem of inscription, as outlined by Latour (1986), includes how to define and mobilize resources (e.g., records of population change, reproductive rates for individual snails) that can be displaced from the object itself, presented, and read. Needless to say, mobilization, presentation, and readability themselves open up layers of complexity. It is not a question of merely having an inscription, but of how one comes up with it, what sense one makes of it, how one explains it, and what others take it to mean (Collins & Pinch, 1993; Latour, 1983; Monk & Nemirovsky, in press; Nemirovsky, in press).

One result of the argument is that, at least as far as the other students are concerned, Scott's assertion is reduced from what, to his mind, was a self-evident fact to a disputable and potentially investigable claim (Latour & Woolgar, 1986). At the same time and as part of the same argumentation process, the class begins to construct norms for what it would take to transform a claim like Scott's into a "fact." These norms argue for evidence that can be mobilized (Latour, 1986) to lift a statement (e.g. "the babies made other babies") outside of the claimant's own subjective assessment into an inspectable and presentable (Latour, 1986) "objective" realm (e.g.

"which ones made babies and which didn't"), one that can be accounted for empirically.[4] Specifically, the standard they are constructing calls for the evidence and the methodology on which Scott's account and its modifications rest. How did Scott come to be convinced of his discovery and for what reasons? Further, it situates Scott's discovery in relation to a specific body of knowledge, that of snail biology, rather than to a more generalized domain of growth and reproduction.

We do not think we can claim that Scott comes to understand fully the implications of the class's emerging norm within the course of the discussion. His own words, "How could I know?," testify more than once that he does not know what to do with the students' challenges. His understanding, however, is not static; by the end of the segment, the certainty of his claim has clearly been shaken. On the basis of his teacher's testimony, moreover, it appears that this conversation proved to be something of a watershed for Scott; rather than withdrawing in the face of a challenge, Scott stayed in the argument, at times fending off the students' challenges, at others moving the discussion forward with his modifications. Scott may not have been able to answer the later, more consequential challenges, but he at least believed he had something worth defending.

In addition, by staying in the argument, Scott helped the class bring to the surface important facets of scientific accountability. Through their discussion the participants put into contact two viewpoints on accountability, one represented by Scott and the other by his challengers, including the teacher. The challengers' perspective—its increasing specificity—emerges dialogically through the interplay between their questions and Scott's modifications. Similarly, Scott's viewpoint is problematized in the process, as he seems to realize by the end when he pleadingly asks: "How could I know? Snails are always small." Earlier he implied he could distinguish snails by their size. In responding to Darlene's challenge, he ends by talking himself into a contradiction.

Thus, the key contrast in the discussions of Scott's claim and of crustal movement lies in the way in which their respective arguments about the relationship of facts to evidence are taken up. In Lemke's earth science lesson, the disputability of a scientific fact is foreclosed and with it the possibility of problematizing assumed relations among theory, fact, and

---

[4]Subject–object relations in scientific practice are not necessarily best conceptualized as dichotomous. In a study of the discursive practices of a university-based physics research group, Ochs, Gonzales, and Jacoby (in press) argue that physicists actively express their subjective involvement with the objects they study through indeterminate referential constructions that mediate their interpretive activity (e.g., "When I come down I'm in the domain state."). The effect is to blur the boundaries between themselves as subjects and physical systems as objects.

evidence. In the discussion of Scott's snails, by contrast, the relations among claim, fact, and evidence are precisely what is negotiated as different points of view are brought into contact with one another. The central underlying problem with which the students grapple is what constitutes accountability in the science they do. Admittedly, these two cases are not entirely equivalent. Scott's claim, for instance, clearly does not carry the same scientific authority as does crustal movement or Hutton's principle. Thus it is not surprising that Scott is energetically questioned by his classmates. Yet in the earth science lesson, the facticity of crustal movement is also disputed, creating what turns out to be an unrealized opportunity for considering the nature of the relationships the students themselves are calling into question.

That argument can function dialogically to help define a community's practice—specifically, its norms of evidence—by bringing into contact differing perspectives and making those differences explicit is supported by Bazerman's (1988) analysis of the emergence and transformation of the written experimental report from 1665 to 1800. He explores the development of this genre of scientific discourse in terms of changing notions of accountability, that is, the constraints operating within particular socially and historically situated communities on how scientists present written accounts of nature. According to Bazerman, within a span of about 150 years, experimental accounts changed in character from uncontested reports of observed events (i.e., "cookbook recipes for creating marvelous effects or effects of practical use," p. 66) to intentional investigations, to tests of theory, and finally to proofs of claims. He describes how the genre developed as experiments began to assume a more argumentative function. For example, challenged by disagreements, scientists such as Newton began to explain more fully the methods of their experiments, the rationales for those methods, and the conditions under which the experiments took place. Thus, argument helped forge norms for accountability within the genre of the experimental report, by pushing "the individual author into recognizing that he is not simply reporting the self-evident truth of events, but rather is telling a story that can be questioned and that has a meaning which itself can be mooted. The most significant task becomes to present that meaning and persuade others of it." (Bazerman, 1988, p. 78). In this sense, the discussion of Scott's claim and that of crustal movement are distinctly different. In the crustal movement discussion, differences in viewpoint and contradictions internal to a given viewpoint are not openly contested. In the discussion of Scott's claim, by contrast, differences are not just expressed, they are fully engaged in argument such that the students specify differences in meaning for crucial terms (e.g., what it means to "grow up") that bear on the model of growth underlying the claim; they question Scott's methods; and they begin to formulate norms of evidence for discovery accounts such as Scott's.

Nevertheless, the discussion of Scott's claim is not without problems. Most crucially, Scott's plea "How could I know?" goes unanswered. The discussion took place in June, just a few days before most of the students graduated from the eighth grade. Consequently, no further work on Scott's claim was undertaken. In theory, however, and no doubt unwittingly on Scott's part, his question creates an opening that could provide him with the means to construct a credible account. It also provides an opportunity for all the students to learn how claims are investigated and established as facts in science. Scott clearly does not know "how to know" in this case; nor is it clear that the other students know any better how to take their challenges and formulate them in relation to Scott's claim in such a way that the claim becomes investigable. In this sense the discussion of Scott's claim brings the class to a critical boundary in the appropriation of scientific discourse, one they perhaps cannot cross by themselves. But their teacher can explicitly coordinate the students' understandings and ways of talking with those of science; it is through such scaffolding that the students can learn to do what they don't already know how to do (Brown & Campione, 1994; Gee, 1994; Palincsar & Brown, 1984).

What direction might such scaffolding take? This question has been raised many times in discussions we have had with teachers and other researchers in the last two years about Scott's claim. From these discussions, we have drawn several implications for practice, specifically, for ways that a teacher might assist the students in seeing Scott's plea in relation to a more elaborated, sociohistorically developed set of practices for empirically investigating claims. In the case of Scott's claim, a teacher might want to affirm publicly the new perspective that the students' challenges have defined in relation to his claim: How much time does it take for a snail to reach sexual maturity? One way to accomplish this would be to engage the students in summarizing explicitly the problems they have exposed with Scott's claim (e.g., the nature of his evidence, his methods, his model of growth), and then to link those criticisms with scientific practices. This kind of analysis could extend to the various students' challenges as well as to Scott's claim itself. In our view, each of the students' criticisms bears importantly on core aspects of scientific practice, for example, on the relation of claims to evidence, on what counts as an explanation in science, and on how questions and hypotheses in science are typically constrained by some view or model of a system of underlying relations, in this case, the reproductive cycle of snails.

One route, for example, might be for the class to uncover the concerns implicit in a challenge like Manel's: "Can you say how many babies they made each day?" As stated, Manel's challenge seems to have rhetorical force, but it is unclear to what extent it has scientific force. Why, according to Manel, is it important for Scott to be able to say how *many* babies *each* snail made *each* day? This is a strong call for detailed quantitative data, but to what specific end? Is Manel asking a question about the nature of the evidence one needs to be persuasive and its relationship to methodology? These questions assume a scientific perspective that has not been made explicit in the discussion. Similarly, the other students, Darlene especially, make the point that it is the particulars of growth in snails—the underlying model of growth— on which any assessment of Scott's claim depends. Darlene situates her criticism in an explanatory framework of snail biology, whereas Scott bases his defense on some general notion of growth. What does Scott make of this distinction? What do the other students make of it? These sorts of distinctions are powerful in delineating scientific from every-day ways of knowing and arguing; making them an explicit part of the public record might help Scott and the other students understand why his use of "grow up" turned out to be vulnerable to a criticism like Darlene's.

Having summarized differences in the meanings and uses of evidence, models, and methods, the class might then proceed to address the question that arose out of their criticisms: How long does it take for snails to become sexually mature? To begin they might discuss different models of growth that could drive their investigation and use these to constrain the investigation's design. How might the class take up this question? In another school that same year, the teachers and students in a combined fifth- and sixth-grade Haitian bilingual class designed and conducted a related study to determine the size at which snails made babies. In developing their study, the students grappled with the always-complicated problem of defining a methodology adequate to their question, how to design a study that would yield the kinds of data they would need to answer their question. They isolated snails of different sizes, ranging from 1mm to 9mm, in nine petri dishes. They discussed the importance of providing each with a suitable environment and comparable food supply. They agreed to observe the snails daily to see if any produced egg masses. They measured the size of each snail once a week to see if they had grown enough to require "reclassification" (transfer to another petri dish containing snails of the next larger size). In the end they decided that on the basis of their data they could safely conclude that snails 7mm to 9mm in length are capable of reproduction. However, they ran into difficulty interpreting their data for shorter lengths because some students mixed snails of different sizes. One group of students combined 3mm and

5mm long snails in one dish. Although egg masses were produced in the mixed case, the class decided to disqualify the result because it violated the design criteria they established for their study; they could not determine which of the different size snails made babies.

In the light of this investigation, work like Scott's, however flawed, can be seen as a useful, preliminary observation or exploration that can lead to more formal inquiry. Learning the differences between these two forms of inquiry is an important move in bringing the students and their work into closer contact with scientific practice. Work along more formal lines also prepares the way for considering core ideas in biology and ecology, for example, relations among niche, reproductive effort and strategies, and natural selection that underlie the question of why snails have so many babies.

There are, in short, at least two important and related directions for teachers to pursue with discussions such as the one this class had about Scott's claim. One is close and public inspection of the substance of the discussions themselves. The purpose is to bring out distinctions in meaning, to construct shared understandings, to make underlying assumptions about methodology, norms of evidence, and explanatory models explicit—broadly, to coordinate the students' ways of knowing and talking with those of science. A second, related direction entails a level of communal reflection and evaluation on the place and function of argumentation in science. Why is argumentation so important? What constitutes a scientific argument? What does it mean to be persuasive in a scientific argument? Why should it matter? Why is it, for example, that the "facts" do not speak for themselves, as Scott would like them to? And in what ways is persuasion in science distinctive or not from everyday forms? Mastering the discourse(s) of science requires action and reflection at both of these levels.

Before concluding, we want to raise a final issue. We alluded earlier to the relation between learning and social identity (Eckert, 1989, 1990; McDermott, 1993), although we have not elaborated the point in this chapter. If one watches the videotape of Scott's claim, however, it is clear that social identity is very much on display and at stake. For example, we talked about the credibility of Scott's claim. But in this analysis we have not linked the intellectual judgment to a more personal one, even though there are strong suggestions in the transcript that we should (e.g., as when Manel accuses Scott of lying). Who is Scott within the social organization of the classroom (not to mention beyond) such that he is seen as not being very credible and such that he has been to this point unwilling to argue his position in a sustained way? What is it about the social organization of science in this class that allows Scott finally to put himself on the line? How is it that science, of all things, may be a means by which Scott can at least attempt to re-constitute his social identity? Are there aspects of the class' discussion or their scientific practice that might need adjusting (e.g., less personalized challenges, more explicit scaffolding of how to construct and mobilize inscriptions) in order for Scott to gain credibility? Or perhaps the personalized forms of argument, in which social intentions are enmeshed in arguing and challenging scientific claims (Ballenger, 1994), are the ways in which the students populate scientific discourse with their own intentions and purposes (Bakhtin, 1981)? Ballenger (1994) suggested, following Bakhtin, that if one cannot populate a discourse with one's own intentions, then perhaps one cannot take on the discourse. We raise these as questions for further thought. At the very least they remind us of the kinds of questions that arise when learning and knowing are viewed as socially organized activity, constructed in relations among people, activities, tools, symbolic systems, and the social world in and with which they act (Lave, 1990). They remind us further that the ways in which resources for learning are structured within any given context will importantly shape participants' identities within that context (McDermott, 1993) and, we might add, the meaning of science itself within any particular community.

In conclusion, we claim, as did Mireille in challenging Scott, that what the students in these two cases learn about the biology of snails or crustal movement on the one hand and about the relations among theory, fact, claim, and evidence on the other is inextricably tied to how they learn and how they use their learning. We think a focus on dialogism may open new perspectives on what it means to say that learning is situated—constituted in and through the activity, context, and culture in which it is developed and used (Brown, Collins, & Duguid, 1989; Lave & Wenger, 1991). We have tried through our analysis of Scott's claim to bring into focus the heterogeneous character of situated activity and its relation to learning (Lave, 1993): in particular, the multiplicity of viewpoints represented by the participants in any given situation and the various ways in which these viewpoints may interact dialogically to deepen, or perhaps more to the point argued here, to problematize understanding.

APPENDIX

Scott's Claim (Haitian Creole transcription)
Lines 1–29
> Scott: OK, kèsyon Murana, m a reponn li, kèsyon Murana two, two, fasil.
> Mr. S: Pale non.
> Scott: Kèsyon Murana, li di konsa, ke, koman m fè konnen gen grann grann. Mwen menm, nan, lè kalmason yo fè zè a, zè a kale, e, lè m gade yon kalmason toujou

rete la, paske, m konn koulè yo, e menm pitit la vinn fè yon lot pitit, kounyea li vinn ponn zè, ti pitit yo vinn ponn zè.

James: //Kèsyon!]

Mr. S: //Men kijan - tann, tann, talè talè...] - kijan pou ou idantifye yo?

Scott: Hunh?

Mr. S: Kijan pou ou idantifye yo?

Scott: Koman?

Mr. S: Yeah.

Scott: M pa konprann.

Mr. S: Non, ou di - ok - ou genyen 30 kalmason.

Scott: A penn de trant yo.

Mr. S: A penn de trant yo. OK. Donk, manman an vinn fe pitit la, pa vre? Li ponn zè. Men kijan ou fè konnen ke, ti pitit grandi yo - pa vre, kounyea-ki gwo, mwen pa konnen, a ki gwosè li fe pitit? Mwen pa konnen. //Eske gen moun ki] ta renmen konnen a ki gwosè yo fe pitit?

Manel: //Wi!]

Scott: Ti pitit, ti pitit yo piti

Mr. S: Non, pale a klas yo non. [ ] mwen pa konnen [ ].

Scott: = ti piti yo pli piti //pase yon foumi.]

Mr. S: //Murana vinn chita.] Pase ki sa?

Scott: Pase yon foumi.

Mr. S: OK.

Manel: Yo fè pitit?

Scott: Non, yo vinn grandi yo fè pitit.

Lines 30–35

Mr. S: Joel, um, James?

James: Yeah, konsa m ap di Scott. E si se pitit ki fè pitit avèk manman?

Scott: Mwen pa fouti di sa. Mwen pa fouti pale de sa. Mwen menm [ ] di [ ] te vinn gen granmanman, granmanman. E sa m te di. E sa m te di. Mwen pa t pale afè pitit al fè sex avèk manman yo.

Lines 36–77

Mr. S: Manel?

Manel: M gen plizyè kèsyon pou Scott.

Scott: Yes?

Claudie: Bay dè.

Manel: Mwen menm m mande ou konsa, ke konben ou te pran la, ou te al lakay ou avè-l an prèmyeman?

Scott: Oh, mwen te pran yon gwo - m te gendwa pran a penn dè, dis oswa senk yo konsa.

Mireille: //[ ] Scott ki te al fe bay [ ]?]

Manel: //Eske ou ka di konben] pitit yo fè pa jou?

Scott: Konben pitit yo fè pa jou? Koman m fè konnen? Se blok zè yo fè.

Manel: Epi ou di //konsa ou gen 30?]
Murana / Mireille://Kijan [ou fè] konte yo?] Kijan [ou fè] konte yo?
Claudie: Non, lè kalmason ponn zè gen plizyè blok, ou pa konn sa?
Manel: No -
Claudie: Konn gen plizyè.
Manel: No -
Mireille: Kite Scott defann tèt li!
Claudie: Non, si m konn wè l, se nomal pou m di l.
Manel: Non, Scott ta sipoze di m konsa //konben pitit ke yo fè] paske, ou te gen 10
Mireille: //Scott ki sipoze defann tèt li.]
   Scott: Ou konn sa ki fè m di apenn de 30 yo? Paske, ti pitit pitit piti yo, sa k menm
          fenk fèt yo, m konte yo. Se sa m konte yo paske, paske m konn wè ke yo konn,
          ke yo konn, ke yo konn kole nan po galon an.
Manel: = OK, Mèt S - Scott, m kwe manti se manti Scott ap bay.
Mr. S: //Poukisa?]
   Scott: //Non, m pap, m pap.]
Manel: Paske, tande, wi! Ou gen 10 - tande, //tande, tande, tande]
Scott: //OK OK OK OK], m ap pote yo pou ou
          demen si dye vè, [ ] tout kalmason
          [ ].
          [Commotion]

Mr. S: Tande, lèse l pale [ ] repons. Pale non.
Manel: Ou gen 10 kalmason. Lè ou gade nan sa ou mete a, ou gen 30. E rès yo, rès yo
       pa fè pitit?
Scott: Mwen te di a penn de 30 yo. E pa sa m te di?
Manel: Non, m mande ou, eske rès yo fè pitit?
Scott: Yes, yo fè pitit.
Manel: [ ] fè pitit?
Scott: Gen <u>enpè</u> ki fè pitit.
Manel: E lot yo?
Scott: Lot yo? M pa konnen.
Manel: [ ]

Line 78
Mireille: Kijan [ou] fè konnen sa k fè pitit sa k pa fè pitit?

Lines 79–101
Darlene: Men kankou si ou di ou gen 30 kalmason
   Scott: Uh hunh.
Darlene: = nan konben <u>tan</u> ke chak kalmason fè pitit? //Kankou,] eske yon kalmason ki
          gen, si l fèt jodia eske demen li ka al fè yon pitit?
   Asline: //Yes Scott.]
   Mr. S: //Bon kèsyon!]

[Commotion, students cry out, some hoot]

Scott: Mwen menm, m di sa! Mwen di konsa lè yo grandi! Mwen di lè yo grandi yo fè pitit.

Mr. S: OK, timoun, m mèt di yon bagay? Sa se yon bagay ke m ta renmen konnen paske nou menm n ap fè rechèch sou sa. M ta renmen konnen - bon kèsyon - Scott reponn [ ]

[Renewed commotion]

Scott: OK, mwen menm, men sa m te di, mwen menm, le [ ] te poze m kèsyon sa, [ ] te mande eske menm lè pitit yo fenk fèt la, eske menm lè a yo al fè pitit anko? Mwen menm m te di non. Mwen menm m te di sa se lè yo grandi, yo vinn fè pitit, paske ke, m konn mete -

Darlene: //Kite m mande ou yon kèsyon anko anvan ou finn reponn.]

Scott: //Ou p ap rèt tann mwen fini?]

Darlene: Anvan ou reponn li konsa, 'te m mande ou yon bagay pandan ou di sa. Kankou si ou di konsa ke yo fè pitit, e sa ou te di m, nan konben tan pou yon kalmason grandi?

Scott: Koman m fè konnen?

Darlene: E ben, //Scott]

Scott: //Kalmason toujou piti.]

ACKNOWLEDGMENTS

The research reported in this chapter was supported by the National Science Foundation (NSF), RED-9153961. The analysis and preparation of this chapter was also supported by The National Center for Research on Cultural Diversity and Second Language Learning under a Cooperative Agreement from the Office of Educational Research and Improvement (OERI), Cooperative Agreement No. R117G10022. The views expressed here do not necessarily reflect the position or policies of the NSF or OERI.

We thank the teacher and students about whom we write in this chapter for their contributions to the Cheche Konnen project during the 1991–1992 school year. In addition, we acknowledge the contribution of our colleague, Faith R. Conant, to the formative stages of the analysis presented here. Ricardo Nemirovsky offered helpful comments on a previous draft, and Bud Mehan, after viewing the videotape of Scott's claim, reminded us of the importance of questions of identity in learning. The comments of our research colleagues, Cindy Ballenger, Mary Bodwell, Costanza Eggers-Piérola, Mark Ogonowski, and Gillian Puttick helped sharpen our thinking on several key points, as did questions from the editors of this volume.

REFERENCES

Bakhtin, M. (1981). *The dialogic imagination.* Austin: University of Texas.

Bakhtin, M. (1984). *Problems of Dostoevsky's poetics.* Minneapolis: University of Minnesota Press.

Ballenger, C. (1996). *Science talk in a Haitian bilingual classroom.* [TERC working paper]. Cambridge, MA: TERC.

Bazerman, C. (1988). *Shaping written knowledge.* Madison: University of Wisconsin Press.

Brown, A. L., & Campione, J. (1994). Guided discovery in a community of learners. In K. McGilly (Ed.), *Classroom lessons: Integrating cognitive theory and classroom practice* (pp. 229–270). Cambridge, MA: MIT Press/Bradford Books.

Brown, J. S., Collins, A., & Duguid, P. (1989). Situated cognition and the culture of learning. *Educational Researcher, 18*(1), 32–42.

Collins, H., & Pinch, T. (1993). *The Golem: What everyone should know about science.* New York: Cambridge University Press.

Cook-Gumperz, J. (Ed.). (1986). *The social construction of literacy.* Cambridge, England: Cambridge University Press.

Eckert, P. (1989). *Jocks and burnouts: Social categories and identity in the high school.* New York: Teachers College Press.

Eckert, P. (1990). Adolescent social categories—Information and science learning. In M. Gardner, J. G. Greeno, F. Reif, A. H. Schoenfeld, A. diSessa, & E. Stage (Eds.), *Toward a scientific practice of science education* (pp. 203–217). Hillsdale, NJ: Lawrence Erlbaum Associates.

Gee, J. P. (1990). *Social linguistics and literacies: Ideology in discourses.* London: The Falmer Press.

Gee, J. P. (1994, April). *Science talk: How do you start to do what you don't know how to do?* Paper presented at the annual meeting of the American Educational Research Association, New Orleans, LA.

Goodwin, M. H. (1990). *He-said-she-said: Talk as social organization among black children.* Bloomington: Indiana University Press.

Heath, S. B. (1983). *Ways with words: Language, life, and work in communities and classrooms.* New York: Cambridge University Press.

Latour, B. (1983). Give me a laboratory and I will raise the world. In K. Knorr & M. Mulkay (Eds.), *Science observed: Perspectives on the social study of science* (pp. 141–170). Beverly Hills, CA: Sage.

Latour, B. (1986). Visualization and cognition. *Knowledge in Society: Studies in the Sociology of Culture Past and Present, 6,* 1–40.

Latour, B., & Woolgar, S. (1986). *Laboratory life: The social construction of scientific facts.* Princeton NJ: Princeton University Press.

Lave, J. (1990). Views of the classroom: Implications for math and science learning research. In M. Gardner, J. G. Greeno, F. Reif, A. H. Schoenfeld, A. diSessa, & E. Stage (Eds.), *Toward a scientific practice of science education* (pp. 251–263). Hillsdale, NJ: Lawrence Erlbaum Associates.

Lave, J. (1993). Introduction. In S. Chaiklin & J. Lave (Eds.), *Understanding practice: Perspectives on activity and context* (pp. 3–32). New York: Cambridge University Press.

Lave, J., & Wenger, E. (1991). *Situated learning: Legitimate peripheral participation.* New York: Cambridge University Press.

Lemke, J. (1990). *Talking science: Language, learning and values.* Norwood, NJ: Ablex.

Lynch, M. (1985). *Art and artifact in laboratory science.* London: Routledge & Kegan Paul.

McDermott, R. (1993). The acquisition of a child by a learning disability. In S. Chaiklin & J. Lave (Eds.), *Understanding practice: Perspectives on activity and context* (pp. 269–305). New York: Cambridge University Press.

Mehan, H. (1993). Beneath the skin and between the ears: A case study in the politics of representation. In S. Chaiklin & J. Lave (Eds.), *Understanding practice: Perspectives on activity and context* (pp. 241–268). New York: Cambridge University Press.

Monk, S., & Nemirovsky, R. (1994). The case of Dan: Student construction of a functional situation through visual attributes. *Research in Collegiate Mathematics Education, 4,* 139–168.

Morson, G. S., & Emerson, C. (1990). *Mikhail Bakhtin: Creation of a prosaics.* Stanford, CA: Stanford University Press.

Nemirovsky, R. (1994). On ways of symbolizing: The case of Laura and the velocity sign. *Journal of Mathematical Behavior, 13,* 389–422.

Ochs, E. (1988). *Culture and language development.* Cambridge, MA: Cambridge University Press.

Ochs, E., Gonzales, P., & Jacoby, S. (in press). "When I come down I'm in the domain state": Grammar and graphic representation in the interpretive activity of physicists. To appear in E. Ochs, E.A. Schegloff and S. Thompson (Eds.), *Interaction and grammar.*

Palincsar, A. S., & Brown, A. (1984). Reciprocal teaching of comprehension-fostering and comprehension-monitoring activities. *Cognition and Instruction, 1*(2), 117-175.

Rosebery, A. S., Warren, B., & Conant, F. R. (1995). Appropriating scientific discourse: Findings from language minority classrooms. *The Journal of the Learning Sciences, 2*(1), 61–94.

Warren, B., & Rosebery, A. S. (1995). Equity in the future tense: Redefining relationships among teachers, students and science in language minority classrooms. In W. Secada, L. Fennema, & L. Adajian (Eds.), *New directions for equity in mathematics education.* New York: Cambridge University Press.

Warren, B., Rosebery, A., & Conant, F. (1994). Discourse and social practice: Learning science in language minority classrooms. In D. Spener (Ed.), *Adult biliteracy in the United States* (pp. 191–210). Washington, DC: CAL and Delta Systems, Inc.

Wertsch, J. (1991). *Voices of the mind: A sociocultural approach to mediated action.* Cambridge, MA: Harvard University Press.

Volosinov, V. N. (1973). *Marxism and the philosophy of language.* Cambridge, MA: Harvard University Press.

Chapter 6

MOVING BEYOND LEARNING ALONE AND IN SILENCE: OBSERVATIONS FROM THE QUASAR PROJECT CONCERNING COMMUNICATION IN MATHEMATICS CLASSROOMS

Edward A. Silver
University of Pittsburgh

In recent years, the professional mathematics education community has been engaged in considerable discussion regarding ways to enhance the form and content of precollege mathematics instruction. Reports from the National Academy of Sciences (National Research Council [NRC], 1989) and the National Council of Teachers of Mathematics (NCTM, 1989, 1991) have stimulated educational practitioners and policymakers to focus their attention on mathematics education reform. These reports have specified new goals for mathematics education and have provided descriptions of mathematical proficiency, using terms such as reasoning, problem solving, communication, conceptual understanding, and mathematical power. At least two things are striking about these new descriptions of mathematics proficiency and new goals for mathematics education. One is that the descriptions do not emphasize procedural facility, which has long been the major goal of school mathematics. Although an emphasis on understanding, reasoning, and problem solving is not new in mathematics education, the degree of emphasis in contemporary discussions of mathematical goals is much stronger than in the past. A second novel aspect of current conceptions of mathematical proficiency and goals for students is the emphasis placed on communication.

It may seem surprising that communication would emerge as such a prominent feature of mathematics learning or teaching. The popular image of a mathematician is someone working in isolation, pondering formulas, and precollege mathematics instruction has generally been designed and delivered as if that were the only way to view mathematical activity. For most students, especially in the middle grades and in high school, conventional mathematics instruction has meant textbooks or worksheets with exercises—typically narrowly prescribed questions, each having a single correct answer—to be solved by students working alone to produce a stylized response, which can then be validated only by teacher approval. Moreover, the answer is expected to be obtained, without much hesitation or reflection, by applying a recently taught procedure. It is little wonder that many studies have suggested that conventional mathematics instruction lacks imagination and invitation to student engagement (e.g., Porter, 1989; Stodolsky, 1988). Silence, memorization, and imitation have long been the hallmarks of conventional mathematics instruction. Although conventional mathematical pedagogy has generally ignored the role of communication, except in the sense of providing technical vocabulary and symbolism as components of a language of mathematics, there is an increasing awareness among educational leaders of the centrality of communication and discourse in mathematics education (e.g., The Mathematical Association [UK], 1987; NCTM, 1991).

In contrast to the situation typically found in mathematics classrooms, documents undergirding the current mathematics education reform effort suggest a view of classrooms as places rich in communication about mathematical ideas. In particular, The *Curriculum and Evaluation Standards for School Mathematics* (NCTM, 1989) identifies "learning to communicate mathematically" (p. 5) as one of the five major goals for students, along with learning to value mathematics, becoming confident in one's own ability, becoming a mathematical problem solver, and learning to reason mathematically. Moreover, communication was designated as one of the four major themes that cut across all of grades K–12; the other cross-cutting themes were problem solving, reasoning, and connections. Communication is also quite prominent in the NCTM's (1991) *Professional Standards for Teaching Mathematics*. In fact, three of the six standards for teaching mathematics identified in this document deal explicitly with notions of classrooms as discourse communities and of teachers as facilitators of mathematical discourse. This view is quite different from that associated with conventional mathematics instruction, in which a teacher's role is to dispense bits of knowledge and to model procedures, and in which the student's role is to work alone, committing the bits to memory and imitating the modeled procedures.

ROOTS OF INTEREST IN COMMUNICATION

There are several interrelated reasons for the emergence of communication as a focal issue in the reform of mathematics instruction. Probably the most fundamental reason is the growing acceptance of a view of mathematics and mathematical knowing that is sociocultural in nature. According to this perspective, to understand mathematics, one must understand the activities or practice of persons who are makers or users of mathematics. This stands in contrast to a more conventional view that understanding mathematics is equivalent to understanding the structure of concepts and principles in the domain and that mathematical knowing is intensely personal and private.

Viewing mathematical knowing as a practice (not in the sense of drill-and-practice but rather in the sense of professional practice) is supported by recent trends in the philosophy of mathematics. For example, Lakatos (1976) portrayed a social process of debate to illustrate the nuances of mathematical discourse and culture, and Kitcher (1984) developed an epistemology of mathematics based on the importance of shared meanings and not simply shared results. Moreover, mathematics educators outside the United States have identified a broad range of sociocultural aspects of mathematics education. For example, Bishop (1988) provided an extensive account of a culturally based view of mathematics education; Bartolini-Bussi (1989, 1992) described the richness of social interaction in primary grade mathematics classrooms; d'Ambrosio (1985) wrote eloquently about the need to consider mathematics from the perspective of the culture of the people who make it, use it, or are asked to learn it; and Mellin-Olsen (1987) dealt with issues of cultural transmission in his consideration of power relationships and ownership of mathematical knowledge. Thus, treating mathematics as a practice as well as a knowledge domain challenges us to confront and examine social and cultural aspects of mathematics, thereby making communication a more salient consideration.

A sociocultural perspective suggests that mathematical knowledge is as much socially constructed as it is individually constructed and that the practice of mathematics is fundamentally a social practice. In brief, the argument is both that mathematics is created using socially appropriated tools and conventions and that mathematical ideas attain validity only when they are accepted within the mathematical community (Tymoczko, 1986). A contemporary illustration of this process of social argumentation and debate within the mathematics community about the suitability of new ideas or new tools and approaches to solving problems can be seen in the controversy and disagreement over the acceptability of a computer-based solution for the famous, and long-unsolved, "Four Color Problem." Simply stated, the problem asks whether or not four colors are sufficient to color any map such that no two adjacent regions have the same color (but regions that share only a common point can have the same color).

This problem was posed in the middle of the 19th century, after which progress was fairly rapidly made in determining that three colors were insufficient for some maps, and it was also soon shown that five regions could not be placed on a map so that each country bordered the other four. Thus, it was long suspected that four colors were sufficient for any map, but no valid proof of this assertion was given until the mid-1970s, when K. Appel and W. Haken announced that they had produced a proof (Appel & Haken, 1977). Their proof, however, generated considerable controversy and debate within the mathematics community, because it made extensive use of the computer to check cases. This aspect of their method, essentially "proof by exhaustion" of possible cases, raised questions not only because of its novelty but also because the computer work was less open to scrutiny and validation. Nevertheless, as a result of extensive discussion within the community, the proof has now been generally accepted, and many other mathematicians are now using computers in similar ways to try to solve problems in other areas of mathematics, such as number theory (Peterson, 1988). As this case illustrates, similar to the development of many mathematical ideas throughout the history of mathematics, one finds that important developments in mathematics often involve communication and social interaction as well as individual reflection and invention (Rowe & McCleary, 1989).

The general theoretical interest in the role of communication and social interaction in mathematical practice is tied to current instructional reform efforts. As noted previously, the reform vision of mathematics classrooms is one of discourse communities in which students engage in doing mathematics rather than having mathematics done to them. In such settings, students would have opportunities not simply to give answers but also to explain and justify their thinking and to discuss their observations. Within these mathematical communities, communication in the form of verification and justification is natural. When students are challenged to think and reason about mathematics and to communicate the results of their thinking to others orally or in writing, they are faced with the need to state their ideas clearly and convincingly. In this way, classrooms are transformed into arenas in which communication and collaboration become central features of activity. The process of communicating ideas within the cultural norms of mathematical practice provides both need and value for mathematical reasoning. Although Fawcett's (1938) pioneering work using social interaction in the teaching of geometry demonstrates that this is not a completely new idea in mathematics education, the current interest in issues of communication is both more widespread than ever before and more central to reform efforts than at any other time in the history of mathematics education. For example, it can be easily argued that the so-called "New Mathematics" reform movement of the 1960s was as silent on issues of communication as the "Back to Basics" reform movement of the 1970s, except that "New Math" had the unfortunate consequence of leading teachers to develop an inflated sense of the importance of ensuring that students were able to spell correctly mathematical terms like "commutative" and "associative."

The current interest in communication is one aspect of a more general contemporary interest in social interaction and its role in supporting learning. Peer collaboration has gradually become recognized as a significant contributor to student learning for both social and cognitive reasons (Cohen, 1984; Webb, 1991). From a cognitive perspective, it has been argued that students can construct knowledge and elaborate understandings through collaborative activity that they would not so readily construct or elaborate via individual work (Noddings, 1985; Schoenfeld, 1989). Many teachers have increased the amount of social interaction and collaboration in their classrooms as a means of coping with student diversity. In fact, the instructional use of cooperative groups, in which more advanced students assist those students who are less advanced or less familiar with the task requirements, is an increasingly common way for teachers to accommodate the wide range of students' backgrounds and abilities in classrooms, which in recent years have become increasingly heterogeneous. This increased frequency of collaborative opportunities in classrooms makes the social dimension of learning more salient, thereby contributing to the emergence of communication as an important issue.

Interest in communication and mathematics has also been engendered by current efforts to develop new forms of assessment. Spawned by fairly intense criticism of the content, form, and consequences of standardized achievement tests, mathematics education reformers have turned their attention to more "authentic" forms of assessment (Silver, 1992). A frequently suggested form of mathematics performance assessment is an open-ended problem, for which the examinee is expected to produce a complete solution and an explanation of the strategy or method used, a justification of the solution obtained, or an elaboration or justification of the problem and its solution. Such problems might be designed to require several days of work, they might involve about one class period, or they might require only about 5 minutes for solution. The open-ended tasks included in pilot testing for the California Assessment Program (California State Department of Education, 1989), the "extended-open-ended" tasks used in the

1992 NAEP Mathematics assessment (Dossey, Mullis, & Jones, 1993), and
the tasks used in the QUASAR Cognitive Assessment Instrument (Lane,
1993; Silver & Lane, 1993) are all examples of 5-minute performance tasks;
the prototype examples and investigations produced by the Mathematical
Sciences Education Board (NRC, 1993) represent performance assessments
that require longer time for completion.

Although an emphasis on communicative aspects of mathematical performance may seem somewhat discordant with the tendency over the last
50 years to test mathematical achievement using short-answer and multiple-choice questions, in which displays of solution methods and explanations or justifications of solutions are not required, there is actually a long
tradition of evaluating students' mathematical proficiency, especially those
thought to be highly capable, through the use of tasks that require not only
solution but also communication about the solution. In particular, communication about one's solutions to mathematical problems has been a feature
of many mathematical competitions for students.

One of the most important competitions in the history of mathematics was
the Eötvös Competition in Hungary, which began in 1894 and ran for most of
the 20th century. This competition for high-school graduates has been credited
with playing a major role in the remarkable number of first-rate Hungarian
mathematicians and scientists, because many of these individuals are former
winners of the competition (Radó, 1932). In the Eötvös Competition, students
were asked to solve three problems in half a day, and the solution of each
problem required insight and creative problem solving rather than the application of well-rehearsed rules and procedures. An important ingredient in
judging the student solutions was the extent to which the solution was
communicated clearly and correctly (Hajós, Neukomm, & Surányi, 1963). For
almost 20 years beginning in 1946, the Stanford Department of Mathematics
sponsored a mathematical competition that was modeled after the Eötvös
Competition. In this competition, high-school seniors were asked to complete
three or four problems in a three-hour time period, and issues of communication
were viewed as being of importance in judging students' responses. In particular,
the directions to contestants stated that "good presentation counts" and that
answers should be "clear, concise, complete" (Polya & Kilpatrick, 1974, p. 2).
Students' solutions were read using a two-stage process, with interjudge
consistency examined at the first stage, consisting of a qualitative analysis of
the solution methods and written presentations. An example of a current
mathematics competition with similar features is the International Mathematical Olympiads. Competitors (eight high-school students from each participating country) are asked to complete a total of six challenging problems during
a two-day period. Their solutions are scored by a jury of judges, and

particular emphasis is placed on originality and elegance in the solution process and on the clarity of communication (Greitzer, 1978). Thus, communication has long been seen as an important issue in judging the quality of the mathematical performance of highly capable students. The current interest in using performance assessments with all students, not simply those few who are exceptional, has increased the salience of communication as an issue for those interested in mathematical performance.

COMMUNICATION-RICH CLASSROOMS AS VEHICLES FOR THE MATHEMATICS EDUCATION OF ALL STUDENTS

As we have seen, the documents that undergird the current reform effort (e.g., NCTM, 1989, 1991) suggest a very different view of mathematics classrooms than the view that has conventionally existed for most teachers and students. These documents not only offer a social view of mathematics instruction but also indicate that such instruction can support the attainment of high-level mathematical goals and outcomes by all students (Silver, 1992). At this point in time, however, the evidence strongly suggests that the rhetoric of reform has far outstripped the reality. Despite evidence that some teachers are struggling to respond to current calls for change, for most teachers and students in this country, classroom instruction in mathematics has changed very little over the past several decades.

It remains the case that forms of *drill-to-kill* or *assembly-line* instruction, consisting of repetitive drill and practice on basic computation and other routine procedures, continues to characterize school mathematics instruction, especially in impoverished urban and rural schools. Data regarding instructional practices suggests that students assigned to the lower tracks of many high schools—predominantly ethnic minority and poor students—tend to receive less actual mathematics instruction, less homework, and more drill and practice of low-level factual knowledge and computational skill than students assigned to middle and higher tracks (Oakes, 1985). Although these instructional practices may be sufficient to support the attainment of basic factual knowledge or proficiency with routine computational skills, they are unlikely to lead to improved performance on more complex tasks requiring mathematical reasoning and problem solving. Moreover, the fact that poor and minority students are largely denied access to instruction that could enhance their communicative competence further disadvantages them with respect to the newer forms of assessment that require clear communication of thinking and reasoning.

There is a growing body of evidence that instructional activities rich in communication and social interaction can be beneficial for students who are not well served by more conventional forms of monologic, teacher-centered instruction. For example, a recent examination of the educational practices used with linguistically and culturally diverse student populations found that collaboration and communication were key elements of effective instructional practice at all levels of the educational system (Garcia, 1991).

Communication was at the heart of a vision of mathematics education for diverse student populations that is portrayed in *Thinking Through Mathematics: Fostering Inquiry and Communication in Mathematics Classrooms* (TTM; Silver, Kilpatrick, & Schlesinger, 1990), a book commissioned by the College Board as part of its Project Equality, which was designed to enhance equity and excellence in secondary-school education. The project was specifically intended to upgrade the quality of educational experiences for those students in the middle half of the ability range in secondary schools. As the title of the book implies, the central message of TTM was that mathematics classrooms can be places in which students regularly engage in thinking. As the subtitle suggests, another theme of the book was that mathematics classrooms can be places rich in communication of and about mathematical ideas, places in which justification and verification are emphasized, and places in which teachers and students engage in authentic forms of mathematical practice. Using commentary on vignettes based on actual mathematics teachers' classrooms, TTM presents several strategies that can be employed by teachers of mid-range, senior- and junior-high school students to create classrooms in which mathematics becomes both an object of thoughtful reflection and an opportunity for meaningful social interaction.

One TTM vignette featured Mr. Westerman's practice of having students explore and discuss multiple solution paths to a single problem. This instructional episode, built around the oral presentation and "publication" of various solution methods, illustrated the explicit use of oral communication and the creation of drawings or mathematical symbolic expressions to accompany the discourse. The example also illustrates how the communicative core of a classroom activity can afford significant opportunity for student reflection. Not only were the solution "publishers" likely to benefit from the reflective opportunity provided in preparing to present a solution to the class, but they and the other members of the class were also likely to benefit from the reflective opportunity provided by the retrospective discussion of the various solution methods.

Another vignette from TTM illustrated a different use of communication. In this example, Mrs. Garcia asked her students to communicate to her, this time in written form, their knowledge and understanding concerning a particular mathematical topic (circles). She then used these responses as the basis for a reflective activity, in which she provided students with various statements that were among those proposed by students in the written exercise, and that the students were expected to examine and then to justify or refute. In this example, the written communication from the student to the teacher afforded material that the teacher subsequently used to engage the students in reflective activity both in the written exercise and in the later reasoning about the peer-generated propositions.

Although some exceptional examples of such classrooms exist today in the United States, a challenge of current reform efforts is to make these kinds of classrooms the norm rather than the exception, especially in settings of greatest need. One project that has been working to effect such changes and to understand the complex challenges embedded therein is the QUASAR project.

THE QUASAR PROJECT: AN OVERVIEW

Quantitative Understanding: Amplifying Student Achievement and Reasoning (QUASAR) is a national educational reform project aimed at fostering and studying the development and implementation of enhanced mathematics instructional programs for students attending middle schools in economically disadvantaged communities. QUASAR was designed to examine seriously the *feasibility* and *responsibility* of the proposition that students in these communities could and would learn a broad range of mathematical content, acquire a deeper and more meaningful understanding of mathematical ideas, and demonstrate proficiency in mathematical reasoning and in solving appropriately complex mathematics problems, if they were provided with appropriately enhanced forms of mathematics instruction. Arguing that the well-documented, low levels of participation and performance in mathematics for poor urban students were not due primarily to a lack of ability or potential but rather to a set of educational practices that blocked them from meaningful experiences with mathematics learning, QUASAR set out to accomplish its goals through the application of effort, imagination, and reasonable financial resources.

Some Design Principles and Features
of the QUASAR Project

From the beginning, QUASAR has recognized the power of approaching school reform from a "bottom up" perspective, thereby tying reform efforts closely to the nuances of local conditions. In particular, QUASAR has chosen to work with educational partnerships centered around middle schools located in economically disadvantaged areas. To select its sites, the project sought partnerships involving a middle school serving an economically disadvantaged community and one or more "resource partners"—mathematics education experts associated with a local university or education agency—who were committed to working in collaboration with the school staff to enhance the mathematics program. Each group was asked to develop plans for enhancing the school's mathematics program with a special emphasis on reasoning and problem solving, plans that were based on sound principles or solid evidence and that appeared to have strong potential for rapid development. In making final selections, the project sought schools in which the climate and general functioning appeared to support and allow the principal and faculty to focus attention on program innovation and academic achievement, but schools that in other ways would be "as typical as possible." Finally, to the extent possible with a small sample, variety was sought with respect to geographic location, ethnicity of student population, and instructional program plans and foci.

During the 1990–1991 school year, QUASAR began its work at four school sites. Subsequently, two additional school sites were added to the project. Thus, there are currently six QUASAR school sites dispersed across the United States. There is diversity across the six QUASAR school sites not only in geographic location but also in various demographic characteristics, such as the size of the school and school district, the number of students per class, the number of classes taught per teacher, and the ethnicity or race of the student populations: two sites serve predominantly African-American students, two serve primarily Latino students, and the other two sites have culturally diverse student populations (Silver, 1994).

These schools and their surrounding communities constitute the operational heart of project activities. Teachers and administrators at the middle schools work in collaboration with their resource partners to enhance the school's mathematics instructional program with an emphasis on mathematical thinking, reasoning, and problem solving. Each site team operates independently in designing and implementing its own plan for curriculum, staff development, and other features of its instructional program. Although each site operates independently, there are regular interactions among representatives from all QUASAR sites. Each site-based, collaborative team is provided with financial support, which will average about $90,000 per year across 5 years by the end of the project. Participants also receive other forms of technical assistance and advice from project staff members.

QUASAR's Instructional Vision

A fundamental premise of the QUASAR project is embodied in the dual assertion that the goal of school mathematics is to help students learn to think and reason about mathematical matters and that the instruction needed to help students attain this goal clearly needs to be different from conventional mathematics instruction, especially for those students who are performing least well in the current system.

QUASAR promotes instruction that blends attention to basic- and high-level mathematical goals, enabling students to develop their capacity to both apply mathematical procedures and understand why. In this way, students learn not only to execute algorithms accurately and to recall factual knowledge correctly but also to know when and why to apply those procedures and that knowledge. They learn to make sense out of complicated situations, to generate hypotheses and critically examine evidence, and to select from among a repertoire of strategic alternatives for formulating and then solving complex problems (Silver, 1994). Moreover, QUASAR attempts to make mathematics relevant by tying instructional content to the life experience, interests, and cultural heritage of students whenever possible (Silver, Smith, & Nelson, 1995). QUASAR is based on the tenet that the content and structure that students bring to the enterprise should be embraced in order to connect the mathematics taught in school and the lives of the children who are asked to learn it.

The QUASAR vision places social interaction and communication at the heart of meaningful learning. The kinds of instructional practices that QUASAR promotes emphasize student engagement with challenging mathematical tasks, enhanced levels of student discourse about mathematical ideas, and student involvement in collaborative mathematical activity. In QUASAR, the mathematics classroom becomes a community of collaborative, reflective practice, in which students are challenged to think deeply about and to participate in the mathematics they are learning by speaking mathematics themselves as they discuss observations and share explanations, verifications, reasons, and generalizations.

This view of mathematics classrooms is compatible with the findings of Resnick (1987), who reviewed research on teaching high-level thinking and reasoning skills and concluded that developing higher order cognitive abilities requires shaping a disposition to thought through participation in a social community that values thinking and independent judgment. Moreover, as noted earlier, this vision of mathematics classrooms has features, such as collaboration and communication, that are likely to be supportive of the learning of linguistically and culturally diverse student populations (Garcia, 1991). Finally, this vision is also consistent with an extensive body of research on learning, which suggests that learners actively construct their own knowledge, individually and through interaction with others, in many complex intellectual domains, including mathematics (Cobb, 1994; Confrey, 1990).

Viewing learners as active constructors of knowledge suggests the intellectual bankruptcy of previous, deficit-based models of low achievers. In fact, this view suggests that the task of teachers and schools is not to detect and remediate students' deficits, but rather to identify and nurture sources of competence in students. Such an education would provide students with the necessary support and materials to refine and enhance the mathematical sophistication of their own constructs and means of building knowledge, as well as having opportunities to appropriate and use mathematical or general academic concepts, principles, and processes contributed by others. This is more than a philosophical position, moreover, because a considerable body of research has identified many of the underlying competencies in the knowledge that children bring with them to the study of mathematics at the elementary- and middle-school levels (e.g., Hiebert & Carpenter, 1992).

This instructional vision is now being realized in QUASAR classrooms where practices are infused with an emphasis on thinking, reasoning, problem solving, and communication. Key features of instruction include student engagement with challenging mathematical tasks, enhanced levels of student discourse about mathematical ideas, and student involvement in collaborative mathematical activity (Silver, Smith, & Nelson, 1995). In addition, teachers and resource partners seek ways to connect the content and form of instruction to children's ways of thinking and reasoning, and to their lives and experiences outside school (e.g., everyday problem settings, culturally relevant teaching activities, Smith & Silver, 1995). Moreover, in line with the general principles espoused in mathematics education reform documents like the *Curriculum and Evaluation Standards for School Mathematics* (NCTM, 1989), the mathematics curriculum at QUASAR sites includes the treatment of a wide array of mathematical topics that stretch beyond computation with whole numbers and fractions, to include topics in measurement, geometry, and statistics. Nevertheless, realizing this instructional vision is a process that takes time and involves confronting a number of substantial challenges.

The struggles, failures and successes of students, teachers, and resource partners to realize this vision of mathematics education constitute an important story in the QUASAR project. This story is being captured through an extensive research effort aimed at documenting the work of project participants and the impact of that work.

QUASAR Research

QUASAR is not only a practical school demonstration project; it is also a complex research study of educational change and improvement. Project research aims to identify critical features of successful programs by examining the implementation of the programs in teachers' classrooms; assessing the impact of the programs on teachers' instructional practices, knowledge, and beliefs; evaluating the impact of the programs on student performance by devising assessment tools to measure students' growth in mathematical reasoning and problem solving; and ascertaining conditions that appear to facilitate or inhibit the success of these instructional reform efforts.[1]

Data and informal observations drawn from the QUASAR project form the basis for the remainder of this chapter. In particular, several issues related to communication and mathematics reform are identified and discussed with reference to observations made within the project. The assumption is that these issues have broader applicability than the confines of this project and that the issues raised here will provide challenges and opportunities not only for those who wish to develop improved forms of mathematics instruction that include attention to communication but also for those who wish to study communicative aspects of mathematics teaching and learning. It is important to stress that the QUASAR instructional programs are very much "works in progress," so this identification and discussion of issues must be viewed as being based on incomplete programs and analyses. Nevertheless, the issues are probably of interest to the field at this point in time, because much remains unknown about how to enrich mathematics instruction in the nation's classrooms.

---

[1]Further details about the design and implementation of the project's research and evaluation efforts can be found in other papers. For example, details regarding the approach taken to documenting classroom instructional activity can be found in Stein, Grover, and Silver (1991) and Stein, Grover, and Henningsen (in press). Details about the approach being taken to measure student outcomes can be found in Lane (1993), Silver and Lane (1993) and Lane and Silver (1994).

COMMUNICATION-RELATED ISSUES
RAISED BY THE EARLY EXPERIENCE
OF THE QUASAR PROJECT

This discussion of issues is comprised of two sections. First, data are presented and discussed regarding evidence of interest among the original applicants to the QUASAR project concerning various aspects or dimensions of communication. Next, the experience of mathematics teachers in the QUASAR project is synthesized to identify some dilemmas and challenges that have been encountered as they have attempted to establish and then orchestrate the dynamics of rich communicative environments for students.

Dimensions of Communication

Data collected early in the QUASAR project suggest that not all dimensions of communication are equally interesting to those willing to undertake school-based instructional reform. Smith, Silver, and Parke (1991) analyzed data available from the formal applications submitted as part of the four-stage site selection process, which included nomination, acknowledgment of interest, formal application, and visitation. They examined the formal application materials submitted at the third stage of the process by 42 middle-school faculties and resource partners. Special attention was paid to responses to questions related to programmatic goals and plans, in which applicants were asked to describe in detail the instructional approach they planned to take to emphasize high-level thinking, reasoning, and problem solving in their middle-school mathematics programs. Smith et al. analyzed the relationship between the plans of the applicants and the ideas espoused in the *Curriculum and Evaluation Standards for School Mathematics* (NCTM, 1989), a draft version of which was available at the time of the application process.

The NCTM Standards (1989) identified "Mathematics as Communication" as one of the 13 standards for grades 5–8. Moreover, the document elaborates six subthemes related to the communication standard.

1. Communicating by modeling situations using oral, written, concrete, pictorial, graphical, and algebraic methods.
2. Using communication to have students reflect on and clarify their own thinking about mathematical ideas and situations.

3. Developing common understandings of mathematical ideas, including the role of definitions.

4. Using the skills of reading, listening, and viewing to interpret and evaluate mathematical ideas.

5. Having students discuss mathematical ideas and make conjectures and convincing arguments.

6. Helping students appreciate the value of mathematical notation and its role in the development of mathematical ideas (NCTM, 1989, p. 78).

For the purposes of this chapter, it is useful to recount the findings of this analysis as it relates to the standard and subthemes associated with communication.[2]

The formal applications submitted by the 42 schools and resource partners offer a glimpse into the thinking of these reform-minded educators about the communication standard and its associated subthemes. According to the Smith et al. (1991) analysis, about 80% of the applications mentioned communication in describing the instructional approaches to be taken or in the educational outcomes for students. Most of the applications contained at least one substantive reference to communication, although many also contained superficial references to the standard or the subthemes. As far as the subthemes were concerned, there was not a uniform level of interest. Some subthemes were very prominent in the applications. For example, more than 75% of the applications referred to subthemes 1 and 5, which deal with modeling using various representational forms and with mathematical discussion and debate. On the other hand, some subthemes were rarely mentioned. In particular, only about 5% of the applications mentioned subthemes 3 or 6, which deal with mathematical definitions and notation.

The variance in frequency of occurrence of various subthemes in the application material may be due to a desire by the applicants to emphasize most heavily those aspects of communication that are most absent in conventional mathematics instruction. In other words, attention to definitions and notation is fairly common in conventional mathematics instruction, whereas attention to student discourse and multiple representations has been far less prevalent. Therefore, the applicants may have intended to

---

[2]For each of the 13 NCTM standards for grades 5–8, explicit references to a standard or to a subtheme corresponding to a standard were noted; implicit references to standards and subthemes were also noted. A reference was considered implicit when the application gave clear indication of concern about a standard or subtheme, but when no explicit reference was made to the NCTM *Standards* document. References in which a standard or subtheme simply appeared as part of a list of student outcomes, topics to be covered, and/or methods of instructional practice were considered "superficial." References were considered "substantive" when an elaboration was provided by giving a detailed example of plans to address the standard or subtheme in the mathematics program.

include the underrepresented subthemes as part of their instructional goals and activities, but they may simply have chosen to emphasize those aspects of their proposed instructional intervention that would be novel. It is, of course, not possible to be completely certain about the thinking of the applicants on this matter, but it is also possible that their attention to communication was intended to *replace* rather than *supplement* more conventional aspects of communication in mathematics instruction. If so, then the applications were largely silent on how matters of definition and notation would be handled in the instruction.

Another interesting finding related to the subthemes associated with communication is the infrequency of mentioning subtheme 2. Only about 20% of the applications referred to the link between communicative and reflective experience as being a goal of the proposed instructional program. It is difficult to know the precise reason for this phenomenon. It may be that the applicants saw opportunities for student reflection as being characteristic of conventional instruction, thereby rendering this subtheme less novel than some others. Yet, it can certainly be argued that conventional mathematics instruction has not provided rich opportunities for either individual or collective reflection and clarification. Another plausible explanation is that advocates of increased communication in mathematics education have made an artificial distinction between communicative and reflective activity rather than emphasizing their interplay.

The dual themes of reflection and communication were identified as being of import by Hiebert (1992) in an article about the research foundations of current mathematics education reform efforts in the United States. Hiebert also commented on a tension regarding the role and importance of individual reflection between proponents of social views of learning and those who view learning as being about individual mental representations:

> It is not clear why reflection on internal representations and communication with others are posed as mutually exclusive or opposing processes in the classroom. I believe that it is more appropriate to think of the processes as describing different features of individual and group life in the classroom. Classrooms that encourage both features create climates that recognize mathematical activity as both a private, introspective experience and a communal, negotiated experience. Moreover, each process can be enhanced by the other. Communication can promote and guide reflection, and reflection can enrich what is shared through communication. (p. 446)

In discussions and debates about instructional reform, communication *qua* communication has often been the object of argument, and this may lead to a view of communication as a process apart from reflection rather than one that is intimately connected to it. Finding the right balance between social communication and individual reflection is just one of several dilemmas that face mathematics teachers as they attempt to teach in ways that mirror the current calls for reform, as is suggested by data collected at the six QUASAR sites finally selected from among the 42 formal applicants.

Some Challenging Aspects of Communication Within Mathematics Instruction

The *Professional Standards for Teaching Mathematics* (NCTM, 1991) identified "the teacher's role in discourse" as one of its six standards for teaching mathematics. In elaborating this standard, the authors develop seven aspects of the teacher's role in discourse: "posing questions and tasks that elicit, engage and challenge each student's thinking; listening carefully to each student's ideas; asking students to clarify and justify their ideas orally and in writing; deciding what to pursue in depth from among the ideas that students bring up during a discussion; deciding when and how to attach mathematical notation and language to students' ideas; deciding when to provide information, when to clarify an issue, when to model, when to lead, and when to let a student struggle with a difficulty; and monitoring students' participation in discussions and deciding when and how to encourage each student to participate" (NCTM, 1991, p. 35). Each of these aspects of discourse presents challenges that must be addressed or dilemmas that must be resolved by mathematics teachers wishing to develop discourse communities in their classrooms.

In many ways, the dicta for mathematics teachers to follow in managing the activity of their classroom discourse communities is reminiscent of the words of a popular song a few years ago about gambling—it is important to "know when to hold 'em, know when to fold 'em, know when to walk away, and know when to run" (Schlitz, 1977). According to the requirements imposed by the NCTM's *Professional Standards for Teaching Mathematics*, it is essential for teachers to know when to tell versus when to withhold information, when to provide explanations versus when to elicit explanations from students, when to appropriate notation and language for shared usage within the class and when to encourage invented symbolism, and when to encourage students to speak versus when to monitor their ideas and challenge them to justify their thinking. As has been noted by others (e.g., Ball, 1991), dilemmas are abundant in the management of mathematical discourse communities, even when teachers believe that discourse is an important component of mathematics teaching and learning.

A perusal of the applications submitted by the six sites chosen to be QUASAR participants revealed that all sites mentioned communication as an issue of concern, and some gave considerable attention to discourse as a feature of the instruction they intended to provide. Moreover, project data suggest that a high level of commitment to communication as a goal has been maintained among project teachers over the first three years. QUASAR teachers responded in each of the first three project years to a survey of beliefs, consisting of 30 statements about mathematics as a discipline, about mathematics teaching, about student learning, about assessment of student learning and performance, and about students from economically disadvantaged backgrounds. Two survey items dealt specifically with communication: (a) "It is as important for students to be able to explain how they obtained their answers as it is for students to be able to obtain the correct answer" and (b) "Verbal and written communication by students are essential components in helping students understand mathematics." Examination of the responses from those who were project teachers at the outset and those who have joined the project since its inception shows a consistently very high level of agreement with each of these communication-related statements (QUASAR Documentation Team, 1993). Thus, an interest in communication and a belief in its efficacy in teaching and learning mathematics has been very much at the heart of the QUASAR effort at the project schools from the beginning.

Despite the high level of interest and commitment to communication as a feature of mathematics instruction, many teachers have struggled during the early years of the project with the challenges embedded in implementing these beliefs in classrooms. Progress has been uneven, with some aspects of discourse communities easier to build than others. Most teachers have found that it has been necessary to spend considerable time encouraging students to speak and discuss in mathematics class. So strong are the traditions and experiences of learning mathematics alone and in silence, especially in schools that serve the children of poverty, that even sixth-grade students enter these middle schools with definite ideas about the way mathematics class is to proceed, and their ideas may not match well the notion of discourse communities. For example, teachers find that most students are used to giving answers without explanation or justification. Building students' capacities to talk about solution strategies or to justify answers does not happen quickly; rather, it happens through a process of negotiation between the teacher and the students gradually over time.

Although the goal is to create discourse communities in which the conversation is rich in mathematical ideas and in debates about the adequacy of assertions, teachers may initially find it difficult to move beyond superficial consideration of activities or problems. In such settings, teachers may struggle with a tension between the reform demand that they encourage students to participate and the reform requirements that they challenge each student's thinking and ask students to justify their ideas. Even as they resolve this dilemma and develop in their students a willingness to see communication as a part of learning mathematics, teachers are faced with other dilemmas.

QUASAR teachers have found that a critical aspect of building classroom learning communities in which students are willing to engage in investigation and discourse is the creation of an atmosphere of trust and mutual respect (Silver et al., 1995). Unless the classroom environment is safe for thinking and speaking, students will be reluctant to posit their tentative ideas and hypotheses, to question assertions that are puzzling to them, or to share their alternative interpretations. Because students often arrive at middle school with the assumption that it is acceptable to criticize fellow students for doing something they would characterize as "dumb" or "stupid" (Barnes, 1976), teachers must establish norms for discourse and social interaction in inquiry-oriented communities. Students must be encouraged to question each other's ideas and assertions, yet teachers must demand that students respect each other as persons. In the classroom communities teachers seek to build, criticizing someone's ideas is acceptable but criticizing the person is not. With middle-school students, who are generally self-conscious and socially anxious, the building of a classroom atmosphere of trust and respect is no small challenge.

The QUASAR experience has also reinforced the role that language plays as an important mediating factor in this effort. In creating safe and supportive environments for children to express their thinking, teachers of multilingual student populations face special challenges. In special bilingual mathematics classes, the teacher and students share more than one language and must negotiate meaning within dialogue that often moves freely between languages. In regular mathematics classes populated at least in part by children whose native language is not English, the challenges are even greater. Secada (1992) discussed ways in which students with limited proficiency in English can be left out of the discourse in communication-rich mathematics classes, even when the lesson is being conducted by an exceptional mathematics teacher. Children may feel most comfortable expressing their ideas in a language other than English, and this may be a language with which the teacher has little or no fluency. Even in settings that are not officially multilingual, we have seen that teachers face a similar issue because children often have informal ways of expressing themselves that may be unfamiliar to the teacher. These situations present substantial challenges as teachers struggle to create supportive classroom environments in which children can express their mathematical ideas freely, yet ensuring that this is done in ways that honor rather than devalue children's non-school-based language and experience.

Students' fledgling communication attempts often need considerable scaffolding by their teacher in order to develop their capacity to engage effectively in meaningful mathematical discourse. Cobb, Wood, and Yackel (1994) differentiated between the classroom discourse practices of "talking about" mathematics and "talking about talking about" mathematics in order to call attention to this kind of teacher scaffolding of student discourse. In talking about talking about mathematics, teachers communicate to students norms for mathematical discourse, as in restricting the kinds of commentary on each other's ideas that will be permitted or in describing the characteristics of good explanations that make them helpful to others. Both kinds of discourse are found in QUASAR classrooms, as teachers attempt to build the communicative competence of individual students and develop in them the capacity to sustain discourse without teacher intervention (Huinker & Moon, 1993). As with many other aspects of classroom discourse, it is often a challenge for teachers to know when to intervene to provide support for a student who is giving an explanation or asking a question and when to allow the discourse to flow freely among the students. Such decisions are related to considerations of the locus of intellectual authority in the classroom community. Teachers and students alike can experience difficulty in allowing intellectual authority to reside within the collective community rather than entirely (or almost entirely) within a single privileged individual (Huinker & Moon, 1993).

Much of the discussion thus far has focused on oral communication as a feature of mathematics classrooms. According to the NCTM (1991) *Professional Standards, for Teaching Mathematics*, another aspect of the teacher's role in discourse is "asking students to clarify and justify their ideas ... in writing" (p. 35). Additional challenges in the establishment of mathematical discourse communities are associated with written communication.

QUASAR teachers view written communication as having a legitimate place in the mathematics classroom, yet they also recognize that writing is often difficult for their students, so they try to encourage writing in various ways. Over the first several years of the project, many teachers have begun to incorporate journal writing as a feature of classroom activity. In fact, the reported frequency of teachers having students write in journals at least once each week increased from about 25% in the second year to nearly 50% by the end of the third year (QUASAR Documentation Team, 1993). In general, the students' journals serve as repositories for their thoughts and feelings about mathematics class activity; students may be also be asked to summarize in their journals important mathematical ideas they are learning. Students' journal entries are read regularly by the teachers, who then write comments in response to the entries. Writing in journals affords students opportunities to present their thinking in written form for another person to read and understand. Oral and written communication have been integrated by other teachers through use of activities that connect mathematics and literature in various ways. For example, some teachers have used poetry or story-telling as a vehicle for presenting mathematically rich situations and then having students produce written solutions to problems embedded in or generated from the story (Silver et al., 1995).

As was the case for oral communication, teachers also face a dilemma in these attempts to foster written communication; namely, how to move students from informal writing to a form of written discourse that is more clearly aimed at the clarification or justification of mathematical thinking. As with oral communication, teachers find that they need first to build a sense of legitimacy for the activity as part of mathematics class and then to develop in students a disposition toward participation. Only after this has been accomplished does it appear possible to move to the kind of activity advocated by the *Professional Standards for Teaching Mathematics* (NCTM, 1991). QUASAR teachers have tended to make oral communication the primary focus of their initial efforts, thereby placing attention to written communication later rather than earlier in the pedagogical stream. Thus, students' competence in written communication develops more slowly than does their oral proficiency. Nevertheless, both oral and written communication are being encouraged in QUASAR classrooms, and students are developing their capacities for both forms of communication. As students' competence in oral and written communication develops over time, corresponding growth can be noted in the maturation of the classroom mathematical discourse communities.

Once students become less reticent to speak and write, teachers can engage them more fully with an interesting array of worthwhile mathematical tasks. Yet, even then, further challenges associated with communication await. For example, teachers are faced with the challenge of pacing lessons built around worthwhile mathematical tasks so that progress is made by students, while resisting the temptation to do the thinking and reasoning for them. Even if the tasks used in the classroom are related to interesting and important mathematical concepts, and even if they are open to multiple routes of exploration, they will be ineffective in promoting learning if students and teachers are not able to use them in an open way to explore and then discuss the emergent mathematicalideas.

Moving Beyond the Challenges:
Effective Communication in Mathematics Classrooms

In the preceding section of this chapter, QUASAR data were used to identify and clarify some dilemmas and challenges associated with the role of communication in mathematics pedagogy, as they have been observed in the classrooms of mathematics teachers in middle schools serving economically disadvantaged communities. In addition to pointing to classroom challenges and dilemmas, our experience in the QUASAR project also provides data demonstrating that it is possible to navigate successfully through the many obstacles.

Despite the challenges to implementing the ambitious, innovative vision of mathematics instruction being promoted within the QUASAR project, teachers have been quite successful in infusing their instruction with an emphasis on thinking, reasoning, problem solving, and communication to a much greater extent than is found in conventional mathematics classrooms. One analysis of nearly 150 tasks used in QUASAR classrooms over a three-year period (Stein, Grover, & Henningsen, in press) found that about three fourths of the instructional episodes observed in QUASAR classrooms involved tasks intended to engage students in matters of conceptual understanding or mathematical reasoning or problem solving. That analysis also revealed that about two thirds of the tasks observed in use in QUASAR classrooms were ones that allowed for the use of multiple solution strategies and multiple representations, and almost that same proportion required students to provide an explanation in addition to finding a solution. Moreover, the analysis also showed that a very high percentage of the tasks were actually implemented in a manner that was compatible with the high-level mathematical goals and cognitive features they were intended to have. Of particular relevance to this consideration of communication was the finding that about three fourths of the tasks intended to require explanations were implemented in a manner that actually called for student explanation.

Beyond this kind of global analysis of instructional emphasis on communication, it is also possible to see the extent to which the challenges are being met in QUASAR schools and classrooms by considering representative examples. As a case in point, consider the issues previously mentioned related to students' primary language. At one QUASAR site, a special effort has been made to employ mathematics teachers who speak Spanish, the primary oral language of the majority of students attending the school. Conversations among students and between teachers and students in many classrooms, not only those officially designated bilingual, are often conducted in Spanish or involve discourse that moves freely back and forth between English and Spanish. Locally developed mathematics instructional materials are prepared in a way that makes both languages simultaneously available, on the same page or on separate pages, thereby affording students the option of reading and/or responding in either language. In addition, some commercial materials available only in English have been translated into Spanish for use at the school.

At another QUASAR site, where students speak a variety of languages and most of the teachers speak only English, teachers work with the students in their classrooms to develop a shared meaning of mathematics vocabulary and rely on students working collaboratively to provide translations to classmates and to the teacher, as discourse often moves among several languages. In this setting, teachers work hard to respect the needs of many children to express their ideas in other languages, to provide an environment that supports such expression by the children, and to assure that the ideas being communicated are in a form that can be understood by all members of the classroom community.

Other challenges related to communication are also being addressed. For example, many teachers have made progress in building safe, supportive classroom environments that promote and scaffold discourse. In their efforts to build such an atmosphere in the classroom, QUASAR teachers are usually supported by school-wide efforts to create trust and mutual respect. These school-wide efforts are probably essential in creating a generally supportive environment, within which the mathematics teachers can create classroom communities where students can explore mathematical ideas freely without fear of error or ridicule. With the combination of a generally supportive environment in the school at large and in the mathematics classroom in particular, students can develop greater confidence in themselves as learners and deeper respect for themselves as human beings. These outcomes are vitally important for QUASAR students whose lives outside school are often filled with the negative images projected on inner-city schools and students. The affective value that support and respect provide for students within the school and classroom is important. The cognitive payoffs for students—helping them to be able to use their minds and express their thoughts freely in exploring and exchanging mathematical ideas with their teacher and their peers—emerge more slowly but are beginning to become evident in many QUASAR classrooms.

Silver et al. (1995) provided excerpts from the classroom of Ms. Healy, a teacher at another QUASAR site, who has established an atmosphere of mutual trust and respect in her mathematics classroom. In Ms. Healy's classroom, students are expected to present their ideas and their solutions to the class, and classmates of the presenter are expected to ask questions if they do not understand the presentation. In her role as facilitator, Ms. Healy tries to help the group achieve consensus through a give-and-take process that often involves several students sharing their thinking amid debate and questioning by peers. In this classroom, students are encouraged to take substantial responsibility for their own learning. Silver et al. (1995) describe a lesson that was observed in this class and make the following comments:

> Several things are noteworthy about this vignette from Ms. Healy's classroom. First, the students were engaged in debate about mathematical assertions, and they used mathematical argumentation to support differing positions. Ms. Healy showed that she valued student ideas by listening carefully to students' explanations. The students, in turn, listened to each other respectfully, though they were not always convinced of another's point. Second, the activity was more about sense making than about generating answers. ... It was clearly "inefficient" [for the teacher] to spend so much time on this single problem. By doing so, however, Ms. Healy was encouraging students to persevere in understanding a problem and in obtaining a sensible solution, which are both important goals in the learning of mathematics. Although painful and difficult at times, such meandering journeys to mathematical outcomes that make sense for students have benefits that can be measured in terms of both cognitive growth and dispositional outcomes. Students in Ms. Healy's class have responsibility for their own learning and they know that their learning depends on their continuing to question until they understand. In Ms. Healy's classroom, she and her students have formed a community in which they work together to develop shared understandings about mathematics. Students felt comfortable sharing their thinking, and they were comfortable challenging each other's ideas. Ms. Healy and her students have created a community in which explanation, questioning, argumentation and sense making are a normal part of mathematics class (pp. 38–39).

This example, and others discussed by Silver et al. (1995), is representative of the attempt in many QUASAR classrooms to create rich communicative environments that are safe and supportive of children learning mathematics and sharing their thinking with others in the classroom community. Nevertheless, the creation of such classroom communities does not occur easily, nor does it occur equally well or at uniform rates of speed across teachers or schools (Silver & Smith, in press). Individual differences among teachers are important mediating influences in the processes of creating and orchestrating classroom communities. Some teachers are better able to adjust their teaching to accommodate more student-centered discourse than are other teachers, and teachers also differ in their willingness to do so. Nevertheless, the examples provided here, drawn as they are from actual occurrences within the QUASAR project, illustrate that teachers can be successful in designing forms of instruction that include a significant role for communication in the learning of mathematics.

The building of safe environments for classroom discourse pertains primarily to the support of students' capacity for oral communication of mathematical ideas. In many classrooms, progress has also been made in the area of written communication. As noted before, the journey to proficiency in written communication about mathematical thinking and reasoning is long and difficult, and it presents many challenges for teachers and students. One way that QUASAR teachers have begun to make progress is by using portfolios for student assessment. Portfolios have emerged as a valuable way for students to engage in written communication. In many cases, portfolio assignments require students to reflect on work they have done and write explanations of their work. Portfolio assignments and requests for written explanations of solutions and reasoning on homework and on tests and quizzes have become more frequent as the project has progressed.

Beyond including writing as a regular feature of classroom assignments and assessments, some QUASAR teachers have more recently begun to engage students with the task of internalizing for themselves the criteria that experts would use to judge their written responses to mathematical tasks. In this way, students are better able to understand the requirements for a clear, complete, and correct written response to a mathematics problem. This is expected to result in students' improved written communication about their mathematical ideas and reasoning. Evidence from the QUASAR project suggests that the transition from oral to written communication proficiency is a journey with many dilemmas and challenges, yet teachers can be successful in assisting students attain greater written communicative competence.

Simply having students engage in conversations or write sentences and paragraphs in the mathematics classroom is not sufficient to develop their capacity for mathematical thinking and reasoning. If an emphasis on communication and discourse is to lead to increased mathematical proficiency on the part of students, then it is critical that the discourse be centered around worthwhile mathematical tasks. As noted earlier, the instructional tasks found in QUASAR classrooms are different from those found in conventional mathematics classrooms, in that a very large percentage of the tasks are accessible to multiple representations and solution strategies, and that they require justifications and not just answers (Stein et al., in press). Key features of instruction in most QUASAR classrooms include student engagement with challenging mathematical tasks, student involvement in collaborative mathematical activity centered around those tasks, and substantial amounts of student-student and student-teacher discourse about the important embedded mathematical ideas.

Many of the QUASAR classroom excerpts presented by Silver et al. (1995) illustrate the powerful ways in which teachers can use communication as a vehicle to support and extend student reflection on mathematical ideas. For example, Silver et al. describe an eighth-grade classroom activity used at one QUASAR site by Ms. Bensen, who provided for her students a dramatic reading of "A Mathematical Tug of War" (Burns, 1982), which is a complex logical reasoning puzzle in story form. Actually, a solution of the task involves not only logical reasoning but also a solid understanding of quantitative equivalence. The students were directed to solve the problem, and then to prepare a written explanation of their method and their reasoning and a justification of their solution. After completing this assignment, students handed in their written work to the teacher who read the solutions and invited selected students to present their solutions to the entire class. The teacher was able to use this activity, which blended attention to oral and written communication, as a way to display a variety of solution approaches. Some students used diagrams and pictures to solve the problem; other students provided natural language descriptions of their deductive reasoning as they worked with logically equivalent quantities in the problem; and other students employed more formal algebraic approaches, in which relationships among quantities were represented with equations.

This classroom excerpt illustrates the way a classroom focus on communication can enhance students' reflection on the mathematical ideas associated with a substantive mathematical problem. Without the opportunities afforded by this activity for students to explore multiple solution paths and representation modes, or to listen to alternative explanations of proposed solutions, the students would have been unlikely to have had more than a superficial engagement with the important mathematical ideas at the heart of the task and its solution. Hiebert (1992) argued that "classroom practice would be altered radically if we took seriously the notion that reflection and communication are essential for learning mathematics" (p. 440). The examples presented here from QUASAR classrooms, the examples from *Thinking Through Mathematics* (Silver et al., 1990) presented earlier, and examples available from other sources (e.g., Lampert, 1990; NCTM, 1989, 1991) illustrate the interplay between communication and reflection within mathematics classrooms where discourse is both a vehicle for and byproduct of students' deep engagement with the learning of important mathematical ideas.

Other evidence from QUASAR shows that students can profit in observable ways from this kind of communications-rich teaching. In particular, there is evidence that students have made progress in their performance on reasonably complex mathematics performance assessments that require solution justification or other forms of written explanation (Lane & Silver, 1994). Moreover, in-depth analyses of responses to selected tasks at several points in time have specifically demonstrated the positive impact of the instructional programs at QUASAR sites on students' communicative competence (Magone, Wang, Cai, & Lane, 1993).

MOVING BEYOND LEARNING ALONE AND IN SILENCE: AN AGENDA FOR RESEARCHERS AND PRACTITIONERS

In this chapter, a rationale has been presented for viewing the mathematics classroom as a site for engagement with mathematical discourse. Then, drawing on data and experience within the QUASAR project, some challenges associated with realizing such a vision have been identified, and some examples to illustrate the possibilities have also been provided. Examples of rich communicative environments for learning mathematics have also been contributed by others. For example, Lampert (1990) described the discourse that characterizes the community of mathematical practice she has developed in her fifth-grade classroom. Others (e.g., Bartolini-Bussi, 1989; Cobb, et al., 1994; Resnick, 1988) described interesting discourse environments for primary-grade children. These examples provide interesting visions of mathematics classrooms in which fundamentally social processes, such as discourse and communication, are viewed as central rather than peripheral to the activity of the class. Yet, relatively few such examples are documented and available for inspection. In fact, Hiebert (1992) argued that theory and advocacy concerning the role of communication in mathematics learning and teaching has outstripped tangible evidence of their centrality in actual school practice:

Although there is a remarkable degree of consensus building among researchers in mathematics learning on the major theoretical points, and although many of the reform documents are quite consistent with current theory, the theoretical speculations are running well ahead of the data. (p. 440)

In order to remedy this situation, researchers and practitioners could together assume collective responsibility for providing useful descriptions and analyses of classroom practices that instantiate the contemporary vision of communication as a central feature of mathematics classrooms. In this way, we will better understand the challenges and dilemmas associated with realizing this vision, as well as understand the nature of the solutions invented in response to the challenges.

It is also important to acknowledge the work that needs to be done to understand the forms of support that may be needed for teachers as they attempt to create communication-rich environments for their students to learn mathematics. Limitations in teachers' subject matter knowledge, and limitations associated with the ways in which they have learned formal mathematics themselves, appear to be intertwined with the dilemmas of managing the dynamics of discourse communities or in helping students make a transition from competence in oral communication to skillful written communication. Not only do teachers need to be technically skillful in orchestrating the dynamics of such classrooms, as previously discussed, but they also need to be deeply knowledgeable about the mathematics they are helping children learn (Silver & Smith, in press).

Limitations in teachers' mathematical content knowledge and associated pedagogical content knowledge present formidable challenges in creating the classrooms envisioned by the current reform documents. In QUASAR schools, as in many middle schools in the nation, many mathematics teachers are certified as elementary-school teachers, as generalists rather than as specialists in mathematics. In fact, nearly 75% of QUASAR teachers are elementary certified. Although generalizations on the basis of surface characteristics are difficult and prone to error, it seems that elementary-certified teachers, though often quite flexible and child-centered in their pedagogy, usually possess quite limited knowledge of mathematics. QUASAR teachers are not unlike teachers in other urban middle schools throughout the nation in this regard. It is clear that limitations in the background preparation of teachers add further complexity to the task of creating a new generation of communications-rich, inquiry-oriented mathematics classroom environments.

Another factor related to the challenge posed by limitations in teachers' content and pedagogical content knowledge is the fact that most teachers have not had experience themselves as participants in collaborative learning communities. Mathematics teachers tend to work in isolation and with little or no motivation to change. For example, a recent survey of mathematics teachers found that only about half of the teachers at all grade levels saw their colleagues as a source of information on new teaching ideas and even fewer saw professional meetings as a source of such ideas (NCTM, 1992). Thus, like the students in traditional mathematics classrooms, mathematics teachers also tend to find themselves also operating alone and in silence.

Helping teachers move beyond a pedagogy of isolation and recitation is likely to require new forms of assistance. As teachers struggle to make fundamental changes in conventional mathematics instructional practice and explore new forms of pedagogy, it is critical that they operate in safe, supportive environments. Teachers need to see themselves as being joined with colleagues within their school and elsewhere in an effort to provide quality mathematical experiences for their students. Teachers could plan together, discuss each other's teaching practice, develop consensus on ways to evaluate their students' thinking, and support each other through difficult points in the change process. As in classroom communities for students, the discourse in these teacher communities would be rich in observations, explanations, verifications, reasons, and generalizations about mathematics as well as about mathematical pedagogical practice. The ability of teachers to deal with the many challenges and dilemmas suggested in this chapter may depend to a great extent on the ability of colleagues to form supportive, collaborative communities of practice in which the discourse of mathematics teaching occurs. A simple version of how this might occur was provided in *Thinking Through Mathematics* (Silver et al., 1990) in the story of Mrs. Holmes, whose entry into new forms of pedagogical practice was closely associated with the formation of community, first with a single colleague and then with a larger group of teachers at her school. Within the community, Mrs. Holmes discussed and reflected on her pedagogical practices in ways that both enhanced and supported her efforts to improve her teaching.

In QUASAR, many examples can be found of teachers and resource partners creating communities of reflective collaboration as teachers develop new forms of instructional practice. For example, teachers and resource partners have used their common meeting times to plan instruction, to visit each other's classes or to watch videotapes of each other's teaching, to reflect on their individual and collective pedagogical practices, and to discuss the work of their students (Brown & Smith, 1994). Moreover, they have examined foundational mathematical concepts and principles, thereby enhancing individually and collectively their mathematical content knowledge. In some cases, the specific assistance activities engaged in by resource partners and teachers within their community are directly supportive of the assistance activities engaged in by teachers and students within the class-room discourse communities (Brown, Stein, & Forman, 1993). But, even when specific connections are not evident, it appears that the general support of teachers is a crucial element in fostering the kinds of changes desired in classroom instruction. In general, teachers and resource partners at QUASAR schools have come to see mathematics instruction as a collaborative practice, improved through communication and discourse with colleagues, which can thereby capitalize on the distributed network of expertise within the community. Unfortunately, there exist too few examples of careful descriptions of such collaborative communities and their work. The creation and study of communities of practice engaged in the improve-ment of education constitutes an important collaborative agenda for re-searchers and practitioners alike.

ACKNOWLEDGMENTS

Preparation of this chapter was supported by a grant from the Ford Foun-dation (grant number 890-0572) for the QUASAR project. Any opinions expressed herein are those of the author and do not necessarily represent the views of the Foundation. The helpful commentary of Mary Kay Stein regarding an earlier version of this chapter is acknowledged, as is the editorial advice provided by Patricia Ann Kenney.

REFERENCES

Appel, K., & Haken, W. (1977). The solution of the four-color-map problem. *Scientific American, 237*, 108–121.

Ball, D. (1991). What's all this talk about discourse? *Arithmetic Teacher, 39*, 44–48.

Barnes, D. (1976). *From communication to curriculum*. London: Penguin.

Bartolini-Bussi, M. (1989). Evaluation of teaching sequences that include individual and collective activities: Two case studies. In L. Bazzini & H.-G. Steiner (Eds.), *Proceedings of the first Italian-German bilateral symposium on didactics of mathematics* (pp. 285–307). Pavia, Italy: University of Pavia.

Bartolini-Bussi, M. (1992). Mathematical knowledge as a collective enterprise. In G. Seeger & H. Steinbring (Eds.), *The dialogue between theory and practice in mathematics education: Overcoming the broadcast metaphor* (pp. 121–151). Bielefeld, Germany: Institut für Didak-tik der Mathematik, University of Bielefeld.

Bishop, A. J. (1988). *Mathematical enculturation: A cultural perspective on mathematics educa-tion*. Dordrecht, Netherlands: Kluwer.

Brown, C. A., & Smith, M. S. (1994, April). *Building capacity for mathematics instructional innovation in urban middle schools: Assisting the development of teachers' capacity*. Paper presented at the annual meeting of the American Educational Research Association, New Orleans, LA.

Brown, C. A., Stein, M. K., & Forman, E. A. (1993, April). *Discourse development: Chains of assistance*. Paper presented at the annual meeting of the American Educational Research Association, Atlanta, GA.

Burns, M. (1982). *Math for smarty pants*. Boston: Little, Brown and Company.

California State Department of Education. (1989). *A question of thinking: A first look at students' performance on open-ended questions in mathematics*. Sacramento, CA: Author.

Cobb, P. (1994). Where is the mind? Constructivist and sociocultural perspectives on mathematical development. *Educational Researcher, 23*(7), 13–20.

Cobb, P., Wood, T., & Yackel, E. (1994). Discourse, mathematical thinking, and classroom practice. In E. A. Forman, N. Minnick, & C. A. Stone (Eds.), *Contexts for learning: Sociocultural dynamics in children's development* (pp. 91–119). New York: Oxford University Press.

Cohen, E. G. (1984). Talking and working together: Status interaction and learning. In P. Peterson, L. C. Wilkinson, & M. Hallinan (Eds.), *Instructional groups in the classroom: Organization and processes* (pp. 172–187). Orlando, FL: Academic Press.

Confrey, J. (1990). A review of the research on student conceptions in mathematics, science programming. In C. B. Cazden (Ed.), *Review of research in education* (Vol. 16, pp. 3–55). Washington, DC: American Educational Research Association.

d'Ambrosio, U. (1985). Ethno mathematics and its place in the history and pedagogy of mathematics. *For the Learning of Mathematics, 5,* 44–48.

Dossey, J. A., Mullis, I. V. S., & Jones, C. O. (1993). *Can students do mathematical problem solving?* Washington, DC: National Center for Education Statistics.

Fawcett, H. P. (1938). *The nature of proof. Thirteenth yearbook of the National Council of Teachers of Mathematics*. New York: Teachers College.

Garcia, E. (1991). *Education of linguistically and culturally diverse students: Effective instructional practices*. Santa Cruz, CA: University of California, Santa Cruz, National Center for Research on Cultural Diversity and Second Language Learning.

Greitzer, S. L. (1978). *International mathematical olympiads 1959–1977*. Washington, DC: Mathematical Association of America.

Hajós, G., Neukomm, G., & Surányi, J. (Eds.). (1963). *Hungarian problem book: Based on the Eötvös competitions, 1894–1905* (E. Rapaport, Trans.). New York: Random House.

Hiebert, J. (1992). Reflection and communication: Cognitive considerations in school reform. *International Journal of Educational Research, 17*(5), 439–456.

Hiebert, J., & Carpenter, T. P. (1992). Learning and teaching with understanding. In D. A. Grouws (Ed.), *Handbook of research on mathematics teaching and learning* (pp. 65–97). New York: Macmillan.

Huinker, D., & Moon, J. (1993, April). *Mathematical discourse as an emerging process: Teacher and student interactions*. Paper presented at the annual meeting of the American Educational Research Association, Atlanta, GA.

Kitcher, P. (1984). *The nature of mathematical knowledge*. New York: Oxford University Press.

Lakatos, I. (1976). *Proofs and refutations: The logic of mathematical discovery*. New York: Cambridge University Press.

Lampert, M. (1990). When the problem is not the question and the solution is not the answer: Mathematical knowing and teaching. *American Educational Research Journal, 27*(1), 29–64.

Lane, S. (1993). The conceptual framework for the development of a mathematics assessment instrument. *Educational Measurement: Issues and Practice, 12*(2), 16–23.

Lane, S., & Silver, E. A. (1994, April). *Examining students' capacities for mathematical thinking and reasoning in the QUASAR Project*. Paper presented at the annual meeting of the American Educational Research Association, New Orleans, LA.

Magone, M., Wang, N., Cai, J., & Lane, S. (1993, April). *An analysis of the cognitive complexity of QUASAR's performance assessments and their sensitivity to measuring changes in students' thinking*. Paper presented at the annual meeting of the American Educational Research Association, Atlanta, GA.

Mathematical Association (U. K.). (1987). *Math talk*. Portsmouth, NH: Heinemann.

Mellin-Olsen, S. (1987). *The politics of mathematics education*. Dordrecht, Netherlands: D. Reidel.

National Council of Teachers of Mathematics. (1989). *Curriculum and evaluation standards for school mathematics*. Reston, VA: Author.

National Council of Teachers of Mathematics. (1991). *Professional standards for teaching mathematics*. Reston, VA: Author.

National Council of Teachers of Mathematics. (1992). *The road to reform in mathematics education: How far have we traveled?*. Reston, VA: Author.

National Research Council. (1989). *Everybody counts: A report to the nation on the future of mathematics education*. Washington, DC: National Academy Press.

National Research Council. (1993). *Measuring up: Prototypes for mathematics assessment*. Washington, DC: National Academy Press.

Noddings, N. (1985). Small groups as a setting for research on mathematical problem solving. In E. A. Silver (Ed.), *Teaching and learning mathematical problem solving: Multiple research perspectives* (pp. 345–359). Hillsdale, NJ: Lawrence Erlbaum Associates.

Oakes, J. (1985). *Keeping track: How schools structure inequality*. New Haven, CT: Yale University Press.

Peterson, I. (1988). *The mathematical tourist*. New York: W. H. Freeman and Co.

Porter, A. C. (1989). A curriculum out of balance: The case of elementary school mathematics. *Educational Researcher, 18*(5), 9–15.

Polya, G., & Kilpatrick, J. (1974). *The Stanford mathematics problem book: With hints and solutions*. New York: Teachers College Press.

QUASAR Documentation Team. (1993). *The QUASAR teacher beliefs inventory: A descriptive summary of responses, 1990–1993*. Pittsburgh, PA: University of Pittsburgh, Learning Research and Development Center.

Radó, T. (1932). Mathematical life in Hungary. *The American Mathematical Monthly, 39*, 85–90.

Resnick, L. B. (1987). *Education and learning to think*. Washington, DC: National Academy Press.

Resnick, L. B. (1988). Treating mathematics as an ill-structured discipline. In R. I. Charles & E. A. Silver (Eds.), *Research agenda for mathematics education: Vol. 3. The teaching and assessing of mathematical problem solving* (pp. 31–60). Hillsdale, NJ: Lawrence Erlbaum Associates.

Rowe, D. E., & McCleary, J. (1989). *The history of modern mathematics. Volume I: Ideas and their reception*. San Diego, CA: Academic Press.

Schlitz, D. (1977). The Gambler [Recorded by Kenny Rogers]. on *Kenny Roger's 20 Greatest Hits*. New York: Liberty Records. (1983).

Schoenfeld, A. H. (1989). Ideas in the air: Speculations on small group learning, environmental and cultural influences on cognition and epistemology. *International Journal of Educational Research, 13*, 71–88.

Secada, W. G. (1992). *Toward a consciously multicultural mathematics curriculum*. Madison, WI: University of Wisconsin.

Silver, E. A. (1992). Assessment and mathematics education reform in the United States. *International Journal of Educational Research, 17*(5), 489–502.

Silver, E. A. (1994, April). *Building capacity for mathematics instructional reform in urban middle schools: Contexts and challenges in the QUASAR project.* Paper presented at the annual meeting of the American Educational Research Association, New Orleans, LA.

Silver, E. A., Kilpatrick, J., & Schlesinger, B. (1990). *Thinking through mathematics: Fostering inquiry and communication in mathematics.* New York: College Entrance Examination Board.

Silver, E. A., & Lane, S. (1993). Assessment in the context of mathematics instruction reform: The design of assessment in the QUASAR project. In M. Niss (Ed.), *Assessment in mathematics education and its effects* (pp. 59–70). London: Kluwer.

Silver, E. A., & Smith, M. S. (in press). Building discourse communities in mathematics classrooms: A challenging but worthwhile journey. In P. Elliott & M. Kenney (Eds.), *Communication in Mathematics, K–12* [1996 Yearbook of the National Council of Teachers of Mathematics]. Reston, VA: National Council of Teachers of Mathematics.

Silver, E. A., Smith, M. S., & Nelson, B. S. (1995). The QUASAR project: Equity concerns meet mathematics education reform in the middle school. In W. Secada, E. Fennema & L. Byrd Adajian (Eds.), *New directions for equity in mathematics education* (pp. 9–56). New York: Cambridge University Press.

Smith, M. S., & Silver, E. A. (1995). Meeting the challenges of diversity and relevance. *Mathematics Teaching in the Middle School, 1,* 442–448.

Smith, M. S., Silver, E. A., & Parke, C. (1991, April). *Voices and visions: The relationship between the NCTM Curriculum and Evaluation Standards and proposals for school-based mathematics reform in the QUASAR project.* Paper presented at the annual meeting of the American Educational Research Association, Chicago, IL.

Stein, M. K., Grover, B. W., & Henningsen, M. (in press). Building student capacity for mathematical thinking and reasoning: An analysis of mathematical tasks used in reform classrooms. *American Educational Research Journal.*

Stein, M. K., Grover, B. W., & Silver, E. A. (1991). Changing instructional practice: A conceptual framework for capturing the details. In R. G. Underhill (Ed.), *Proceedings of the Thirteenth annual meeting of the North American chapter of the International Group for the Psychology of Mathematics Education* (pp. 36–41). Blacksburg, VA: Virginia Polytechnic & State University.

Stodolsky, S. (1988). *The subject matters: Classroom activity in mathematics and social studies.* Chicago: University of Chicago Press.

Tymoczko, T. (Ed.). (1986). *New directions in the philosophy of mathematics.* Boston: Birkhauser.

Webb, N. (1991). Task-related verbal interaction and mathematics learning in small groups. *Journal for Research in Mathematics Education, 22,* 366–389.

Chapter 7

TOWARD A PRACTICE OF "CONSTRUCTIONAL DESIGN"

Mitchel Resnick
MIT Media Laboratory

Charlene loved amusement parks, especially Ferris wheels. So when I brought a big box of LEGO bricks into her fourth-grade classroom, Charlene knew exactly what she wanted to build. She spent two class sessions building a Ferris wheel out of LEGO bricks. She put little LEGO people in the seats of her Ferris wheel and connected the axle of the Ferris wheel to a LEGO motor. Finally, Charlene connected the LEGO motor to a computer and typed a command: on. She expected the Ferris wheel to move, but it didn't. Something was wrong.

Great, I thought. This is a perfect opportunity to explain mechanical advantage. Charlene had not used the gears correctly. A large gear on the motor was connected to a small gear on the Ferris wheel. With that combination, there was not enough torque to turn the Ferris wheel. If Charlene exchanged the two gears, the Ferris wheel would work.

I tried to engage Charlene in a discussion about gears, but she was not interested. Instead, she started to build a little LEGO box next to the Ferris wheel. The little box gradually became a refreshment stand. I was feeling frustrated. Part of me wanted to shout out: "Don't waste your time on a refreshment stand. You can't learn about gears that way. And you can't control the refreshment stand from the computer." But I kept quiet. Charlene finished her refreshment stand, then she built a wall around the amusement park and finally a parking lot outside the wall.

It was only after Charlene finished the refreshment stand, the wall, and the parking lot that she returned to the Ferris wheel, to try to figure out why it was not moving. She played around with the gears, tried different combinations, and (with a bit of help) got her Ferris wheel spinning smoothly. Later, she wrote several computer programs to control the movements of the Ferris wheel. In one program, the Ferris wheel started moving whenever anyone pressed a particular LEGO touch sensor. Another program asked the user to type a number into the computer, which made the Ferris wheel turn that number of revolutions.

DESIGNING FOR DESIGNERS

In recent years, there has been a surge of interest in this type of classroom activity, in which students learn through design, invention, and construction. A growing number of researchers and educators have argued that design activities provide rich opportunities for learning (e.g., Harel, 1991; Lehrer, 1993; Papert, 1991; Soloway, Guzdial, & Hay, 1994). There are many reasons for this interest in design-based learning:

- Design activities engage students as *active participants*, giving them a greater sense of control (and responsibility) over the learning process, in contrast to traditional school activities in which teachers aim to "transmit" new information to the students.
- Design activities encourage *reflection and discussion*, because the artifacts that students design can serve as "props" for students to reflect on and talk about.
- Design activities encourage a *pluralistic epistemology*, avoiding the right/wrong dichotomy prevalent in most school mathematics and science activities, suggesting instead that multiple strategies and solutions are possible (Turkle & Papert, 1990).
- Design activities are often *interdisciplinary*, breaking down the barriers that typically separate subject domains in school.
- Design activities provide a sense of *authenticity*, suggesting stronger connections to real-world activities (because most real-world activities involve design-oriented strategies, not the rule-driven, logic-oriented analyses that underlie many school activities).
- Design activities can facilitate *personal connections*, because students often develop a special sense of ownership (and caring) for the artifacts that they design.
- Design activities promote a *sense of audience*, encouraging students to consider how other people will use and react to the artifacts they create.

Unfortunately, most classroom-based design projects do not live up to these ideals. In many cases, educators propose highly restrictive design tasks or even cookbook-style recipes for constructing particular artifacts. Students are given little opportunity to redefine and restructure the tasks. In such cases, students are less likely to make personal connections with the design activities or with the domains of knowledge underlying the activities.

Consider Charlene and her amusement park. If Charlene had been instructed to build a particular machine, it is unlikely that she would have gained much insight into concepts such as mechanical advantage. Charlene was not interested in the bare Ferris wheel. Charlene wanted to tell a story about her Ferris wheel. She created a story about a family spending a day at the amusement park. She imagined the family driving into the parking lot, walking through the main gate, and buying cotton candy at the refreshment stand, before ever going on the Ferris wheel. For Charlene, the refreshment stand and the parking lot were just as important as the Ferris wheel itself. In order to become engaged with the ideas of gearing and mechanical advantage and computer programming, Charlene needed to embed her Ferris wheel in an environment, in a context. Only in that way could Charlene form a personal relationship with the Ferris wheel and with the scientific ideas underlying the workings of the Ferris wheel.

The story of Charlene and her amusement park provides a glimpse of the complexities involved in bringing design tools and activities into the classroom. Unfortunately, there are few established theories for managing these complexities. The field of instructional design is biased toward more traditional teaching strategies. Although it includes a wealth of theories and strategies to guide the development of curriculum materials, the field of instructional design offers little guidance for the development of design-oriented tools and activities.

What is needed, in parallel with research on instructional design, is a new research program on what might be called "constructional design."[1] Rather than focusing on new strategies and materials to help teachers instruct, constructional design focuses on new strategies and materials to help students construct. Constructional design is a type of meta-design: It involves the design of new tools and activities to support students in their own design activities. In short, constructional design involves designing for designers.

Successful constructional design involves a tricky balancing act. It must support and encourage two very different sorts of "connections": connections to important intellectual ideas, and connections to students' own personal interests and passions.

---

[1]The phrase constructional design was first suggested to me by Nobiyuki Ueda, an educator and museum designer in Japan. It is inspired by the constructionist theories of Seymour Papert (Papert, 1991).

The challenge (and it is a significant challenge) is to create design-oriented tools and activities that support both types of connections. The tools and activities must make important intellectual ideas salient and accessible, so that students are likely to engage meaningfully with these ideas as they go about their design work. At the same time, the tools and activities must provide enough flexibility so that all students can follow their own personal fantasies and build on their own personal experiences. This challenge can be met only through a thorough mixing of research and practice: Each must be guided by the other.

In the next two sections, I discuss two computational construction kits, LEGO/Logo and StarLogo, as case studies in constructional design. I describe not only the tools themselves but the ways in which the tools have been used, focusing particularly on how teachers and students have related to these tools and how the tools have helped users form new relationships with various domains of knowledge.

LEGO/LOGO

In 1985, I began working with Steve Ocko and Seymour Papert on a new type of construction set. We envisioned a construction set that would allow children to construct buildings and machines, as they had done for years with erector sets, Tinker Toys, and LEGO bricks. In addition, we wanted children to be able to program and control the things they built. After building a model house, a child should be able to add lights to the house and to program the lights to turn on and off at particular times. The child should also be able to add a garage and to program the garage door to open whenever a car approaches.

The idea was to combine several different design activities. Children would not only design architectural structures and gearing mechanisms, they would also design computer programs to control them. So we formed a collaboration with the LEGO toy company, and we began to link LEGO building bricks with the Logo programming language (Papert, 1980), a combination that we called LEGO/Logo (Resnick, Ocko, & Papert, 1988). Whereas traditional LEGO bricks form a type of structural construction kit, we view LEGO/Logo as a "behavior construction kit" (Bourgoin, 1990; Granott, 1991; Martin, 1988; Resnick, 1993).

LEGO/Logo includes new types of LEGO blocks for building machines and new types of "Logo blocks" for building programs. In addition to the familiar LEGO building bricks, there are new LEGO pieces such as gears, pulleys, wheels, motors, lights, and sensors. There are optosensors that detect changes in the level of light and touch sensors that detect pressure.

As its programming language, LEGO/Logo uses an expanded version of Logo. Just as students can build increasingly complex structures and machines by snapping together LEGO bricks, they can build increasingly complex computer programs by "snapping together" Logo commands.

LEGO/Logo is now in use in more than 15,000 schools across the United States, and teachers use the materials in many different ways. In some classrooms, the teacher instructs every student to build an identical car based on building instructions from the LEGO company. In other classrooms, the teacher might focus on a theme—for example, instructing each student to create some type of insect (if the class happens to be studying insects).

We have found that LEGO/Logo offers the richest learning opportunities when students work on projects that connect more closely with their own interests and passions. When we first designed the LEGO/Logo system, we explicitly tried to create a diverse set of project activities that would appeal to a wide variety of students with a wide variety of interests. In our suggested projects, we included not only cars and traffic lights, but Ferris wheels and merry-go-rounds. We thought we were being open-minded, but we never thought to include refreshment stands and parking lots with the amusement park rides. It was only by working in classrooms, with students such as Charlene, that we began to develop a new, broader vision of LEGO/Logo. While some students are satisfied with building individual machines such as cars or Ferris wheels, other students want to design entire environments, entire scenarios. Not only do they want to make their LEGO contraptions move, they want to tell stories about them.

The limitations of our initial vision became particularly clear to me during a summer workshop that we organized for classroom teachers (Resnick, 1991). The teachers began working on "conventional" LEGO/Logo projects: cars, merry-go-rounds, conveyor belts. Then a visiting researcher suggested that the teachers might use LEGO/Logo to create moving sculptures, pieces of kinetic art (Adamson & Helgoe, 1989). Several teachers responded with immediate enthusiasm. By combining the LEGO bricks with a variety of non-LEGO materials that they brought in from home (pipe cleaners, reflective paper, hair curlers), the teachers began to construct wonderfully eclectic sculptures. Next, the teachers connected their artistic creations to the computer, and they wrote Logo programs to make the sculptures whirl and spin. They even added sensors, so that the motions of the sculptures depended on interactions with the surrounding environment.

Sharon Beck, one of the teachers at the workshop, wanted to build something that would evoke the carnival-like atmosphere of the annual Mardi Gras celebration in New Orleans. She combined LEGO motors and gears with pipe cleaners and flashy colored paper with optical patterns. One

LEGO motor catapulted confetti into the air, while also controlling the dance of a pipe-cleaner turtle. A second motor spun a dazzling array of optical patterns. With both motors on, the LEGO machine turned into a lively and colorful work of art.

At some abstract level, the moving sculptures were very similar to traditional LEGO/Logo projects. The teachers used the same LEGO motors, gears, and sensors that they would have used in making a LEGO car. The teachers controlled the sculptures with the same programming-language constructs. The teachers also needed to think about all of the same scientific concepts (such as mechanical advantage, friction, and sensory feedback) to make their creations work.

For these teachers, the kinetic-art project fundamentally changed the way they viewed LEGO/Logo. It was not until they began working on their kinetic-art projects that they became truly excited about LEGO/Logo. Kinetic art resonated with these teachers. Finally, they had something that they really *wanted* to make. As a result, the teachers seemed to make deeper connections with the scientific concepts underlying their work with LEGO/Logo. They cared about friction because they really wanted their sculptures to move. They cared about sensory feedback because they really wanted to interact with the sculptures.

These same issues arise when children use LEGO/Logo in the classroom. When students design and construct LEGO/Logo projects that are meaningful to themselves (or to others around them), they tend to approach their work with a sense of caring and interest that is missing in most school activities. In doing so, students are more likely to explore, and to make deep connections with, the mathematical and scientific concepts that underlie the activities. Building and programming a merry-go-round is based on the same underlying principles as building and programming a classic robot—but for a child who cares more about merry-go-rounds than robots, the merry-go-round project offers a much richer learning experience. For LEGO/Logo activities to have any real meaning, children must be given the freedom to follow their fantasies but also the structure and support to make those fantasies come to life.

Consider, for example, the LEGO/Logo project created by George, a third-grade student at a Boston public elementary school. George began his LEGO/Logo work by building a simple LEGO car. First, he connected the car's motor to a battery box and watched the car roll forward. Next, he connected the motor to the computer and began experimenting with some of the new Logo commands. After a while, George put several commands together in the following expression:

repeat 4 [onfor 20 rd]

When George executed this expression, the computer turned on the motor for two seconds (**onfor 20**), reversed the direction of the motor (**rd**), then repeated those commands three more times. The result: the car moved forward and back, then again forward and back, completing two forward-back cycles.

Next, George changed the numerical input to the repeat command. He tried **repeat 3** and **repeat 6** and **repeat 7**. After this experimentation, George noticed a pattern:

When I use an even number, the car ends up where it began.

When I use an odd number, it ends up away [from where it started].

George paused for a moment and then added:

So that's why there are even and odd numbers!

Clearly, George had previously learned about even and odd numbers in the classroom. But George's experimentation with the LEGO car provided him with a new (and more personally relevant) representation of the concept. Moreover, the LEGO activity allowed George to relate to numbers in a new way: He played with the ideas of even and odd. This new relationship with even and odd numbers helped George develop a new level of understanding.

STARLOGO

In recent years, there has been a growing fascination with decentralized systems and self-organizing phenomena. Increasingly, people are choosing decentralized models for the organizations and technologies that they construct in the world and for the theories that they construct about the world. Researchers are recognizing that many patterns are formed not by centralized authority but by local interactions among decentralized components.

Almost everywhere you look these days, there is evidence of the growing interest in decentralization. You can see it every time you pick up a newspaper. On the front page, you might see an article about the failure of centrally planned economies in Eastern Europe. Turn to the business page, and you might find an article about the shift in corporate organizations away from top-down hierarchies toward decentralized management structures. The science section might carry an article about scientific research on decentralized models of the mind, or maybe an article about engineering research on distributed approaches to computing. In the book review section, you might read an article suggesting that literary meaning itself is decentralized, always constructed by readers, not imposed by a centralized author.

Even as decentralized ideas spread through the culture, there is a deep-seated resistance to such ideas. In trying to understand natural systems, people often assume centralized control where none exists. For example, many people assume that a "leader bird" guides the rest of the flock when, in fact, flocking patterns typically arise as a result of local interactions among the birds. In constructing artificial systems, people often impose centralized control where none is needed—for example, using top-down, hierarchical programming structures to control a robot's behavior or using hierarchical organizational structures to manage a large company.

To probe how people think about decentralized phenomena, and to help them develop new ways of thinking about such phenomena, I developed a new simulation environment called StarLogo (Resnick, 1992; Resnick, 1994). Other researchers have used so-called "cellular automata" (such as the "Game of Life") to explore these sorts of phenomena (e.g., Toffoli & Margolus, 1987). Cellular automata are, indeed, a rich framework for exploring self-organizing behaviors. Simple rules for each cell can lead to complex and unexpected large-scale patterns. Cellular automata seem best suited as a tool for computer aficionados, not for novices. The idea of writing transition rules for cells is not an idea to which most people can relate. Other decentralized computational models (such as neural nets) have similar drawbacks. In most cases, the objects being programmed, such as nodes and cells, seem too low level. These models are a great way for computer hackers and mathematicians to explore decentralized phenomena, but they seem ill-suited for people who have less experience (or less interest in) manipulating formal systems.

I wanted to create a system in which the objects were more familiar, more related to people's experiences. In developing StarLogo, I decided to focus on how colony-level behaviors arise from interactions among individual creatures—for example, how ant-colony behaviors arise from interactions among individual ants. People are quite familiar with both of these levels (the creature level and the colony level). So I expected that people would be more interested in (and have a better chance at understanding) situations involving these levels.

StarLogo is a type of construction kit, with which students can construct their own self-organizing systems.[2] Rather than just a few graphic "turtles" (as in traditional versions of Logo), StarLogo has *thousands* of turtles.

---

[2]The idea of constructing a self-organizing system might seem like a contradiction. By definition, a self-organizing patterns are created without a centralized designer. But there are ways to construct self-organizing systems. Users can write rules for lots of individual components, then observe the larger-scale patterns that arise from all of the interactions. This is a different sort of design: Users control the behaviors of the parts, not of the whole.

StarLogo is designed as a *massively parallel* language, so all the turtles can perform their actions at the same time, in parallel. StarLogo also introduces a new type of object: the patch. A patch is a piece of the environment in which the turtles live. Just as turtles can execute Logo commands, so too can patches. For example, a patch might control the growth of food within its borders, or the diffusion of a chemical. StarLogo has commands for controlling all types of interactions: interactions among the turtles, interactions among the patches, and interactions between turtles and patches.

Students have used StarLogo turtles and patches to model many different types of dynamic systems: ants in a colony, birds in a flock, antibodies and antigens in an immune system, buyers and sellers in a market, molecules in a chemical reaction. With such a range of possibilities, students can find their own personal paths for exploring the idea of self-organization.

As an example, consider the StarLogo project created by Ari and Fadhil, two high-school students. At the time Ari and Fadhil started working with StarLogo, they were also taking a driver's education class. Each had turned 16 years old a short time before, and they were excited about getting their driver's licenses. Much of their conversation focused on cars. So when I showed StarLogo to Ari and Fadhil, they imagined the turtles as cars, and they decided to work on a project involving cars and traffic.

Traditional studies of traffic flow rely on sophisticated analytic techniques (from academic fields like queuing theory). But many of the same traffic phenomena can be explored with simple StarLogo programs. To get started, Ari and Fadhil decided to create a one-lane highway. (Later, they experimented with multiple lanes.) Ari suggested adding a police radar trap somewhere along the road to catch cars going above the speed limit. He also wanted each car to have its own radar detector, so cars would know to slow down when they approached the radar trap. After some discussion, Ari and Fadhil decided that each StarLogo turtle/car should follow three basic rules:

- If there is a car close ahead of you, slow down.
- If there aren't any cars close ahead of you, speed up.
- If you detect a radar trap, slow down.

Ari and Fadhil expected that a traffic jam would form behind the radar trap, and indeed it did (Figure 7.1). After a few dozen iterations of the StarLogo program, a line of cars started to form to the left of the radar trap. The cars moved slowly through the trap, then sped away as soon as they passed it. Ari explained, "First one car slows down for the radar trap, then the one behind it slows down, then the one behind that one, and then you've got a traffic jam."

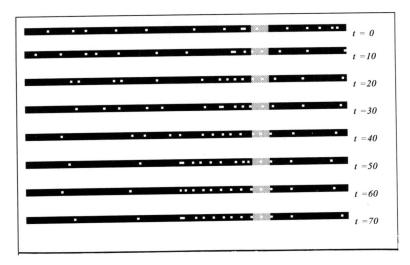

FIG. 7.1. Traffic jam caused by radar trap. (Cars move left to right.)
t = the number of iterations of the program.

I asked Ari and Fadhil what would happen if none of the cars had radar detectors—or, equivalently, if the radar trap were removed entirely? With no radar trap, the cars would be controlled by just two simple rules: if you see another car close ahead, slow down; if not, speed up. The rules couldn't be much simpler. At first, Fadhil predicted that the traffic flow would become uniform: cars would be evenly spaced, traveling at a constant speed. After all, without the radar trap, what could cause a jam?

I showed the StarLogo traffic program to several other high-school students, and they all had similar reactions. All the students expected the cars to end up evenly spaced along the highway, separated by equal distances. No one expected a traffic jam to form. Some of their predictions:

Emily: [The cars will] just speed along, just keep going along...they will
            end up staggered, in intervals.

Frank: Nothing will be wrong with it. Cars will just go ... There's no
            obstacles. The cars will just keep going, and that's it.

Ramesh: They will probably adjust themselves to a uniform distance from
            each other.

In fact, when we ran the StarLogo program, a traffic jam began to form (Figure 7.2), much to the surprise of the students. In their comments, most students revealed a strong commitment to the idea that some type of "seed" (like a radar trap or an accident or a broken bridge) is needed to start a traffic jam. Perhaps Frank expressed it best, "I didn't think there would be any problem, since there was nothing there." In other words, if there is nothing there, if there is no seed, there should not be a traffic jam. Traffic jams do not just happen; they must have localizable causes. These reactions are evidence for what I call the *centralized mindset*—the tendency of most people to assume centralized causes or centralized control for the patterns they see in the world.

As Ari and Fadhil worked with their StarLogo program, they began to move beyond this centralized mindset. After trying the program several times, Fadhil made an important change: He altered the program so that the cars *started out* evenly spaced and with equal velocities, rather than at random positions along the road. Sure enough, when he ran the program, the cars remained evenly spaced, and no traffic jam formed. Now, Fadhil understood what had happened in the original program: The random initial positioning of the cars had provided a "seed" from which a traffic jam could form. Fadhil explained, "Some of the cars start closer to other cars. Like,

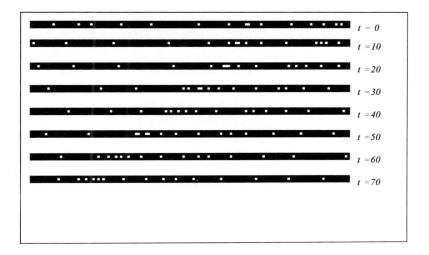

FIG. 7.2. Traffic jam without radar trap. (Cars move left to right, but jam moves right to left).
t = the number of iterations of the program.

four spaces between two of them, and two spaces between others. A car that's only two spaces behind another car slows down, then the one behind it slows down."

Ari and Fadhil reintroduced some randomness in the initial conditions of the StarLogo program, and the traffic jams returned. Watching the traffic jams more closely, Ari and Fadhil noticed that the jams did not stay in one place, but tended to move with time. In fact, the traffic jams tended to move *backwards*, even though all of the cars within them were moving forward. Fadhil described it, "The jam itself moves backward. If you keep your eye on one car, it leaves the traffic jam, but the jam itself, I mean where you see the cars piling up, moves backward."

The backward movement of the traffic jam highlights an important idea: Collective structures (such as traffic jams) often behave very differently from the elements that compose them. This idea is true not only for traffic jams, but for a much wider range of phenomena, including waves. Ideas about waves are generally very difficult for students to grasp. One reason is that waves are often presented in unmotivated contexts (e.g., perturbations moving along a string) and through difficult mathematical formalisms (such as differential equations).

StarLogo seems to provide a more accessible introduction to wave-like phenomena. As with differential equations, StarLogo can be used as a formal system for expressing ideas about wave behavior. But the StarLogo representation is different in several important ways. For one thing, StarLogo programs seem easier to understand and manipulate. In addition, StarLogo programs are executable, so that students can watch their programs run and revise their ideas based on what they see. Perhaps most important, StarLogo offers students a chance to explore wave phenomena in personally meaningful contexts. The fact that Ari and Fadhil developed strong intuitions about traffic flow while working on their StarLogo project was due, in no small part, to their deep interests and experiences with cars.

TOWARD EMERGENT
LEARNING EXPERIENCES

As these examples suggest, LEGO/Logo and StarLogo offer rich opportunities for learning. But as students and teachers have used LEGO/Logo and StarLogo, their specific learning experiences have been quite different than we (as developers of LEGO/Logo and StarLogo) expected. When we developed LEGO/Logo, we did not have kinetic sculptures in mind, and we did not expect students to gain new insights into even and odd numbers. And when I developed StarLogo, I was not thinking about traffic jams or wave phenomena.

This unpredictability is characteristic of good constructional design. Developers of design-oriented learning environments need to adopt a relaxed sense of control. It is neither possible nor desirable to control each aspect of the learning experience. Educational designers cannot control exactly what or when or how students will learn. The point is not to make a precise blueprint. Rather, practitioners of constructional design must create fertile environments in which interesting activities and ideas are likely to grow.

In some ways, the design of a new learning environment is like the design of a StarLogo simulation. In creating StarLogo simulations, users write simple rules for individual turtles, then observe the large-scale patterns that emerge. Users do not program the patterns directly. So too with constructional design. Developers of design-oriented learning environments cannot program learning experiences directly. The focus, instead, is to create frameworks from which interesting experiences are likely to emerge. The goal is *emergent learning experiences*, not imposed learning experiences.

It is still possible, of course, for constructional designers to emphasize and highlight particular concepts in the tools and activities that they create. In LEGO/Logo, ideas about mechanical advantage and feedback are particularly salient. In StarLogo, ideas about self-organization and emergence are particularly salient. But salience is not enough. As the examples presented here suggest, students (and teachers) are most likely to become deeply engaged in thinking about these concepts when they can form their own personal connections to the concepts. The challenge for constructional designers is to create tools and activities that not only highlight important concepts but also facilitate personal connections.

ACKNOWLEDGMENTS

Steve Ocko, Fred Martin, Randy Sargent, Brian Silverman, and Seymour Papert have been major contributors to the LEGO/Logo project. Hal Abelson, Seymour Papert, Brian Silverman, Randy Sargent, Andy Begel, and Uri Wilensky have provided encouragement, inspiration, and ideas for the StarLogo project. The LEGO Group and the National Science Foundation (Grants 851031-0195, MDR-8751190, and TPE-8850449) have provided financial support. All student names in this chapter are pseudonyms.

REFERENCES

Adamson, E., & Helgoe, C. (1989). Exploring art and technology. In G. Schuijten & M. Valcke (Eds.), *Teaching and learning in logo-based environments: Proceedings of the EuroLogo Conference.* Gent, Belgium: IOS Press.

Bourgoin, M. (1990). *Children using LEGO robots to explore dynamics.* Cambridge, MA: MIT Media Laboratory.

Granott, N. (1991). Puzzled minds and weird creatures: Spontaneous inquiry and phases in knowledge construction. In I. Harel & S. Papert (Eds.), *Constructionism* (pp. 295–310). Norwood, NJ: Ablex.

Harel, I. (1991). *Children designers.* Norwood, NJ: Ablex.

Lehrer, R. (1993). Authors of knowledge: Patterns of hypermedia design. In S. P. Lajoie & S. J. Derry (Eds.), *Computers as cognitive tools* (pp. 197–227). Hillsdale, NJ: Lawrence Erlbaum Associates.

Martin, F. (1988). *Children, cybernetics, and programmable turtles.* Unpublished master's thesis, MIT Media Laboratory, Cambridge, MA.

Papert, S. (1980). *Mindstorms: Children, computers, and powerful ideas.* New York: Basic Books.

Papert, S. (1991). Situating constructionism. In I. Harel & S. Papert (Eds.), *Constructionism* (pp.1–27). Norwood, NJ: Ablex.

Resnick, M., Ocko, S., & Papert, S. (1988). LEGO, logo, and design. *Children's Environments Quarterly, 5*(4), 14–18.

Resnick, M. (1991). Xylophones, hamsters, and fireworks: The role of diversity in constructionist activities. In I. Harel & S. Papert (Eds.), *Constructionism* (pp.151–158). Norwood, NJ: Ablex.

Resnick, M. (1992). *Beyond the centralized mindset: Explorations in massively parallel microworlds.* Unpublished doctoral dissertation, Massachusetts Institute of Technology.

Resnick, M. (1993). Behavior construction kits. *Communications of the ACM, 36*(7), 64–71.

Resnick, M. (1994). *Turtles, termites, and traffic jams.* Cambridge, MA: MIT Press.

Soloway, E., Guzdial, M., & Hay, K. (1994). Learner-centered design. *Interactions, 1*(2), 37–48.

Toffoli, T., & Margolus, N. (1987). *Cellular automata machines.* Cambridge, MA: MIT Press.

Turkle, S., & Papert, S. (1990, Fall). Epistemological pluralism: Styles and voices within the computer culture. *Signs, 16*(1), 128–157.

Chapter 8

A CLASSROOM ENVIRONMENT FOR LEARNING: GUIDING STUDENTS' RECONSTRUCTION OF UNDERSTANDING AND REASONING

Jim Minstrell
Virginia Stimpson
Mercer Island School District

The central charge in the writing of this chapter is to create a vision of what it is like to teach with a focus on engaging students and teachers in the bidirectional nature of learning rather than the unidirectional transmission of knowledge from teacher to student. We posit that learning is an active cognitive undertaking in which the student and teacher reconstruct understanding and reasoning from the classroom subject matter. In this environment, the teacher follows students' thinking and attempts to guide student experience. In such an environment, a student's question or comment may change the teacher's goal or create subgoals that affect the teacher's decisions about what to do next. Teaching from this perspective is an ill-defined problem, that is, "...there is no unique solution and no standard, universal method of finding solutions" (Bruer, 1993, p. 32). To create classrooms that focus on student learning rather than information transmission, there are many questions that need to be addressed. Among them are: How might curricular materials or the ways materials are used differ from the past? How might the strategies of teaching, the ways students and teachers interact in the classroom, be different from the dominant perspective of teacher and textbook as teller and student as the receiver of predigested knowledge? How might making understanding accessible to all be achieved given the diversity of students in our classes? How might assessments be made consistent with these perspectives on learning and teaching? What type of support encourages implementation of such a vision? In this chapter, we consider these factors, among others, that affect learning in school and in the extended school community.

Before we begin painting a vision of the relevant attributes of an environment for constructing understanding, we need to make evident some of our assumptions. The first is that by understanding, we mean understanding not only the products, results, and conclusions of the discipline, but also understanding the nature and processes of the discipline. In mathematics, Lampert (1992) called the latter "responsible teaching of mathematics," and addresses the question of whether "what is being learned is authentic mathematics." Do the skills and knowledge being acquired contribute to the students' ability actually to perform in the discipline (p. 296–297)?

To reflect the discipline appropriately, in-depth investigations into the nature and content of the discipline replace superficial coverage that is told or read and then memorized by rote (Arons, 1983). In our classes the teacher acts as a guide and, occasionally, as a summarizer of past activities with an emphasis on depth of coverage that has implications for the activities, teaching strategies, and the assessment of understanding. The text provides a resource that extends understanding developed through class activities. The learning environment becomes an issue-driven, investigative one, not the passive environment of a training school. The teacher represents the professional world and helps mediate between the professional world and school activities, guiding students in moving toward the professional world.

Others use the term "constructivist teaching" to describe an approach that engages students in meaningful experiences and discourse (von Glasersfeld, 1991). Although we avoid labeling our approach to teaching, we share some assumptions with constructivists. Teaching for learning is different from training; the latter focuses on performance and observable actions while the former focuses on performance with understanding. Teaching for students' understanding may yield a student saying or doing things in ways that are compatible with understanding, but the teacher cannot be sure the goal of understanding has been achieved. We can train students to deliver a particular explanation, but we cannot be certain the student understands the event and related ideas the same way we do.

That is not to say that we cannot attempt to assess for understanding. We look for observables that might indicate understanding, such as applying learned information in new and novel ways. In our assessments, the more our observations are consistent with a deep understanding, the more confident we are that the individual understands.

Conceptual knowledge is the result of constructing a relational network of perceptions from experiences. The conceptual knowledge of a particular individual depends on the salient perceptions and the particular mental organization, and to the extent that the experiential perceptions are unique, the conceptual understandings of each individual will be unique. Thus, conceptual knowledge cannot be reliably transferred by words. Yet, developing vocabulary in the context of a set of shared experiences increases the likelihood of developing a common understanding. This focus on learning implies that the teacher needs to know something about the initial and intended understandings of the student. When the teacher guides learners to select a common set of salient features on which to focus their perceptions, there is an increased likelihood that the resulting conceptions of different learners are compatible. From this learning perspective, then, the purpose of teaching is brought out naturally: How might I create an environment (physical and social) to address present understanding and effect the intended, or at least a deeper, more powerful, understanding?

When good instruction focuses on student learning, new perceptions, inconsistent with articulated initial conceptions, will arise and are more likely to be held in common among the learners in the classroom. Clever teachers can create the experiences and the environment in which the resulting group-shared conception is likely to be more consistent with the phenomena and likely more compatible with the conceptions of the professional scientist. Students report various factors that influence a change in their understanding. They include hearing the different ideas and points of view of fellow students, being given time and encouragement to think about the situation, seeing that their prediction did not work, being able to experiment and see first-hand what does happen, being reminded of experiences that were not consistent with their ideas, and seeing how the newly initiated ideas relate to other knowledge and experiences in and out of school.

It is important to note that this view relies on the possibility of developing a collective understanding (conception, explanation, theory, and so forth). From the class experiences, each individual will create her or his own understanding. Moreover, it is against this collective understanding that students' answers and rationale might be judged wrong or not wrong. A conception consistent with the commonly shared experiences and resulting perceptions may be incomplete but not incorrect. In fact, an evolving conception of a phenomenon reflects the tentative nature of scientific knowledge and the epistemological processes by which scientific knowledge is derived. Our view fosters a social dynamic in which students desire to develop understanding consistent with collective experience.

It follows from these basic assumptions that teachers need to have opportunities to develop a deep understanding of the subject matter of the discipline. Clearly they also need to know about their students' initial and developing understanding and reasoning in order to guide students' learning toward understanding and reasoning (Minstrell, 1989). Thus, addressing learning in the classroom requires at least three types of instructional expertise: managing and conducting activities with groups of children; understanding deeply the subject matter, that is, the epistemological processes of the discipline and its interconnectedness with other areas of knowledge and with the day to day world; and understanding the nature of learning in humans.

Presented here are our views on what it means to create an environment that fosters student reconstruction of understanding and reasoning. We begin with a fictionalized account—a story based on experiences we encountered when attempting to reform our teaching. The students' statements and questions reflect their attempts to negotiate meaning from experiences in and out of the classroom. We hope this vignette provides insight into teaching for learning, reconstructing understanding and reasoning from prior ideas and experiences, and relating new experiences to students' initial ideas. Within the story we share the sorts of concerns and decisions that are addressed by teachers and students.

Our teaching is based on some assumptions about the cognition of learners. We debrief the story by discussing these assumptions and then by considering aspects of curriculum, teaching strategies, and assessment that are consistent with these assumptions. We refer to the story as an example of how these aspects get played out in the classroom. Although the story is about a science classroom, there are implications for most school disciplines that involve conceptual understanding and reasoning. We conclude by talking about the benefits and concerns of educational reform based on a teaching for understanding perspective.

A STORY ABOUT AN ENVIRONMENT FOR BUILDING UNDERSTANDING AND REASONING ABOUT ELECTRICITY

On the first day of the study of electricity, students looked at typical electrical devices in their day-to-day world. Mr. Jones set out various devices that had been somewhat dismantled such as a toaster, an old calculator, a desk lamp, and a couple of different flashlights. Outside he had parked his car close to the classroom, so the students could see the many wires, the battery, and other electrical devices under the hood. Students were encouraged to think about general questions they had about electrical devices. Being able to give complete answers to these questions would be a major goal of the new unit.

On the second day (which is described in detail later), students began their formal exploration by conducting an investigation using common flashlight cells (batteries) and bulbs.

While Mr. Jones checks the adequacy of the equipment he has set out for his next class, he reflects on how much more interesting and satisfying his work has become during the past 10 years. Early in his teaching, he typically began a unit by having students read a specific chapter in the assigned text and answer the questions in the book. He had believed that they needed to have an appropriate vocabulary and the main ideas before they could follow lab procedures. He remembered his instruction as being dominated by teacher talk at the chalk board and students reading and doing generally mindless end-of-chapter exercises. Being a good student meant taking the time to memorize facts from the text and the steps to getting the answers to the exercises. Occasionally the students had performed experiments, but, as they filled in the blanks of their lab books, they did not seem to be excited by the phenomena. There were times when an interesting opportunity to apply the new ideas did come up, but he remembered how woefully superficial and inadequate the students' understandings were. Students bided their time through his class, apparently saving their interesting observations and conversations for other parts of the day. While his administrators had thought of him as a good teacher, Mr. Jones mostly found his job uninteresting. Now, his current methods of teaching are as challenging to him as he hopes they are to his students.

Mr. Jones used to think of himself as a very good teacher. However, when he used some of the new assessment questions with his students, they performed very poorly, yet he had been convinced that he had done a admirable job presenting the ideas to the students. This apparent inconsistency piqued his curiosity. When opportunities arose for him to work with researchers and curriculum developers, he signed up. In one case, a project bought part of his time to think more about the nature of learning and implications for the reform of his teaching. These activities had moved him from centering on his own presentations to focusing on students' learning: what thinking students brought to the classroom, what thinking was more desirable, and what activities might help students develop in their thinking.

Mr. Jones smiled, reflecting on the demands of paying attention to students' thinking and reasoning, and his own impatience with his initial ability to design questions which revealed students' ideas. Those early changes in teaching had been pretty overwhelming but revitalizing for him and for his students. The shift in perspective had come slowly. How could he have taught so long without seeing that his students weren't really understanding? Mr. Jones shook his head thinking how obvious it was that it takes time for learning, for teachers as well as for children.

His own learning had been facilitated by the time he shared his classroom expertise with university researchers, working together to better understand students' thinking and to design lessons that fostered learning. A grant to his school district from local business and industry released him from half of his teaching day during one school year to allow him time to reflect, with the research team, on how to address learning in his classroom. Their work resulted in curriculum activities that worked with his students. Because he had participated in the research and development, he knew firsthand the purposes of each lesson and how the lessons would play out in the classroom. He was further motivated and encouraged by reports of reform efforts at the national, state, and local levels. He was now feeling valued as a team member in the efforts to reform schools.

Mr. Jones' efforts and intellectual challenges were sustained by regular conversation with his teacher and researcher colleagues. The group focused on the classroom as a learning community in which experiences interacting with the natural and human-made worlds could serve as contexts for exploring ideas with each other. On electronic mail and in face-to-face meetings, he and his colleagues discussed phenomena of the classroom, implications about students' thinking, and implications for design of instruction to address students' understanding and reasoning. Now, 4 years since he began rethinking his teaching perspective, the reward for the investment of time and effort was paying off in terms of the empowerment of his students. From recent assessments, there was evidence that his students were now exhibiting greater depth of understanding. From his interactions with learning researchers and with curriculum developers, he was improving his own knowledge of students' thinking and the principles of developing lessons that address students' understanding and reasoning. The activities in his classroom now seemed to have a much greater sense of purpose.

[Note how the activities of the curriculum, the assessment, and the teaching strategies in the following scene are integral parts of meaning-making in the science lessons.]

Getting Started

Mr. Jones hands out a sheet of paper on which are drawn a few simple arrangements involving one flashlight cell, one bulb, and one or two wires. Mr. Jones shows the class a typical flashlight bulb, battery, and some ordinary wire. He asks the students to consider what they already know about arrangements of electrical devices. What each student writes will become an initial assessment of that student's understanding and reasoning in the conceptual arena of current electricity. This brief probe, and others that follow, inform the teacher's decisions about appropriate instructional activities. As importantly, the students quickly realize that they begin this unit with some knowledge and many unanswered questions which they are now motivated to get answered.

> Mr. Jones:　This is a situation where what you know and understand may change considerably. Yesterday you began a record of your ideas when you wrote down questions about electrical devices. Now I would like you to consider the arrangements of batteries and bulbs represented on this sheet. In which cases do you think the bulb would light? In which cases would it not light? Would it be brighter or dimmer in some? As best you can, write a summary of your ideas. How did you decide which would light, how bright? What are your present ideas about electricity that help you make your predictions?

These are questions that will help unpack the issues of the unit. Essentially they ask for prediction and for explanation. Mr. Jones hopes that these questions will focus students on common electrical occurrences such as the lighting of a bulb. The diagrams on the paper reflect arrangements frequently made by students as they attempt to light the bulb. Although such sheets were part of the curricula of the 1960s and 1970s, today more is known about the implications for students' conceptions in electrical interactions. Some students' choices will reflect a "source-receiver" model, others a "two kinds of electricity interacting" model, and others a "complete circular flow" model. By knowing which students exhibit which sorts of ideas, Mr. Jones can set up group work such that discussions will be seeded by a variety of perspectives competing for which will best account for the phenomena.

Mr. Jones walks among the students, clarifying the task and noting students' answers and rationale. Some students predict that a single wire used to connect one end of the battery to the tip of the bulb will light the bulb. This suggests that those students believe that the battery is a source of the electricity and the bulb is the receiver. Even though Mr. Jones knows this prediction is incomplete, his experience suggests that students will see the inadequacy of this idea as they design and perform tests of their predictions.

Mr. Jones: Once you have made your predictions and given your reasons, begin comparing your answers and ideas with other students. Don't change what you have written on the sheet. Rather, on another sheet begin writing questions you want to investigate or ideas about the nature of electricity that you want to test.

Students begin sharing their ideas with each other in small groups:

Sara: I think if you make the wire, like a pipe, from the top of the battery to this pointy thing on the bottom of the bulb, then the wire will carry the electricity to the bulb and make it light.

Martin: I don't think it will work. I heard on a TV show that you have to make a electrical circle, so the only ones that will light are when you have two wires helping make a circle with the battery and the bulb.

Sara: I don't know. I want to try my idea and see if I can make it work.

Martin: I think it's the circle idea that works. Mr. Jones, isn't that right? You have to make a circle to make the bulb light, right?

Mr. Jones: Well ... Ann and Chris, you two have been listening to Martin and Sara, but you have been pretty quiet, what do you think?

Mr. Jones wants his students to take responsibility for their learning, and since they have not sufficiently discussed their ideas, he chooses to reflect Martin's question to other students who have not yet spoken their ideas.

Ann: Uh ... it seems like both are right. I know you gotta have a power source like a battery or things won't work, but maybe the more wires you have the brighter the bulb, so the ones with two wires will make the bulb light brighter.

Chris: I think Sara's idea is right. The other day when my dad and I were trying to fix the taillight on the car, I noticed there was only one wire to the bottom of the bulb.

Sara: Let's quit talking and see what does happen.

In working with his students and in conferences with the fellow educators and researchers with whom he works, Mr. Jones has learned to search for value in what the students bring to the learning situation. The source-receiver idea, expressed by Sara, is generally a useful intuition since even the energy company expresses electrical distribution as the flow of electricity from the powerplant to the consumer. Ann has suggested another generally useful intuition, "the more of one thing gives more of another." Even though these two ideas do not fully apply to the situations at hand, Mr. Jones sees this statement as evidence that the student is exploring possible relations between variables. He is confident that the students will sort this out as they experiment with the battery, wire, and bulb. Mr. Jones also knows that Chris failed to observe all of the relevant variables when he looked at the car battery. Since relating classroom work to out-of-class experiences is a priority for Mr. Jones, he notes that this context will provide a nice challenge once students have dealt with less complicated classroom phenomena. He will ask Chris to talk about it again after the students have additional shared experiences involving somewhat structured observations and inferences.

Martin has suggested the circular idea that will eventually be the precursor of "circuit." Just as with the other students, Mr. Jones does not signal Martin about the correctness of his ideas. This student's knowledge may be based on an incomplete understanding of something he has seen or heard, but not observed. Mr. Jones has learned that knowledge built on superficial experiences is less likely to generalize to new situations.

Mr. Jones: That's good that you all have brought so many ideas and experiences to the situation. What could you do to find out which of these ideas, if any, work?

Sara: Can we try it? Can we try the experiment?

Mr. Jones: Go to it! But, as you are setting up the situation, be sure you think about how your experiment will help you decide which of the ideas you have discussed so far seem to work. In the end you will need to be able to describe not only your ideas but also how the experiments you did tested your ideas.

Getting Started opens a giant box of issues. In the process of Getting Started, the students become aware of the variety of ideas they have about electricity. As their study progresses, some of these ideas will be rejected, others will be modified as they begin to account for new phenomena. Additional contexts will cause students to refine further their emerging reconstructed understanding. Though he is aware of the limitations of some of the students' understandings, Mr. Jones avoids thinking of the students' ideas as either right or wrong. He knows which questions to encourage early in the study of electricity and which should be postponed. Mr. Jones thinks about phenomena which can be observed by the students. He applauds Sara's impulse to investigate. The tentative, evolutionary nature of ideas developed from such idea-testing investigations will be reflective of the nature and processes of science.

The Investigation

Each group uses flashlight batteries, bulbs, and wires. Mr. Jones knows his students are capable of dealing with the variables in this situation, so he elects to have them identify relevant factors and design investigations to test their initial ideas. Chris and Sara have teamed up. Chris holds a battery in one hand and a bulb in the other. A thumb holds one end of the wire to the top of the battery while the other thumb holds the other end of the wire to the bottom tip of the bulb. Sara holds the tip of a bulb directly to the top of a battery. Neither bulb lights.

Ann places one wire from the bottom of a battery to the tip of the bulb and another wire from the top of the battery to the threaded part of the bulb. Her bulb lights. Martin holds the same arrangement except that the ends of both wires are touching the bottom tip of the bulb. His bulb does not light.

Martin wishes Mr. Jones would just tell him the answer like his last science teacher did. He has always earned good grades when he knew exactly what answers to study. He is concerned that his grades will go down because instead of giving him answers, this teacher keeps asking him to think about everything. Mr. Jones holds high expectations for this capable person but is sensitive to the time the student will need to adjust to being expected to describe the phenomena and to justify his answers and ideas.

Ann, by contrast, is pleased to have a class where she actively explores ideas and justifies her thinking. She is beginning to recognize the limitations of her past experiences, how little equipment she has had the opportunity to play with and use outside of school. Though her initial ideas on prein-struction quizzes have proven to be incomplete, she has performed excep-tionally well on tests at the end of the first few units. Mr. Jones and the research team who occasionally observes his class have found that involving students in lab activities that answer student-posed questions has had a leveling effect in terms of making up for inequities in students' backgrounds.

Mr. Jones moves from group to group noting the varied explorations and the quality of the students' techniques. This embedded assessment helps

Mr. Jones monitor the students' development of skills in investigation. The check-sheet on which he takes notes will become part of a longer record, the analysis of which will help Mr. Jones improve his teaching about scientific investigation processes.

The building principal, on her way down the hall, stops by the classroom to admire the level of engagement and activity of the students and teacher in this "controlled chaos," as she calls it. Because of the efforts of Mr. Jones and other educators and researchers in the partnership, this school has improved on several measures of performance. As she leaves, the principal recounts the extra efforts it has taken to convince the rest of the school district to commit the necessary resources to support the new programs, professional development opportunities, and facilities. The extra equipment and the time for teachers to plan has proven to be a worthwhile expense. Excellence does not come without a price.

Down the hall the principal passes the mother who heads the Schools' Foundation. Officers in the Foundation assumed leadership in developing understanding and support for reforms in mathematics, science, and technology education. In addition to written explanations providing a rationale for planned changes, these members of the community worked with the teachers to provide Family Nights when parents could experience the excitement and frustrations of exploring ideas. Change is a process that takes time, so parents are just now beginning to value the growing depth of understanding, facility with reasoning, and investigation capabilities of their children. Each woman expresses appreciation for the invaluable support the other has provided for the teachers and students.

Meaning-Making

Mr. Jones encourages the students to share their observations. Sharing requires the students to re-present their understandings. In this way a common (to the class) understanding can be constructed, an understanding that may generalize across a broader range of experiences.

Mr. Jones: OK, so what did you find out? What factors must be present in order for the bulb to light?

Chris: Sara and I found that even though we know the battery is important and needed, you can't just connect the bulb to one end of the battery.

Mr. Jones: Do you agree, Sara? Did you find any way to light the bulb?

Sara: Yeah, but it was more like Martin and Ann said.

Mr. Jones: What do you mean? How was it like what Martin and Ann said?

Mr. Jones reflects her comment back to her, asking her for clarification, encouraging Sara to be more precise.

Sara: Well, Martin said you need a circle to get the bulb to light. When Chris and I tried their idea, we got it to light most of the time.

Martin: Except that to get it to light, you have to touch the wires to two parts of the light bulb, not just to the tip on the bottom. Mr. Jones, please just tell us the answer.

Mr. Jones: You're doing fine. You don't want me around for the rest of your lives to tell you when you are right or wrong. You all are finding out that you can learn from your own investigation and from talking with others about their investigations and experiences. That's how paid scientists learn too. I want you to continue to learn about the world around you even after you are out of school and away from teachers. I will say, however, what's been said so far is consistent with my experience, too.

Mr. Jones coaches the students to think about their own experiences, to listen and share experiences with others, and to gain confidence in their skills of meaning-making together.

Mr. Jones: In the situations that light the bulb, what is important about the arrangement?

In learning and problem solving, Mr. Jones knows it is important to have learners identify perceptually salient characteristics by which they can later recognize when principles, findings, or conclusions will apply and when they will not.

Sara: You need a circle.

Martin: But you also need to touch two parts of the bulb and both ends of the battery.

Mr. Jones used to be relieved when a single student suggested this essential part of the pattern. He now realizes that if he is patient enough, several students will share this observation.

Ann: Yeah, it's like you have to have both the plus electricity and the minus electricity to come from the ends of the battery to go to the bulb and have a reaction at the filament.

From working with the research group and from last year's experience, Mr. Jones has been expecting the "two kinds of electricity" model to be suggested.

Martin: But, it has to go to the tip of the bulb and to the threaded part of the bulb.

Ann: Yeah, one wire to each, because the tip of the bulb is connected inside to one end of the filament and the threaded part of the bulb is connected to the other end of the filament.

Chris: How do you know that?

Ann: Cuz, I asked Mr. Jones if it would be okay to break open a bulb, so we did it, and I saw what was connected to what inside.

Sara: But how do you know there is a reaction from the two electricities crashing in the bulb. I think it is like Martin said. There is a circle from one end of the battery to one end of the bulb, through the bulb out the threaded part to the other end of the battery. Maybe that is how electricity flows, around the circle.

Mr. Jones: OK, so let's see what we've found out so far. It sounds like some of you are suggesting that we need to involve two connection places on the battery, two connection places on the bulb, and, that the whole arrangement has to form a circle. Did any of you find an arrangement that shows that any of these parts are unnecessary? (Mr. Jones pauses to learn if the students agree to these essential parts.) The conclusions you have come to so far are very important. Most common electrical devices we encounter daily have two endedness. And most have one or more circles, technically called circuits. Notice that the words circle and circuit are very similar.

Mr. Jones has learned that technical terms are best understood when rooted in shared, prior experience. That is why he did not introduce the terms earlier in the unit as he once had done.

Martin: That's the word I was trying to think of. That was the word they used on TV.

Mr. Jones: Yes. That's probably what you heard, Martin. So, two endedness and a circle arrangement. Those important factors seem to be common for us all now. Those things we could see. Now what about these ideas that Ann and Sara are suggesting? Has anyone seen any evidence for one of these and not the other, whether two different electricities meet and react in the bulb or that electricity goes around in a circle through the bulb?. . . No? Perhaps we'll have to keep thinking about that and see if we can come up with any evidence to support or reject one or the other.

Although Mr. Jones has read about electron drift theory, he has not seen any evidence for this idea that would be accessible to his students. There are other ideas that are more likely to be relevant and applicable to their lives so he chooses to ignore the more sophisticated idea unless a student mentions having read or heard about it.

Chris: But, I'm still confused about when I worked on the taillight. I know I saw only one wire to the back of the bulb holder.

Mr. Jones waits 5 seconds to see if there is anyone who addresses Chris's concern. Not getting an answer, Mr. Jones primes the discussion again. One of his goals for classroom interaction is to have students address each other's concerns and questions.

Mr. Jones: Can anybody help Chris out on that concern?

Sara: I think maybe the metal car acts like the other wire. The electricity might go from one end of the car battery through a wire to the bulb. Then, maybe it goes from the other end of the bulb to the metal part of the car and through the metal car back to the other end of the battery.

Chris: Ohhh, maybe that is why the other end of the battery goes through a big wire to the metal engine of the car. I noticed that the other day when we were looking at Mr. Jones' car.

Extending Activities

The Teacher Guide that Mr. Jones is using is based on the same sort of research on students' understanding in which he participated. By observing and recording the sequence of issues that became salient to students during their investigations, developers could write teacher guides that included descriptions of expected behaviors of students, included implications for what the behaviors mean about students' thinking, and included next issues and rationale for choices for needed lessons. From that research-informed guidance and from his own classroom experience, Mr. Jones knows that a next big issue regarding current electricity will be whether the electricity gets used up by a bulb or flows through the bulb. He will use another preinstruction assessment, asking students to predict the relative brightness of two bulbs in series. That usually primes the discussion for considering these major alternatives. This will initiate another instructional cycle of Getting Started, Investigation, and Meaning-Making. These cycles have proven useful even if the shapes of the particular activities differ. For example, in order to explore this next idea, he has a particular critical experiment for every student to do. The students will not be engaged in an open investigation this time.

For another week or two, the emphasis will be on working qualitatively with ideas. At some point the students will make measurements, and at that time numerical data analysis will become integrated with the qualitative ideas. That will offer a natural opportunity to integrate learnings in mathematics with those in science. As numbers are introduced, it will be important for the students to revisit ideas and experiences that made sense earlier to see the consistency between concepts and formulas.

After students have shared a common set of experiences, each student will engage in a computerized assessment designed to diagnose problematic understandings or reasoning. Because the questions and expected answers are derived from the same research and integrated with the material in the Teacher's Guide, the diagnosis will assist Mr. Jones in making instructional decisions about what ideas need to be addressed by further activities with the whole group or smaller groups of students. This diagnosis and prescribed instruction increases the probability that certain key ideas will get developed. It also makes students aware of areas where they need further study.

By experiences such as these, students' understandings of classroom situations are elaborated. Their understandings are extended into new situations which were not explored by the full class. They are reminded of contexts in which additional constraints need to be imposed.

At some point, the students will go back to the devices available the first day and show that they understand aspects critical to the working of these devices. Given batteries, bulbs, switches and wire, they will have an opportunity to wire a makeshift house addressing problems such as turning off lights in one room while being able to leave them on in another and some appliances requiring twice the voltage to operate them. Striving for this more authentic assessment seems to help students retain their understanding and bridge the gap to being able to see the world more like the professional.

ASSUMPTIONS ABOUT
THE COGNITION OF LEARNERS

Research on students' conceptual understanding suggests that students come to a learning situation with existing ideas. In the context of our story, "battery is the source, bulb is the receiver" is one dominant idea. Associated with this idea is "each bulb uses up electricity that comes from the battery." Another more generic reasoning pattern is "the more influence the more effect" which gets applied in the electrical context in the form of "the more wires, the brighter the bulb," "the more batteries the brighter the bulb," or "the more bulbs you use, the more electricity gets used." These are initial ideas that are predictably present at the beginning of a unit on electricity. When teachers and students are aware of initial understandings and reasoning, experiences can be designed that challenge and extend these initial ideas.

These understandings and reasoning are pervasive and often robust. Conceptual questions have been asked internationally with similar resulting understanding and reasoning exhibited (Driver, Guesne, & Tiberghien, 1985; Jung, 1984; Viennot, 1979; White and Gunstone, 1992). Without implementing instruction that addresses students' understanding and reasoning, they will continue to exhibit their old ways of thinking in new contexts (McDermott, 1984). Students need to observe first-hand the limitations of their initial ideas.

Telling students they are wrong is not effective. At one point in his career, one of us (JM), knowing well the conceptual ideas invoked by students, attempted to tell his students about the misconceptions they had and why those ideas would not work. He spent extra time talking about the scientifically accepted ideas and contrasting them with the initial ideas described in the research and apparently held by his students. Although the students seemed to follow the arguments as they were told the correct ideas and the troubles with the alternative ideas, still there was very little change in the students' thinking on the next assessment. Telling the accepted ideas and the difficulties with the alternative ideas did not help most students change their conceptions (Minstrell, 1984).

Experience alone is nearly as ineffective as telling. Merely creating the first-hand experience does not necessarily lead to conceptual change. Early in the experience of one of us (JM) this truth was forcefully brought home. During an initial assessment wherein a large proportion of the students indicated that the "earth is in the way" was a dominant explanation for the crescent phase of the moon. Without being told a better explanation, the students were instructed in making a chart of observations of the moon.

The data tables included the phase of the moon, the approximate direction and angle of elevation of the moon, similar data for the sun at the same time of day, if it could be seen, the date and time of day or night of the observation. After 2 months the students had accumulated an impressive array of data, including many observations wherein the crescent moon and the sun were in the same region of the sky. Without having been prompted, only a few students came forward spontaneously with the concern that the earth couldn't be "in the way" if both the sun and moon were in the sky at the same time. After the 2 months of observations, students were asked individually to explain the crescent phase of the moon. Nearly all the students gave the same "earth in the way" explanation. The experience of making observations over the long term did not effect a change in the initial conception of the students. These sorts of experiences have convinced us that students do not necessarily learn from first-hand experiences alone.

One reason why the ideas are robust is that they often work in some circumstances, so the student may come to believe that they are always valid. The limitation of students' ideas often resides in the contextual application of the ideas rather than in the ideas themselves. "The more batteries used in the circuit, the brighter the bulb" applies if the batteries are arranged in series, but not if they are arranged in parallel. "Heavier falls faster" works when dropping a coin and a feather from the ceiling, but not if a wooden ball and steel ball are dropped from that same height. However, if the wood and steel balls are dropped from a height of a hundred meters above the ground, the heavier steel ball will hit the ground sooner. Unless one wants to rely on knowing and remembering a vast number of observations, a deeper sense of the mechanisms influencing effects is necessary to accurately predict the relative fall times for various objects under various conditions. One goal of teaching is to help students build an understanding that incorporates knowing when (in what contexts) certain ideas apply and when they do not.

There are valuable aspects of students' knowledge and experience that they bring from their everyday experiences, aspects that can help them as they move toward a professional's view of the world. Questions and observations from fellow students or from the teacher can help students clarify what aspects of earlier understanding are valid and in what contexts and can help identify more specifically where earlier thinking may be flawed.

Students have ideas or beliefs about teaching and learning in addition to ideas specific to the discipline (Gunstone, 1991). "The teacher's job is to tell me what I need to know. My job is to study hard to remember what she told me" was a belief represented through the voice of Martin in the story. Instructional systems need to address these notions, if students are to make a smooth transition from their daily world where they occasionally may be expected to think and make decisions to the professional world where they regularly will be expected to think and make decisions. Our teacher, Mr. Jones, resisted the temptation to tell Martin the answer, but Mr. Jones also guided the learning situation so that Martin might begin to feel empowered by his success at investigating the ideas which he generated.

Learners exhibit a confirmation bias. Seeking evidence that supports their existing ideas takes precedence over looking and accounting for disconfirming evidence. They "see" the heavier ball fall faster, partially because they believe that "heavier falls faster." Even when students note discrepancies, they tend to discredit its source. Our students, for example, after noting disconfirming evidence can be heard to say "I can never do science right anyway" or "our equipment isn't working right." Perhaps there is an ecology among their existing ideas, an ecology that is so strong that it becomes difficult to modify one aspect without attending to the others. Perhaps in an attempt to avoid being overloaded with perceptual cues, learners avoid dealing with apparent discrepancies. For whatever reason, the knowledge system of learners tends to be conservative with respect to change, especially with respect to attending to and resolving inconsistencies between articulated expectations and classroom observations. In our story, Mr. Jones knew what to expect in the way of students' thinking; he asked questions to get students to reconsider their initial ideas in light of the new experiences and in consideration of ideas and experiences expressed by fellow students. He persisted, encouraging students through classroom conversations to recognize and resolve differences between their expectations that reflected their initial ideas and the new experiences that suggested a need for a reformed conception. When students are convinced that the new observations during the learning experiences are valid, that their initial ideas and reasoning are inconsistent with the believed experiences, and a new way of thinking about the situation is understandable and seems viable, the probability for change in understanding is more likely (Posner, Strike, Hewson, & Gertzog, 1982).

CURRICULAR ACTIVITIES

What is taught and what is done in the classroom, typically called the curriculum, has been traditionally embodied in the textbook. As we address learning, as we take students' understanding and reasoning into account, and as we attempt to reflect the questions, issues, and activities of the discipline, our view of the curriculum becomes more dynamic. What we investigate and how we investigate it, in terms of the activities of the class, depends on the assessed needs of the students, on the resources available, and on the interests and capabilities of the students and teacher.

Curriculum activities should address the understanding and reasoning of students. Camp and Clement (1994), for example, devoted an entire book to lessons addressing students' preconceptions in mechanics. In our story, Mr. Jones used a preinstruction quiz and related discussion to help make students aware of their initial expectations and ideas. We find that asking our students to make predictions or initial interpretations prepares them mentally to listen more critically to the ideas of others and to be more likely to note differences between expected results and the actual results of demonstrations or lab experiences. In the story, students had an opportunity to identify and clarify their initial ideas and to test, change, and further develop their ideas. Lessons that open up the issues in the unit or subunit, that get students suggesting and conducting investigations to test their ideas, and that initiate new understandings we have come to call Benchmark Lessons (diSessa & Minstrell, in press). Like surveying benchmarks, they serve as reference points for later discussions and investigations.

After the initial investigation, Mr. Jones asked all students about a particular situation (two bulbs in series) because learning their ideas around that situation was critical to the teacher's choice of subsequent instructional activities. Thus, embedded in the curriculum are cycles of diagnosis of potential difficulties and prescription of activities designed to address those potential difficulties. The larger instructional cycle involved Getting Started, Investigation, Meaning-Making, and Extending Activities. This cycle represents phases of identifying potentially relevant ideas, testing the ideas, resolving differences, and then trying the reformed understanding in new contexts from which the cycle repeats.

The curriculum should reflect activities consistent with intellectual practice of the discipline. Investigation (including questioning, predicting, experimenting, and interpreting results) involves the processes of the discipline called science. We foster and facilitate activities that incorporate aspects of scientific investigation. In the story, the students designed their own experiments to test alternative ideas about electricity.

Problems which might require further investigation provide opportunities to apply and extend ideas. Rather than assigning ten repetitious exercises using $V = IR$ and solving for voltage (V), current (I) or resistance (R), students might encounter and use the conceptual ideas behind Ohm's Law as they design circuitry to meet the voltage and current requirements of appliances in a home.

The issues involved in coming to new understandings and reasoning need to be revisited in subsequent activities. Arons (1990) recommended revisiting new ideas in no fewer than five contexts. Some memory research suggests spacing the review opportunities (Loftus, 1980). In our situation, the two-endedness and simple circuit idea will be revisited each day in the early part of the unit, then arise later in the house and appliance circuits, and even later in a subsequent unit that focuses on energy.

Good curricular activities correctly and appropriately represent the substance and nature of a subject and use a context that focuses attention on relevant aspects of the concept being developed. The activities must be comprehensible to the particular pupils being taught. A lesson that works well with one group of students may bomb with a group that has had very different earlier experiences. Finally, the activities should focus on a particular change in students' thinking, so much so that students can articulate the puzzling questions that they are working to resolve. In order for teachers to create, know, and implement useful curricular activities, they need to understand the subject matter in a rich flexible way, and they need to have a knowledge of learners and learning (McDiarmid, Ball, & Anderson, 1989). Within the curriculum materials, there need to be opportunities for teacher learning as well as student learning.

TEACHING STRATEGIES

A Critical but Supportive Environment

To create an environment for reconstructing understanding and reasoning, we suggest using teaching strategies that foster a critical, yet comfortable, risk-taking environment. Students are more likely to attend to the results of a new investigation if they consider those results in light of their initial ideas and expectations (Jung, 1984). We want students to express their predictions or interpretations openly. We also want students to critically analyze those ideas that do not make sense to them. Part of the artistry of teaching is bringing these purposes together within the same classroom. Lampert (1986) described her role as working "to bring students' ideas about how to solve or analyze problems into the public forum of the classroom, to referee arguments about whether those ideas were reasonable, and to sanction students' intuitive use of mathematical principles as legitimate" (p. 339).

We want to foster a willingness to make and correct errors rather than to avoid and deny them (Resnick, 1987). We also want students to be thinking and to be critical of conclusions that seem inconsistent with their experiences. In our story, Mr. Jones was neutral in his responses to students' suggested interpretations or predictions. He kept the argument focused on the phenomena and on ideas rather than on people or on whose ideas were right. Students seem to feel less threatened with sharing their initial ideas when they respond to ideas individually or in small groups before sharing them in large groups. This gives them a smaller arena in which to articulate their ideas and a preliminary opportunity to evaluate the viability of those ideas. Finally, the ideas may be written on the board. By then they are usually owned by several members of the class.

When discussing ideas in the large group, we first allow people to cite evidence in support of a particular idea. We may ask people to hold their counterarguments or questions until after we have heard the supportive arguments. By the time we are ready for counterarguments, two things usually have happened. One is that several of the arguments begin to look viable. Another is that ideas are further separated from the people who suggested them. When we turn to counterarguments, we are now challenging the ideas, not the person. The students who originally suggested the idea are usually the first to be allowed to raise objections to it. Thus, we hope that the private understandings of individuals are developed in the arena of public evidence in support or against various ideas. When we are finished we find there is a public consensus of workable understanding and reasoning. In our story, the group concluded that the circle and two-endedness were both important principles related to the circuit phenomena.

Questioning in the Discipline

When learning is viewed as accruing information, teacher as teller is an associated view of teaching. If learning is viewed as constructing understanding, the role of teacher changes to guide in the disassembling and reconstruction of understanding. Under the latter perspective, questioning becomes a key activity, initiated early in the course by the teacher but progressively adopted by the students as they begin to take responsibility for their own learning. At the start of an investigation, the questions may center around descriptions of what will happen or what did happen. Associated with predictions are questions of "How do you know?" or "How did you decide?" Associated with interpretations or explanations are questions such as "What is your evidence?" or "Why do you believe that?" The first are phenomenological questions and the second are related to the reasoning associated with that phenomenon. We have built a computerized DIAG-NOSER that asks these associated questions in sets (Hunt & Minstrell, 1994). For both teacher and students, these types of questions reinforce the importance of having a rationale associated with any pronouncement. Notice this same approach applies equally well in literature or social studies. What conclusion would you make about?... How did you decide, or what evidence do you have to support that conclusion?

Questioning About Learning

In building environments for conceptual change, there are also questions relevant to learners encountering phenomena during investigation. In generating new knowledge (or revising existing knowledge), there are critical questions for the learner to ask: Do I identify any inconsistencies between what I am observing and what I would expect from what I already know? If I observe an inconsistency, is the resolution of the inconsistency (between observation and what I presently believe to be true) of value? Is resolution worth the intellectual effort that it will take to understand the limitations of my earlier thinking? These questions have to do with deciding whether to further engage in intellectual practice or to shunt it, in favor, perhaps, of being told. Sometimes it is not worth the effort to engage or the differences are too vague to articulate and resolve. Most learners choose to engage in intellectual practice at some times and determine that it may not be worth the effort in others. We attempt to increase the chances that they will engage by bringing the inconsistencies into the public arena.

Questions associated with generating knowledge are a bit different from questions related to applying accepted knowledge. Consider looking at a set of data and attempting to identify and interpret the patterns in the data. What is nature trying to tell us? What factors are related to the observed effects? What is the quantitative relation between the variables? Now, consider applying what has been learned from answering the first questions. What are the implications of that relation, if we have certain known initial conditions? Emphasis in schools has been more on accepting conclusions from the past and applying them. In the reformed system, skills in generating knowledge (the first set of questions) are being emphasized as well.

Verbal Interaction

In the dominant questioning cycle, it is typical for the teacher to ask a question, the student to respond, and the teacher to evaluate the student's response. As an alternative, we work to have our students talk to each other about the issues and questions. We use what we have come to call a "reflective toss" (vanZee & Minstrell, in press). After asking a thinking question, the teacher listens to a response from a student; then, rather than evaluating it, the teacher reflects the response back to that or a different student. Notice in the story that Mr. Jones encouraged students to talk among themselves. Intellectual practice among professionals involves colleagues suggesting ideas and evaluating them as a team, rather than waiting for a response or input from a supervisor.

Perhaps no single finding from science education research has received as much attention as the lack of wait-time in the average classroom. The average teacher waits less than one second after asking a question before calling on another student to respond. Similarly, after a student gives an answer, the average pause-time before evaluating the answer or calling on another student is typically less than one second (Rowe, 1974). It takes time to listen to a question and to develop an articulate response. The quality and length of answers increases with an increase in the wait or pause-time of a few additional seconds. Teachers and students need to consciously wait to respond for 3 to 5 seconds while all students have an opportunity to formulate or reformulate their responses.

ASSESSMENT OF UNDERSTANDING
AND REASONING

Assessment, by focusing both teacher and students on what is known and not known, can guide instructional decision making. Short quizzes or observations of discussions and lab work may indicate concepts and skills that need further development by the full class or by individual students. In the past, tests have been used largely as instruments for grading students at the end of a unit or a course, not as diagnostic instruments that help determine learners' needs. We feel the need to refocus assessment to be primarily in the service of instruction to guide learning.

In the service of learning, assessment becomes more embedded within the instruction. For example, in our story, Mr. Jones administered a preinstruction, diagnostic quiz to identify what understandings and reasoning students had at the beginning of the unit. That gave him an initial reading of who had what ideas, and it gave his students some preview of the issues that would be involved in activities of the next few days instruction. As indicated, in our classes we are using a computerized DIAGNOSER that assesses the sorts of understanding of phenomena and associated reasoning used by our students (Hunt & Minstrell, 1994). This assessment is late in the unit when students might believe they understand the ideas; it allows them to check their understanding. Our unit tests are considered assessments of understanding at a given point in time; the ideas and situations included in those tests remain open for further discussion during the rest of the school year.

The questions or situations used in the assessment ought to reflect significant ideas that students might use in their everyday lives. Our long-range purpose for building the understanding and reasoning should be addressed by assessment tools. In the story, Mr. Jones asked students to deal with flashlight bulbs and batteries, yet the ideas about circuitry and electrical devices that were learned with this equipment can be later applied to circuits in the home, car, and other contexts as well.

When students learn particular understanding and reasoning, they should also know the conditions under which those particular ideas are sufficient. For example, we want our students to understand and be able to interpret and explain various situations of objects being moved under the influence of natural forces like gravity and the pushes by the surrounding air (or another more viscous medium like water). We want learners to be able to identify when air resistance can be considered to be negligible and when that is not an appropriate assumption. What are the conditions under which a particular explanation is sufficient? What alternative explanation is more appropriate if those conditions do not exist? How might the conditions change from one sort to the other? What factors are involved? In mathematics, under what data conditions would it be appropriate to assume a straight line equation would describe the relation between variables? Too frequently, we prescribe the conditions for the learner. We teach them how to perform the needed action, but not how to identify when it is appropriate to apply that action. These considerations should be built into our assessment of learning as well as our instruction. Do our students know when it is appropriate to apply the ideas they are studying?

Our assessments should include questions that are situated in real-world problems. Learners should be asked to apply their knowledge in more authentic circumstances than the typical paper and pencil test in multiple-choice format. Mr. Jones' end-of-unit assessment involved a practical situation: Teams of students were instructed to set up the circuits to address the needs of a pretend house. In our science and mathematics classes at the high-school level, we give students blood alcohol content data for an arrested driver to consider as they wrestle with the issues of measurement. To high school students, drinking and driving are relevant issues in their lives.

In creating an environment for reconstructing understanding and reasoning, students' reasoning needs to be expressed and assessed. In his verbal interaction with students, Mr. Jones asked for the experiences and rationales that supported students' answers. Students should be expected to justify their answers based on observations and inferences. Even when a quiz uses multiple-choice questions, each question can be supplemented with an additional question asking students to "Briefly explain how you decided on the answer you chose." In large projects such as the circuitry of a home, students could be asked to interpret the results of particular configurations of bulbs and wires. "What does it mean that the fuse gets hot when we have lights on in several rooms?"

BENEFITS AND CONCERNS
ABOUT THIS ENVIRONMENT

Benefits

Why would a teacher want to create an environment for reconstructing understanding and reasoning that incorporates the attributes described in this paper? As some teachers have become frustrated by the superficiality of students' understanding that often results from more traditional teaching, they have sought ways to change what happens in their classrooms. Those with whom we have worked report having found significant changes in their students' actions and performance once they began really to focus on their students' learning. The level of conversation increased as students were encouraged to reduce the use of jargon and discuss issues and ideas. As students were expected to explicate their rationale, the length of written responses increased. Questions related to the everyday world, that required a deeper understanding of scientific concepts and an ability to identify relevant variables, were answered in thought-provoking ways. Students have begun to feel empowered as they come to believe that they too have valuable ideas about the world. In many cases, program enrollment has increased. Students are exiting the program demonstrating that they understand physical concepts as they arise in rich and varied contexts.

Teachers feel revitalized about their own teaching and learning. Not being responsible for presenting knowledge to students gives some teachers permission not to have to know everything. As a result, they may enter into investigations with their students. The authors confess to learning much physics and mathematics from students as a result of complex and interesting questions and ideas raised during class discussions. The focus shifts to learning how we can come to know, how we can determine what might occur when a given set of circumstances are postulated.

Concerns

It seems appropriate that we share concerns that might be raised by this practice. Even when the students seem to be quite engaged in a classroom discussion, they may resist this approach to learning and teaching. Many students believe in the role of teacher as knower, demonstrator, and teller and student as empty vessel, note-taker, and memorizer. They feel uncomfortable with questions that extend beyond one period's exploration and the lack of closure that can extend for a period of days or longer. It seems unfair to some students that they might be held responsible for ideas for the entire length of a course, let alone until an assessment for certificate of mastery might be completed. Yet, many investigations in professional life take days and even years to complete.

If the individual teacher's program is the only one in the school system in which students are expected to be accountable for their learning, the teacher may encounter resistance from outside the classroom. Parents, and even other educators, may not understand or appreciate the approach and may resist its implementation. Some parents do not believe that students should make decisions for themselves on the basis of their experiences. They may challenge basic assumptions that underlie the course. Our experience suggests that creating opportunities for parents to participate in similar learning situations, in which their risk-taking is supported and in which they have an opportunity to learn some content, helps these parents become advocates for creating such learning environments. There are those parents and community members whose beliefs are so contrary to this approach that they are not convinced by any experience inconsistent with their beliefs. Parents have a right to know what is going on in school. The school system has an obligation to create a process by which parents can become informed about programs and ask questions and voice their concerns as they arise. Then, the administration and school board need to consider and act on those concerns. The individual teacher is obliged to participate in this district process but not to revise program on the basis of each and every suggestion by the parent community. The reflective practitioner needs to create a coherent, principled classroom program that is supported by the school and community in general, even though it may not be supported by every individual parent.

Even when this new approach is perceived as valid and is supported by the community, it can be difficult to implement if a teacher is working alone. Most existing curriculum and assessment materials are not consistent with this approach and creating them can be time consuming. As national reforms in mathematics and science education result in pressure on publishers to modify their curriculum, this is likely to change. To challenge and reconstruct students' understanding and reasoning, teachers need to know students' existing ideas and be able to guide the development of more powerful concepts. By learning more about the results of research on teaching and learning and about fostering development of ideas, teachers can become better prepared to teach in ways suggested in this chapter. While classroom discussions are fascinating, the ability to skillfully lead discussions takes time to develop. All of these changes require time and commitment from the education community in general.

For the authors, the benefits of engaging students in genuine learning far outweigh the costs. As our approaches have evolved in the directions described in this chapter, our own teaching has been revitalized. We have become actively involved in teacher leadership and research and development efforts. Our work has been supported by our administrators, and although some parents and students do not yet understand the environment we are creating, for the most part we have their confidence. We have a broader range of students and a larger percentage of the student body taking physics than ever before. As teachers, when we compare our current students' performance with what we used to expect and accept, we believe that the effort has been a worthwhile investment.

ACKNOWLEDGMENTS

An earlier version of this chapter was prepared for a presentation at the Conference on Curriculum and Assessment Reform in Education, Boulder, Colorado, June 1992. That conference was supported by The U. S. Department of Education. Preparation of this chapter was supported in part by the James S. McDonnell Foundation Program in Cognitive Studies for Educational Practice. The ideas presented here are those of the authors and do not necessarily reflect the beliefs of the foundations just mentioned.

REFERENCES

Arons, A. (1983). Achieving wider scientific literacy. *Daedalus, 112*(2), 91–122.
Arons, A. (1990). *A guide to introductory physics teaching.* New York: Wiley.
Bruer, J. (1993). *Schools for thought: A science of learning in the classroom.* Cambridge, MA: MIT Press.
Camp, C., & Clement, J. (1994). *Preconceptions in mechanics: Lessons dealing with students' conceptual difficulties.* Dubuque, IA: Kendall Hunt.

diSessa, A., & Minstrell, J. (in press). Cultivating conceptual change with benchmark lessons. In J. Greeno (Ed.), *Thinking practices: A symposium in mathematics and science education.* Mahwah, NJ: Lawrence Erlbaum Associates.

Driver, R., Guesne, E., & Tiberghien, A. (1985). *Children's ideas in science.* Philadelphia, PA: The Open University Press.

Gunstone, R. (1991). Constructivism and metacognition: Theoretical issues and classroom studies. In R. Duit, F. Goldberg, & H. Niedderer (Eds.), *Research in physics learning: Theoretical issues and empirical studies, Proceedings of an international workshop* (pp. 129–140). Kiel, Germany: IPN at the University of Kiel, Germany.

Hunt, E., & Minstrell, J. (1994). A cognitive approach to the teaching of physics. In K. McGilly (Ed.), *Classroom lessons: Integrating cognitive theory and classroom practice* (pp. 51–74). Cambridge, MA: MIT Press.

Jung, H. (1984). *Preinstructional conceptual frameworks in elementary mechanics and their interaction with instruction.* Unpublished doctoral dissertation, University of Washington, Seattle.

Lampert, M. (1986). Knowing, doing and teaching multiplication. *Cognition and Instruction,* 3, 305–342.

Lampert, M. (1992). Practices and problems in teaching authentic mathematics in school. In F. Oser, A. Dick, & J. L. Patry (Eds.), *Effective and responsible teaching: The new synthesis* (pp. 295–314). San Francisco: Jossey-Bass.

Loftus, E. (1980). *Memory.* Reading, MA: Addison-Wesley.

McDermott, L. (1984). Research on conceptual understanding in mechanics. *Physics Today,* 37, 24–32.

McDiarmid, G. W., Ball, D. L., & Anderson, C. W. (1989). Why staying one chapter ahead doesn't really work: Subject-specific knowledge. In M. Reynolds (Ed.), *The knowledge base for the beginning teacher* (pp. 193–205). Elmsford, NY: Pergamon.

Minstrell, J. (1984). Teaching for the development of understanding of ideas: Forces on moving objects. In C. W. Anderson (Ed.), *Observing science classrooms: Observing science perspectives from research and practice. 1984 AETS Yearbook* (pp. 53–73). Columbus, OH: Ohio State University.

Minstrell, J. (1989). Teaching science for understanding. In L. Resnick & L. Klopfer (Eds.), *Toward the thinking curriculum: Current cognitive research. 1989 Yearbook of the Association for Supervision and Curriculum Development* (pp. 129–149). Washington, DC: Association for Supervision and Curriculum Development.

Posner, G., Strike, K., Hewson, P., & Gertzog, W. (1982). Accommodation of a scientific conception: Towards a theory of conceptual change. *Science Education, 66*(2), 211–244.

Resnick, L. (1987). *Education and learning to think.* Washington, DC: The National Academy Press.

Rowe, M. (1974). Wait-time and rewards as instructional variables: Their influence on language, logic and fate control. *Journal of Research in Science Teaching, 11,* 81–94.

vanZee, E., & Minstrell, J. (in press). *Using questioning to guide student thinking.*

Viennot, L. (1979). Spontaneous reasoning in elementary dynamics. *European Journal of Science Education, 1,* 205–221.

von Glasersfeld, E. (1991). A constructivist's view of learning and teaching. In R. Duit, F. Goldberg, & H. Niedderer (Eds.), *Research in physics learning: Theoretical issues and empirical studies, Proceedings of an international workshop* (pp. 129–140). Kiel, Germany: IPN at the University of Kiel, Germany.

White, R., & Gunstone, R. (1992). *Probing understanding.* New York: The Falmer Press.

Chapter 9

CHALLENGING PROSPECTIVE TEACHERS' UNDERSTANDINGS OF HISTORY: AN EXAMINATION OF A HISTORIOGRAPHY SEMINAR

G. Williamson McDiarmid
Michigan State University

What is history and what does it mean to know history? Addressing these questions, vital to teachers at all levels, is particularly critical for those involved in the preparation of teachers, both in the arts and sciences and in teacher education. For teachers' beliefs about the nature of historical knowledge and what it means to know history are the foundations on which they will build both their curriculum and their pedagogy, shaping what and how they teach, including the ways—texts, activities, assignments, evaluations—they choose or devise to represent history as well as how they find out what students know and learn. If, for example, they conceive of history as a more or less agreed-upon account of past political developments, as history is typically portrayed in high school textbooks (Axtell, 1987; FitzGerald, 1979; Gagnon, 1988; Sewall, 1987), then knowing history means knowing the details—actors, events, dates—of this account.

Such a conception is, however, but one view of history. Historians and philosophers of history have argued forcefully for a wide range of perspectives on the past (see Abelove, Blackmar, Dimock, & Schneer, 1984; Appleby, Hunt, & Jacob, 1994; Berlin, 1954; Braudel, 1980; Carr, 1962; Collingwood, 1956; Gagnon, 1988; Geyl, 1962; Handlin, 1979; Hexter, 1979; Himmelfarb, 1987; Holt, 1990; Novick, 1988; Schama, 1991; Walsh, 1984). Because different, sometimes competing, accounts of the past are possible, history, in this view, is a debate about the past—what events and evidence mean—and how best to make sense of these (Geyl, 1962). The meaning of events is not self-evident, inherent somehow in the events themselves. Rather, the historian's purposes or questions determine the account that gives the individual events or conditions their meaning. Historians, in turn, take their cues from what Fish (1980) termed "interpretative communities," professional communities to which historians belong.

Theorists of narrative history (the kind of history found in most school textbooks) such as Ricouer have argued that a past event "receives its definition from its contribution to the development of a plot" (quoted in White, 1987, p. 51). The plot is the story line, the sense the historian makes of the surviving record of the past and the line of rhetorical development necessary to make an historical argument.[1] This is not to say that the narrative historian merely imposes a plot onto events. Rather, as White (1987) explained, "It is as if the plot were an entity in process of development prior to the occurrence of any given event, and any given event could be endowed with historicality only to the extent that it could be shown to contribute to this process" (p. 51). From this point of view, to understand history "is to 'grasp together,' as parts of wholes that are 'meaningful,' the intentions, motivating actions, the actions themselves, and their consequences, as reflected in social and cultural contexts" (p. 50).

Such a view of history is shared in various shades by a number of contemporary historians (Appleby, Hunt, & Jacob, 1994; Jacoby, 1992; Novick, 1988; Rosenau, 1992) and stands in contrast to history as a singular account of the past. In this view, history is not a conglomeration of facts that, when amassed and ordered chronologically, tell a particular story. History is, instead, accounting, persuasively and plausibly, for what we know about the past. From this point of view, historians impose meaning on the past and they do so from particular moments in time, cultural perspectives, epistemological standpoints, "interpretative communities." As a consequence, historians frequently differ about what past events mean. As they disagree about the plot, they also disagree about the definition of particular events and the roles of particular groups and individuals. These disagreements arise from a variety of differences: in the questions historians address, in the historical moment from which they write, in sociocultural perspectives, in individual epistemes, and in the methods they employ, what they consider evidence, and how they weigh evidence. In vital ways, these differences constitute the essence of history as a social and political con-

---

[1]Historical accounts by cliometricians and annalist historians such as Braudel, not only those by narrative historians, also could be said to have "story lines."

struct; they attest to the constructed and, hence, the contestable and contested nature of historical knowledge.

If history is a debate about what the past means, then to *understand* history means more than to accumulate information about the past, in the hope that the information would eventuate in understanding. To understand history requires that learners create, for themselves, a particular story that accounts for what is known of the past. A critical aspect of such understanding recognizes that events assume their relative significance from the story. The meaning and significance of particular events, consequently, vary from story to story. The opening chapter of Mattingly's (1959) account of the Armada is a dramatic rendering of the execution of Mary, Queen of Scots; in Fernandez-Armesto's (1989) treatment of the Armada, Mary is only mentioned twice, in passing. Determining what learners should know about the past depends on the story, or stories, they encounter.

Schools invert this view of historical knowledge as contested and understanding as creating accounts that confer significance on events. In schools, historical events and actors are treated as important in and of themselves as though they had significance outside of some account that affords them significance and as though wide agreement exists about the significance of events. Students are rarely assessed on their understanding of the relationships among events, on their comprehension of the significance of events within some account of the past. They are most often assessed on their ability to recall discrete events and people abstracted from any account that would afford them their historical significance. For example, beyond the sheer human tragedy of Lincoln's death, what is the significance of his assassination? Is it historically significant outside the circumstances in which it occurred: the debate over the political and economic reconstruction of rebellious states, the jockeying for power within the Republican party, the struggles of African Americans to secure economic and political rights, and the federal government's unprecedented assumption of political and economic power?

The view of learning history as accumulating information on isolated events and the actions of heroic or demonic, larger-than-life individuals dominates in schools in part because textbooks dictate the curriculum in many, if not most, classrooms (Goodlad, 1983; Perrone, 1985). Under increasingly strident and polarized political pressures, publishers seem more unlikely than ever to produce texts that are other than desiccated catalogues of facts, drained of the lifeblood of historical writing—controversy, conflict, dilemmas, moral conviction, and most importantly perhaps, story lines or plots that afford events their meaning (FitzGerald, 1979; Gagnon, 1988; Sewall, 1987). However historically unfashionable and racist by contemporary standards, textbooks from the 1930s and 1940s are animated by the authors' scarcely disguised convictions and prejudices and by story lines—the progression of democratic institutions, the "redemption" of the Reconstructed South by the Democrats, and so on (see Adams & Vannest, 1935; Wirth, 1945). Authors of these textbook at least have identifiable stances with which readers can engage and agree or disagree. Textbook writers today, wary of offending various interest groups and powerful state-level textbook committees, generate accounts deceptive in their apparent neutrality. They contribute to the view of history as a conglomeration of discrete bits of information about the past.

Evaluative instruments such as the National Assessment of Educational Progress (NAEP) and Scholastic Aptitude Test (SAT) have also contributed to the denaturing of history in schools. Until recently, these assessments reinforced the piecemeal treatment of historical events and actors, communicating and reinforcing the idea that history is a collection of isolated bits of information. Many teachers, committed to serving their students, by necessity focus instruction on this limited view of historical knowledge.

Teaching pupils history as discrete bits of information about past events is what many teachers have been trying to do, and the results are discouraging. As Ravitch and Finn's (1987) analysis of the NAEP data reveal, secondary students' grasp of individual facts of the United States' past is much less than impressive. Moreover, most students dislike history and social studies. Shug, Todd, and Berry (1984), for instance, found that only 17% of the elementary and secondary pupils in their sample rated social studies as the most important subject they were taking while only 13% rated it their favorite subject. Such data challenge those who contend that history-as-true-information-about-past-events is the version of historical knowledge pupils are most likely to be able and inclined to learn.

Some of those who subscribe to this view might even agree that history is, at some level, subject to interpretation and that different stories can be told about the past. Although such a view of history might be appropriate for advanced undergraduates and graduate students in history, it is unnecessarily academic and elitist for elementary, secondary, and most college students who probably could not understand it anyway and, as the vast majority will not become professional historians, would have no use for it. What these students need to learn is the information about the past taught in schools. Once they have mastered this information, then they can, if they choose and are capable, learn about interpretation.

Are proponents of this view of history right? Are attempts to teach history as contested, as interpretative, as a debate necessarily arcane, mandarin, elitist? What does an experience look like whose purpose is to help students develop such a view of history? My purpose is to describe and analyze such an experience—in this case, a undergraduate historiography seminar required of all history majors including prospective teachers. The focus of my analysis is the relationship between the instructor's understanding of what it means to know history and how history is learned, on the one hand, and the design of the course, on the other. Elsewhere, I have examined the understandings of history that students in the course developed and found that most of them did, in fact, develop views of history as interpretation (McDiarmid, 1994). Here, I wish to learn more about how the instructor may have contributed to the development of his students' understanding.

DESCRIPTION OF THE STUDY

The Undergraduate Historiography Course As the Object of Study

I selected the historiography seminar because I wanted to study an experience in which students would encounter critical epistemological questions such as what is historical knowledge and how is it produced and validated, as these understandings underlie the curricular and pedagogical decisions history teachers make. I was interested both in how prospective teachers think about such questions as well as in how history instructors treat them. I was also interested in how students think about such epistemological questions under *promising* circumstances, a best case. Consequently, I wanted to choose an instructor who had a reputation as a successful pedagogue. Finally, I wanted a required course, one considered essential for all students and one that is typically taken early in students' sequence of courses. This latter stipulation enabled me to follow the students for at least a year to see how their thinking developed subsequently. This was posited on the assumption that the ideas whose development I wish to follow are difficult, requiring time to comprehend.

A section of the required undergraduate historiography course offered by the History Department at Michigan State University (MSU) taught by Professor Peter Vinten-Johansen met all these criteria. He has taught at MSU for 15 years. (For an autobiographical account of Vinten-Johansen's development as a teacher, see McDiarmid & Vinten-Johansen, 1994.) Enrollment in the course is limited to 25 students per section and reflects the history department's commitment to maximize history majors' interactions with senior faculty. Prior to and after this seminar, the students typically attend classes with 50 or more students. They may not encounter such a small class again until their senior-level research-paper seminar.

The section of the course I studied is taken by students in the Honors College at MSU. Consequently, some of the students were likely to be highly motivated and had succeeded in their past encounters with history. Others in the course were not Honors College students. In subsequent observations of a nonhonors course Vinten-Johansen teaches, I found that in all essential respects the courses were similar in organization, procedures, activities, assignments, evaluation, and pedagogy. The presence of the Honors College students, for our purposes, enhanced its qualifications as a best case test of whether a history course could enable students, including prospective teachers, to develop an appreciation for the contested and constructed nature of historical knowledge.

Of the 20 students who started the seminar, 16 completed it. Of the 14 students for whom we have base line data, 8 were third-year students, 2 second-year, and 4 first-year. Eight were males and six were females and all were White. They had taken an average of two history courses prior to the historiography seminar; three of the third-year students had taken as many as four courses. Although they had taken no previous college-level history courses, two of the first-year students had taken Advanced Placement American History courses in high school. The courses students had previously taken were, by and large, survey courses taught in large-lecture formats with weekly discussion sections taught by graduate students. The most common survey course taken was the two-term sequence in American History. All but three of the students were history majors. Eight of the original 14 planned to teach high school history after graduation. Two planned to teach history at the university level. Hence, only 2 of the 14 in the base line sample were considering careers as professional historians.

Description of the Data on Teaching

I documented the students' opportunities to learn, the instructor's rationale for the purposes and opportunities he orchestrated, and the students' understandings of critical ideas over time. To document opportunities to learn, I attended and took notes on all but 2 of 19 meetings of the seminar. I also made tape recordings of the classes that were subsequently transcribed, interviewed the instructor formally twice, tape recorded the instructor's conferences with the students, and collected course documents and copies of the instructor's comments on students' written work.

I conducted two formal interviews with the instructor as well as several informal conversations about the course and specific students. The first structured interview focused on the instructor's rationale for the course—the sequence of activities, the texts, and the assignments. The second interview focused on his assessment of how much progress students made toward the goals he had set for them. In this interview, we returned to some of the themes of the earlier interview such as the purpose of various activities and texts.

In taking field notes, I focused on the classroom discourse—that is, the issues that were discussed and how these were related to prior and subsequent issues or questions, the roles of various participants in the discussion, the kinds of questions asked and explanations offered, and other ways in which history was represented.

Data Analysis

I analyzed the data on teaching, especially the interviews with the instructor and the transcriptions of the course meetings, along several dimensions. One was the instructor's ideas about what history is and what it means to know history. A second dimension was the instructor's goals and purposes for the historiography course. A closely related, third dimension was the way that the instructor represented history through the design and organization of the seminar—choice of texts, assignments, activities, and evaluations—and the discourse he promoted. Finally, I analyzed the data for evidence of the instructor's assumptions about what his students believe about history and learning and knowing history.

Beginning with the full transcripts of the interviews, I reduced the data on each dimension to summaries with illustrative quotations and, then, to a single summary. I looked for patterns or themes across the individual summaries. To check for reliability, another member of the research team independently followed the same procedure. Comparing our summaries, we discussed and resolved the few minor differences in our analyses of the data.

Limitations

My purpose in this study is to understand more about the opportunities that undergraduates in general and prospective teachers in particular encounter to understand history. Specifically, I purposively sought out an opportunity, in the arts and sciences, for prospective teachers to learn a view of history that might lead them to think about teaching in ways that differ from current pedagogical conceptions, particularly in history. Consequently, the course and the students in it constitute a purposive, not random, sample. I am less interested in making broad generalizations about how history is taught than in examining the relationship between a faculty member's views of the nature of history, historical inquiry, and learning history, and the opportunities that the faculty member orchestrates to enable students to learn.

Although I purposely selected the historiography seminar to examine, the study was conducted at a large, land-grant state university, a setting in which many teachers are currently prepared. The students—mostly middle-class Whites from small towns and suburbs—are representative of the majority of students who enter teaching. Currently, few detailed descriptions or analyses of history teaching designed to challenge students' ideas about the nature of history and historical method exist (Holt's [1990] is an exception). Yet, just such investigations are needed if we are to begin to understand the relationship among instructional design, instructor's purpose, and students' understandings. I hope this chapter spurs interest in, discussion of, and more investigation of these issues.

DESCRIPTION OF THE
HISTORIOGRAPHY SEMINAR

Pedagogy

On first encountering Professor Vinten-Johansen, students who are unacquainted with his reputation are a bit unsettled. He expects them to speak up in class, to argue for the views they express, and to argue *from* evidence *with* others students. They are unprepared for the close scrutiny he gives their written work, for his extended, detailed comments, for the revisions he expects. Nor are they prepared for the amount of work he demands—not merely to have done the assigned reading but to have determined the author's thesis and the supporting evidence. To help them learn to identify how historians construct arguments, muster evidence, develop context, Vinten-Johansen provides worksheets that prompt students to look for certain elements in their readings. As one of the students—who, despite receiving a failing grade, regarded Vinten-Johansen as his best history teacher—said, "He puts us through hell." Even those students who eagerly take any course he offers agree: Vinten-Johansen is demanding and the work in his courses is exacting and time consuming.

The historiography seminars, true to form, tended to be lively. As early as the second meeting, students needed little prompting to discuss the thesis of Mattingly's account of the Armada. After soliciting students' reactions to the text, he listened, asked for clarification, and restated but offered no judgments. Early in the discussion, two students disagreed as to whether Mattingly was "pro-Protestant." Vinten-Johansen listened without intervening. As other students gave their reactions, Vinten-Johansen asked if they found Mattingly biased. When a student, Bill (this, like all student names in this chapter, is a pseudonym), suggested that the book was really about an "ideological conflict" between Protestants and Catholics and about "politics and church," Vinten-Johansen offered a two-minute monologue in which he described the Counter-Reformation, comparing the Catholic counterattack to the "reverse in momentum" in a basketball game. (The night before this particular class, MSU had come from behind to defeat favored and much despised University of Michigan).

After another student admitted to feeling "weak" because he did not know who the Huguenots were, Vinten-Johansen took five minutes to describe how the purpose for reading dictates the level of attention to the text, concluding: "I did not want you to look at the book [Mattingly] as one that you had to examine closely because we should get the general drift of the argument and think more about the author's major thesis than worrying about particulars—at this point." As an example, he wrote the word "ultramante" on the board, discussed its meaning, and suggested that if such a word appeared more than once in the text, it might be worth looking up. He then described how the connotations of words change over time and why it might be important to track down the meaning that a word or phrase had at a particular time in the past.

At this point, Kim, anxious to pick up the thread of debate, argued that Mattingly viewed religion as a pretext for England to attack the Spanish. Vinten-Johansen turned to Bill and asked, "What do you think about that?" By calling on different students and drawing attention to the points or questions individuals raised, Vinten-Johansen guided the discussion for the remainder of the time.

Many of the subsequent seminars followed this format; Vinten-Johansen or, later in the term, a student, would raise a question or problem. This led to a discussion that produced additional questions or issues. By the questions he asked, the carefully structured assignments he made, the student comments to which he attended, and the brief monologues he delivered, Vinten-Johansen guided the discussions and activities. Later in the term, after introducing the "packet" of documents concerning the Good-win–Fortescue conflict, Vinten-Johansen changed the format. Before the class began, he would arrange the tables so that students could meet in their research groups. When students arrived, they organized themselves into groups and began to discuss what they had found in the materials Vinten-Johansen had put on library reserve, documents and secondary sources, to answer questions they had posed in the previous class. During these classes, Vinten-Johansen circulated about the room, stopping to listen in on discussions, ask and answer questions, suggest sources, nag individuals for late or missing assignments. (Students were also unprepared for his vigilance: He always knew who owed him which assignments, who had missed which classes, who had come to class unprepared.) As the time waned, he would remind students of what they were expected to do before the next meeting.

Vinten-Johansen played several roles, regardless of format. He often began seminars by summarizing the discussion during the previous class. During discussions, he often acted as a moderator, highlighting differences in views and directing the discussion ("I think Dick is disagreeing with you, Karen. This is Karen, Dick. You can speak directly to her.") He also posed questions and problems: "What's Mattingly arguing here? What's the basis for his argument? Do you buy his argument? Kim thinks Fernandez-Armesto is blowing smoke, that there's no real evidence for his assertion. What do you think?" Occasionally, he delivered monologues—on the process of reading, different types of historical accounts, his own experience as a reviewer of historical work.

Much of what characterized Vinten-Johansen's instruction occurred off-stage. Over the years, he has developed activities to help his students become the kind of readers, writers, and thinkers he would like them to become. For the third meeting of the historiography seminar, students completed a worksheet designed to help them identify the thesis of Mattingly's book (see appendix A). Discussions during the third meeting focused on the worksheet. After students read the Fernandez-Armesto account of the Armada, they completed another worksheet designed to help them compare the theses of the two works, the structure of the argument in each, and the author's choice and use of evidence. Consequently, the discussions in class were the fruit of much preparation and work, on both students' and instructor's part, outside of class. The worksheet comparing the two accounts formed the basis for the comparative papers, the first draft of which the students turn in at the beginning of the sixth week of class.

Instructional Design

The centerpiece of the seminar is a puzzle—an apparently obscure early 17th century dispute over a seat in Parliament between two Englishman, one named Goodwin and the other Fortescue. Vinten-Johansen described the course as consisting of two "chunks." The history workshop on the Goodwin–Fortescue controversy constituted the second, and central, chunk. The other chunk was to set up and assist students in their investigations into the case. During the first three weeks, students analyzed Mattingly's (1959) classic narrative account of the defeat of the Spanish

Armada in 1588 and, subsequently, compared this account with Fernandez-Armesto's (1988) revisionist analysis. This chunk presented students with the opportunity to learn both how historical interpretations are constructed and that historians can argue cogently and persuasively for differing, even competing, accounts of the same event or events.

Analysis of Mattingly's Armada and Comparison With Fernandez-Armesto's Text. Vinten-Johansen focused classroom discussions of Mattingly on the purpose for which the author wrote *The Armada*. As described earlier, during the second class meeting, students reacted to Mattingly's characterization, in his preface to the 1959 edition, of the battle in the English Channel as part of an "ideological war." Vinten-Johansen, midway through the class, called attention to the context in which Mattingly wrote:

Mattingly is writing in a time [*The Armada* was originally conceived in 1940] in which this ideological struggle is going on and so, therefore, in his mind—even though economics may be an issue, even though nationalism may be an issue—in his mind, this ideological . . . conflict going on in the 1940s is causing him to go back and look at an earlier period of time. . . . Do you think that is wrong? He is in a way imposing something from the present onto past. Why? What does that mean? What does that say about history?

When a student responds that "you can never have completely unbiased history," Vinten-Johansen agrees that as human beings "come from different backgrounds and experiences" they will write biased history. The classroom discussion focused on Mattingly's thesis.

Discussions of Fernandez-Armesto's account of the Armada similarly focused on identifying his thesis and the evidence on which he based this argument. From the beginning, however, students used Mattingly's account as the standard against which to judge Fernandez-Armesto's thesis. Discussions explored differences in the treatment of evidence on which the two historians rely. For instance, the students noted that whereas Mattingly's account is devoid of footnotes, including instead a General Note on Sources section, Fernandez-Armesto meticulously documents his sources, chapter-by-chapter, in endnotes.

Toward the end of the third class on Fernandez-Armesto (the seventh class meeting), debate on his thesis reached its climax. Several students argued that Fernandez-Armesto's thesis is that the English and Spanish were more evenly matched than they had previously been portrayed and that characterizing the battle as the English "David" defeating the Spanish "Goliath" misrepresented what actually occurred. Leading up to this debate were extensive conversations about the two texts as well as the written assignment in which students identified Mattingly's thesis and his evidence. In addition, by the way he has orchestrated conversations in prior meetings of the seminar, Vinten-Johansen had created a climate in which most students appeared free to speak their minds.

Kathy: I don't think [Fernandez-Armesto] says they were equal. I think he says Spain won.

Vinten-
Johansen: Okay, do you, do you. . .

Gary: I think he says it right here on page 236 when he says "the deficiencies of Spanish strategy above all, as I have suggested, the failure to provide a northern port of refuge bears some responsibility for the Armada's failure. The English made a contribution of sorts to their own salvation, the weather did much of the rest, but the Armada would still have been reckoned a remarkably successful venture but for the work of the Irish siren." . . . I think that's such a stupid thing to say . . . . How can he claim success—just success that they made it out of there? I mean, that wouldn't have made it a successful voyage.

David: I'll take a shot. I think that he was arguing that they could claim success because [Fernandez-]Armesto mentions early in the book that, really, possibly, the main purpose behind the Armada might have been just to end English provocation [a reference perhaps to Drake's raids on the Portuguese coast] and not so much, you know, the success and the total invasion. So I think that in those terms, that argument stands up a lot more strongly.

Gary: Well, I know he says that maybe they didn't plan to invade and maybe they just went to scare the English into doing something. But, I mean, how can you consider all the time that they spent as being successful and nothing really happened to the English?

Kara: I would argue against that because I think what I got from what he's saying . . . that the Spanish were successful because they were able to keep most of their ships together and the English weren't really able to sink them or really harm them in any way. Most of their problems came from the weather and not having enough food and the English didn't accomplish their goal of destroying the Armada.

Gary: But how's that successful when the Spanish were on the offensive?

Dick: But it's not thinking like winning or losing—the Spanish were defeated, or the English didn't succeed because they couldn't destroy the Armada and the Spanish succeeded because the English weren't able to. It's not like win or lose.

Gary: I think that's a cop out to say that—

Vinten-
Johansen: Jump in, Sean.

Sean: That's what I was thinking too. . . . I mean, why call it "The Armada?" Why not call it like a "little sailing fleet?" Just for the heck of it, they went out and sailed . . . If that's all they wanted to do, why do they go to all the trouble . . . ? If it's all just going to be some type of feint to quell England's provocation into Spanish territory or anything like that, they didn't have to go to such extremes to do that, probably. And all they did was go up there and sail around and then get a couple of ships lost and . . . . . I don't see it as a Spanish victory.

Vinten-
Johansen: You do not?

Curt: . . . This assumption's ridiculous because . . . I read at the beginning how [Fernandez-Armesto] said the only reason for the Armada was possibly to get bargaining power over the English. Well they certainly didn't. I mean, the English think that they won. So, I mean, it's not like the English were beaten up and said, "Well, at least we got them out of here." I mean, the English didn't get touched at all and got them out of there. So, I mean, Spain really has no bargaining power. If they came back, I mean, maybe the weather would change but England seemed [stronger]. . . [Fernandez-Armesto] is not looking at it . . . from the English point of view. But to me, the English seemed that they know that they won and they're not going to bargain.

Diane: I have to admit that I agree that the Spanish lost it, but I don't think by that much because . . . the Spanish only lost like four or five ships. . . . After the battle, I mean, the weather took out most of the ships. And I think maybe [Fernandez-Armesto] is suggesting that Philip was just testing his power against the English and they got up there and they got in a fight and they came out a lot better than maybe Philip thought that they would come out and then that way it was a victory and then that way maybe if the ships would have been able to get down back through the channel and back to Spain and they could have improved it, gone back up, challenged the English again and won.

Curt: What I don't understand is if he's arguing that Spain was the victor in this battle, why didn't they have the guts to come back down the channel to go home?

Vinten-
Johansen: They couldn't, it was not a matter of guts, the wind was—

Kathy: Why didn't Spain turn around and attack, attack the English? Why didn't, if they were the victors, you know, why didn't they, why didn't they do something to England? They had to sail all the way back to Spain and then say, "Ha-ha, we won" . . . .

This exchange illustrates the kinds of conversations that took place around the Mattingly and Fernandez-Armesto texts. Nine of the 18 students present took part in this particular exchange. Professor Vinten-Johansen's role appeared minimal—indeed, when he tried to interject information into the discussion, Kathy interrupted him to make her point. Yet, this exchange took place because of the way he had organized the seminar: the texts he had chosen, the worksheets he devised to help students understand the historians' arguments, a classroom culture that valued students' informed views.

Besides illustrating Vinten-Johansen's instructional design, this exchange could also be examined for evidence of student understanding: Students evidenced the capacity not only to identify the thesis of historical accounts but also to critique the evidential and logical bases for the thesis. Lest the reader conclude that this type of conversation is possible because this was a honors section, only four of the nine involved in this exchange were honors students.

The History Workshop: The Goodwin–Fortescue Controversy.   During the eighth class meeting, one third of the way through the course, the history workshop portion of the seminar commenced with the distribution of "the packet," a collection of primary documents relating to the Goodwin–Fortescue dispute. Consisting of some 46 single-spaced, typed pages, the packet contained various documents that bear on the dispute: court accounts of events in the case; reports of the dispute in Parliament from the journal of the House of Commons and private diaries kept by Members; various state papers; correspondence between James I, the recently installed and first Stuart monarch, and the House of Commons; letters written by Members of Parliament; and correspondence among diplomats from European capitals. (In our first interview, Professor Vinten-Johansen acknowledged that the idea for the packet and parts of the packet itself came from Professor Jack Hexter with whom Vinten-Johansen studied as a graduate student at Yale in the 1970s. For more on this experience, see McDiarmid & Vinten-Johansen, 1994.)

The students' first task was to order the documents chronologically and by source. Simple but for the fact that, as the students discovered, England was, at the beginning of the 17th century, on a different calendar (Julian) from the Catholic states of the continent (Gregorian). Immediately, then, students encountered a problem in accomplishing what appears to be the most straightforward task historians undertake: establishing the temporal order of events.

Subsequently, Professor Vinten-Johansen assigned each of the students to two types of groups: primary and topical. Primary groups consisted of four or five students randomly assigned. Topical groups consisted of one student from each of the primary groups who was responsible for gathering information on a specific topic. During the ninth class meeting, Vinten-Johansen worked with the class to identify topics about which they would need additional information if they were to make sense of the documents and, ultimately, the controversy itself. The topics for research identified included: biographical information on the principals in the controversy; organization of the government and the elections process; legal terminology; and the social structure of England at the beginning of the 17th century.

In their topical groups, students collaboratively decided what information they needed to sort out the controversy, found the information in primary and secondary sources that Vinten-Johansen had put on reserve in the library or other sources, and also tracked down information requested by their primary group. Students, working in their topical groups, reported the information they gathered to their classmates in their primary group. In these groups, students pooled their information and understandings in an effort to make sense of the dispute.

These collaborative efforts provided the data students needed to write their individual accounts of the controversy. The first draft of these papers was due following the 13th class meeting, some 4 weeks after the packet had been introduced. After receiving Vinten-Johansen's comments and meeting individually with him to discuss their drafts, students turned in a second draft in lieu of a conventional final examination.

Context for the Packet

To provide context for the students' inquiries into the Goodwin–Fortescue controversy, Vinten-Johansen assigned two additional texts: G.R. Elton's (1974) *England Under the Tudors* and Joyce Youings's (1984) *Sixteenth Century England*. Whereas discussions of Mattingly and Fernandez-Armesto had focused on the arguments the authors made and the evidential bases of their arguments, these two texts were treated as sources of information. Vinten-Johansen assigned each student a chapter from one of the books on which to make a presentation to the seminar and lead a discussion. The books represented contrasting types of histories. Elton's work is a classic political history that focuses on the policies, personalities, political alliances and conflicts, and events of the Tudor reign. Youings, on the other hand, examines the social context, particularly the class structure, of England during the period. Presenters were responsible for answering questions that classmates might have about the topic. Classroom discussions also focused on differences in the two texts and how differences in the historian's questions lead to different types of histories.

Papers

Students wrote three short papers and a longer research paper on the Goodwin–Fortescue case. The short papers included an analytical review of Mattingly's *Armada*, a analytical review comparing Mattingly's account with that of Fernandez-Armesto, and a revision of the latter. These written assignments were distinguished by two features: Vinten-Johansen treated all papers as drafts, and review of the papers was an occasion for him to meet with individual students and discuss their progress. For instance, Vinten-Johansen required students to turn in a first draft of their research papers after the 13th class meeting and a second draft at the time set aside for the final examination.

The short papers, like the classroom discussions, required the students to attend to historical arguments and the bases for these. In the first paper, for example, students had to identify Mattingly's thesis in *The Armada* and the logical and evidential foundation for his thesis. The assignment required students to compare the theses and the substantiations of the two authors. Vinten-Johansen wrote extensive comments both in the margins and on separate sheets of paper. The following example, randomly selected, is typical of the comments Vinten-Johansen wrote on a first draft, comparative essay, submitted after the ninth class meeting:

Opening paragraph is one of your most clearly written to date, Dick. Need to flesh it out more, however—from your personal orientation to each of the author's major thesis and your final integration. Also you need more analysis (where I write "because...")—esp. concerning which (or both) of the arguments you consider persuasive.

Substantiation needs reorganization. The first paragraph has far too many topics. Reduce the number of paragraphs, then discuss M[attingly]'s view vs. F[ernandez]-A[rmesto]'s view and *explain* why you consider F[ernandez]-A[rmesto]'s more reasonable. You point out different perspectives and simply choose the one you like. Rough transition to Mattingly. In the next long paragraph, your organizational logic is unclear. We'll need to think of ways to help you set this up in the revision.

Throughout, you need clearer explanation of the standards you employ for determining "better," etc. There's a difference between a particular perspective on the Armada and a clearer, more persuasive explanation. The key to that comes in your thesis—the analytical part especially.

The five-page paper on which this comment appears contained an additional 15 comments or questions.

Conferences

Another critical experience in the course was the required conferences that Vinten-Johansen held with individual students about their papers. These conferences focused on the student's written work and involved the themes and issues that recurred in classroom discussions. Students signed up for appointments on a schedule Vinten-Johansen brought to class. As he afforded 15 minutes for each conference, the discussions were sharply focused. Limiting conferences to a quarter of an hour each made this a manageable component of the course for Vinten-Johansen who, in addition to teaching and research, had considerable administrative responsibilities and edited a national journal of Scandinavian studies.

Following is an excerpt from the conference that he had after he returned Dick's paper with the comments that were presented earlier:

Vinten-
Johansen: So you're stacking the deck against Mattingly.

Dick: I guess so. I didn't think, I thought Fernandez[-Armesto] was better, that's why I guess.

Vinten-
Johansen: Yea, okay, but, "better?" What's "better?"

Dick: A more persuasive. . . .

Vinten-
Johansen: Why?

Dick: 'Cause of the way he, umm, examined the Armada itself.

Vinten-
Johansen: Because you liked it more?

Dick: Not really. When I read it I didn't like it as much. I kind of felt
             like he was ripping off the English. But then I thought at the end
             he did a better job.

Vinten-
Johansen: Okay, now what we need to do is get that word "better" out of
             there and come up with something where we can really compare
             the writing. In other words, we've got to compare the two theses.
             Then, unless there is a problem with the way in which Mattingly
             sets up the notion of the larger conflict. . . .

Dick: The narrative?

Vinten-
Johansen: No. . . you say here, "In his book, Mattingly does not examine
             the Armada with its real goal in mind." You're telling the reader
             that Mattingly's got it screwed up. Instead of focusing on the
             "real goal" which you've set up here, to essentially invade
             England, . . . you're saying that Mattingly's gone off on a tangent.
             He's all concerned about . . . the Armada's role within the larger
             crusade. . . . There's absolutely no doubt in your mind that that's
             the case?

Dick: Well, when you put it that way I'm not sure, but the way he set
             up France and the Netherlands, and what was happening in
             Spain, what was happening in England, I think that's, and then
             he just fit the Armada into it.

Vinten-
Johansen: Okay. Do you have any standard by which you can judge which
             one is the real goal, which one is closest to coming up with the
             real goal? . . . Other than yourself and how you feel about it?

Dick: Yea, I think, the documents that Fernandez-Armesto used.

Vinten-
Johansen: What about the documents that Mattingly used?

Dick: I think they both said, kind of said the same thing.

Vinten-
Johansen: Okay, what, how did you decide what was the real goal? . . . You're
             convinced that the real goal, the actual mission, was to make
             this crossing, to assist in the crossing [i.e., the Armada assisting
             the Duke of Parma in bringing his troops across the Channel
             from the Netherlands to attack England]. Tell me precisely, what
             evidence caused you to arrive at that conclusion?

Dick: I can't remember that exact thing from the book, but the way
             he said, to meet [the Duke of] Parma.

Vinten-
Johansen: Okay, but whose goal was that? Is this something that Mattingly
             or Fernandez-Armesto invented?

Dick: Philip [II of Spain]'s goal.

Vinten-
Johansen: Okay, so what . . . is imbedded in here, but not clear yet, is that
             you're going to evaluate the two authors in terms of, at least
             initially, how well each one reconstructs Philip's goal back then,
             in 1587–88. And then how the rest of this story that they tell,
             whether or not it seems to carry out Philip's goal or whether they
             wander off. What you're suggesting is, Philip II's true goal,
             actual, real goal, whatever you want to word it, was what? . . . .

The exchange exhibits a pattern typical of the conferences: Vinten-Johansen was persistent in questioning students about the claims they make
in their papers and how they substantiate their claims. It also demonstrates
that I could have analyzed the seminar as a course in teaching writing.

These five elements—the packet and the attendant research and discussions in small groups, the books about the Armada and the accompanying
worksheets and discussions of the authors' theses and substantiation, student presentations from the Youings and Elton texts, the short papers and
the longer research paper, and the conferences on the papers—constitute
the opportunities that Vinten-Johansen has created for students to learn.

But why these elements? Where do these come from? In particular, what seems to be the relationship between Vinten-Johansen's understanding of his subject—including his ideas about the nature of the historical knowledge, how one comes to know history, and how new knowledge and understandings are generated—and the purposes and opportunities to learn he created?

SOURCES OF THE PEDAGOGY AND WORK-SHOP DESIGN: VIEWS OF HISTORY

Underlying Vinten-Johansen's pedagogy and curricular design are both his understandings of what history is and his understandings of his students and how they learn. In the data I identified eight ideas that appear central to his view of history:

1. An accurate chronology of events is an essential first step in constructing an historical account;
2. the record of the past lends itself to multiple interpretations;
3. a given event can only be understood in the context in which it occurred;
4. central to the historian's task is to link a given event to its context in a way that produces an interpretation of the event;
5. a critical aspect of writing history consists in placing oneself, to the extent possible, in someone else's shoes and seeing the world as he or she saw it;
6. historians impose an orderliness on past events that belies both the confusion and uncertainty with which events were actually experienced as well as the essentially contingent nature of events;
7. historical accounts and interpretations should be judged on their own terms according to how well the historian substantiates his or her thesis; and
8. history is written for the present generation and, hence, the past needs to be periodically re-interpreted.

These ideas are not merely idiosyncratic beliefs; they coincide with the views expressed by other historians and philosophers of history, particularly those who have been categorized under the label "idealist" (Walsh, 1984). Idealist historians have been defined as such to distinguish them from "positivists" who believe, in Tosh's (1984) words, "the essence of historical explanations lies in the correct application of generalizations derived from other disciplines supposedly based on scientific method such as economics, sociology and psychology" (p. 110). Idealist historians, on the other hand, distinguish human events, which have an "inside"—that is, at the core of human events are human motives, beliefs, feelings, and so forth which must be apprehended if the events are to be understood—from natural events that are amenable to the inductive methods of science (for further discussion, see Collingwood, 1956; Croce, 1921; Walsh, 1984).

As Novick's (1988) recent treatment of the development of the historical profession reveals, historians in the U.S. have moved away from earlier, less sophisticated conceptions of objectivity. That the conceptual framework of the historian, built up through his or her experiences in particular cultures during a particular period, shapes not merely interpretation but what he or she chooses as the object of study has become a commonplace.

In addition to his "idealist" stance, Vinten-Johansen appeared, both as a teacher and as an historian, partial to narrative forms of history. For instance, he opens his study of Johan Ludvig Heiberg (a work in progress) with the following:

> Monday was always hectic at Reitzel Publishers. One customer after another dashed into the front office with book requests than had accumulated over the Sabbath. Christian Kramer was already behind with morning deliveries, yet the stack of additional orders to fill was larger every time he returned to the stockroom. Kramer would locate the desired items, wrap them in brown paper, and sort them for delivery by city quarter, of which Copenhagen was divided into twelve, all situated within wide moats and tall ramparts erected in the mid-seventeenth century. (Vinten-Johansen, n.d., p. 6)

For Vinten-Johansen, history is a story. As a committed narrativist, he would seem to share with certain analytical philosophers such as Danto (1985), Mink (1969), and Walsh (1984) an abiding interest in what White (1987) termed "the epistemic status of narrativity, considered as a kind of explanation especially appropriate to the explication of historical, as against natural, events and processes" (p. 31). White (1987) distinguished this view of history as narrative from the social science orientation of the French *Annales* group, represented by Braudel (1975, 1981, 1992), and from the "semiologically oriented literary theorists" such as Foucault and Derrida who view narrative as another "discursive code."

For historians of the *Annales* school, narrative, particularly political narrative, is something of a distraction, a misrepresentation of what is truly significant about the past. For them, doing history involves explicating the long-term and shorter-term "structures"—geographic, climatic, demographic, economic, social, and cultural—that underlie the events chronicled in narratives. For instance, the chapters in Braudel's (1981) renowned *The structures of everyday life: The limits of the possible* include "Weight of Numbers" (about demographics), "Daily Bread" (about agricultural techniques), "Superfluidity and Sufficiency" (about eating habits, housing, and clothing), "The Spread of Technology," "Money," and "Towns and Cities." The literary theorists, on the other hand, focus their attention on the text, which can be the text of historical documents (as in Foucault's [1965] *Madness and Civilization*), the text historians write (as in LaCapra's [1989] essay, "Chartier, Darnton, and the Great Symbol Massacre,") or the past itself as a text (as in LaCapra's [1982] *Madam Bovary*). These theorists are preoccupied with language and the form of the text. For instance, LaCapra, who readily acknowledges his debt to Derrida (LaCapra, 1989) wrote a study of Gustave Flaubert's trial in 1857 on charges of offending public morality with the publication of *Madam Bovary* (LaCapra, 1982). Much of the book is devoted to an analysis of the novel itself. LaCapra's main point seems to be that while the trial focused on an interpretation of the novel as a celebration of adultery, *Madam Bovary* was actually a far greater threat to the moral certainties of the mid-nineteenth century. The threat was manifest more insidiously in what LaCapra terms Flaubert's "dual" style than in the content of the story. He concluded that

> . . . the problem of narration or modes of "representation" in *Madame Bovary* is indeed complex . . . One minimal point I have tried to establish is that one cannot take the most lapidary statements concerning pure art . . . from the letters [of Flaubert] and interpret the novel as their unproblematic realization. (LaCapra, quoted in Jacoby, 1992, p. 416)

As one critic of this school has pointed out, the products of its proponents often sound more like literary criticism than what is conventionally regarded as history (Jacoby, 1992).

Examining both Vinten-Johansen's pedagogy and his historical writings, I conclude that he aligned with a group that White (1987) identified as "defenders of a craft notion of historical studies." Mentioning Hexter and Elton in this group, White wrote:

> . . . this group does not so much represent a theoretical position as incarnate a traditional attitude of eclecticism in historical studies—an eclecticism that is a manifestation of a certain suspicion of theory itself as an impediment to the proper practice of historical inquiry, conceived as empirical inquiry. (p. 31)

I draw attention to the similarities between Vinten-Johansen's views and those of historians in the idealist and "eclectic" traditions to place him in the debate over the nature of historical knowledge and the place of narrative. I am not suggesting either that Vinten-Johansen sees himself as an idealist or an eclecticist nor that his views consistently line up with those identified with these traditions. I examine next the ideas that seem to underlie both his views of history and his pedagogy. Although I have relied primarily on interview data in developing these ideas, I have also drawn on other sources such as transcripts of classes and student conferences as well.

The Record of the Past Lends Itself
to Multiple Interpretations

Underlying Vinten-Johansen's commitment to the workshop approach is his view that the past can be ordered, interpreted, "read" in a number of ways. This is evident in the rationale Vinten-Johansen offered, during our post-course interview, for assigning the essay that students write comparing the two accounts of the Armada:

> History is a series of interpretations and viewpoints that are based in evidence, but various readings of the very same evidence—issues of selectivity, the background of the historian—would eventuate in different outcomes. . . . [The students] needed to see that history is not simply a series of chronological recapitulations. That it involves a process of understanding not just what happened but how and why it happened as it did. I wanted them to see that Mattingly had . . . not just come up with a view of the Armada based upon . . . his own interests or proclivities, but that the range of evidence that he looked at eventuated in a certain interpretational point of view and one that I hoped that some of them would take issue with. To kind of pique that a bit, I made sure that Fernandez-Armesto had some different points of view so that they could see that intelligent and reasonable people could disagree without turning to fisticuffs. So [the paper served] two purposes: one, to see that all history is a process of interpretation, and two, that if they're going to do history themselves, they've got to develop interpretations. Not just simply recount what happened. It's not just a—what's the word I want—it's not just a chronology but chronicle.

Vinten-Johansen echoes others who have attempted to define the study of history. For example, Walsh (1967) defined history as a "significant" narrative of the past. A narrative in which the historian has labored to uncover the "intrinsic" relationship among events in order to produce a coherent whole from the events studied:

[The historian's] way of doing that, I suggest, is to look for certain dominant concepts or leading ideas by which to illuminate his facts, to trace connections between those ideas themselves, and then to show how the detailed facts become intelligible in the light of them by constructing a "significant" narrative of the events of the period in question. (Walsh, 1967, p. 61)

In researching the Goodwin–Fortescue controversy, students soon found that several interpretations were possible for the evidence they uncovered. On the one hand, evidence suggests that Parliament was justified in asserting its right to manage its own internal affairs, including determining who has the right to sit in the House of Commons. The Tudor monarchs, Elizabeth I, in particular, had granted Parliament certain privileges that empowered it to decide matters related to its internal governance. James I, however, claimed a monarch's prerogative, by divine right, to override any decision Parliament might reach and to decide, in particular, who might sit in Parliament. The facts do not, to the students' dismay, speak for themselves. None of the documents nor the secondary sources they perused identify this particular controversy as an instance of burgeoning Parliamentary privilege bumping up against traditional royal prerogative. In their research papers, they must account for what they have learned about the dispute and, in so doing, argue for and support a particular interpretation. The notion that history *is* interpretation is no longer an abstraction; interpret the students must.

A Given Event Can Only Be Understood
Within the Context in Which It Occurred

In describing historical inquiry, Walsh (1967) placed at the heart of the enterprise delineating the "intrinsic" relationship between one event and others. Vinten-Johansen gives expression to this by the way he situates the Goodwin–Fortescue case within the overall organization of the course and within history:

Students are forced, first, into a sense for a broader context, that even if they . . . look at a particular event such as the Armada they have to recognize that the Armada cannot be viewed in isolation . . . . So the first goal of doing history is to have a sufficient sense for background, setting, the broader contextual developments. To be able to know more or less where a particular event might be situated.

In fact, all the readings in the course had as a primary purpose providing students with a context for the case. The accounts of the Armada set the stage for the transition from the Tudors to Stuarts and England's emergence as a Protestant power counterbalancing Catholic power on the continent. Elizabeth withstood intrigue and warfare with the Catholic continent but at a price. Parliament provided her the wherewithal to hold off the Catholics in exchange for greater self-determination. Once out of the barn, the horse that was Parliament's desire for greater power was not about to be reigned in by the imperial Scot, James I. The internecine struggle between the Stuart monarchs and Parliament would culminate a half century later in the Civil War, regicide, and Cromwell's Commonwealth. The Elton (1974) and Youings (1984) texts offered details of the political, diplomatic, and social milieu in which the controversy occurred. The use of the topic-specific groups to gather information was precisely to delineate and fill out the context of the controversy.

The Historian's Task Is to Link a Given Event to Its Context in a Way That Produces an Explanation for the Event

This is most clearly expressed in Vinten-Johansen's purpose for the research paper that students wrote on the basis of their investigations and discussions of the Goodwin–Fortescue controversy. In our first interview, Vinten-Johansen explained:

> Students need to recognize that particular events are confusing to the participants at the time. The clarity that we often impose historically is an artifact. . . . They need to go back and, in a sense, become absorbed in the uncertainty, in contingency, the lack of perspective in an event itself. Once they have . . . that confusion, then the goal is to essentially recognize that the role of the historian is to impose clarity on the past for a particular purpose. The purpose is: first, clarity for the individual investigating the event to try to understand what he or she thinks occurred. The second is clarity in terms of communication to others. Why would this event, in which one has invested one's time and energy and understanding, be of significance to other people?

Vinten-Johansen's idea that historians "impose clarity on the past for a particular purpose" comports well with Walsh's (1967) observation that the historian's task is to construct a "significant" narrative of events and Burston's (1976) assertion that historians seek to "elucidate the individual event" (p. 32). Carr (1962) argued that "[t]he facts of history cannot be purely objective, since they become facts of history only in virtue of the significance attached to them by the historian" (p. 120). These views of "facts" and the historian's relation to them differ markedly from the views of those in the positivist tradition who hold that the historian's beliefs and values are largely irrelevant (cf. Benson, 1972).

Just as the texts in the course, particularly Elton and Youings, and the topic-specific groups were the vehicles for filling out the context of the case, the primary groups were the forum in which students pooled information on the context and individual insights to make sense of the data gleaned from the packet documents. Again, the process of inquiry and collaborative "sense-making," more than either the primary documents or the secondary sources, constituted the principal opportunity for students to develop understandings of the nature of historical knowledge and inquiry.

Writing History Involves Placing Oneself in Someone Else's Shoes and Seeing the World As He or She Saw It

In discussing this component of his view of history, Vinten-Johansen described during our first interview how he has used *To Kill A Mockingbird* in another course he taught:

> There's one point in [the novel] when [the little girl] stops and says, "You know, suddenly I can step inside the shoes, and I can walk around in them for a few minutes, and I could understand that Boo was not that different from me where it counted," or something like that. . . . I use that, and [I urge my students] to "use your feelings and your intuitions not as the basis for your judgment, but as the vehicle for getting yourself out of your present, and at least making a pass [at getting] into these very strange waters of the past."

In describing his use of literature, especially novels, in his history courses, Vinten-Johansen explained why he tries to create opportunities for students to experience, imaginatively, someone else's reality:

> What is the context that would help explain why they did that? There's usually an explanation for what human beings do. Even a serial killer you can figure out. There's a lot of detective work, I suggest to [my students], even though I don't like the whole notion of history as detective [work]. . . . There is that sense of what a good detective has to do in order to try to understand, to solve a problem, a murder or what have you, that a historian also can make use of, and that tends to work. But because of the difficulties that students have with [putting themselves in someone else's place]. . . . you'll see how

chock full [my courses] are of literature. . . . And that's largely because I have found literature is one of the most effective ways of getting students into a different world view.

Such imaginative projection into the hearts and minds of others in the past is, for a number of philosophers and historians, a critical requirement for understanding and doing history. In particular, idealist historians such as Croce (1921) and Collingwood (1956) argue that historical truths are not generalizations of the sort that the physical scientists seek but rather historical truths are individual, applying to a particular event rather than to a category of events. Understanding individual events is possible because these experiences are a consequence of human thought and actions that are accessible to the historian. According to Walsh (1967), the historian can "re-think or re-live" the thoughts and experiences of individuals in the past: "This process of imaginative re-living . . . is central to historical thinking, and explains why that study can give us the individual knowledge which other sciences fail to provide" (p. 44). Elton (1967), in distinguishing between amateur and professional historians, observed that "[t]he purpose and ambition of professional history is to understand a given problem from the inside" (p. 18).

Wineburg (1994) pointed out the dilemma inherent in achieving historical empathy. Successful empathy, "finding home in a foreign country" as Wineburg called it, can generate false historical parallels between the past and present. He cites Mink's (1987) observation that doing history consists in discovering "the world we have lost rather than rediscovery of the world which survives in our culture" in arguing that greater knowledge about the past makes us aware of the uniqueness, the irreproducibility of the past. The more we know about the past, the less we apprehend in it analogies with the present. The teacher's challenge is to encourage students to identify imaginatively with historical actors to achieve some level of empathy but, at the same time, to ensure they explore the past sufficiently to understand the particularities that afford events their uniqueness and irreproducibility. The detailed investigation students conduct in Vinten-Johansen's course is intended, in part, as an antidote to facile and misleading analogies.

At the same time, Vinten-Johansen views the experience of imaginative re-thinking and re-living as a critical antidote to the presentism common not merely among his students but throughout our society. The issue arose in the first seminar discussion of *The Armada* when a female student objected to an analogy Mattingly uses to compare the way Elizabeth I managed the people of England to the way a woman manages her lover. The student accused Mattingly of sexism. After soliciting other students' views of this observation, Vinten-Johansen discussed the charge:

If you are going to stand back and try to be objective, it is a sexist description, by our current standards. But then, as a practicing historian, you have to stop and say, "Wait a minute. What kind of society was this?" In so far as that society was sexist by our standards, then it is possible that Mattingly has captured sexism in the society. If Mattingly had written this book thirty or forty years later than he did, it is very possible that he would have figured out a way to let us know whether he approved or disapproved of that sexism, but writing in the 1950s—actually he started writing in the 1940s—was essentially a decade before the full popular explosion, so to speak, of the notion of sexism.

Notice that in this class, the second of the term, Vinten-Johansen was already including students in the category of "practicing historians," explaining to these novitiate historians the culture and the conventions of the historical community and modeling a process of reasoning characteristic of historians. Vinten-Johansen, in class, frequently asked questions intended to alert students to their use of contemporary beliefs, knowledge, moral standards, and attitudes to judge the actions of individuals in the past. In discussing students' first drafts of their research papers, he often questioned students about their judgments of Members of Parliament or James I, asking what purpose is served by characterizing James, as one student did, as "stupid" because he insisted on the divine right of kings.

The Apparent Orderliness of Historical Accounts Is an Artifact of the Written Form in Which History Is Represented, Not of Past Events

Vinten-Johansen is well aware of the distortions of the past created by written accounts and by the way history is frequently taught. By their very nature, historical accounts omit the fine-grained details, the minutiae, that are the basic unit of human experience. Consequently, the picture of the past created in historical accounts, particularly textbooks, is highly overdetermined. As it is taught, the past is often portrayed as a single, unified story, a chronicle of political events that follow one another as night follows day. This leads students, and others, to believe that events in the past were inevitable, that one event led inexorably to the next as so often appears to be the case in historical writing.

Viewing the past as inevitable, as predetermined by a present that had to be as it is, both misrepresents the past and drains the past of its drama, its tension. Stephen Jay Gould (1989), addressing the idea of contingency in his book on the reinterpretation of the evidence in the Burgess shales, argued that, while the inevitable and the random leave us cold, we are fascinated by what did not have to be:

> When we realize the actual outcome did not have to be, that any alteration in any step along the way would have unleashed a cascade down a different channel, we grasp the causal power of individual events. We can argue, lament, or exult over each detail—because each holds the power of transformation. Contingency is the affirmation of control by immediate events over destiny, the kingdom lost for want of a horseshoe nail . . . . Contingency is a license to participate in history, and our psyche responds. (Gould, 1989, pp. 284–285)

This is Vinten-Johansen's goal: To have students appreciate the contingent nature of historical events. Both the Armada and the Goodwin–Fortescue case are vehicles for developing such appreciation. A shift in wind direction as the Armada sailed through the Channel totally altered the plans of the Duke of Medina Sidonia, commander of the Armada. Had the wind not shifted, the outcome of the expedition may have been quite different, and the future of Europe itself changed. Slight alterations in any one of the numerous details of the Goodwin–Fortescue case—a different membership in the Privy Council, a shift in leadership in the Parliamentary party, and so on—could have resulted in quite altered circumstances, affecting the development of parliamentary government. By working with the details, reconstructing events, creating their own interpretations, Vinten-Johansen reasons, students come to appreciate this critical aspect of historical knowledge.

Historical Accounts Should Be Judged on Their Own Terms According to How Well the Historian Substantiates His or Her Thesis

This component of Vinten-Johansen's view of history was central to the total experience of the course. Many of his comments on students' papers, such as the quotation from his comments on Dick's paper, focused on this issue. This parallels Vinten-Johansen's insistence that historical events be understood, as much as possible, from the "inside," although he acknowledges, as Berlin (1954) argued, that our capacity to do so is restricted by the degree to which our understandings are framed by the historical moment in which we live.

The emphasis on judging historians in the terms of the purposes and methods that they set for themselves appeared to be Vinten-Johansen's way to help students think about the importance of internal consistency and overall coherence to the persuasiveness of the arguments they make in their research papers. His comments on students' papers and to students in individual conferences and class focused on the viability of the arguments they were attempting to make, rather than on whether the interpretation was right or wrong.

In the following student conference, Vinten-Johansen addressed his comments to Kathy's criticisms of Mattingly in the comparative essay:

Kathy: I guess I'm judging Mattingly by. . . .

Vinten-
Johansen: By Fernandez-Armesto's criteria? Is that fair?

Kathy: I guess not.

Vinten-
Johansen: Would you want somebody to decide whether you have had a successful undergraduate career on the basis of your buddy's standards of what makes success, your parents' standards of success, or your own standards of success?

Kathy: My own.

Vinten-
Johansen: All right. Then you've got to extend the same courtesy to Mattingly. What was he trying to do in his book? Does he do that well? What was Fernandez-Armesto trying to do? Does he do that well?

History Is Written for the Present Generation and, Hence, the Past Needs to Be Periodically Re-interpreted

A critical aspect of Vinten-Johansen's view of historical knowledge is that our understanding of the past changes as circumstances in the present change. This was evident when he discussed the use of both Mattingly's and Fernandez-Armesto's accounts of the Armada. Published some 38 years apart, they offer contrasting interpretations of the event:

It becomes a . . . perfect instance in which one can show the need for constant historical revision. That we are writing for a present generation and that present generation is never the same. So that even if no new material is unearthed on a subject like the Armada, let's say, one can go back and—with different eyes, different assumptions, with different goals in mind—can make a very valuable contribution in trying to [understand the events].

The experience of the workshop itself was designed to convey the idea that "different eyes" may produce different interpretations. As Postan (1970) argued, "[t]he facts of history, even those which in historical parlance figure as 'hard and fast,' are no more than relevances: facets of past phenomena which happen to relate to the preoccupations of historical inquirers at the time of their inquiries" (p. 51).

In sum, Vinten-Johansen's view of history stands in sharp contrast to the view purveyed in most history classrooms, whether university or precollegiate, and textbooks. His view places students, as creators of their own accounts and as consumers of others' accounts, center stage. He has designed the seminar so that students experience directly the vicissitudes of doing history as well as the disputed nature of historical knowledge. In so doing, he creates an opportunity for prospective teachers and others to come to view history less as an accumulation of information about the past and more as an argument, a debate shaped by the preoccupations of the present.

SOURCES OF THE PEDAGOGY AND WORKSHOP DESIGN: VIEWS OF LEARNERS AND LEARNING

Vinten-Johansen's views of history are but one source of his course design and pedagogy. Of equal importance are his views of learners and learning. These seem to have developed over his career as a teacher, beginning with his brief stint as a high school government teacher in Rhode Island. As his pedagogy has evolved and he has created opportunities for students to express their ideas, he appears to have learned from his students.

Although Vinten-Johansen's views of history were clearly expressed in his syllabus, the design of his courses, the discourse he encourages, and the interviews, his views of learning were more covert. Students can hardly take any of his courses without becoming aware of his views of history; yet, his beliefs about learning appear to be less accessible (McDiarmid, 1994). The difference seems to be that whereas he explicitly called students' attention to his beliefs about history, he did not do the same for his ideas about learning. This is not intended as a criticism:

Vinten-Johansen is responsible for helping students learn history and about the nature of history, not about the teaching and learning of history. At the same time, however implicit, he has a clear theory, the tenets of which are delineated next.

All Students Are Capable of Appreciating the Nature of Historical Knowledge and Inquiry

Vinten-Johansen designed his course to raise epistemological issues that some would consider proper only for graduate students in history. That the history faculty required students, as one of their first courses in history, to take a historiography seminar attested to the belief that all majors, at an early point in their studies, are capable of engaging in epistemological question. Nowhere in our interviews or in his interactions with students did Vinten-Johansen betray the belief that the ideas and activities in the course were beyond the capacity of any of the students.

Although the slogan "all students can learn" has become a mantra for elementary and secondary educators, university faculty appear more willing to blame students' failures on their lack of ability. Indeed, some faculty seem to assume that the best measure of the intellectual rigor of a course is the proportion of the students who fail—the greater the number of Fs, the more rigorous the course. The irony is, of course, that faculty are paid to teach; if students fail to learn, shouldn't faculty shoulder at least some of the responsibility? Vinten-Johansen, like other faculty, went out of his way to work with those students who were not keeping up with the work in the course. Early in the term, he scheduled conferences with two students who were clearly struggling and spoke with them informally before and after class to maintain contact and express his concern. He did not assume, at first, that the difficulty was solely the students'.

Developing an Appreciation for the Nature of Historical Knowledge and Inquiry Requires That Students Engage—in a Limited and Bounded Fashion—the Problems and Issues That Historians Face

This is the central tenet of Vinten-Johansen's teaching. His purpose is not to develop "junior historians." Rather, he believes that in the process of creating their own accounts of the past, students encounter many of the same difficulties as do professional historians: often fragmented and frequently contradictory information about what happened in the past; the need to decide which evidence to consider and which to ignore; the necessity of reaching tentative conclusions in spite of the absence of critical evidence; the need to decide when to stop pursuing additional evidence; and so on. Encountering these problems, students come to understand the profound uncertainty of historical knowledge and the plausibility of competing interpretations. His hope is that doing history will make his students more critical consumers of history.

Critics most frequently attack such approaches on the grounds that students simply do not have enough background information about the past to do what professional historians do (Burston, 1976). Vinten-Johansen organized the seminar so that students accumulated a lot of information about the past while they were developing and defending a thesis. A primary criterion for the papers they wrote on the Goodwin–Fortescue controversy was how well they analyzed the evidence available. Moreover, by working in teams, students benefited from the background information that their classmates gathered. In our interviews with the students, they impressed us with their extensive and detailed knowledge of England at the beginning of the 17th century, even though this was not a primary goal of the course (McDiarmid, 1994).

By placing critical primary and secondary sources on reserve in the library, Vinten-Johansen made the task manageable. This saved students time and frustration in trying, for example, to figure out where to find information on the membership of Parliament in 1604. In addition, after the first 2 weeks, he devoted large portions of the seminar to small group work. This enabled students to figure out, in conversation, what additional information they needed and afforded Vinten-Johansen the opportunity to listen to each group and suggest additional sources.

The Instructor's Role Is Designer, Research Guide, Critic, and Orchestrator of Discussion

Vinten-Johansen's beliefs about learning history led him to assume particular roles in the classroom. Because of his views, his most important role may have occurred before he even met his students: designing the experience. Choosing and setting up the problem, that is, the Goodwin-Fortescue case, was critical. This involved a variety of considerations: What is a fruitful historical question; what will engage students at this level; what data should be within easy reach and which should students have to search for; what should be the foci of the different research groups; and so on. In addition, he developed worksheets that guided students in identifying authors' theses, how they structure historical arguments, and how they muster evidence.

Once the course began, Vinten-Johansen then had to listen carefully to students, their questions, hypotheses, ideas, and decide what would be most helpful. This required a good grasp of the primary and secondary literature as well as a sensitivity to individual students. As students wrote in response to Vinten-Johansen's assignment, he had to provide comments that would encourage students but push them toward more focused, better organized, and more thoughtfully written work. Throughout the term, Vinten-Johansen had to orchestrate the seminar discussions in ways that addressed students' ideas and challenged their thinking.

In sum, underlying Vinten-Johansen's pedagogy seemed to be the belief that history can be learned but not taught. This accounts for the "workshop" design in which students must struggle together to understand primary sources and the context from which they have been abstracted. This also accounts for his roles. Rarely did he assume the conventional role of lecturer. When he did, the focus of his comments was on doing history, particularly writing history rather than information about the past. He assumed that students could collect for themselves pertinent information about the past from the materials he put on reserve or required as readings for the class. His role was to help them sort through and organize this information.

CONCLUSION

In the case of teaching history I have described here, the attempt to teach students the contested, uncertain, and interpretative nature of historical knowledge requires, paradoxically, that students examine and interrogate the details of the past. Rather than teaching generalizations about the nature of historical knowledge, the instructor designed an experience in which students would confront the difficulties that are the coin of the professional historian's realm. Working back and forth between primary documents and secondary accounts, relying on each other's investigatory work, writing and rewriting attempts to make and support a thesis about past events, students did not need to be told that historical knowledge is uncertain, perspectival, contested. This is what they experienced (McDiarmid, 1994). As I have argued, the design of the experience and the instructor's pedagogy derive from particular beliefs about both the nature of history and how history is learned.

What is the value of university students' developing such a view of history? A tenet of recent school reform efforts is that *all* students should develop knowledge and understandings that differ from those typically cultivated in the past. Intellectual flexibility, critical judgment, and the capacity to work collaboratively have come to overshadow, in the eyes of reformers, the acquisition of a particular body of knowledge as the desired cognitive outcome of schooling (see American Association for the Advancement of Science, 1989; Holmes Group, 1990; National Commission on Social Studies in the Schools, 1989; National Council of Teachers of Mathematics, 1989). Logically, the teachers themselves must have this kind of knowledge and understanding if they are to help their students develop it. Rarely, however, do prospective teachers encounter opportunities to develop such understanding.

Why not? University faculty appear no less concerned about "coverage" than their precollegiate counterparts. University faculty who teach introductory undergraduate courses seem to feel that they cannot afford the time required for the fine-grained, intensive work described in this chapter. The assumption is that such intensive work would take time away from the more critical work of surveying events, people, and so on across time. These faculty ignore evidence that students rarely retain much of the information they cram in order to pass exams. Perhaps more critically, some faculty hold the view that historical knowledge consists solely in information about the past; they appear to consider debates about the nature of historical knowledge unnecessary or unsuitable for undergraduates. As a consequence, universities seem likely to continue graduating prospective history teachers whose understandings will perpetuate the view that history is just "one damn thing after another." Without changes in the way history is taught at university, changes that seem highly unlikely (McDiarmid, 1988, 1990, 1992), reformers who argue that the purpose of teaching history in schools is to help students develop the judgment so vital to a democracy are unlikely to see their goal realized (Gagnon, 1988).

Despite calls for more emphasis on undergraduate teaching, research universities continue to value research activities above teaching. Given the increasingly tight financial straits most universities face, this seems unlikely to change. Faculty who bring in outside research funds are prized. Faculty who devote themselves to teaching undergraduates and work to improve their practice generally are not, unless they also bring in outside funding. In the disciplinary fields, academics make their reputations, earn prestige and rewards through publication, not teaching. In short, the reward systems of universities and disciplinary communities clearly favor research and publication over teaching excellence and innovation. Faculty, like Vinten-Johansen, who invest heavily in their teaching practice do so against the grain of their institutions and their fields.[2]

Yet, teachers such as Vinten-Johansen create precisely the opportunities students, especially those who plan to teach, need to understand particularly instructive historical moments or events in detail and, in the process, develop an appreciation of the nature of historical knowledge and accounts. Underlying his pedagogy is his conviction that not only are undergraduates capable of understanding sophisticated epistemological ideas about the nature of history but school pupils are as well.

The historiography seminar also represents an opportunity for students to learn more about pedagogy. If Vinten-Johansen felt he had the time and responsibility to help students' interrogate his pedagogical moves, and the rationale for these, in the same way they interrogate historical accounts, he could help them begin to develop an understanding of teaching and learning history to rival the sophisticated views of history they develop. Helping students understand the teaching and learning of history is not, however, his brief. In the division of labor common to most universities, these understandings are considered the responsibility of teacher educators. Methods courses, however, rarely locate examination of teaching and learning in the context of interrogating or developing historical accounts. Just as history faculty do not regard as their responsibility helping students learn about teaching and learning history, methods faculty do not regard teaching students history or about the nature of history as theirs.

The impediment to improving undergraduate teaching and teacher preparation is not a lack of information on how to teach better. Ideas for improving undergraduate teaching have been around for years (see Chickering & Gamson, 1987; Elbe, 1972, 1980, 1988; Gullette, 1982; Levinson-Rose & Menges, 1981; McKeachie, 1978; Menges & Svinicki, 1991; Runkel, Harrison, & Runkel, 1969; Weaver, 1989; Weimer, 1987). The impediments appear to be, rather, the culture of institutions that continue to value funded research over teaching, the accumulation of information over understanding of how knowledge is developed, and the maintenance of a division of labor in which the questions of greatest relevance to prospective teachers fall between the cracks.

---

[2]One of Vinten-Johansen's colleagues in the history department told me that Peter had "nearly ruined" his career by focusing so much attention on his teaching.

APPENDIX

Book Title: _____ Student's Name _____

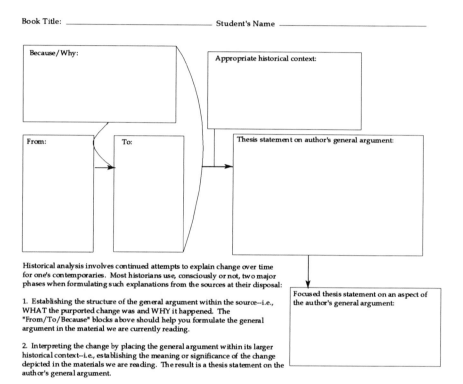

Historical analysis involves continued attempts to explain change over time for one's contemporaries. Most historians use, consciously or not, two major phases when formulating such explanations from the sources at their disposal:

1. Establishing the structure of the general argument within the source--i.e., WHAT the purported change was and WHY it happened. The "From/To/Because" blocks above should help you formulate the general argument in the material we are currently reading.

2. Interpreting the change by placing the general argument within its larger historical context--i.e., establishing the meaning or significance of the change depicted in the materials we are reading. The result is a thesis statement on the author's general argument.

REFERENCES

Abelove, H., Blackmar, B., Dimock, P., & Schneer, J. (Eds). (1984). *Visions of history*. New York: Pantheon Books.

Adams, J. T., & Vannest, C. G. (1935). *The record of America*. New York: Charles Scribner's Sons.

American Association for the Advancement of Science. (1989). *Science for all Americans: A Project 2061 report on literacy goals in science, mathematics, and technology*. Washington, DC: Author.

Appleby, J., Hunt, L., & Jacob, M. (1994). *Telling the truth about history*. New York: Norton.

Axtell, J. (1987). Europeans, Indians, and the Age of Discovery in American history textbooks. *American Historical Review, 92*, 621–632.

Benson, L. (1972). *Toward the scientific study of history*. Boston: Lippincott.

Berlin, I. (1954). *Historical inevitability*. London: Oxford University.

Braudel, F. (1992). *The Mediterranean world in the age of Philip II.* New York: HarperCollins. (Original work published 1949)

Braudel, F. (1975). *Capitalism and material life 1400–1800.* New York: Harper Colophon. (Original work published 1967)

Braudel, F. (1981). *The structures of everyday life: The limits of the possible.* New York: Harper & Row. (Original work published 1979)

Braudel, F. (1980). *On history.* Chicago: University of Chicago Press.

Burston, W. H. (1976). *Principles of history teaching* (Rev. ed.). London: London & Home Counties Branch of the Library Association.

Carr, E. H. (1962). *What is history?* New York: Penguin.

Chickering, A. W., & Gamson, Z. F. (1987). Seven principles for good practice in undergraduate education. *American Association for Higher Education Bulletin, 39*(7), 3–7.

Collingwood, R. G. (1956). *The idea of history.* London: Oxford University. (Original work published 1946)

Croce, B. (1970). *History as the story of liberty.* Lanham, MD: University Press of America. (Original work published 1921)

Danto, A. C. (1985). *Narration and knowledge.* New York: Columbia University.

Elbe, K. E. (1972). *Professors as teachers.* San Francisco: Jossey-Bass.

Elbe, K. E. (Ed.). (1980). *Improving teaching styles* (New Directions for Teaching and Learning No. 1). San Francisco: Jossey-Bass.

Elbe, K. E. (1988). *The craft of teaching* (2nd ed.). San Francisco: Jossey-Bass.

Elton, G. R. (1967). *The practice of history.* London: Sydney University.

Elton, G. R. (1974). *England under the Tudors.* London: Routledge.

Fernandez-Armesto, F. (1989). *The Spanish Armada: The experience of war in 1588.* London: Oxford University.

Fish, S. (1980). *Is there a text in this class: The authority of interpretative communities.* Cambridge, MA: Harvard University Press.

FitzGerald, F. (1979). *America revisited.* Boston: Atlantic-Little, Brown.

Foucault, M. (1965). *Madness and civilization* (R. Howard, Trans.). New York: Random House.

Gagnon, P. (1988, November). Why study history? *Atlantic Monthly,* pp. 43–66.

Geyl, P. (1962). *Debates with historians.* London: Collins. (Original work published 1955)

Goodlad, J. I. (1983). *A place called school.* New York: McGraw-Hill.

Gould, S. J. (1989). *Wonderful life: The Burgess Shale and the nature of history.* New York: Norton.

Gullette, M. M. (Ed.). (1982). *The art and craft of teaching.* Cambridge, MA: Harvard University, Harvard-Danforth Center for Teaching and Learning.

Handlin, O. (1979). *Truth in history.* Cambridge, MA: Harvard University.

Hexter, J. H. (1979). *On historians: Reappraisals of the masters of modern history.* Cambridge, MA: Harvard University.

Himmelfarb, G. (1987). *The new history and the old.* Cambridge, MA: Belknap.

Holmes Group. (1990). *Tomorrow's schools: Principles for the design of professional development schools.* East Lansing, MI: Author.

Holt, T. (1990). *Thinking historically.* New York: College Entrance Examination Board.

Jacoby, R. (1992). A new intellectual history? *American Historical Review, 97,* 404–424.

LaCapra, D. (1982). *"Madam Bovary" on trial.* Ithaca, NY: Cornell University Press.

LaCapra, D. (1989). *Soundings in critical theory.* Ithaca, NY: Cornell University Press.

Levinson-Rose, J., & Menges, R. (1981). Improving college teaching: A critical review of research. *Review of Educational Research, 51,* 403–434.

Mattingly, G. (1959). *The Armada.* Boston: Houghton Mifflin.

McDiarmid, G. W. (1988). Values and liberal education: Allan Bloom and the education of teachers. *Colloquy, 2*(2), 9–16.

McDiarmid, G. W. (1990). The liberal arts: Will more result in better subject matter understanding? *Theory Into Practice, 29,* 21–29.

McDiarmid, G. W. (1992). *The arts and sciences as preparation for teaching* (Issue Paper No. 92–3). East Lansing, MI: Michigan State University, National Center for Research on Teacher Education.

McDiarmid, G. W. (1994). Understanding history for teaching: A study of the historical understanding of prospective teachers. In J. Voss and M. Carretero (Eds.), *Cognitive and instructional processes in social sciences and history.* (pp. 159–180). Hillsdale, NJ: Lawrence Erlbaum Associates.

McDiarmid, G. W., & Vinten-Johansen, P. (1994). *Teaching and learning history—from the inside out* (Special Report.). E. Lansing, MI: Michigan State University, National Center for Research on Teacher Education.

McKeachie, W. J. (1978). *Teaching tips: A guidebook for the beginning college teacher* (8th ed.). Lexington, MA: D.C. Heath.

Menges, R. J., & Svinicki, M. D. (1991). *College teaching: From theory to practice.* San Francisco: Jossey-Bass.

Mink, L. O. (1969). *Mind, history, and dialectic.* Middletown, CT: Wesleyan.

Mink, L. O. (1987). *Historical understanding.* Ithaca, NY: Cornell University.

National Commission on Social Studies in the Schools. (1989). *Charting a course: Social studies for the 21st century. Washington, DC: Author.*

National Council of Teachers of Mathematics. (1989). *Professional standards for teaching mathematics: Working draft.* Reston, VA: Author.

Novick, P. (1988). *That noble dream: The "objectivity question" and the American historical profession.* New York: Cambridge University.

Perrone, V. (1985). *Portraits of high schools.* Princeton, NJ: Carnegie Foundation for the Advancement of Teaching.

Postan, M. M. (1970). *Fact and relevance.* Cambridge, UK: Cambridge University.

Ravitch, D., & Finn, C. E., Jr. (1987). *What do our 17-year-olds know? A report on the first national assessment of history and literature.* New York: Harper & Row.

Rosenau, P. M. (1992). *Post-modernism and the social sciences.* Princeton, NJ: Princeton University Press.

Runkel, P., Harrison, R., & Runkel, M. (Eds.). (1969). *The changing college classroom.* San Francisco: Jossey-Bass.

Schama, S. (1991). *Dead certainties: (Unwarranted speculations).* New York: Knopf.

Schug, M. C., Todd, R. J., & Berry, R. (1984). Why kids don't like social studies. *Research in Social Studies Education, 48,* 382–387.

Sewall, G. T. (1987). *American history textbooks: An assessment of quality.* New York: Columbia University, Teachers College, Educational Excellence Network.

Tosh, J. (1984). *The pursuit of history.* New York: Longman.

Vinten-Johansen, (n.d.). *The reluctant vaudeville master: Johan Ludvig Heiberg in Denmark's golden epoch.* Unpublished manuscript.

Walsh, W. H. (1984). *An introduction to the philosophy of history* (3rd ed.). Westport, CT: Greenwood Press. (Original work published 1967)

Weaver, F.S. (Ed.). (1989). *Promoting inquiry in undergraduate learning* (New Directions for Teaching and Learning No. 38). San Francisco: Jossey-Bass.

Weimer, M. G. (Ed.). (1987). *Teaching large classes well* (New Directions for Teaching and Learning No. 32). San Francisco: Jossey-Bass.

Wineburg, S. S. (1994). Contextualized thinking in history. In J. Voss & M. Carretero (Eds.),
    Cognitive and instructional processes in social sciences and history (pp. 285–308). Hillsdale,
    NJ: Lawrence Erlbaum Associates.
White, H. (1987). *The content of the form: Narrative discourse and historical representation.*
    Baltimore, MD: Johns Hopkins.
Wirth, F. P. (1945). *The development of America.* Boston: American Book.
Youings, J. (1984). *Sixteenth-century England.* Harmondsworth, UK: Penguin Books.

Chapter 10

SCHOOLS FOR THOUGHT: OVERVIEW OF THE PROJECT AND LESSONS LEARNED FROM ONE OF THE SITES

Mary Lamon
Schools for Thought Project, St. Louis, MO

Teresa Secules
Vanderbilt University

Anthony J. Petrosino
Vanderbilt University

Rachelle Hackett
University of the Pacific

John D. Bransford
Vanderbilt University

Susan R. Goldman
Vanderbilt University

Our goal in this chapter is to describe a project designed to combine the resources of three different research teams in an effort to create middle-school classrooms that support extraordinary student achievement. Called Schools For Thought (SFT), the project is named after John Bruer's (1993) award winning book. The SFT project is based on the goal of extraordinary achievement for all students, not just a select few (Resnick, 1987). Reports such as the Secretary's Commission on Achieving Necessary Skills, and the Report for America 2000 (U.S. Department of Labor, April, 1992), emphasize that in a high performance workplace workers will need a solid foundation in literacy, computational, and technological skills. Beyond these enabling tools, future workers will need expertise in critical thinking, reasoning, and decision making. Finally, they will need the ability to communicate and collaborate with others. SFT is dedicated to the goal that students will develop the ability to think, reason, and learn throughout their lives (e.g., Bereiter & Scardamalia, 1987; Bransford, Goldman, & Vye, 1991; Bruer, 1993).

The idea to begin the SFT project arose in the context of meetings sponsored by the James S. McDonnell Cognitive Studies of Educational Practice program (CSEP). Participants in the CSEP program had each developed and studied individual school-based programs that data showed were quite effective (see McGilly, 1994). Nevertheless, a number of CSEP grantees speculated that their results were limited by the fact that, at most, their programs involved only 1–1-1/2 hours of a student's day. In many settings, the philosophy of teaching and learning that was characteristic of the remainder of each student's day was antagonistic to the CSEP programs that had been implemented. What would happen if the major portion of each student's day involved the kinds of teaching and learning activities that were congruent with the overall theoretical orientation that was emerging in the CSEP group?

As discussions progressed, it became clear that a number of individual CSEP programs looked extremely promising (see McGilly, 1994) and had the potential to be combined with one another. But these programs also spanned a broad age range extending from kindergarten to high school. It seemed too large a first step to attempt to restructure an entire K–12 system. Because we had to focus our efforts, only a few of the CSEP programs were involved in the first step of SFT.

The focus we eventually chose was to begin in sixth grade and gradually move both upward and downward. The decision to begin in sixth grade arose, in part, because of an opportunity in St. Louis, Missouri (home of the McDonnell Foundation), to build a new middle school that would be connected to the St. Louis Science Center. Dennis Wint, President of the St. Louis Science Center, wanted to create a school that would integrate informal science learning of the kind that takes place in community institutions with science education. The construction of the school was a few years in the future. If we could show that it was possible to successfully organize an entire school day around programs founded on state-of-the-art cognitive theory, and further show that integrating these programs produced extraordinary student achievement, we had a chance to convince the St. Louis system to design their school along cognitive lines. The James S. McDonnell Foundation was excited about this possibility and agreed to fund the first steps of what we now call Schools for Thought.

In the remainder of this chapter we focus on the following:

1. Descriptions of the three core programs that form the basis of SFT.
2. Analysis of the educational features that make the three core programs synergistic.
3. Descriptions of the initial attempt to create SFT classrooms at one of the sites (Nashville).
4. Discussion of the lessons we have learned and next steps.

DESCRIPTION OF THE THREE CORE PROGRAMS THAT FORM THE BASIS OF SFT

Our goal in this section is to describe the three CSEP programs that comprise the core of the Schools for Thought collaborative: The Adventures of Jasper Woodbury, Computer Supported Intentional Learning Environments (CSILE), and Fostering Communities of Learners (FCL). Each of these programs is discussed in this section.

The Jasper Woodbury Problem Solving Series

Vanderbilt's Adventures of Jasper Woodbury program is a powerful approach to teaching mathematical problem solving. Through quality video dramas, students are presented with complex, realistic problems that call for the types of mathematical thinking required in real life. Links to science, history, and social studies are evident as well (Cognition and Technology Group at Vanderbilt [CTGV], 1990, 1992a). Using video technology to provide a context for mathematics is in accord with one of the Curriculum and Evaluation Standards published by the National Council for Teachers of Mathematics (NCTM): "the mathematics curriculum should engage students in some problems that demand extended effort to solve." (NCTM as cited in CTGV, 1993b).

The adventures are not meant to replace the mathematics curriculum. Instead, they provide a realistic context for problem solving, for realizing the relevance of mathematics to everyday life, and for grounding mathematics concepts and procedures in authentic situations. The following brief synopsis of one video adventure "The Right Angle" is presented to illustrate the series. (This is one of three "Jaspers" that emphasizes geometry; other triplets emphasize introductory statistics, trip planning, and introductory algebra.)

Paige Littlefield, a young Native American, has been left a challenge by her grandfather, to find a cave with a family heirloom. Paige wants to find the heirloom in time for the powwow which is coming up soon. As the story unfolds, the viewer learns about topographic maps, as well as about important concepts of geometry (e.g., isosceles right triangles) and their usefulness for measurement. At the end of the story, the students need to use the information about maps and geometry to locate the cave by following Paige's grandfather's directions which, in part, require that students use geometric principles to estimate the height of objects. They then need to determine the fastest way to get to the cave (Zech et al., 1994).

Solving this multifaceted challenge requires that students formulate goals, devise strategies, find relevant data (all the data needed are embedded in the video along with additional distractor data), and construct mathematical arguments. Perhaps most significantly, the challenges in the video make mathematics an object for discussion.

Teachers use related activities to extend and reinforce mathematical knowledge and skills. Teachers often have students extend their learning from the Jasper adventures by using a variety of geometry-based methods to estimate the height of real objects such as the school flagpole or the school building. All estimation procedures require students to use geometric concepts, but the methods are not equally accurate. Teachers use this extension both for teaching geometry and as an opportunity for helping students acquire an understanding of estimation. Insofar as estimation is rarely covered in middle-school mathematics, the video based extension is a nice example of how experience and embedded teaching can lead to mathematical insights.

The Adventures of Jasper Woodbury series now includes nine episodes (three additional episodes will provide an introduction to algebra and are in the process of being scripted and filmed). The nine existing stories are organized as triplets around three thematic and mathematical content areas: complex trip planning involving relationships between distance, rate, and time; constructing business plans, involving the use of probability and statistics; and way-finding, relying on the use of geometry.

Extensions accompany each adventure. They include "what if" problems designed to allow students to consider the implications of varying problem constraints. The adventures deliberately contain links to other curricular areas as well. For example, "The Right Angle" can be used for geography and topography and in history for exploring native American cultures. Jasper is currently in use throughout the United States and is showing impressive results in both conventional mathematics and in complex problem solving (e.g., B. Barron et al., 1995; CTGV, 1992a, 1992b, 1993a, 1994, in press). Examples of data relevant to Jasper appear in Table 10.1.

TABLE 10.1
The Adventures Of Jasper Woodbury

Measure	Outcome
Standardized Achievement Tests: Mathematics	Students using Jasper score as well as and in some cases have a significant advantage compared to matched control groups.
One and two-step word problems	Significant advantage for Jasper students compared to students who had received instruction in solving word problems.
Broad scale assessment of problem solving	Highly positive results across gender and ethnicity for Jasper students compared with students who had a traditional curriculum.
Attitude toward mathematics	Jasper students are more positive about mathematics and problem solving.
Transfer to analogous and partially analogous problems	Positive transfer to items analogous and partially analogous to problems presented in an adventure.

Note: Adapted from "Anchored instruction and situated cognition revisited," by the Cognition and Technology Group at Vanderbilt (1993b), *Educational Technology, 23*(3), 52–70.

Fostering a Community of Learners (FCL)

The conceptual basis of the Berkeley Fostering Communities of Learners (FCL) program stems from two sources. The first is based on research that has clearly shown that learning is a matter of discovering and exploring fruitful ideas for oneself. Therefore, the program is designed to encourage students to be partially responsible for designing their own curriculum. The second comes from the well-founded idea that disciplines develop from fundamental principles. Through the curriculum, and through classroom structures, students are systematically guided into discovering these deep principles. Although these two may seem to be contradictory, the following example from a unit in biology will help illustrate how these conceptual underpinnings play out in the classroom (The description here is taken from A. L. Brown, 1992; A. L. Brown & Campione, 1990, 1994; A. L. Brown, Ash, Rutherford, Nakagawa, Gordon, & Campione, 1993).

Students first participate in a "benchmark" lesson on a curriculum theme (e.g., changing populations). This lesson is designed to captivate students' interest in the topic and raise important issues about it. From this lesson students will generate as many questions as they can (usually 100 or more are produced). The teacher and students categorize these questions into approximately five subtopics (e.g., extinct, endangered, artificial, assisted, and urbanized populations). About six students form a research group; each group takes responsibility for one of the five or so subtopics.

Using texts, trade books, magazines, newspapers, videos, and electronic-mail consultations with outside experts, students write up summaries of what they are learning. Students engage in small group discussions of articles and texts relevant to the overall theme as well. Discussions are structured along the lines of four key strategic activities: summarizing, clarifying, questioning, and predicting. These activities originated in a reading comprehension program called Reciprocal Teaching (Palincsar & Brown, 1984) in which students take turns leading the discussion. Reciprocal Teaching has been found to produce dramatically elevated reading comprehension scores in a variety of settings and for all types of students.

In addition, the program uses a greatly modified version of the Jigsaw method (as in jigsaw puzzle) of cooperative learning. As students prepare preliminary drafts of their reports, they engage in "crosstalk" sessions (a whole-class activity where the groups periodically summarize where they are in their research and get input from other groups). If they cannot answer their peers' questions, they do additional research and incorporate it into their writing. Also, they conduct "mini-jigsaws" (small group activities) during the unit. Again, if other students do not understand what the students in the group are writing about, the writers have to go back to revise.

Reading and writing are integrated; students are writing about what they are reading, and they may need to do additional reading to buttress their writing. One purpose of writing is to help clarify thinking, and another purpose is communication.

Finally, students regroup into reciprocal teaching seminars in which each student is expert in one subtopic, and each student holds one fifth of the information necessary to understand the whole topic. Each fifth needs to be combined with the remaining fifths to make a whole unit, hence "jigsaw." All children in a learning group are "expert" on one part of the material, teach it to others, and take part in constructing questions for the test that all students take at the end of each unit. Students finish the unit with a well-written summary of what they have learned. Results show that students improve dramatically in their ability to do this over a series of extended units. Students show impressive understanding and flexible use of content knowledge. The project has resulted in elevated reading, writing, and problem solving scores. Examples of data relevant to FCL appear in Table 10.2.

The CSILE Project

The Computer Supported Intentional Learning Environments (CSILE) Project developed at Toronto provides a rich computer environment aimed at creating a certain kind of school environment in which the focus is on

TABLE 10.2.

Fostering Communities of Learners (FCL)

Measure	Outcome
Reading comprehension/factual questions	No differences between research and control students
Reading comprehension/inferential questions	Research students improved significantly over the year while control students showed no improvement
Short answer pre- and post-tests: content knowledge	Community of Learners students score significantly higher than control groups
Critical thinking on novel application questions.	Research students introduce significantly more novel variations of taught principles and more novel ideas
Analogical reasoning	Research students use structural similarities in problem solving by analogy but control students rely on superficial characteristics

Note: Adapted from "Guided discovery in a community of learners," by A. L. Brown and J. C. Campione (1994). In K. McGilly (Ed.) *Classroom lessons: Integrating cognitive theory and classroom practice* (pp. 229–272). Cambridge, MA: MIT Press/Bradford Books.

problems rather than on categories of knowledge: not "the digestive system" but "how does the digestive system work?" (Bereiter & Scardamalia, 1989; Scardamalia & Bereiter, 1994; Scardamalia et al., 1992; Scardamalia, Bereiter, & Lamon, 1994, Scardamalia, Bereiter, McLean, Swallow, & Woodruff, 1989).

The standard CSILE classroom has eight networked computers per classroom, connected to a file server, which maintains the communal database for the whole school. The core of CSILE is the communal student-generated database that encourages students to articulate their theories and questions, to explore and compare different perspectives, and to reflect on their joint understanding. In CSILE, students work individually and collaboratively, commenting and building on one another's understanding. Anyone can add a comment to a note or attach a graphic note (e.g., picture, diagram) to another note, but only authors can edit or delete notes. Authors are notified when a comment has been made on one of their notes.

The CSILE environment offers an additional avenue for communication and collaboration in addition to the usual one of face-to-face discussions. Although personal discussions are clearly important, the written medium made possible though CSILE is important as well. CSILE provides a highly literate form of communication. Articulating ideas in writing encourages students to formulate their theories explicitly, it clearly facilitates memory, and it supports reflection and revision. Also the written records live on, creating resources for others, and so knowledge is progressively transformed.

The CSILE database consists of text and graphical notes, all produced by the students and accessible through database search procedures. One of the most distinctive features of CSILE is the provision of different ways of representing knowledge, all of which are accessible in the same database (Scardamalia & Bereiter, 1994). The following example of work done by a combination fifth/sixth grade class shows the kinds of exploration encouraged in CSILE.

> In a unit on ecology, one group worked on the topic of fossil fuels. This group started with a kitchen scene that one of the students had previously created as a CSILE note. They took as their challenge to identify the uses of fossil fuels represented in an ordinary kitchen. Different students tackled different parts of the kitchen, researching such matters as the manufacture of plastic wrap, the generation of electricity, and the origin of natural gas. This information was used in creating subsidiary notes consisting of pictures of the relevant kitchen object with text explaining how fossil fuels were involved. The system permits linking such notes in a hierarchical fashion, so that a reader could start with the kitchen scene and for instance, click on the refrigerator. This would open a picture of the interior of the refrigerator; clicking on the various items in the refrigerator would bring up pictures and text presenting the fossil fuel information. The result was a museum-like demonstration that dramatized the extent to which virtually every detail of daily life involves some dependence on fossil fuels (Bruer, 1989).

By writing a note in CSILE or by commenting on others' notes, students become contributors to the knowledge of the class and so gain an overview of how understanding grows. Students working in CSILE classrooms become aware that a true measure of learning is understanding something that you did not already know and consequently that learning is a matter of taking a deep approach to a question, studying for a long time, and finding more and more questions (Scardamalia et al., 1994). Examples of data relevant to CSILE appear in Table 10.3.

ANALYSIS OF THE EDUCATIONAL FEATURES THAT MAKE THE THREE CORE PROGRAMS SYNERGISTIC

The individual programs discussed previously share features that make them compatible and, we hope, synergistic. In particular, each of the programs involves fundamental changes relative to typical classroom instruction in curriculum, instruction, assessment and sense of extended community.

TABLE 10.3

Computer Supported Intentional Learning Environments (CSILE)

Measure	Outcome
Standardized achievement tests: Language	Each year in a CSILE classroom adds a significant gain. CSILE students consistently have an advantage compared to control groups
Standardized achievement tests: Mathematics	No difference between CSILE and control groups
Depth of explanation	CSILE students score significantly higher than control groups
Reading difficult text/Problem Solving	CSILE students score significantly higher than control groups
Beliefs about learning	Each year in a CSILE classroom significantly shifts attitudes toward a deeper conception

Note: Adapted from "The CSILE Project: Trying to bring the classroom into world 3," by M. Scardamalia, C. Bereiter, & M. Lamon (1994). In K. McGilly (Ed.),*Classroom lessons: Integrating cognitive theory and classroom practice* (pp. 201–228). Cambridge, MA: MIT Press/Bradford Books.

Changes in Curriculum

The three core programs in SFT emphasize the importance of sustained thinking about authentic problems that form the basis of extended in-depth inquiry in domains such as science, social studies, and mathematics. Because of this emphasis, materials that attempt to provide a breadth of factual coverage must be replaced with ones that involve opportunities for in-depth exploration. As Brown et al., 1993 argued, existing curricular guidelines of the scope and sequence variety are insufficient. These guidelines, often correlated with standardized test questions, result in disjointed survey courses.

As an illustration, consider the traditional objectives for middle-school science. Typically, objectives are concerned with categories: classifying organisms into taxonomic categories, comparing and contrasting the characteristics of living things, and identifying the forms of energy. Adequate coverage requires that each topic is a focus for a matter of days. Assessment is based on fact retrieval. Projects are typically book-like productions with sections on the various types of living things, with information about their properties, habitats and so on, mostly taken directly from an encyclopedia. Traditional objectives, thus, minimally meet cognitively based goals.

Contrast these traditional objectives with those from a unit in a Fostering Communities of Learners (FCL) classroom (A. L. Brown et al., 1993; A. L.

Brown & Campione, 1994). In this unit, the main theme is interdependence. The subthemes include photosynthesis, energy exchange, decomposition, food consumers, and food competition. Inquiry is extended over a period of months. Students generate the questions, and multiple resources including community experts are consulted. The class produces a substantial communal project, and students are involved in self-assessment.

Like FCL, the Jasper program focuses on the use of problem-based and project-based activities that sustain students' interest for four to eight weeks (e.g., CTGV, 1994). There is a preference for beginning with problem-based activities prior to moving to student-generated projects because the former provide models of effective thinking and problem solving that allow students to begin their subsequent projects on a more conceptually sophisticated level (e.g., CTGV, 1994).

The Jasper adventures are organized around sets of big ideas such as sampling in the domain of statistics, measurement in the domain of geometry, and the construction of smart tools in the domain of prealgebra and algebra. The use of Jasper videos as anchors for additional research by students permits a great deal of flexibility. Students are encouraged to identify and define their own issues that are related to anchors and to then seek relevant resources. This is very different from always being told when, where, and what to study and read.

The CSILE project does not involve a curriculum per se, but its emphasis on knowledge building rather than knowledge telling is consistent with both FCL and Jasper. Pilot studies conducted by Lamon (1993) suggest that CSILE can enhance the learning that typically takes place in contexts like Jasper and FCL where problem solving is usually face-to-face. With CSILE, face-to-face interactions can be augmented by activities that involve writing and that occur over extended periods of time. CSILE greatly enlarges the possible set of entry points through which students can participate in classroom and community activities.

It is also noteworthy that Jasper, FCL, and CSILE all support inquiry that crosses traditional subject boundaries. For example, figuring out what it means to say that an animal is endangered may mean considering problems of estimating populations, problems of sampling, and other issues more strictly considered topics in mathematics. In integrating the three projects, efforts have been made to develop cross-domain curricular units on substantive problems affording in-depth and extended study. Demonstration curricula have been developed that integrate geography, geology, topography, environmental and physical science, ancient and American history, and language arts and reading.

Changes in Instruction

All three of the SFT programs involve a change in the instructional climate of classrooms. In typical classrooms, students adopt the role of receivers of information that is dispensed by teachers, textbooks, and other media (A. L. Brown, 1992). The role of the teacher is to deliver information and manage learning. Usually, everyone is taught the same thing at the same time. Assessments typically measure how much each student learned about what was taught. As Greeno (1993) stated, "In most schools, what students mostly do is listen, watch, and mimic things that the teacher and textbook tell them and show them."

All three of the CSEP projects in SFT were informed by analyses of successful, informal learning environments that exist outside of school (e.g., B. Barron et al., 1995; Bransford & Heldmeyer, 1983; J. S. Brown, Collins, & Duguid, 1989; Lave & Wenger, 1991; Resnick, 1987; Rogoff, 1990; Senge, 1990). For example, students who participate in successful informal learning environments typically do not spend most of their time simply memorizing what others teach them. In many settings (e.g., apprenticeships), there is little formal teaching yet a great deal of learning occurs (Holt, 1964; Lave & Wenger, 1991; Sternberg & Wagner, 1986).

In SFT, students are provided with opportunities to plan and organize their own research and problem solving, plus opportunities to work collaboratively to achieve important goals (e.g., A. L. Brown et al., 1993, A. L. Brown & Campione, 1994; Collins, Hawkins, & Carver, 1991; CTGV, 1994; Lamon, 1993). In addition, these projects are consistent with an emphasis on the importance of distributed expertise (e.g., B. Barron et al., 1995; A. L. Brown et al., 1993; Pea, 1993; Pea & Gomez, 1992). Students are allowed to specialize in particular areas so that the community can capitalize on diversity. An emphasis on distributed expertise is distinctively different from environments where all students are asked to learn the same things at the same time.

Overall, the instructional strategies in SFT involve strategies for organizing the intellectual activities of students rather than strategies for delivering information. The overall goal is to help students learn to explore ideas, evaluate data, and consider opinions in a reciprocal interchange with peers, teachers and experts.

It is important to note that SFT environments are not discovery environments. A great deal of structure is necessary in order to make them work optimally. For example, teachers and other community experts maintain their focus on deep principles of the domains being studied (e.g., science, mathematics). They constantly work to help reframe student-generated questions from the perspective of these principles (e.g. A. L. Brown et al.,

1993). In this way they guide the direction of the inquiry such that students discover the deep principles of the domain. Nevertheless, within a domain such as science or mathematics, the exact issues defined by the students in the community are allowed and expected to vary from year to year. This provides an advantage of ownership and distributed expertise while also ensuring that the students learn the deep principles experts in the domain use to organize their thoughts.

Changes in Assessment

We noted earlier in this chapter that the major goal in developing Jasper, FCL, and CSILE was not to enhance scores on traditional achievement tests. If the latter were adopted as the major goal, the programs would look very different. For example, they would involve a great deal of practice with the component concepts and skills typically included on standardized achievement tests.

Three major characteristics of assessment that are common to Jasper, FCL, and CSILE are their emphasis on (a) assessment of complex, authentic performances (e.g., reading for the purpose of answering research questions; writing to build knowledge about new areas); (b) frequent opportunities for formative assessment and revision; and (c) attempts to make assessment as seamless as possible with respect to instruction and learning (e.g., Frederiksen & Collins, 1989). In all three programs, the ideal is to help students develop the ability to independently self-assess their progress and make adjustments depending on their results. By designing activities that make students' thinking visible to others, and by creating performance goals that are clear and motivating, students have frequent opportunities to "debug" their thoughts, assumptions, and arguments (cf. Goldman, Pellegrino, & Bransford, 1994).

Jasper, FCL, and CSILE are also consistent with an emphasis on outside evaluations that are summative as well as formative. These activities involve real deadlines, and they let students see how well they have accomplished particular goals. For example, the Cognition and Technology Group at Vanderbilt (CTGV) has experimented with several interactive, video-based "public performance challenges" that have been extremely motivating for students and teachers and have provided them with real deadlines and with important sets of feedback about their learning (B. Barron et al., 1995; CTGV, 1994; Goldman et al., 1994; Kantor, Moore, Bransford, & CTGV, 1993). These public performance arenas make available to the teacher many of the advantages available to coaches and music and art teachers—their students actually perform and get opportunities to reflect on their performances and decide whether and how they need to improve. Ideally, students also have opportunities to revise their ideas and to try again (much like playing the same team a second time).

All of us involved in the SFT collaborative also acknowledge the need to be accountable to larger constituencies, and hence to be subjected to traditional summative evaluations. How to generate such evaluations is a major issue. Traditional achievement tests assess the acquisition of basic skills and knowledge, but they do not assess more sophisticated levels of thinking, reasoning, or communicating, and they do not assess learning to learn. Furthermore, traditional tests are based on the assumption that everyone has had a chance to learn the same things (an assumption that is diametrically opposed to the assumptions underlying the concept of distributed expertise). Nevertheless, for the moment they are a reality that must be considered.

To meet mandated curricular objectives, projects are organized in ways that are designed to cover the objectives of each local system (e.g., a project on "Mission to Mars" covered almost 50% of the curriculum objectives in science and some of the objectives in social studies, mathematics, and health that were specified by the Nashville school system). In addition, we are currently attempting to use the problem-solving strengths of students in SFT to prepare for standardized achievement tests. This includes helping students identify how knowledge needed for the tests is potentially relevant to the projects that they have pursued in the context of SFT.

SFT also allows room for more traditional activities such as skill building. Students need to learn facts and skills that allow them to read, compute, and spell with fluency (e.g., Bransford, et al., 1988; Goldman, Mertz, & Pellegrino, 1989; Goldman, Pellegrino, & Mertz, 1988; Hasselbring, Goin, & Bransford, 1988). Knowing an answer is more efficient than computing an answer. Consequently, lack of fluency takes attentional resources away from thinking about other aspects of problems. As an illustration, consider students who have to compute the dollar value of four, six, and eight quarters rather than simply retrieve the answers from memory. Unlike most approaches to skill building, in SFT teachers and students identify and choose the sets of skills needing practice. These processes of identifying areas where one needs help, and finding ways to work on them, are extremely important for lifelong learning (e.g., Bransford & Stein, 1993).

Changes in Community

Most classrooms and teachers operate in isolation from one another and from other segments of the broader community. The Jasper, FCL, and CSILE programs each emphasize the importance of helping students and teachers see themselves both as a team and as part of a larger community. The sense of team emerges from opportunities to work collaboratively with peers on issues that students believe are important.

Within the classroom, whole-class discussions consist of interchanges among students in which the teacher is one participant. A question from either a student or the teacher initiates the discussion. The questioner calls on a volunteer to answer the question; the volunteer then "hands off" to another contributor. If the teacher wishes to contribute, he or she raises a hand and may be called on. This custom stands in sharp contrast to the traditional whole-class discussion in which the teacher poses the question, calls on a student to answer the question, often reframes or rewords the student's answer, and then provides feedback. The "passing off" interaction both reflects and fosters the sense of community in the classroom.

Technology can help break the isolation of traditional classrooms and hence provides a promising vehicle for helping students and teachers feel part of a large community. Jasper, FCL, and CSILE all encourage electronic communication with peers and outside experts. Successful technology trials have included the electronic sharing of CSILE databases, desktop videoconferencing to link groups working on common problems, as well as e-mailing outside experts. There are also useful strategies for community building that are designed to integrate classrooms with the larger community. For example, a powerful strategy is to have adults attempt to solve problems that the SFT students are working on, and let the students act as expert guides. Another is to encourage students to engage adults in discussions about the topics that they have been working on, or to let adults see examples of written discussions by students. Because of the depth of knowledge developed by the students, these strategies have worked extremely well (Brown & Campione, 1994; CTGV, 1992a, in press; Scardamalia et al., 1994).

A sense of team can also be enhanced by creating interesting, extrinsic challenges that students and teachers prepare for (e.g., B. Barron et. al., 1995; CTGV, in press). These challenges provide deadlines for meeting particular performance objectives, and this motivates teachers, students, and often entire school systems to work to meet important goals. For example, in one such challenge students across several states prepared for satellite transmission of a game show in which they were to "Pick the Expert." Contestants on the show professed to be experts in the same topic areas in which the students had been working. The challenge for the students was to use their own expertise to detect the imposters. Such challenges are most effective and motivating when they are accompanied by opportunities for students to revise their thinking and try again (B. Barron et al., 1995).

INITIAL ATTEMPTS AT IMPLEMENTATION

The preceding discussion of Jasper, FCL, and CSILE suggests that they should fit together and complement one another. There are, however, large gaps between shoulds and realities. In particular, as the proposed starting date for implementing SFT drew near (September 1993), we began to doubt whether there would be enough time in the day to attempt all three programs. And if there were, would teachers *want* to integrate the three programs? The only way we knew to answer these questions was to try.

A workshop for prospective teachers was held in August 1993. All the teachers involved in this initial phase of the SFT experiment were volunteers who shared an enthusiasm for reinventing schools according to cognitive principles. They came from Toronto, Canada; several cities in California; St. Louis, Missouri; and Nashville, Tennessee. Many had considerable experience with at least one of the three CSEP projects that formed the core of SFT; none had experience implementing all three projects: Jasper, FCL, and CSILE.

The teachers joined representatives from the three CSEP projects and participated in a one-week summer institute in which they worked with the three projects. They solved a Jasper, worked with CSILE, and learned about the FCL project from Oakland, California students who had participated in FCL. The level of knowledge and enthusiasm of the Oakland students was an inspiration to everyone. After learning about the three separate programs, the teachers developed plans for implementing SFT in their classrooms and began to establish an ongoing network for professional development.

The need for ongoing professional development became increasingly clear as the workshop proceeded. As discussions moved from theoretical overviews and data to issues of actually doing each program, the gap between theory and applications began to become clear. It gradually dawned on the researchers in the group that, as participants in the McDonnell Foundation's CSEP program for 6 years, we knew a great deal about the theoretical and empirical aspects of the three projects that comprised SFT (Jasper, FCL, CSILE). However, except for the program that each of us had developed, we discovered that we had little idea about how to get the other programs up and running with sixth-grade students. We could talk about these programs, but we could not do them. These experiences were humbling but also immensely important. They helped us develop a much deeper appreciation of the challenges faced by new teachers who were attempting to implement SFT.

It is beyond the scope of this chapter to report on the implementation efforts at all the original SFT sites. Therefore, we focus on the sites in Nashville, Tennessee. Other members of the SFT project will produce their own chapters that report on their experiences with SFT.

The Nashville Classrooms and Development Plan

We decided to focus on only two sites in Nashville and to begin with the sixth grade. The classrooms were in two different schools in the Nashville area; both were inner-city schools that served a large number of traditionally underserved students. Achievement levels of students in each classroom were in the same range as were levels throughout each school (from very low to very high). The classes included mainstreamed special education students and students identified as attention deficit disordered or learning disabled. Both classes were well balanced for gender and ethnicity. In both classes, students came from the low-income neighborhood surrounding the school; in one class additional students were bused from an integrated working-class neighborhood. The Metropolitan Nashville School System was interested enough in the project to supply the technology needed for the SFT classrooms. For each classroom, they supplied eight networked computers, a server, a printer, and a scanner plus a laser disc player and phone line for access to wide-area networks.

One of our teacher-collaborators had extensive experience with Jasper but had never used CSILE or FCL in his classroom. Our second teacher-collaborator had never worked with any of the three programs. We tried to make it clear that this was an experiment for everyone involved, that we needed the teachers' expertise, and that we greatly appreciated the teachers' willingness to take the risk of helping us invent SFT.

In an effort to ensure as much success as possible, we arranged with Nashville principals for our two teachers to have self-contained classrooms. We all thought that this would make it easier to create flexible scheduling of classtime in order to permit sustained thinking about one topic or content domain before moving on to another. We also hired project staff who served as part-time permanent team teachers. This allowed our staff to take over classrooms while the Nashville teachers met with one another and with members of our research team. These meetings were held weekly and were intended for curriculum construction, for reflecting on particular cases and episodes, and for developing progressive models of integration.

Members of our local research team visited classrooms periodically and talked with teachers about what they observed. Teachers and members of the research teams from other sites also visited our Nashville classrooms, and we visited theirs. Observing how implementation occurred in different sites allowed teachers and researchers to separate variations that remain faithful to cognitive principles of SFT and those that do not. Haertel (personal communication) has called the latter variations "lethal mutations."

Integrating the Programs

The weekly meetings, plus feedback from other SFT sites, helped us develop models for how Jasper adventures could be integrated with CSILE and FCL. In this section, we describe the curriculum units developed collaboratively by the teachers and research staff. Nashville classrooms began with a relatively short (3-week) starter unit. The purpose of this unit was to introduce the participation structures of SFT and have the students experience the research *process* from start to finish. We were less concerned about getting at deep principles with this first starter unit.

By way of example, Nashville classrooms began with the Jasper adventure "Rescue at Boone's Meadow," which involves the use of an ultralight to save a wounded eagle (CTGV, 1992a, 1993b). In addition to solving the adventure, in one class (the experienced Jasper teacher's class) students used reciprocal teaching and jigsaw groups as they conducted research on topics relevant to the adventure (e.g., eagles, principles of flight, first aid). Students also used CSILE to communicate about their topics and draw pictures to illustrate their ideas. By the middle of November, this sixth-grade class had produced a report (complete with CSILE graphics) on their topics. The other class was not equipped with computers until the beginning of November and so they only solved the adventure using some of the participation structures.

During the remainder of the year, two major units were undertaken, each lasting approximately 3 months. In November, the SFT classrooms began a "Mission to Mars" unit that dealt with issues in physical science, mathematics, health, social studies, and language arts. The unit was anchored around a video designed to help students generate questions relevant to a trip to Mars and back without giving them solutions (Hickey et al., 1992; Sherwood, Petrosino, Lin, Lamon, & CTGV, 1995). Students also related this video to Jasper adventures involving trip planning, the use of geometry for wayfinding, and business planning (to fund worthy projects).

History was covered by considering similarities and differences between possible colonization on Mars and colonization of Rome. If there were resources on Mars, what would we do with them? What did the Romans do with natural resources in their colonies? Throughout this unit, students engaged in reciprocal teaching to understand difficult texts that they were using in their research; they recorded their research and their questions in CSILE; and jigsaw sessions were used for revising their written reports.

The third major project undertaken in Nashville sites involved an extensive unit on endangered species. By this point in the year (spring 1994), students were quite familiar with Jasper, FCL, and CSILE, and their research and collaborative editing went quite smoothly. In addition to social studies, literature that emphasized some of the important underlying themes from the science and social studies units was included in the curriculum as well.

By the end of the school year, all members of our SFT team (the teachers, researchers, and support staff) were convinced that the idea of SFT classrooms was both revolutionary and exciting. What convinced us were the levels of knowledge and enthusiasm of the students. Students in one of the classrooms reached levels of achievement in speaking, reading, writing, and technology that were extraordinary. Students in the second classroom did not advance quite as much, but their progress was nevertheless noteworthy.

The slower progress of the students in the second classroom was due to several reasons. First, their ability to implement SFT was delayed because of overcrowding and lateness in delivery of computer equipment and security devices. It was not until November that the physical and technological situation in the classroom stabilized. Second and more important, it took members of our research team a considerable amount of time to learn how to interact with the teacher in a way that worked. Both teachers had to make monumental changes to implement SFT. Our research group was more familiar with one of the teachers and, inadvertently, undermined the confidence of the second teacher during the first several months of the project. We think we have repaired the situation, and the second teacher is implementing SFT this year during a portion of the school day. She has completed a major unit on recycling and is focusing SFT activities around science and math content areas. But our research group had to learn some hard lessons about ways to provide feedback without seeming overly critical.

Indicators of Achievement

Due to the extremely time-consuming process of simply attempting to get our SFT classrooms up and running, we were not able to be as systematic about collecting data as we would have liked. Nevertheless, there are some tangible signs of the progress that students made. Our discussion focuses primarily on one of the classrooms because the second had only a partial year implementation of SFT due to the delays in getting started discussed earlier.

The students themselves were excited by their progress and eager to continue in the SFT program. Talking with them in person is the best way to become convinced of the value of the program. Unfortunately, the present medium does not allow interaction of this kind.

A proxy for talking with the students is to consider the reactions of people who had this opportunity. An important set of reactions came from the superintendent and other officials of the Nashville School System who met with the SFT students. The system representatives decided that the SFT students should have the option of continuing in SFT classrooms when they went on to the seventh grade.

Another group that had opportunities to talk with the SFT students was their parents. Although some were worried about the program at the beginning of the year, they were extremely enthusiastic by the year's end. Parents reported a number of interactions with their children that impressed them. A frequent example involved amazement that their children now had something to talk about when asked, "What did you do in school today?" Students brought home the substantive issues they were researching to discuss with their parents. They reported interesting information, discussed issues, and made connections to their own world. They regularly brought in resources from home or the library. Students' attendance improved over previous years and several parents even avoided moving so their children would not have to transfer to another school.

Parents made known to Metropolitan School System administrators their enthusiasm about the program and conveyed their delight at their children's changed attitudes toward school. Their dedication, together with the students' extraordinary products and performances, convinced Metropolitan School System administrators to develop a corridor by expanding the program for the next year into the seventh grade and providing technology funding for six additional classrooms. A continuing grant from the McDonnell Foundation allows us to provide support staff for this growth in implementation.

A second way to understand the value of SFT is to explore the students' products. They were extremely impressive, especially the ones produced in the second half of the school year. In the Appendix, we present some sample pages from the student-generated publications that constituted the culminating projects for the "Mission to Mars" and for the "Endangered Species" units. These products were developed almost entirely through student collaboration. Students worked in "expert" groups to develop and research ideas and write about their topics. Then they used jigsaw groups to evaluate and revise what they had written. Teachers managed the process but did not explicitly edit the texts.

The "Endangered Species" product was a 180-page illustrated research report that was better than almost anything we have seen from sixth-grade classrooms. The sample pages provided in the Appendix illustrate this quality. Equally impressive were students' abilities to explain in person what they had learned from their research projects.

Written products collected from students showed a marked increase in quality over the course of the school year for every student. A comparison of one student's first drafts of short reports of field trips taken in August and in February gives a sense of these changes:

August: Mr. (Teacher's Name)'s class went to Vanderbilt. When we got there. We heard a presentation about Jasper. We eat papa Johns pizza the we left. I liked the chairs and Vanderbilt.

February: Recently the Maclearner classroom was working on a mission to Mars. At the Cumberland Museum and worked with Commander Bradshall to the mission to Mars. In the spacecraft you had 6 groups working on different things. The six groups are surface, crew, health, spacecraft, history, and trip. We need surface to tell us a good place to land on Mars. The crew gave us our food to eat when we were hungry. The health group video and interview all of the groups to find out how they were doing. Spacecraft would fix little things on the spacecraft. History gathered us information about the past flights. Trip gets everything together for the mission. Technology gives us information about storms. By all of us working together we succeeded with our mission.

Students wrote more, organized better, used better and more complex sentence structure, and improved in punctuation, capitalization, and usage. This is not to say their writing was error free. However, the depth of their knowledge and their abilities to express it were impressive. This improvement has carried over to the next year, where their new teachers can pick second year SFT students out of the class by looking at writing samples.

We conducted a diagnostic assessment of students' reading strategies twice during the year, once in February and once in June.[1] We focused on the extent to which the strategies students used in reciprocal teaching were reflected in their individual reading behavior. We had students read expository passages of approximately 300 words and provide us with think-aloud protocols (cf., Coté et al., 1994; Goldman, Coté, & Saul, 1994; Saul, Coté,

---

[1]Nathalie Coté, Leilani Gjellstad, Julie Keeton, Carolyn Millican, Kristen Gottschalk, and Mark Frymire were instrumental in conducting this phase of the project.

& Goldman, 1993). We were particularly interested in the degree to which they engaged in self-explanation, made predictions about the text, and monitored their comprehension. These three kinds of activities are integral to the reciprocal teaching process. These kinds of behaviors index active "seeking after meaning" and are associated with superior comprehension and the formation of more coherent representations of the information (e.g., Chi, deLeeuw, Chiu, & LaVancher, 1994; Coté et al., 1994; Goldman, Coté et al., 1994; Saul et al., 1993).

The total number of events (i.e., comments) coded from the think-alouds was approximately equal at the two testing times. The percentage of events that were self-explanations increased (from 63% to 72%) while the percentages of monitoring decreased (from 22% to 17%). There was a smaller decrease in paraphrasing (from 7% to 4%). Predicting (6% to 4%) and associations irrelevant to the meaning of the text (approximately 2% at both times) stayed about the same. This pattern of changes is consistent with improvements in the children's active and strategic behavior in developing coherent representations of the information.

Particularly important is the decrease in paraphrasing and the increase in self-explaining. Paraphrasing merely rearranges the words in the sentence; it does not add anything to it. In contrast, self-explanations make connections to prior knowledge, among different sentences in the text, and include questions about the kinds of information that the reader would still like to know. These questions reflect a type of comprehension monitoring that we distinguish from comments such as "I don't get that," monitoring statements that do little to augment representations of the information and that decreased from the first to second testing. We also differentiated among the self-explanations in terms of using prior knowledge to reason about presented information and attempts to cross-connect among sentences in the text. All these behaviors increased from the first to second testing.

An example of the kind of changes that occurred is illustrated by one student's protocol. For this student, the percentage of paraphrases dropped from 56% to 8% from the first to second assessment and the percentage of self-explanations increased from 16% to 77%. Put another way, paraphrases occurred on 18 of the 28 sentences during the first assessment but on only 3 during the second assessment. The following excerpts provide examples of comments made during the first think-aloud (sentences from the text are numbered; the student's comments are preceded by S):

13.   Eating too much processed sugar can be harmful to our health in three ways.
      S: It says if you eat too much processed sugar, it'll be harmful.

25. Eating too much sugar can lead to being overweight.
S: Sugar can cause you to be overweight.

28. In fact, many foods that have a lot of processed sugar also contain fat.
S: Food with processed sugar contains fat.

Comments from the second assessment illustrate the changes:

7. But our bodies only need a very small amount of fat to be healthy.
S: So I don't need a lot of fats.

12. Plant foods usually have less harmful kinds of fat.
S: So, salads are good for you.

17. If we eat too much of it, it will slowly clog the walls of our blood vessels.
S: Like, blood won't be able to shoot to different parts of the body because of saturated fat.

Similar kinds of changes occurred in many of the other students' protocols. It is also interesting to note that the coherence of this student's recall of the information increased as well, although the total number of statements recalled did not increase.

Systematic interviews conducted with a subset of the SFT students throughout the course of the year indicated important changes in their perspectives on research and learning. For example, at the end of the year students often laughed about their earlier ideas of research, which had consisted of finding a paragraph or two in an encyclopedia and copying it. Each of the students interviewed commented on the changes in their appreciation of thorough rather than superficial research.

Students also showed increased sophistication in their views about research as a process of knowledge building rather than knowledge telling. When asked what they would do when reading about a new topic, a typical response was "find out what I don't understand and write it in my field journal." The idea of focusing on areas in need of further work is extremely positive. It reflects a culture of "knowledge building" that is emphasized in CSILE (Bereiter & Scardamalia, 1989; Scardamalia et al., 1992; Scardamalia, Bereiter, & Lamon, 1994) as well as the other programs involved in SFT. It is the kind of attitude needed for lifelong learning. The development of a classroom culture that emphasized knowledge building was an extremely positive development.

The students also developed a good intuitive grasp of the nature and purpose of experimentation in science. Students participated in a number of different types of experiments. For example, the "Mission to Mars" theme and the Jasper adventures lent themselves to experimentation with wing design (for paper airplanes) as well as principles of flight and reentry (for model rockets). One student's description expresses the view held by most of them by the end of the year: "You test out what you have read about in your research."

The SFT students developed a commitment to thorough research—they liked the challenge of doing it. We did not simply learn this from their statements, we also saw it in their behavior when we visited classrooms. Students were clearly engaged in the hard work of finding relevant articles for their research, reading (often using reciprocal teaching to work collaboratively) and writing. In interviews at the end of the year, many echoed the sentiments of one student who said: "They don't do the work for us. We *get* to do the research."

Students also became extraordinarily proficient with technology. This was one of the most visible aspects of the SFT program, and one to which students, parents and administrators could easily relate. Other teachers in the schools often visited the classrooms to ask students to do technology-related tasks for them, such as creating banners, posters, and flyers. The technology allowed the students to create real products that others in the school valued and used. Students were very proud of their technological proficiency, which was never taught as an end in itself, but only as a tool for recording research, creating graphics, or other useful products.

The cohesion of the students was extraordinary. The participation structures established by the teacher emphasized the importance of developing expertise in specific areas. The topics that individual groups researched were designed so that each group would find something important for their work in the work of the other groups. This interdependence among the groups fostered a classroom culture in which students learned to listen to each other and respect each other's ideas. In this regard, CSILE played an important role. Students reported that they enjoyed being able to find out what all their classmates thought, rather than just what the "talkers" thought. CSILE also allowed students who had been absent due to illness to quickly catch up with the class and with their group.

The fact that the SFT classrooms involved technology also helped build group cohesion. Different students became experts at different aspects of the technology. In CSILE, for example, some students were especially good at graphics and helped others learn about this aspect of communication. Other students were more proficient at writing and organizing verbal information. Different students also became the class experts (and teachers) in additional areas of technology such as specific CD-ROM programs and databases that were available in the classroom, particular software programs such as graph- and banner-making software, and specialized software such as desktop videoconferencing and other connections to wide-area networks.

The use of groups for most activities also increased the value of group management and interpersonal skills. For some students, this was the first time that their social/interpersonal expertise was integral to the work of the classroom. The fact that their expertise in these areas was valued and acknowledged by the other students in the class seemed to spur their academic work.

The fact that students could specialize in different areas had another effect that we had not anticipated initially. We had expected that the ability to specialize would build self-esteem because each student would discover that he or she was able to contribute something to the community. However, we also found that the multiple opportunities for learning made available in SFT classrooms also provided students with opportunities to be novices who initially had difficulty. For some of the students in the SFT classrooms, this was a "first time" experience. One girl wrote in CSILE that she was frustrated by not being able to make faster progress in learning some computer skills. She then wrote that she now knew what it felt like to be a beginner, a feeling she had never consciously experienced before. Experiences such as these seemed to help students better understand the struggles of their classmates who had less experience in particular domains.

The students' collaborative spirit was an aspect of the program that was apparent to observers. After a 3-day field trip to a conservation camp, the camp director asked the teacher what was being done differently than in previous years. The teacher wondered why the director had asked the question, and reported the director's response: "We have school groups through here every day, and I have to tell you that your group is one of the most integrated I've seen. I didn't see any cliques. They didn't separate themselves into boys and girls or black and white. All I saw were kids walking together, talking together, working together" (Monin, 1994).

The students' accomplishments were evident to themselves as well as to us and other observers. Data collected on self-esteem are relevant to this point. Petrosino, Secules, Goldman, Lamon, and Bransford (in progress) measured changes in self-esteem of students in one SFT class as they progressed through the school year and compared those changes to a closely matched control class. Children in both the SFT and control classes were tested in early November 1993 (two months after SFT had started) and in mid-June 1994 using the "What I Am Like" scale developed by Harter

(1985). This scale assesses the degree to which children like themselves as people and are happy with the way their life is progressing. The November assessment indicated that the SFT students had higher self-esteem scores than the control classroom. Because students had been assigned randomly to the SFT and control classes, we assume that these early differences were due to the fact that the SFT program had been in operation for two months.

Even more important, the mid-June data showed a significantly greater increase in self-esteem for students in SFT compared to students in the comparison class. Analysis of covariance, using the November performance as the covariate, indicated that SFT students reported significantly higher estimates of global self-worth than students in the control class. This was true across genders and there was no interaction between group and gender.

Although limited in scope, these results accord well with informally collected parent, teacher, and student reports about student perceptions of themselves as learners. We are currently pursuing additional data collection on self-esteem, including questions posed to students to respond to in the CSILE environment.

Other Indicators of Achievement: Standardized Tests

The previous discussion focused on observations of student understanding and motivation that are theoretically consistent with the SFT philosophy. Our work in Nashville also provided us with an opportunity to assess how SFT students would look when reflected through a different set of lenses—those involved in the Tennessee Comprehensive Assessment Profile (TCAP). Many observers of SFT classrooms believed that SFT students would knock the top off the TCAPs. Others (ourselves included) were concerned that the tests would fail to reflect the sophisticated gains in skill, knowledge, and motivation that seemed so apparent when one talked with the SFT students (e.g., Frederiksen & Collins, 1989; Goldman, Pellegrino, & Bransford, 1994). Our hopes for the TCAP during the first year of SFT were that we would "do no harm" (i.e., that SFT students would not score lower than other students, especially those in their school).

There are several reasons why we did not expect extraordinary scores on the TCAP. First, administration of the TCAP occurred in early April, 2 months prior to the end of school and before some of the most exciting SFT activities were begun. Second, students did not spend the year explicitly practicing skills for the test nor did the teacher gear the curriculum to the test (cf., Frederiksen & Collins, 1989). Third, SFT classrooms are concerned with deep understanding of a few topics rather than shallow coverage of many topics. As a result, there was the potential that content tapped by the

Grade 6 TCAP would not have been covered by our SFT classrooms. We noted earlier that one of our units, "Mission to Mars," covered about 50% of the Tennessee science objectives, as well as some of the objectives in other content areas. But our curricula did not necessarily encompass all of the objectives. Furthermore, the TCAP is designed as most achievement tests are: to have no ceiling. As a consequence, students covering only Grade 6 curricula should not score at the top of the scale, i.e., 90th percentile plus.

These caveats notwithstanding, the performance of the SFT sixth graders was above the national norms in the five areas for which these comparisons are provided by the state of Tennessee: math, reading, language, social studies, and science. The TCAP also reports gain scores that reflect how much has been learned during the year. Compared to other students in their own school in these five areas, SFT students' gain scores were comparable in overall math and reading scores. But the gains were not extraordinary.

Mathematics. In math, SFT students showed no gains in math computation but impressive gains in math concepts. These data fit our expectations. SFT students did not frequently drill computation skills during the year. The SFT students' work on Jasper should have helped them develop an understanding of mathematical concepts that, at least in part, were assessed on the TCAP test (e.g., CTGV, 1992b; Pellegrino et al., 1991).

Reading Comprehension, Vocabulary, Spelling. Reading comprehension, vocabulary, and spelling all showed gains over fifth-grade performance. (Data on the subtests are not available for the national normative sample nor for the other sixth-grade classes in the school.) Gains in these areas should be expected; SFT students did a great deal of reading and writing about complex subject matters. Still, the gains were not extraordinary. One reason may be that it took considerable time to get activities such as reciprocal teaching to proficient levels. A. L. Brown and Campione (1994) are much better at helping teachers and students learn to engage in reciprocal teaching than we are—we have considerable room to improve. Another reason why gains for the SFT students were not extraordinary probably involves mismatches between SFT activities and the TCAP. For example, reading comprehension measures on the TCAP do not assess students' abilities to define a topic, select research articles, read them for the purpose of learning about that topic, and then write about one's findings and about needs for more information. Similarly, vocabulary items tested on the TCAP did not assess the sophisticated levels of knowledge that students acquired given their deep exploration of a few content domains.

Language Mechanics.   The language mechanics portion of the TCAP measures punctuation, grammar, and usage. The SFT students showed a slight drop in this area. The SFT students' performances on the language mechanics test stands in marked contrast to their writing samples and oral performances in class (see our earlier discussion). This contrast is most easily understood by considering the kinds of competencies tapped by each. On the TCAP, language mechanics is a multiple choice test. A sample item from the preparation materials for this test gives a sense of the test:

Choose the adjective or adverb that completes the sentence CORRECTLY.

He can work   than I can.

a) oftener
b) less often
c) least often
d) most often

An emphasis on mechanics rather than on important ideas is the opposite of the SFT philosophy. In SFT, students' write for real audiences (their peers, teachers, and members of the community). Their primary goal is to make sure that they have something meaningful to say. They also have access to resources such as dictionaries and peers who can help them with mechanics.

Our comparisons of individuals' writing samples from the beginning to the end of the year showed dramatic changes in sophistication of ideas communicated, and also showed clear improvement in mechanics even when students had no access to other resources while generating their writing samples. Nevertheless, these improvements did not show up on the mechanics portion of the TCAP test. Tennessee is currently piloting a writing test. We expect SFT students to show significantly higher scores than the average on this new test in future years.

Science and Social Studies.   There were two scales on the TCAP on which SFT students performed particularly poorly: the science and the social studies scale. We think performance on these scales reflects the breadth versus depth of coverage issue.

The SFT students' performance in science knowledge did not reflect any gains while their nonSFT peers registered small gains in performance. In contrast, when we interviewed the SFT students about adaptation and endangered species, a very different picture of their science knowledge emerged. They had acquired well-differentiated ideas about endangerment, the importance of preserving habitat, recovery, the impact of economic and political forces on the environment and scientific exploration, interdependence among life support systems, and so forth. And, as described before, their appreciation and understanding of the nature of the scientific research process had changed enormously. Gains of these types were not measured by the TCAP.

The SFT students' gains in social studies were considerably lower than social studies gains by the other students in the school. This is understandable for several reasons. First, we had originally intended to exclude social studies from the SFT curriculum and teach it in a traditional matter. However, after 2 months the teacher decided that the SFT philosophy should be used for the entire curriculum, not just science, math, and language arts. As a consequence, the social studies units were not as carefully prepared as they might have been had there been more time for planning and preparation of these units. In addition, during previous years of teaching the teacher had been departmentalized, teaching primarily math for a number of years.

After a year of experience, it is clear to us that the SFT philosophy is as applicable to social studies as it is to science, mathematics, and language arts. We also have much better ideas of how to integrate social studies instruction with other aspects of the SFT curriculum. Nevertheless, when it comes to tests such as the TCAP, it seems clear that the issue of breadth versus depth of coverage is going to be as problematic in social studies as it is in all the other areas of the test.

LESSONS LEARNED AND IMPLICATIONS FOR EXPANDING SFT

Our goal in this section is to discuss some lessons learned and some ways we plan to address the issues raised by these lessons. We draw primarily on our experiences with the two Nashville classrooms, but the issues we discuss have arisen at all of the sites.

Lessons About Synergy

The major lessons we learned are that it is indeed possible to integrate FCL, CSILE and Jasper within a single classroom and that the three programs have the potential to operate synergistically. In our experience, each of the three programs adds something important to classrooms. A summary of our perspective on these contributions appears in the following list.

From Jasper:
• Complex, authentic problems with links across the curriculum,
• Assessment challenges
• Anchors for community building

From FCL:
• Students as researchers
• Focus on deep principles
• Distributed expertise and support for it (i.e., reciprocal teaching & jigsaw)

From CSILE:
• Emphasis on knowledge building
• Avenues for reflective communication
• Opportunities for connectedness and assessment of progress

The Jasper series provides complex, authentic problems that focus on "big ideas" in mathematics and that provide links to other subject areas such as science, history, and social studies. In addition, the Jasper assessment programs provide a model for encouraging ongoing, formative assessment as teachers and students work together to prepare for relevant, interesting challenges that come from outside the classroom (our assumption is that "nothing unites like a common enemy"). In addition the fact that Jasper videos are short, interesting, and complex to solve make them ideal environments for helping teachers, parents, administrators, and other community members build a sense of community. Ideally, the adults attempt to solve the challenges collaboratively and students act as their guides (CTGV, 1994).

FCL provides an emphasis on community that is based on the notion of students as researchers who focus on deep principles. This focus is important because it gives students access to fundamental concepts that help them see underlying similarities between one aspect of a domain (e.g., research on whales) and another (e.g., research on eagles). The FCL culture also emphasizes distributed expertise. In our experience, this is an extremely important concept that plays a fundamental role in developing a sense of community and collaboration. The activity structures of reciprocal teaching and jigsaw provide support for the interactions needed to help students collaborate.

CSILE provides an emphasis on knowledge building, plus a mechanism for reflective conversations and communication. Many students do not talk a great deal in face-to-face situations and seem to prefer an environment such as CSILE. Other students like face-to-face conversations, but also appreciate the opportunities that CSILE provides to reflect on their thoughts. The development of wide-area CSILE also has the potential to promote a connectedness among classrooms and schools that is beneficial for both students and teachers. In addition, teacher tools such as the ones developed by Cohen (1994) and the CSILE team allow teachers to efficiently search the CSILE database in order to identify fruitful conversations as well as keep track of who is contributing and who needs a push.

Lessons About Student Potential

The classroom communities developed through the integration of Jasper, FCL, and CSILE have been exciting to observe and have convinced us that it is indeed possible for students to reach extraordinary levels of achievement. At this point in time it is extremely difficult for us to be satisfied with anything less than the levels of achievement that we have seen.

We do not wish to argue that only FCL, CSILE, and Jasper are capable of producing these levels of achievement. It seems clear that many other programs have the potential to produce similar outcomes. Our point is simply that we have witnessed a level of student engagement and achievement that we had never seen before.

Lessons About the Challenges of Change

A third major lesson we have learned is that it is extremely challenging to create SFT classrooms. Learning FCL, CSILE, and Jasper simultaneously was overwhelming for teachers across all the sites involved in the first-year implementation of SFT. Even teachers who already had experience with one component of the program discovered that the need to develop expertise in the other programs was still time-consuming and exhausting. All teachers spent considerably more than eight hours per day in strenuous intellectual and emotional efforts.

Readers familiar with school reform efforts will recognize that the SFT teachers in Nashville invested a great deal more personal time in the SFT project than many teachers will want to invest. In addition, the teachers had access to opportunities and resources that are rarely available. For example, only a very small number of teachers have opportunities to meet weekly with their colleagues in order to plan and discuss new ideas—*and* do this during school time while qualified people who know their students take over their classrooms. Furthermore, only a small number of teachers have access to other important aspects of SFT classrooms such as computer technology and content experts who can help them and their students acquire complex subject-matter knowledge.

During the second year of our work (which now covers five classrooms in Grade 6 and four in Grade 7), we have continued to supply resources such as planning time (made possible by staff who cover the teachers' classes) and access to expertise in both pedagogy and content knowledge. We realize that the availability of resources such as these represent the rare exception rather than the rule, and that it will be hard to maintain this level of support as the SFT program expands to even more classrooms in subsequent years. A major challenge is to explore ways to maintain the quality of the SFT experience while simultaneously making it easier for newcomers to develop their own SFT classrooms. Clearly, this issue of "scaling up while ensuring quality" is an issue for any attempt to restructure education—it is not simply an issue for SFT. This brings us to the fourth lesson.

Lessons About the Need for Tools for Community Building

A fourth lesson we have learned is that teachers need tools to help them get started in the process of developing SFT classrooms. We are fortunate to have received funding from the Mellon Foundation for a program of research that intersects perfectly with the SFT project and is helping us develop such tools.[2] The Mellon project is funding a consortium of researchers who are all focusing on ways to help both preservice and inservice teachers re-invent Brown and Campione's FCL project in their own classrooms.[3] Because FCL is such an integral part of the SFT project, the Mellon project informs the SFT project, and vice versa.

The Nashville role in the Mellon consortium is to design and study ways that technology can provide tools for the community building needed for FCL and SFT classrooms. Our discussions with our collaborators on the Mellon project, as well as our experiences with the SFT project, have suggested a need to develop "starter units" that provide scaffolds for teachers who are new to FCL and SFT classrooms. Furthermore, we need to provide them with "performance support tools" that they can continually refer to as they work in SFT classrooms. We discuss each of these in the next section and explain how their development is related to our experiences with SFT.

---

[2]In addition to John Bransford, Susan Goldman, and Teresa Secules, Ted Hasselbring, Katherine Burgess, and Bunny Bransford are working on this project.

[3]Collaborators on the Mellon Project are Steve Athanases, Ann Brown, Joe Campione, Marilyn Chambliss, Ed Haertle, Milbrey McLaughlin, Nancy Sato, Judy Shulman, Lee Shulman, Lauren Sosniak, Joan Talbert, Joel Westheimer, and Jennie Whitcomb.

STARTER UNITS FOR FCL AND SFT

The idea that new teachers of FCL or SFT have to begin somewhere does not seem particularly controversial. However, the idea of developing starter units becomes more interesting and controversial when one explores how the goals of FCL and SFT relate to different ways that teachers might start.

One approach to the development of starter units is to provide new teachers with descriptions of the theoretical basis of a program and expect them to generate examples that fit their classrooms. As we discussed earlier, the initial workshop on SFT taught us that this approach does not work. As researchers, we were very familiar with the theory of FCL and CSILE, and our colleagues were familiar with the theory behind Jasper. But when it came to translating theory into practice, all of us hit a blank wall. We needed lots of help.

A second approach to the development of starter units is to augment approach 1, with at least one example of a well-developed unit complete with support for curriculum (e.g., a list of appropriate deep principles to emphasize plus some research materials for exploring these principles), instruction (e.g., explanations for how to do reciprocal teaching and jigsaw), and assessment (e.g., materials and procedures for making students' thinking about the curriculum visible). There are many advantages to this approach, but there are disadvantages as well (see Collins, 1996, for examples of design-decision tradeoffs).

The advantage of providing teachers with a worked-out unit is that they have a concrete example that they can use in their classrooms. The disadvantage is that the teachers are simply given a prescription for how to teach that they can follow relatively passively. In Brophy's terms, they are being taught to "follow the prescriptions of absentee curriculum developers" (Brophy & Alleman, 1992). This approach to working with teachers directly contradicts the idea of collaborative community building that is fundamental to FCL and SFT.

The approach to starter units that the Mellon collaborative is beginning to explore is one that focuses on *tools for community building*. We begin by providing a group with a common experience that serves as a basis for researching interesting questions that are generated by the group (community), and explored by using activity structures such as reciprocal teaching and jigsaw teaching. In short, we want to allow teachers and other community members (administrators, business leaders) to experience what it is like to do FCL and SFT. This involves helping them discover that the resources are within them to begin to generate interesting questions and make use of the distributed expertise of their current group (community). This is very different from simply being handed a curriculum unit plus a teaching script to follow.

Our initial starter unit is organized around *Bridging the Gap,* a specially designed Jasper adventure developed in collaboration with Ann Brown, Joe Campione and other members of the Mellon collaborative. It features principles of sampling and statistics in the context of an endangered species theme. The adventure gives teachers the option of focusing on many different levels of mathematics. In addition, or as an alternative, teachers can focus students' attention on issues of endangered species that are introduced in the video.

Accompanying the Jasper video are CD-ROM-based text and video materials that can be used to research issues suggested by the video. These materials are being developed so that multiple sources must be consulted in order to explore issues adequately. Our goal is to make hard-to-find research materials easily accessible. However, students have to search through numerous documents in order to conduct their research. We do not want to provide documents that give "the answer" to a set of math or science questions that the community may ask.

Based on our experiences (CTGV, 1994), the use of *Bridging the Gap* as an anchor for learning about FCL or SFT is an excellent way to begin professional development workshops. Everyone first watches the video and then collaboratively generates issues and explores them. Discussions of the theory that underlie these activities come later in the workshop. The availability of CD-ROM research materials (which can also be distributed as text materials) means that people who attend the workshops can actually "do" FCL or SFT rather than simply be told about it. Teachers can then take these materials and try them in their own classroom community.

Because issues and interests are generated by the community rather than supplied by the teachers, the classroom experience of using the Jasper anchor will not be identical to what happened when the teachers used the anchor with their peers. The Jasper anchor video is relatively short (approximately 17 minutes), and, therefore, teachers can also use it to help administrators, parents, and other members of the community experience what it is like to do FCL or SFT. Ideally, experienced FCL or SFT students will act as guides for the adults (CTGV, 1994).

A major goal of the Mellon project is to conduct research on the strengths and weaknesses of various designs for starter units. Our research plans include audiences of both preservice and inservice teachers. We expect to need several design-test-redesign cycles in order to create starter units that are beneficial.

PERFORMANCE SUPPORT TOOLS (PSSTs)
FOR FCL AND SFT

In addition to developing and testing starter units, the Mellon project includes plans for the design of performance support tools (PSSTs) that are accessible to teachers whenever they want them. Some of these tools will take the form of CD-ROM-based video, audio, and text materials. Others will take the form of networks that link SFT teachers with one another as well as with sources of content and pedagogy expertise. Work by other members of the research community is very valuable for helping us think about the design of such tools (e.g., L. Barron & Goldman, 1994; Duffy, in press; Kinzer, 1993; Lampert & Ball, 1990; Pea & Gomez, 1992; Risko, 1993).

We propose to make PSSTs available to teachers because numerous questions about FCL and SFT begin to arise only after teachers have tried particular activities in their classrooms. Teachers need support in order to evaluate their efforts and relate them to the theoretical principles that underlie FCL and SFT. Teachers also need to see that there is not simply one way to achieve the objectives of FCL and SFT. We want to avoid mere procedural recipes for how to do FCL and SFT, and instead, promote conceptual understanding. One way to achieve this goal is to provide teaching vignettes that illustrate flexibility of procedures without creating "lethal mutations" (E. H. Haertel, personal communication June, 1994).

An initial PSST that we are developing focuses on one component of FCL and SFT that is very important yet difficult to get started: reciprocal teaching. The concept of reciprocal teaching can be understood at many different levels. Particularly challenging is the goal of helping new teachers understand the purposes of reciprocal teaching at a conceptual level rather than simply think of it as a procedure (e.g., questioning, clarifying, summarizing, and predicting) that must always be followed in strict linear order.

Our work to create a PSST for reciprocal teaching is just beginning. We are fortunate to have video of both Ann Brown and Ann Marie Palincsar explaining the purposes and genesis of the procedure. We also have video of groups of adults and students doing reciprocal teaching. However, we find that simply watching videos of groups of students engaged in reciprocal teaching is not sufficient for achieving the goal of doing reciprocal teaching in a flexible manner. We are in the process of designing multimedia systems that provide teachers with simulations that let them lead a reciprocal teaching session and, over time, fade themselves out of the picture. After teachers make decisions about how to proceed, they have the option of receiving expert commentary about different moves that the experts might have made in each situation and why.

A second PSST that we are developing attempts to provide a bigger picture of FCL and SFT classrooms and is organized around the Jasper video *Bridging the Gap*. It goes beyond the starter units by including visual examples of different ways to use this anchor in the classroom, plus explanations of how these examples relate to key theoretical principles. In addition, we are including expert discussion of the deep principles of biology and ecology (e.g., biodiversity, interdependence) that can be developed within the context of the topic of endangered species, plus samples of content experts and master teachers building on and deepening the ideas that students have discovered in their research.

An especially important feature of the PSST we are developing is that it provides video access to teachers who are at various stages of attempting to implement FCL or SFT in their own classrooms. What did they find difficult? What strategies did they use to help them get started (e.g., many began with only one or two of the programs in SFT before adding the second or third)? What are some changes they saw in students that gave them the courage to keep going even though they knew that things were not perfect? How did they inform parents about the goals of SFT? How did they deal with issues of giving grades? How did they keep up with new technology and debug existing technology that was not working? What happened when students took standardized tests, and how could one ensure that student test scores would be good?

There are multiple answers to each of the preceding questions, and there are additional questions that new SFT teachers face almost daily. We are in the process of documenting these and cataloguing different approaches taken to each one. For example, in some SFT classrooms the students are being encouraged to take some time at the end of each unit to map sample test items from the state mandated standardized tests into the projects that they are currently working on, and to make sure that everyone understands how to solve these problems. As an illustration, consider the following sample test item:

Traveling at the rate of 900 kilometers in 1 hour, how many kilometers could one travel in 15 minutes?

a) 225 km
b) 270 km
c) 3,600 km
d) 13,500 km

Students work in expert groups to focus on different types of problems and then jigsaw in order to teach one another about their relevance and how to solve them. For example, the preceding problem is directly relevant to some of the trip-planning scenarios involved in Jasper adventures such as *Journey to Cedar Creek, Rescue at Boone's Meadow*, and *Get out the Vote*. Focusing on relationships between the achievement tests and Jasper helps students learn to look for the potential relevance of decontextualized problems, and it adds a reason for practicing the basic skills involved in Jasper. The exercise can also broaden students' learning. For example, in the preceding problem the units involve kilometers; in the Jasper adventures they involve miles.

In other classrooms, students and teachers are taking a distributed expertise approach to learning about key aspects of technology. Some groups learn how to use the Jasper software, some become experts in CSILE graphics, others learn how to access the Internet, and so forth. Then they teach one another in jigsaw groups. Similar strategies can be applied to the goal of developing expertise in common problems that arise in classrooms, for example, problems involving the network. One of the goals of our PSSTs is to help teachers and students learn to use the power of the community to handle common problems and challenges that arise.

We also want our PSSTs to include information about basic infrastructure support that is needed for SFT classrooms. For example, there is a level of infrastructure support needed for any classroom to be equipped with upwards of eight computers and other technological gear. Infrastructure needs include technological support personnel who can design and implement networks, troubleshoot problems involved with telecommunications, and generally handle hardware kinds of problems that go beyond the specific applications with which students and teachers are working. Through our McDonnell support, we are currently able to furnish such a person, but the school district clearly needs to take a leadership role in this area. Eventually, we need ways to help district experts work with the students in the classroom in order to distribute the district's expertise.

BEYOND STAND-ALONE SYSTEMS

No matter how much information we put into our PSSTs, we believe that something more will be needed, namely, the ability to communicate with others around the country in order to raise questions and receive suggestions and advice. Therefore, we plan to supplement our stand-alone tools (Starter Units and PSSTs) with networking tools.

Simple examples of networking tools involve e-mail connections among teachers at other SFT sights. Others involve the possibility of a wide-area TeleCSILE for teachers and other professionals that is being developed by Scardamalia, Bereiter, and colleagues. We also want to experiment with the advantages of Internet resources such as the World Wide Web and desktop videoconferencing to connect various sites. One of our goals is to explore the possibility of enhancing the quality of electronic communication by encouraging people to make reference to the stand-alone Starter Units and PSSTs that we provide them. We also want to provide simple ways for people to add multi-media information to our PSSTs.

SUMMARY AND CONCLUSIONS

Our goal in this chapter has been to describe the Schools for Thought (SFT) collaborative and our early attempts to implement it in two classrooms in Nashville, Tennessee. The SFT collaborative emerged from the integration of three independent research projects funded by the James S. McDonnell Foundation's CSEP program: Jasper, Fostering Communities of Learners (FCL), and Computer Supported International Learning Environments (CSILE). These programs had been successful when tested in isolation, but a synthesis of them had never been tried.

Initial efforts to create SFT classrooms began in September 1993 and were carried out in several different sites in North America. For purposes of the present chapter, we concentrated on the implementation efforts in two sixth-grade classrooms in Nashville, Tennessee. One classroom got off to a faster start than the other, and, ultimately, was more successful. Nevertheless, our experiences in both classrooms convinced us of the potential benefits of classrooms organized around the principles of SFT. We discussed a number of indicators of the kinds of achievement reached by SFT students. We also noted that the extraordinary levels of achievement that were so visible to us, parents, and school administrators were not necessarily evident on the standardized achievement tests.

Our initial attempts to create SFT classrooms have taught us some important lessons. The two most important ones stemmed from convincing demonstrations that sixth-grade students are indeed capable of extraordinary achievement and that attempts to create SFT classrooms are extremely time and resource intensive. We are experiencing this at an even greater level as we work with additional sites this year.

In closing we discussed work funded by the Mellon foundation that involves building and testing tools that are designed to support the development of classroom communities such as FCL and SFT. We are focusing on two types of tools: Starter Units and Performance Support Tools (PSSTs). Both are designed to help teachers with the daunting task of re-inventing FCL and SFT classrooms.

We are attempting to create tools that are consistent with the principles of FCL and SFT. Therefore, we are creating tools for community building rather than prepackaged curriculum units that can be used like recipes. Some of our tools are designed to be stand-alone units that teachers and others can access as needed. Other tools are in the form of networks that allow teachers to communicate with others around the country. We believe that both the stand-alone and network tools are necessary. Research to be conducted over the next several years will allow us to better understand optimal functions and designs for tools.

Appendix

MISSION TO MARS

Excerpt from a 76-page document created by the sixth grade "MacLearner" Schools for Thought classroom in Nashville, TN, February 1994.

Flight Scenarios or Possible Trajectories

There are many ways of going to Mars. Each and every one of these ways has it's own advantages and disadvantages. These different ways are called trajectories. Trajectories are the flight paths of objects. In this case, objects in space. One of the possible missions to Mars is called a sprint mission. Sprinting to Mars is going to Mars and coming back to Earth as fast as you can. On the sprint mission you stay in space the shortest amount of time and the risk of equipment malfunctioning is minimized. However, the disadvantage to this mission is the cost of the fuel and the weight. The rockets will be firing all along the way, so you use more fuel. The total sprint mission length will vary to 1 and 1.5 years.

Another type of mission takes the sprint mission, but sends a cargo ship ahead of the main spacecraft. This means the main ship will go faster using up the same amount of fuel. The cargo ship will carry a small shuttle for the descent down to Mars, the fuel for the return trip home, oxygen for the return trip home, and other needs of the crew. The cargo ship plan still uses a lot of fuel, but it allows the spacecraft to move faster minimizing your time in space.

All of the ships involved in the cargo ship plan will be assembled on the future space station Freedom, in orbit around Earth. The estimated weight of the mother ship, supplies, fuel and the lander ranges to about 770 to 1100 tons. All of these components are essential for the future Mars mission to succeed. The current space shuttle launch plan can only deliver 19.03 tons into Earth's orbit. The estimated number of launches is 58. The total launch time and assembly is estimated to be about 5 years. NASA is working on a new launch system that is capable of lifting 154 tons into Earth's orbit. Another proposed mission to Mars plan is an opposition class mission. To do this type of mission we must wait until Mars and the sun are on opposite sides of the Earth. The phase angle between Earth and Mars during an opposition is 90 degrees. An opposition class mission requires more fuel for the launch than a conjunction class mission explained later on. Also an opposition class mission takes a longer travel time to Mars from Earth than a conjunction class mission. Despite these large disadvantages, the big difference results in a larger time savings than a conjunction class mission in the total mission duration period which is below 700 days.

One proposed plan to make up for the fuel loss in the launch is to fly toward Venus in the direction of the sun instead of flying to Mars working against the sun's gravity. As the spacecraft flies toward the sun it gains the necessary velocity to catch Mars at a time that allows a shorter surface stay. The space craft heads in the wrong direction by heading toward Venus. It gains speed as it gets closer to the sun. Venus's gravity turns the spacecraft around and sends it toward Mars. This maneuver is called a Gravity Assist Maneuver or a Hyperbolic Flyby.

A conjunction class mission is another kind of mission plan. To take this mission we must wait until Mars and Earth lie 180 degrees apart in space. This is the name of the mission because Earth is headed toward a conjunction at the same time the spacecraft reaches Mars. Conjunction class missions offer a great difference in fuel savings than the other class missions. Both coming and going from Mars will be on a Homan Transfer. A Homan Transfer is going directly to a planet, not necessarily meaning non-stop. Each trip from or to Mars will take 259 days. Once the crew reaches Mars, they must wait between 400 to 500 days for the "Return to Earth" launch window to open.

The disadvantage to this mission is the total duration period which is 918 to 1018 days. That is the equivalent to about three years. This length in time may be too long for the first mission. Currently space biologists don't believe in the human body's ability to perform physically after being used to weightlessness and radiation. A true analogy to this would be like spending 259 days in the best water bed you can find. Then one day you decide to get up and go for a 12 mile run.

Another fact that doesn't support this mission is that the longer a mission lasts, the greater the chance of your vital equipment failing. It would be very tragic if you died in space, and a waste of money.

Conclusion

In this report we learned that there are many possible ways to get to Mars. Also that a launch window selection is needed. We have also learned that aerobraking is just as important as orbit selection. If something goes wrong with the trajectory you found out how to get back on course in the section about mid course correction. In conclusion, we decided to take the opposition class mission. The reason why we chose the opposition class mission is because it is one of the shorter missions and it does not take a lot of fuel.

WE HOLD THE ANSWER

Excerpt from a 171-page document created by the sixth grade "MacLearner" Schools for Thought classroom in Nashville, TN, May 1994.

Saving Habitat

Today, there are thousands of reserves around the world protecting forests, grasslands, wetlands, mountains, seashores, and coral reefs. They range in size from tiny sanctuaries of a few acres, perhaps protecting a patch of woodland, or a single marsh, to giant national parks covering thousands of square miles where a variety of different habitats are preserved.

Reserves are very important for saving the best bits for wilderness that are left but we must also find ways of letting wildlife live alongside us. Even good reserves are not enough to save the greatest variety of wildlife on our planet well into the future. Less than 4% of all the world's land is protected. If the remaining 96% became suitable for only human beings to live in, we would lose countless numbers of species.

There are various things that can be tried. Timber companies, for instance, can cut down and remove trees in ways that do not destroy the whole forests. Trees can be replanted where they used to grow and better methods can be found of getting rid of the waste that we produce, so that it does not pollute the rivers. More people realize the importance of doing something for wildlife now before it is too late. In 1992, governments from all around the world met in Rio de Janeiro to discuss the future of our planet. One of the things that they agreed on was for wealthy countries to help others protect their plant and animal species.

Habitat Destruction

Mountains are being worn away or eroded by wind, water, and extreme changes in temperature. Over thousands of years, mountains, can be re-duced to small rolling hills. Humans cause the quickest and most drastic changes, to the mountain's habitat.

Logging companies that take away trees without replanting can destroy the mountains. The small layer of soil that was held in place by the trees is quickly washed away by rain water. A nice forested slope can turn into a dreadful cliff in a little less than one year. Different human activities can destroy the mountain habitat. Some of them are farming, hydro-electric projects, mining, road building, ranching, hunting, and even mountain climbing can threaten the plants and animals that live in mountains.

Mountains are one of the last refuges for animals. Many kinds of small creatures have learned to live in mountain areas to escape humans. Some have their natural habitat taken from them because of humans. Others are left stranded in mountain areas when regions around them are destroyed or changed. Some animals are being pushed further up on a mountain to survive.

Habitat destruction is the main mover behind extinction of animals today, as people disturb other animal or plant species with their numbers and activities. According to a report by the World Resources Institute in Washington, some 67% of all endangered, vulnerable, and rare species of vertebrates are threatened by habitat destruction. These factors also pose the greatest threat to invertebrates.

What Can We Do?

We can stop littering and stop dumping toxic waste into the oceans, lakes, ponds, mountains and other places. We also need to stop the killing of animals and help the animals that need us. We reject them, so help undo things we've already done and the things we are about to do! Pitch in and help save the earth!

ACKNOWLEDGMENTS

For an update on the Schools for Thought project in Nashville, please access our Web site at: http://peabody.vanderbilt.edu/projects/funded/sft/general. We wish to acknowledge and thank our colleagues Julie Keeton and Carolyn Millican, who were invaluable in the implementation of Schools for Thought (SFT) in Nashville, and the teachers and students in our SFT classrooms. James Pellegrino, Dean of Peabody College, has been instrumental in obtaining community support for the project and stimulating the intellectual agenda of Learning Communities in Nashville. We are extremely appreciative of the collaboration surrounding the concept and implementation of the Schools for Thought project and wish to acknowledge our collaborators on this project: Carl Bereiter, Ann Brown, John Bruer, Joe Campione, Marlene Scardamalia, and Dennis Wint. Support for the collaboration project is provided by the James S. McDonnell Foundation, and in Nashville by Metropolitan Nashville Schools and the First American Bank.

REFERENCES

Barron, B., Vye, N. J., Zech, L., Schwartz, D., Bransford, J. D., Goldman, S. R., Pellegrino, J., Morris, J., Garrison, S., & Kantor, R. (1995). Creating contexts for community based problem solving: The Jasper challenge series. In C. Hedley, P. Antonacci, & M. Rabinowitz (Eds.), *Thinking and literacy: The mind at work* (pp. 47–71) Mahwah, NJ: Lawrence Erlbaum Associates.

Barron, L. C., & Goldman, E. S. (1994). Integrating technology with teacher preparation. In B. Means (Ed.), *Technology and education reform: The reality behind the promise* (pp. 81–110). San Francisco, CA: Jossey-Bass.

Bereiter, C., & Scardamalia, M. (1987). An attainable version of high literacy: Approaches to teaching higher-order skills in reading and writing. *Curriculum Inquiry, 17*(1), 9–30.

Bereiter, C., & Scardamalia, M. (1989). Intentional learning as a goal of instruction. In L. B. Resnick (Ed.), *Knowing, learning, and instruction. Essays in honor of Robert Glaser* (pp. 361–392). Hillsdale, NJ: Lawrence Erlbaum Associates.

Bransford, J. D., Goin, L. I., Hasselbring, T. S., Kinzer, C. K., Sherwood, R. D., & Williams, S. M. (1988). Learning with technology: Theoretical and empirical perspectives. *Peabody Journal of Education, 64*(1), 5–26.

Bransford, J. D., Goldman, S. R., & Vye, N. J. (1991). Making a difference in peoples' abilities to think: Reflections on a decade of work and some hopes for the future. In L. Okagaki

& R. J. Sternberg (Eds.), *Directors of development: Influences on the development of children's thinking* (pp. 147–180). Hillsdale, NJ: Lawrence Erlbaum Associates.

Bransford, J. D., & Heldmeyer, K. (1983). Learning from children learning. In J. Bisanz, G. Bisanz, & R. Kail (Eds.), *Learning in children: Progress in cognitive development research* (pp. 171–190). New York: Springer-Verlag.

Bransford, J. D., & Stein, B. S. (1993). *The IDEAL problem solver* (2nd ed.). New York: Freeman.

Brophy, J., & Alleman, J. (1992). Planning and managing learning activities: Basic principles. In J. Brophy (Ed.), *Advances in research on teaching: Planning and managing learning tasks and activities* (Vol. 3, pp. 1–45). Greenwich, CT: JAI.

Brown, A. L. (1992). Design experiments: Theoretical and methodological challenges in creating complex interventions in classroom settings. *The Journal of the Learning Sciences, 2*(2), 141–178.

Brown, A. L., Ash, D., Rutherford, M., Nakagawa, K., Gordon, A., & Campione, J. C. (1993). Distributed expertise in the classroom. In G. Salomon (Ed.), *Distributed cognitions: Psychological and educational considerations* (pp. 188–228). New York: Cambridge University Press.

Brown, A. L., & Campione, J. C. (1990). Communities of learning and thinking or a context by any other name. *Human Development, 21*, 108–125.

Brown, A. L., & Campione, J. C. (1994). Guided discovery in a community of learners. In K. McGilly (Ed.), *Classroom lessons: Integrating cognitive theory and classroom practice* (pp. 229–272). Cambridge, MA: MIT Press/Bradford Books.

Brown, J. S., Collins, A., & Duguid, P. (1989). Situated cognition and the culture of learning. *Educational Researcher, 18*, 32–41.

Bruer, J. (1989). *1989 Annual Report*. St. Louis, MO: James S. McDonnell Foundation.

Bruer, J. (1993). *Schools for thought: A science of learning in the classroom*. Cambridge, MA: MIT Press.

Chi, M. T. H., deLeeuw, N., Chiu, M., & LaVancher, C. (1994). Eliciting self-explanations improves understanding. *Cognitive Science, 18*, 439–477.

Cognition and Technology Group at Vanderbilt. (1990). Anchored instruction and its relationship to situated cognition. *Educational Researcher, 19*(6), 2–10.

Cognition and Technology Group at Vanderbilt. (1992a). The Jasper series: A generative approach to mathematical thinking. In K. Sheingold, L. G. Roberts, & S. M. Malcolm (Eds.), *This year in science series 1991: Technology for teaching and learning* (pp. 108–140). Washington, DC: American Association for the Advancement of Science.

Cognition and Technology Group at Vanderbilt. (1992b). The Jasper series as an example of anchored instruction: Theory, program description, and assessment data. *Educational Psychologist, 27*, 291–315.

Cognition and Technology Group at Vanderbilt. (1993a). Anchored instruction and situated cognition revisited. *Educational Technology, 23*(3), 52–70.

Cognition and Technology Group at Vanderbilt. (1993b). The Jasper experiment: Using video to furnish real-world problem-solving contexts. *Arithmetic Teacher, 40*, 474–478.

Cognition and Technology Group at Vanderbilt. (1994). From visual word problems to learning communities: Changing conceptions of cognitive research. In K. McGilly (Ed.), *Classroom lessons: Integrating cognitive theory and classroom practice* (pp. 157–200). Cambridge, MA: MIT Press/Bradford Books.

Cognition and Technology Group at Vanderbilt. (in press). The Jasper series: A design experiment in complex, mathematical problem solving. In J. Hawkins & A. Collins (Eds.), *Design experiments: Integrating technologies into schools*. New York: Cambridge University Press.

Cohen, A. (1994). *The effect of a teacher-designed assessment tool on an instructor's cognitive activity while using CSILE.* Unpublished manuscript.

Collins, A. (1996). Design issues for learning environments. In S. Vosniadou, E. DeCorte, R. Glaser, & H. Mandl (Eds.), *International perspectives on the psychological foundations of technology-based learning environments* (pp. 347–362). Mahwah, NJ: Lawrence Erlbaum Associates.

Collins, A., Hawkins, J., & Carver, S. (1991). A cognitive apprenticeship for disadvantaged students. In B. Means, C. Chelemer, & M. S. Knapp (Eds.), *Teaching advanced skills to disadvantaged students* (pp. 216–243). San Francisco, CA: Jossey-Bass.

Coté, N., Goldman, S. R., Gjellstad, L., Keeton, J., & Millican, C. (1994, November). *Children's use of prior knowledge and experience in understanding informational text on nutrition.* Paper presented at the annual meeting of the Mid-South Educational Research Association, Nashville, TN.

Duffy, T. M. (in press). Strategic teaching framework: An instructional model for learning complex interactive skills. In C. Dills & A. Romiszowski (Eds.), *Instructional development state of the art, Volume 3: Paradigms.* Englewood Cliffs, NJ: Educational Technology Publications.

Frederiksen, J. R., & Collins, A. (1989). A systems approach to educational testing. *Educational Researcher, 18*(9), 27–32.

Goldman, S. R., Coté, N., & Saul, E. U. (1994, January). *Children's strategies for making sense of informational text.* Paper presented at the Fifth Annual Winter Text Conference, Jackson Hole, WY.

Goldman, S. R., Mertz, D. L., & Pellegrino, J. W. (1989). Individual differences in extended practice functions and solution strategies for basic addition facts. *Journal of Educational Psychology, 81,* 481–496.

Goldman, S. R., Pellegrino, J. W., & Bransford, J. D. (1994). Assessing programs that invite thinking. In E. Baker & H. F. O'Neil, Jr. (Eds.), *Technology assessment in education and training* (pp. 199–230). Hillsdale, NJ: Lawrence Erlbaum Associates.

Goldman, S. R., Pellegrino, J. W., & Mertz, D. L. (1988). Extended practice of basic addition facts: Strategy changes in learning disabled students. *Cognition and Instruction, 5,* 223–265.

Greeno, J. G. (1993). For research to reform education and cognitive science. In L. A. Penner, G. M. Batsche, H. M. Knoff, & D. L. Nelson (Eds.), *The challenge in mathematics and science education: Psychology's response* (pp. 153–194). Washington, DC: American Psychological Association.

Harter, S. (1985). *The self-perception profile for children.* Denver, CO: University of Denver.

Hasselbring, T., Goin, L., & Bransford, J. D. (1988). Developing math automaticity in learning handicapped children: The role of computerized drill and practice. *Focus on Exceptional Children, 20*(6), 1–7.

Hickey, D. T., Petrosino, A., Pellegrino, J. W., Goldman, S. R., Bransford, J. D., Sherwood, R., & CTGV. (1992, July-August). *The MARS mission challenge: A generative, problem-solving, school science environment.* Paper presented at the NATO Advanced Study Institute on Psychological and Educational Foundations of Technology: Based Learning Environments, Kolymbari, Greece.

Holt, J. (1964). *How children fail.* New York: Dell.

Kantor, R. J., Moore, A. L., Bransford, J. D., & CTGV. (1993, April). *Extending the impact of classroom-based technology: The satellite challenge series.* Paper presented at the annual meeting of the American Educational Research Association, Atlanta, GA.

.inzer, C. K. (1993, October). *What do teachers/administrators learn from video cases?* Research Working Group at a Working Conference on Case-based Teaching, University of Nevada, Las Vegas, NV.

.amon, M. (1993). *St. Louis Science Center/St. Louis Public Schools: Middle school curriculum collaborative.* Unpublished manuscript.

.ampert, M., & Ball, D. L. (1990). *Using hypermedia technology to support a new pedagogy of teacher education* (Issue Paper 90–5). East Lansing, MI: Michigan State University, National Center for Research on Teacher Education.

.ave, J., & Wenger, E. (1991). *Situated learning: Legitimate peripheral participation.* New York: Cambridge University Press.

AcGilly, K. (1994). *Classroom lessons: Integrating cognitive theory and classroom practice.* Cambridge, MA: MIT Press/Bradford Books.

Aonin, B. (1994). Schools for thought. *Peabody Reflector, 65*(1), 18–21.

'alincsar, A. S., & Brown, A. L. (1984). Reciprocal teaching of comprehension-fostering and comprehension monitoring activities. *Cognition and Instruction, 1,* 117–175.

'ea, R. D. (1993). Practices of distributed intelligence and designs for education. In G. Salomon (Ed.), *Distributed cognitions: Psychological and educational considerations* (pp. 47–87). New York: Cambridge University Press.

'ea, R. D., & Gomez, L. M. (1992). Distributed multimedia learning environments: Why and how? *Interactive Learning Environments, 2,* 73–109.

'ellegrino, J. W., Hickey, D., Heath, A., Rewey, K., Vye, N. J., & CTGV. (1991). *Assessing the outcomes of an innovative instructional program: The 1990–1991 implementation of the "Adventures of Jasper Woodbury"* (Tech. Rep. No. 91–1). Nashville, TN: Vanderbilt University, Learning Technology Center.

'etrosino, A. P., Secules, T., Goldman, S. R., Lamon, M., & Bransford, J. D. (in progress). *Self-esteem enhancement in the schools for thought classroom: Initial findings.*

.esnick, L. (1987). Learning in school and out. *Educational Researcher, 16*(9), 13–20.

.isko, V. J. (1993). *What do teachers/administrators learn from video cases?* Research Working Group at a Working Conference on Case-based Teaching, University of Nevada, Las Vegas, NV.

.ogoff, B. (1990). *Apprenticeship in thinking.* New York: Oxford University Press.

.aul, E. U., Coté, N., & Goldman, S. R. (1993, April). *Students' strategies for making text make sense.* Paper presented at the annual meeting of the American Education Research Association, Atlanta, GA.

.cardamalia, M., & Bereiter, C. (1994). Computer support for knowledge-building communities. *Journal of the Learning Sciences, 3*(3), 265–283.

.cardamalia, M., Bereiter, C., Brett, C., Burtis, P. J., Calhoun, C., & Smith, L. N. (1992). Educational applications of a networked communal database. *Interactive Learning Environments, 2*(1),45–71.

.cardamalia, M., Bereiter, C., & Lamon, M. (1994). The CSILE Project: Trying to bring the classroom into world 3. In K. McGilly (Ed.), *Classroom lessons: Integrating cognitive theory and classroom practice* (pp. 201–228). Cambridge, MA: MIT Press/Bradford Books.

.cardamalia, M., Bereiter, C., McLean, R. S., Swallow, J., & Woodruff, E. (1989). Computer supported intentional learning environments. *Journal of Educational Computing Research, 5,* 51–68.

.enge, P. M. (1990). *The fifth discipline: The art and practice of the learning organization.* New York: Doubleday.

.herwood, R. D., Petrosino, A. J., Lin, X., Lamon, M., & CTGV. (1995). Problem-based macro contexts in science instruction: Theoretical basis, design issues, and the development of applications. In D. Lavoie (Ed.), *Towards a cognitive-science perspective for scientific problem solving* (pp. 191–214). Manhattan, KS: National Association for Research in Science Teaching.

Sternberg, R. J., & Wagner, R. K. (1986). *Practical intelligence.* New York: Cambridge University Press.

U.S. Department of Labor. (1992). *Secretary's commission on achieving necessary skills report for American 2000.* Washington, DC: Author.

Zech, L. K., Vye, N. J., Bransford, J. D., Swink, J., Mayfield-Stewart, C., Goldman, S. R., & CTGV. (1994). Bringing geometry into the classroom with videodisc technology. *Mathematics Teaching in the Middle School, 1*, 228–233.

Chapter 11

PSYCHOLOGICAL THEORY AND THE DESIGN OF INNOVATIVE LEARNING ENVIRONMENTS: ON PROCEDURES, PRINCIPLES, AND SYSTEMS

Ann L. Brown and Joseph C. Campione
University of California at Berkeley

During the course of this century, there have been major changes in the aims and goals of education. Whereas the early goal was to produce graduates who possessed basic literacy skills, more recently the stakes have been increased to emphasize higher levels of literacy, greater understanding of traditional subject matters and technology, and the capability to learn and adapt to changing workplace demands.

During the same period, theories of learning have also undergone significant change. For the first half of the century, psychology was dominated by behaviorist analyses that sought laws of learning of great generality. These laws were thought to be species-, age-, and content-independent. Learning was viewed as an individual, primarily passive activity, involving the formation of simple associations governed by external reinforcements. Complex behaviors were seen as involving the extension and combination of those associations.

More recently, theorists have emphasized the active, reflective, and social nature of learning. Following the "cognitive revolution," the model of the human learner, including the child, was transformed. Learners came to be viewed as *active constructors*, rather than passive recipients of knowledge. Learners were imbued with powers of introspection; they were granted knowledge and feelings about learning, sometimes even control of it, *metacognition* if you will. And, although people are excellent all-purpose learning

289

machines, equipped to learn just about anything by brute force, like all biologically evolved creatures, humans come *predisposed* to learn certain things more readily than others.

In place of rote learning of simple associations, psychologists began to study the acquisition of disciplined bodies of knowledge characteristic of academic subject areas (e.g., mathematics, science, computer programming, social studies, and history). With the emphasis on understanding within rich content areas, it also became necessary that higher order thinking be returned as a subject of inquiry.

At the same time, psychologists began to consider learning settings outside the laboratory and even beyond classroom walls. Consideration of these alternative settings highlighted the richness of learning as it occurred in different situations. This in turn forced psychologists to consider input from other branches of cognitive science, such as anthropology, sociology, and linguistics. It became clear that a strictly laboratory-based and purely psychological theory of learning is, and always was, a chimera (A. L. Brown, 1994).

These advances notwithstanding, it has become increasingly clear that we need a new type of learning theory to inform the design of learning environments, including those that are situated in settings of formal schooling. By the same token, the best way to contribute to the development of such emergent theories of learning is through careful study of innovative settings for learning.

In this chapter we describe the theoretical bases of an instructional program, Fostering Communities of Learners (FCL), that we have been developing for the past decade (A. L. Brown & Campione, 1994). Set in the inner city elementary schools, FCL is designed to promote the critical thinking and reflection skills underlying multiple forms of higher literacy: reading, writing, argumentation, technological sophistication, and so forth. Although billed as a thinking curriculum (Resnick & Resnick, 1992), the FCL program is embedded in deep disciplinary content. One cannot think critically, or otherwise, in a vacuum; food for thought is needed to nourish critical thinking and reflection.

A major part of our research agenda has been to contribute to a theory of learning that can capture and convey the essential features of the learning environments that we design (A. L. Brown, 1992). Aspects of the design, implementation, and evaluation of the FCL program, from its inception to the present day, have been guided by the development of a situated learning theory, one grounded in the day-to-day milieu of regular schools. This theory or, more precisely, set of learning principles (A. L. Brown, 1994; A. L. Brown & Campione, 1994), has evolved over the course of the project. The development of a theory of learning to capture the essence of innovations such as FCL, and other programs that share a family relation to FCL, is critical for two reasons: conceptual understanding and practical dissemination. The development of theory has always been necessary as a guide to research, a lens through which one interprets, that sets things apart and pulls things together. But theory development is essential for practical implementation as well. We need to specify FCL in sufficient detail to communicate its essential features to: (a) ourselves, so we can refine the design of the environment; (b) our colleagues, so they can elaborate, help clarify, and criticize our views; and (c) teachers and administrators, so they can put the program into place in their classrooms, schools, and districts.

It is for these reasons that we have been concerned with the development of a set of first principles of learning to guide research and practice. Without adherence to first principles, surface procedures tend to be adopted, adapted, and ritualized in such a way that they cease to serve the "thinking" function they were originally designed to foster. This proceduralization of surface activities has been the fate of many innovations, notably cooperative learning. We use as an example of this the fate of one of our own innovations, reciprocal teaching (Palincsar & A. L. Brown, 1984), an activity system designed to enhance comprehension-monitoring while reading. Reciprocal teaching has received widespread dissemination, and is quoted as a success story by reports put out by such learned bodies as the National Research Council and the National Academy of Education. But, too often something called reciprocal teaching is practiced in such a way that the principles of learning it was meant to foster are lost, or at best relegated to a minor position. The surface rituals of questioning, summarizing, and so forth are engaged in rituals divorced from the goal of reading for understanding that they were designed to serve. These "strategies" are sometimes practiced out of the context of reading texts. Quite simply, if one wants to disseminate a program on the basis of principles of learning rather than surface procedures, one must be able to specify what those principles are in such a way that they can inform practice. We attempt such a description in this chapter.

Research-based programs of the latter part of the century have emphasized the central role of process. In FCL, for example, students are required to practice research-like activities, to become involved in systems of activity that lead them to engage in understanding texts, writing to communicate, engaging in domain-situated problem solving, and so forth. To put these processes into practice, theorists and practitioners often devise specific procedures aimed to introduce and support them. These procedures are based on, and embody, specific learning principles. It is the embodiment and enactment of these principles, rather than the surface procedures, that is

important. But this in turn requires that those using the procedures understand the underlying principles, else the procedures can degenerate into a
modified activity unrelated to the guiding principles. Some modifications
so depart from the original philosophy that they can be termed "lethal
mutations" (E. H. Haertel, personal communication, 1994).

Lethal mutations were not a major problem for the translation of behaviorist views of learning into classroom activities. Understanding was required of neither the teacher nor the student. Skills hierarchies could be
developed, basic exercises constructed, reinforcement principles laid out,
and related assessments conducted. Much of what went on in the classroom
could be scripted.

But philosophies are hard to script. Learning principles need to be
understood and internalized if flexible use and creative adaptation is the
goal. There are by now many procedures available that were designed to
foster thinking. These procedures are part of the teacher's toolbox. But the
procedures are understood as unrelated tools, not as systems of interdepend-
ent activities. This leads to the practice of selecting tools following a Chinese
menu approach, with teachers choosing some subset of the available candi-
dates. Teachers may, for example, decide to include forms of cooperative
learning, the use of long-term projects, a writer's workbench approach, and
so on. The problem we see is that such an approach ignores the potential
power of creating a classroom system of activities, activities that mutually
influence and reinforce each other. Thus, in addition to understanding the
principles underlying individual procedures, it is necessary to understand
the ways in which the principles embodied in sets of procedures themselves
cohere. We address the interdependence of activities in FCL in the next
section.

THE COMPONENTS OF FCL:
THE SIMPLE SYSTEM

First and foremost, FCL should be viewed as a system of interacting activities
that results in a self-consciously active and reflective learning environment.
Some descriptions of FCL, even those written by the current authors, paint
an unnecessarily complex picture. At its simplest level, there are three key
parts. Students engage in independent and group *research* on some aspect
of a topic of inquiry, mastery of which is ultimately the responsibility of all
members of the class. This requires that they *share* their expertise with their
classmates. This sharing is further motivated by some *consequential task* or
activity (Scardamalia, Bereiter, & Fillion, 1981) that demands that all

students have learned about all aspects of the joint topic. This consequential task can be as traditional as a test or quiz, or some nontraditional activity such as designing a "biopark" to protect an endangered species. These three key activities—(a) research, (b) *in order* to share information, (c) *in order* to perform a consequential task—are all overseen and coordinated by self-conscious reflection on the part of all members of the community. In addition, the research–share–perform cycles of FCL cannot be carried out in a vacuum. All rely on the fact that the participants are trying to understand *deep disciplinary content* (Shulman, 1986). Thus, the backbone of an FCL class is captured in Fig. 11.1.

To make this schematic concrete, let us consider a second-grade class. Children are engaged in research on animal survival mechanisms. They begin their research sharing a common piece of information, an anchoring event (Cognition and Technology Group at Vanderbilt [CTGV], 1992) if you will. They read a well-written, beautifully illustrated children's book such as *The Tree of Life*, by Barbara Bash (1989), in which the theme is animal/habitat interdependence. Individual students then adopt an animal or plant mentioned in the book. With help from their colleagues, they write and illustrate a paragraph on why their animal is dependent on the tree of life (the baobab tree) and why the baobab tree is in turn dependent on the

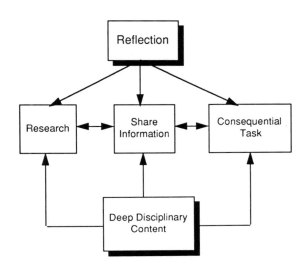

FIG. 11.1. Community of learners: the basic system.

animal or plant. They post their illustrated text on a large mural of the tree for all the class to see and share. Although individually prepared, the tree and all its inhabitants belong to the community. Children can describe to an array of visitors why their animal or plant is dependent on the tree and vice versa. Over time they become able to describe not only their own choices, but also those of their classmates. The class owns the tree and the lives that depend on it.

The research process is then expanded as students build on their emerging knowledge by exploring subtopics that have surfaced, such as food chains or defense mechanisms; the *big idea* underlying their research is that of animal/habitat interdependence. Six research groups are formed and begin working concurrently. Their chosen subtopics are food chains, predator/prey relations, defense mechanisms, protection from the elements, animal communication, and reproductive strategies. Children in each research group write and illustrate booklets about their subtopic. Periodically, the groups gather as a whole class and check their progress, a procedure known as *cross-talk* (A. L. Brown & Campione, 1994) because the students are sharing information across research groups. Opportunistically during the unit, and always at the end of the unit, the students divide up into Jigsaw (Aronson, 1978) teaching groups. Each Jigsaw group consists of one designated member of each research group. These designated members have the responsibility of teaching the remaining members about their research topic in order to complete the consequential task, in this case, to design an animal of the future that has evolved a solution to the six research group questions—reproductive strategies, protection from the elements, and so forth. In each group someone knows about predator/prey relations, someone else can talk wisely on the strengths and weaknesses of possible methods of communication, and so forth. All pieces are needed to complete the puzzle, to design the "complete animal," hence Jigsaw.

Design groups then display illustrated text about their animal of the future to classmates, to the previous year's second graders, and to a variety of visiting adults. When exhibiting their animal and telling their research story, the children are required to put on a performance. Regular exhibitions to a variety of audiences are an important component of FCL. Audiences demand coherence, push for higher levels of understanding, require satisfactory explanations, request clarification of obscure points, and so on. The sense of audience is not imaginary, but palpable and real.

These opportunities to display provide an element of reality testing that is also an important feature of many successful out-of-school activities, such as dramatic plays put on by boys' and girls' clubs (McLaughlin, Irby, & Langman, 1994). Such groups typically engage in seasonal cycles of planning, preparing, rehearsing, and performing. There are deadlines, discipline, and most important, reflection on performance (Heath & McLaughlin, 1994). So, too, in an FCL classroom, we have cycles of planning, preparing, practicing, teaching, and exhibiting. Deadlines and performance demand reflection and the setting of priorities—What is important to know? What is important to teach? What of our newfound knowledge do we display (A. L. Brown, 1994)?

FCL: ACTIVITY STRUCTURES THAT SUPPORT THE SYSTEM

These cycles of research–share–perform are the backbone of FCL. The particular activity structures of FCL are chosen to motivate, enable, and support the central research–share–perform cycles. The activities that we have used serve these support functions, but they could be replaced by others, as long as they also serve the same functions, thus preserving the system. A sample of activities we have used repeatedly is shown in Table 11.1. We describe these briefly here (for more details, see A. L. Brown & Campione, 1990, 1994).

Research Activities

In order to conduct their research, even the youngest students (thus far first graders) need to be able to engage in reading, writing, listening, or viewing activities to select critical material on their chosen topic. Key participant structures that support these activities are:

TABLE 11.1
Elements of FCL

Research	Share Information	Consequential Task
Reading/Studying (Reciprocal Teaching) (Research Seminar)	Jigsaw	Exhibitions
Guided Viewing	Cross-Talk	Tests, Quizzes
Guided Writing	Distributed Expertise	Design Tasks
Consulting Experts (face-to-face)	Majoring	Publishing
Consulting Experts (electronic mail)	Help-Seeking	Transparent Assessments
Peer- and Cross-Age Teaching/Research	Exhibitions	Authentic Assessments

1. Reciprocal teaching (RT) reading, listening, or viewing sessions for younger children that evolve into research seminars (RS) for older students;
2. Guided writing and composing;
3. Consultation with experts, either face-to-face or via electronic mail to remote sites, including other classes within the school, other schools, museums, laboratories, and so forth; and
4. Peer- and cross-age teaching.

Reciprocal Teaching and Research Seminars

Reciprocal teaching reading groups (Palincsar & A. L. Brown, 1984) were designed to help students monitor their comprehension. They can be led by teachers, parents, older students, or peers. Six or so participants form a group with each member taking a turn leading a discussion about an article, a video, or other materials the group needs to understand as part of its research process. The leader begins a discussion by *asking a question* and ends by *summarizing* the gist of the argument to date. Attempts to *clarify* any problems of understanding take place when needed, and a leader can ask for *predictions* about future content when appropriate. These activities promote comprehension monitoring. Obviously, someone who cannot summarize or ask a question after reading has a clear comprehension problem.

Reciprocal teaching was designed to provoke zones of proximal development (Vygotsky, 1978) within which readers of varying abilities can navigate at various levels and at various rates. Everyone is trying to arrive at a consensus concerning meaning, relevance, and importance, which helps ensure that understanding occurs, even if some members of the group are not yet capable of full participation. Because thinking is externalized in the form of discussion, beginners can learn from the contributions of those more expert than they. It is important that adults or older students take their turns being the leader, so that younger students are exposed to mature modeling of comprehension-monitoring strategies. Collaboratively, the group, with its variety of expertise, engagement, and goals, gets the job done; usually the text is understood. The integrity of the task, reading for meaning, is maintained throughout. The task is simplified by the provision of social support through a variety of expertise, not via decomposition of the task into basic skills (A. L. Brown & Palincsar, 1989).

With repeated experiences in the RT mode, groups of older students (sixth and seventh grade) created a version they called Research Seminar (RS). In RS, the four RT activities (questioning, clarifying, predicting, and summarizing) are resorted to only in times of trouble. They are replaced by a variety of more intellectually demanding activities. Increasingly powerful comprehension-extending activities, such as those shown in Table 11.2, are modeled and practiced. In RS, adults model and students practice the use of analogies to note recurrent themes or to explain mechanisms. Causal explanations are proffered, challenged, and refined, not just in response to comprehension breakdowns (impasse driven), but also spontaneously, in the search for deeper understanding. Argumentation formats are developed, in which different points of view and defensible interpretations are compared. Warrants and backings (Toulmin, 1958) are expected in support of arguments. The nature of what constitutes evidence is discussed. On occasions, discussions include a consideration of negative evidence. A variety of plausible reasoning strategies (Collins & Stevens, 1982) begins to emerge. The nature and importance of prediction evolves, with students going beyond predictions of simple outcomes to considering possible worlds and engaging in thought experiments about them.

TABLE 11.2

Discourse Elements Involved in Research Seminar

Analogy:

    To note recurrent themes

    To explain mechanism

Causal Explanation:

    Impasse driven

    Resolving inconsistencies

    For deeper understanding of mechanism

Explanation and Evidence:

    Claims and premises

    Warrants and backings

    Negative evidence

Argumentation:

    Different points of view

    Different interpretation

Predictions:

    Of possible outcomes

    Of possible worlds

    Of perturbations in the system

    Thought experiments—What if? Imagine that, etc.

    Plausible reasoning

Note: From A. L. Brown and Campione (1994).

Guided Writing

In FCL, research is embedded in writing and vice versa. Writing serves to encourage students to clarify their ideas, to set priorities, and to communicate the fruits of their research to others. In preparation for teaching others and displaying their knowledge, research groups produce illustrated texts (A. L. Brown & Campione, 1990). These texts go through many revisions, some guided by an expert (the classroom teacher, a researcher, or an older student). The idea again is to create zones of proximal development in which students can operate at the cutting edge of their competence. An expert or older student sits with each group on a regular basis. Younger children often dictate their material to the guide, who types the students' suggestions to speed up the input process. In all cases, the guide helps the group progress to higher levels of discourse using such prompts as: "Do you think the reader will be able to understand that?" "Have you said how your animal gets food?" "Have you told us how it communicates?" "Remember that the reader hasn't read about echo location; is this enough to make it clear?" "Is this in your own words?" "What's the main point of this paragraph?" "Do you think this is important enough to include?" Repeated exposure to these external prompts, first by a teacher and then by other children, eventually leads to internalization in the form of self-editing procedures.

Consultation With Experts

In support of their research activities, students rely on the distributed expertise that is the result of Jigsaw activity and their own research (Brown, Ash, et al., 1993). But in our original FCL work (A. L. Brown & Campione, 1990), we found that this was not enough. Students repeatedly confronted issues of fundamental importance to the discipline, on occasion inventing scientific misconception; but there was no one there to help them push to higher levels of understanding or rectify a misunderstanding. For these reasons, we decided to introduce domain-specific expertise into the system. Therefore, in addition to the expertise that is generated in the classroom, FCL participants now have access to a broader level of information, both face-to-face and online via electronic mail.

Face-to-Face Consultation: Benchmark Lessons. Elementary school teachers are rarely subject-area specialists, and this has been true in most of our FCL classrooms. In light of this, FCL has adopted the procedure of providing a subject-area specialist who works with teachers to develop units and subtopics, to select a variety of research materials and artifacts, and to deliver occasional benchmark lessons (diSessa & Minstrell, in press). We note in passing that these benchmark lessons also serve a professional development function. With increasing exposure to the visitor's lessons, the classroom teachers learn more about the content area and increasingly take over responsibility for the benchmark lessons.

Benchmark lessons serve several important functions. First, the visiting expert (or classroom teacher when appropriate) uses the format to introduce a new unit. At the beginning of a unit of study, the benchmark lesson serves to introduce the class to the big ideas and deep principles that they will be studying. Ideally, the first benchmark centers around some common knowledge that the class as a whole has developed in preparation for the first benchmark (a video viewed, a play enacted, a powerful text read, an experiment performed). This common knowledge (Edwards & Mercer, 1987) can be referred back to by all students once they start their idiosyncratic research odysseys.

Subsequent benchmarks occur when the classroom teacher or visiting expert feels the class is ready to progress toward higher levels of abstraction. The adult leads the class to look for higher order relations, encouraging the students to pool their expertise in a novel conceptualization of the topic. For example, if they have discovered the notion of energy and amount of food eaten, the expert might lead them toward the biological concept of metabolic rate.

Another benchmark activity involves the teacher modeling thinking and self-reflection concerning how she would go about researching a topic, or how she might reason with the information given, or not given, as in the case of reasoning on the basis of incomplete information (Bruner, 1969; Collins & Stevens, 1982). Finally, a simple but imperative type of benchmark lesson is when the adult teacher asks the group to summarize what is known and what still needs to be discovered, thereby helping students set new learning goals to guide the next stage of inquiry.

Online Consultation.   Another way that FCL classrooms have the benefit of wider experience is via electronic mail. It has always been recognized that any learning community is limited by the combined knowledge of its members. Within traditional schools, members draw on a limited knowledge capital if the faculty and students are relatively static. Or they face jarring discontinuity if there is rapid turnover, as is the case in many inner city schools. In addition, both teachers' and students' expectations concerning excellence, or what it means to learn and understand, may be limited if the only standards are local. Experts coaching via electronic mail provide FCL with an essential resource, freeing teachers from the sole burden of knowledge guardian and allowing the community to extend in ever widening circles of expertise.

Linking the teachers and students to a wider community of scholars helps teachers handle the domain-expertise problem that often impedes investment in deep content knowledge in elementary school classes. In the last several years, FCL has been involved in recruiting local expertise within the community to join forces with classroom teachers and students to extend the learning community of which all are members (A. L. Brown, Ellery, & Campione, in press; Campione, A. L. Brown, & Jay, 1992). The essential underlying principle is that all members are co-researchers, colearners, and coteachers, who listen to and respect each other.

Face-to-face and online experts are not merely providers of much needed information, they act as role models of thinking, wondering, querying, and making inferences on the basis of incomplete knowledge. The metaphor we have used to explain varieties of expertise within the classroom extends to the wider community, supported by electronic mail. We conceive of both communities, the face-to-face and the electronic, as supporting multiple, overlapping zones of proximal development, with the expert acting as model, guide, and supportive other, as well as a knowledge source, pushing the student to higher levels of understanding. Extending the learning community beyond the classroom walls to form virtual communities across time and space not only enriches the knowledge base available to students but also exposes them to models of reasoning and reflection about the learning process itself (A. L. Brown, Ellery, & Campione, in press; Campione et al., 1992).

Children Teaching Children

Cross-age teaching is an important support for FCL; the community is enriched to the extent that we can rely on the expertise of the children themselves. FCL uses cross-age teaching, both face-to-face and via electronic mail, and also uses older students as discussion leaders guiding the reciprocal teaching and Jigsaw groups of younger students (A. L. Brown & Campione, 1994; Nakagawa, Brown, Kennedy, Walker, & Felgenhauer, 1994). Cross-age teaching not only increases the knowledge capital of the community, but it also provides students invaluable opportunities to talk about learning. We agree with Bruner (1972) that the higher goal of tutoring is the building of community. Cross-age teaching gives students responsibility and purpose, and reinforces collaborative structures throughout the school.

Our cross-age teaching program to date has involved fifth- to seventh-grade students working with first to third graders. The older students have expertise in reciprocal teaching procedures, guided writing using computers, and the content area of interest to both ages (note that both older and younger students focus on endangered species in their environmental science units). They are subsequently given systematic training in tutoring and the rudiments of ethnographic methods—what to look for, field notes, interviewing tutees, and so forth (Heath & Mangiola, 1991).

Older students are then divided into teachers and observers. The teachers are assigned two tutees whom they assist in undertaking all aspects of their research: reading, discussing important points, composing on the computer, setting new learning goals, and so on. The remaining students work as ethnographers, taking field notes, and interviewing tutors and tutees. The roles are then reversed, with the student teachers becoming ethnographers and vice versa.

Older students also act as teachers when they lead RT or Jigsaw sessions for the younger students, thereby providing much needed group leaders and role models (A. L. Brown & Campione, 1994). The use of older children to assist the research efforts of their younger colleagues contributes to the self-esteem of the older students, provides individualized attention to the younger students, helps relieve the teaching burden on the classroom teacher, and contributes to the building of a sharing community.

Sharing Information

The second prong in the FCL system is that of motivated sharing. Students undertake their research activities for the purpose of sharing information in order eventually to perform a consequential act. This sharing occurs informally face-to-face and online, but it also occurs by design because of the Jigsaw and cross-talk participant structures.

Jigsaw has already been described. It is a principle participant structure of FCL, modeled after Aronson's classic procedure. Students are divided into research groups, and then regroup into Jigsaw units composed of one member of each of the research groups. These "experts" share the benefits of their research so that all will be prepared for the consequential task, whatever it might be. By definition, the consequential task demands the compilation of all subunits of the knowledge unit under inquiry.

Cross-talk is a whole-class activity designed and led by the students themselves (A. L. Brown & Campione, 1994). In the initial FCL classes (A. L. Brown & Campione, 1990), Jigsaw actually occurred quite late in the research cycle. Students complained that by the time they began teaching in Jigsaw, it was too late for them to shore up their understanding or to do major revisions to their written work. Asked questions by their peers that they could not answer, they felt inadequate and at the same time realized they did not understand completely themselves. Teaching others is an extremely powerful test of comprehension. So the students designed cross-talk, whereby members of the various research groups periodically report in about their findings to date. Students from other working groups then ask questions of fact, clarification, or extension. Students carefully record knowledge or explanations they lack in their field notes and use these indicators as the basis for the next round of research. The various groups thus talk "across groups" and provide comprehension checks for each other.

Expertise is deliberately shared via Jigsaw and cross-talk. Because students depart on idiosyncratic research agendas, varieties of expertise arise, and students make use of this distributed expertise. We refer to this phenomenon as *majoring* (A. L. Brown et al., 1993). Children are free to major in a variety of ways, free to learn and teach whatever they like within the limits set by their selected subtopic. Children select topics of interest—some become resident experts on disease and contagion; others major in animal communication strategies or animal communities; still others become concerned with animal versus human rights. Some students become technology mavens; others specialize in illustration; some are known and rewarded for their skills as social facilitators. Within the community of the classroom, these varieties of expertise are recognized and used for the joint good.

The Consequential Task

A main ploy of an FCL classroom is to trap students into thinking deeply. One such trap is the consequential task. Everyone is held responsible for the entire knowledge unit through the requirement that each research cycle end with an activity that demands consideration of all aspects of the unit. In our first FCL classrooms (A. L. Brown & Campione, 1990), we used two such tasks: a traditional test at the end of each of three units (defense mechanisms, changing populations, habitat destruction) and a choice of long-term projects that tapped knowledge gleaned in all three units, for example, design a biopark to protect an endangered species, a biosphere, or a habitat for an invented species. The consequential task in the second-grade class mentioned earlier had the students inventing an animal of the future, complete with habitat and solutions to the six design criteria mentioned earlier—method of communication, protection from the elements, reproductive strategy, and so on. These consequential acts bring the research cycle to an end, force students to share knowledge across groups, and act as occasions for exhibition and reflection.

In addition to the consequential acts that seal the end of the research–share–perform cycle, FCL uses a variety of other assessment procedures that are to some extent intended to be transparent to the students and to reinforce the type of guided learning to which they are exposed. These assessments include clinical interviews, dynamic assessment, transfer tests, and thought experiments (for details of these assessments, see A. L. Brown, 1992; A. L. Brown & Campione, 1990, 1994; Campione, Shapiro, & A. L. Brown, 1995).

These guided assessments are collaborative learning experiences in their own right. The philosophy of negotiation and appropriation within zones of proximal development is just as much a part of our assessment procedures as of our instructional activities. Often the two are hard to distinguish. Both are based on the same loosely translated Vygotskian theory.

Guided assessment methods present children with problems just one step beyond their existing competence and then provide help as needed for the child to reach independent mastery. Again, competence is fostered in social interactions before individual mastery is expected. The degree of aid needed, both to learn new principles and to apply them, is carefully calibrated and measured. The amount of aid needed is a much better index of students' future learning trajectories in a domain than static pretests (A. L. Brown, Campione, Webber, & McGilly, 1992; Campione & A. L. Brown, 1990).

In many ways the guided assessment procedure mirrors the RT instructional procedure. As can be seen in Table 11.3, both are based on the same type of learning theory but differ in their primary goals—instruction or assessment of a student's level of understanding. The primary difference rests in the nature and timing of the adult aid. In assessment, aid is metered out only as needed, permitting students to demonstrate independent competence when they can and permitting adults to gauge the extent of that competence. In the RT instructional mode, help is given opportunistically as a result of the teacher's online diagnosis of need. Four main principles are involved in the design of both guided instruction and assessment:

1. Understanding procedures rather than just speed and accuracy are the focus of instruction and assessment.

2. Expert guidance is used to reveal as well as promote independent competence.

3. Microgenetic analysis permits estimates of learning as it actually occurs over time.

TABLE 11.3
Guided Instruction and Assessment in a Zone of Proximal Development

Main Similarities
Based (loosely) on Vygotsky's Learning Theory
Involve guided collaboration with expert feedback
Strategy modeling by experts (apprenticeship model)
Externalizing mental events via discussion formats
Online assessment of novice status
Help given, responsive to student needs
Aimed at problem solving at the level of metacognition
Understanding measured by transfer, flexible use of knowledge

Main Differences			
Guided Instruction (Reciprocal Teaching)		*Guided Assessment* (Clinical Assessment)	
Goal:	collaborative learning	Goal:	individual assessment
Test:	knowledge and strategies	Teach:	knowledge and strategies
Aid:	opportunistic	Aid:	standardized hints
Hints:	easy-to-hard to scaffold student progress	Hints:	hard-to-easy to measure student need

Note: Adapted from Brown et al. (1993).

4. Proleptic teaching (Stone & Wertsch, 1984) is involved in both assessment and instruction, for both aim at one stage beyond current performance, in anticipation of levels of competence not yet achieved individually but possible within supportive learning environments.

A METACOGNITIVE ENVIRONMENT

On the Importance of Reflection

In Fig. 11.1, the research–share–consequential task scheme is subsumed under the overarching concept of reflection. FCL is historically and intentionally a metacognitive environment. The roots of FCL, including RT, Jigsaw, guided writing, guided assessment, and exhibitions and performances are all designed as metacognitive activities, occasions for students to monitor their own and others' comprehension, and reflect on progress to date. The classroom talk in FCL is largely metacognitive: "Do I understand?" "That doesn't make sense," "They [the audience] can't understand X without Y," and so forth.

Even when an aspect of the simple system is not inherently metacognitive, it is rendered so by one means or another. For example, in the early version of FCL (A. L. Brown & Campione, 1990), the teachers demanded that quizzes and tests be given at the end of each of the research units that corresponded not accidentally to their district's grading period. In order to comply with the need for quizzes, FCL staff, in collaboration with the classroom teachers, designed short-answer quizzes that tapped factual material, inferential material, and flexible use of knowledge. In order to make this an occasion for reflection, the normal procedure for designing tests was modified in several ways. First, the students were fully aware of the reason why tests were given; the concept of accountability and teacher responsibility was explained and discussed. Second, the students were asked to make up one-half of the questions to be asked on their research subtopic. This occasioned much reflection concerning what was important to test, what was a "thinking question," and what was a "picky, detail question." Some students at this stage realized that what they thought most important to test had received short shrift in their texts, and subsequently revised them to place greater emphasis on important information at the expense of trivia, beloved trivia, but trivia all the same. Third, the students designed quiz-like games to prepare themselves and their colleagues to take the whole test. And fourth, debriefing after the test consisted of discussions about why questions were fair, or "thinking questions," as much as why an answer was correct or not. Even traditional tests can be made objects of reflection and occasions for thinking and learning. An atmosphere of querying, wondering, inferring, and reflecting is a mainstay of a well-functioning FCL classroom even when certain activities would not necessarily lend themselves to this end.

On the Importance of Discourse

Discussion is essential to the FCL classroom in which we explicitly aim to simulate the active exchange and reciprocity of a dialogue. Our classrooms are intentionally designed to foster interpretive communities of discourse (Fish, 1980). FCL encourages newcomers to adopt the discourse structure, goals, values, and belief systems of a community of research practices. Ideas are seeded in discussion, and migrate throughout the community via mutual appropriation and negotiated meaning. Sometimes they lie fallow, and sometimes they bloom (see A. L. Brown et al., 1993, and A. L. Brown &

Campione, 1994, for examples). The FCL community relies on the development of a discourse genre in which constructive discussion, questioning, querying, and criticism are the mode rather than the exception. In time these reflective activities become internalized as autocriticism (Binet, 1909) and self-reflective thought (A. L. Brown, 1978).

On the Importance of Disciplinary Content

Although billed as a thinking curriculum (Resnick & Resnick, 1992), FCL relies heavily on disciplinary content units of suitable rigor to sustain in-depth research over substantial periods of time. One cannot expect students to invest intellectual curiosity and disciplined inquiry on trivia; there must be a challenge, there must be room to explore, to delve deeply, to understand at ever deepening levels of complexity. Four main points have influenced our choice of domains of inquiry. The units should: (a) be informed by research on developmental trajectories in a domain, both in terms of knowledge and reasoning strategies; (b) support intermediate and long-term instructional goals; (c) foster sharing; and (d) encourage diversity and multiple ways to participate (Lave & Wenger, 1991).

Knowledge and Development

An FCL unit should lead students to conduct research, read, write, and think about a compelling, deep theme at a developmentally appropriate level. It is precisely because we know something about the development of children's theories of biology (Carey, 1985) that we initially selected the biological underpinnings of environmental science as our focus. The idea is to understand children's emergent theories about biology and lead them gradually toward deep principles of the discipline, such as interdependence, biodiversity, evolution, and adaptation. In principle, the same should be true of areas of the social sciences, but there is, at present, a paucity of developmental research to inform this endeavor.

Although we believe it to be somewhat romantic to think of young children entering the community of practice of adult academic disciplines (J. S. Brown, Collins, & Duguid, 1989), awareness of the deep principles of academic disciplines should enable us to design intellectual practices for the young that are stepping stones to mature understanding or at least are not glaringly inconsistent with the end goal. For example, in the domain of ecology and environmental science, we realize that contemporary understanding of the underlying biology would necessitate a ready familiarity with biochemistry and genetics that is not within the grasp of young students.

Instead of watering down such content to a strange mixture of the biological and the biochemical, as do textbooks for the young, we invite young students into the world of 19th-century naturalists, scientists who also lacked modern knowledge of biochemistry and genetics. The idea is that by the time students *are* introduced to contemporary disciplinary knowledge, they will have developed a thirst for that knowledge, as indeed has been the case historically.

Practically speaking this means that as we revisit, for example, the topic of endangered species across grade, we gradually reach toward increasingly sophisticated disciplinary understanding. We refer to this as a *developmental corridor*. Children remain in the program for several years, during which time they delve more deeply into the underlying principles of the domain. Second, fourth, sixth, and eighth graders may be working on extinct, endangered, and rebounding populations, and all will be guided by the basic disciplinary principles of interdependence and adaptation. But different levels of sophistication will be expected at each age. This procedure has much in keeping with the notion of a spiraling curriculum such as that intended by Bruner (1963, 1969). Topics are not just revisited willy-nilly at various ages at some unspecified level of sophistication, as is the case in many curricula that are described as spiraling, but each revisit is based on a deepening knowledge of that topic, critically dependent on past experience and on the developing knowledge base of the child. It should matter what the underlying principles are at, say, kindergarten and grade two; it should matter that the sixth-grade students have experienced the fourth-grade curriculum.

We take seriously the fact that an understanding of the growth of children's thinking in a domain should serve as the basis for setting age-appropriate goals. As we learn more about children's knowledge and theories about the biological and physical world (Carey & Gelman, 1991), we can be more precise about designing age-sensitive curricula. It is for these reasons that in our environmental science/biology strand we seek guidance from developmental psychology concerning students' evolving biological understanding (Carey, 1985; Hatano & Inagaki, 1987; Keil, 1992; Wellman & Gelman, 1988). We know that by age six, children can fruitfully investigate the concept of living things, a topic of great interest that they refined over a period of years. It is not until approximately age 10 that they begin assimilating plants into this category (Carey, 1985), and perhaps not even then (Hatano & Inagaki, 1987). By second grade we begin to address animal/habitat mutuality and interdependence. Sixth graders examine biodiversity and the effect of broad versus narrow niches on endangerment. By eighth grade the effect of variation in the gene pool on adaptation and survival is not too complex a topic. Whereas second graders begin to consider adaptation and habitats in a simple way, sixth graders can distinguish structural, functional, and behavioral adaptations, biotic and abiotic interdependence, and so forth.

A similar developmental guideline governs our approach to reasoning within the domain. For example, we initially permit teleological reasoning (Keil, 1992) and an overreliance on causality in general, but then we press for an increasingly more sophisticated consideration of chance, probability, and randomness (A. L. Brown, Metz, & Campione, in press). Personification as analogy (Carey, 1985) is a powerful, if limited, reasoning strategy used by the young (and by the old, for that matter). It supports inductive reasoning and helps children distinguish between natural kinds and artifacts (Gelman & Markman, 1986). We allow children to reason on this basis, putting off until later discussion of the limitations of this way of thinking.

It is of no small theoretical interest to developmental psychologists that by deliberately aligning instruction to the child's developing theories about biology, we face a theoretical and practical issue about developmental sensitivity. The lion's share of our knowledge of young children's theories of the biological and physical world has been provided by developmental psychologists. True to the tradition of this discipline, cross-sectional or microgenetic data are taken from children divorced from the culture in which they are developing, a culture that includes school. We know a great deal about what the average (usually upper middle class) child knows about what is alive, not alive, never alive, at age five, eight, ten, and so forth. What is not known, however, is the influence of instruction on these developmental milestones, a basic research topic in itself. If we target children's developmental theories as the essence of instruction, what will change developmentally, and what will be resistant to such change?

We have introduced the term developmental corridor to capture the notion that units of FCL should be revisited at ever increasing levels of complexity. This allows us to ask whether, after 4 or 5 years in the program, sixth graders will be capable of performing at much more mature levels of reasoning, capable of acquiring and using domain knowledge of considerably greater complexity than that of sixth graders in the program for the first time. In a very fundamental sense, to the degree FCL is successful, we should be mapping a moving target. Units once thought suitable for sixth graders will now be found more appropriate for fourth grade, and so on. Of considerable theoretical interest to developmental psychologists is what, if any, forms of knowledge and process are immutable in the face of carefully tailored instruction (Gelman & Baillargeon, 1983).

Knowledge and Instructional Goals

We would like teachers to share the biggest of big pictures concerning knowledge and development, that is, to understand the entire developmental corridor that we envision for a topic of inquiry. Ideally, teachers should know that the reason we concentrate on the concept of interdependence with the baobab tree and animal survival mechanisms in Grades 1 and 2 is that this will be an important foundation for students studying urban wildlife in Grade 3, endangered species in Grade 5, and changing populations in Grade 6. The entire developmental corridor, and links supporting it across grade, should be known to participating teachers; they should have a vision of what went before and what will come next (in the case of, for example, a third-grade teacher, what was covered in second grade and what will be expected of the students in fourth grade). This cross-age consideration is routinely given to skill acquisition in grade schools but rarely to matters of content.

Although this big picture is undoubtedly helpful in building the knowledge community within a school, an understanding of the big picture within a year-long curriculum is also necessary. Thus, within a grade level, we have found it helpful to provide each unit starting, intermediate, and final goals. A concrete example from a novice fifth/sixth-grade class is shown in Fig. 11.2. Students began research on endangered species by adopting a particular animal and finding out all they could about it. Once this activity was well under way, the teacher, in a benchmark lesson, pushed the students to

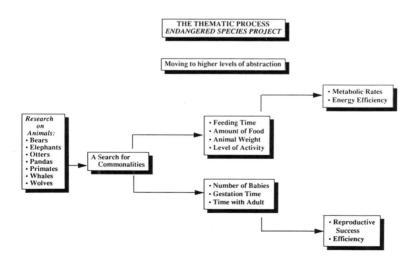

FIG. 11.2. A concrete example from a novice fifth/sixth-grade class..

consider common problems the various endangered animals might share. Students discovered that their animals, although living on different continents, in different types of habitats (rainforests, oceans, and so on), did share common problems such as number of babies, gestation time, degree of parenting, among others. These commonalities can be harnessed in the service of introducing a big idea in biology, in this case reproductive success or efficiency. Another set of common problems the children readily identified—the amount of food consumed, the notion of energy conservation, and size of a vanishing habitat—led to another big idea, metabolic rate. Providing examples of such stepping stones toward a big idea within the reach of a particular grade level helps FCL teachers know where they hope to go and recognize when they get there.

Fostering Sharing

Because of the centrality of sharing in the simple research–share–perform cycle, another requirement for an FCL unit is that it be sharable. That is, the unit should be sufficiently rich that it can support five or so sustained research subunits, the products of which combine in some way to form a coherent whole.

An FCL unit should support Jigsaw activity, that is, it should have a purpose and a goal that would be helped by sharing. It should support majoring. Each unit should begin with a set of shared materials to build common knowledge before the students branch off on their subunits. This common knowledge could be based on one item if students are young, for example, the baobab tree mentioned earlier, or four or five items if the students are older. For example, in the fifth/sixth grade we introduce endangered species with a play (*The Day They Parachuted Cats onto Borneo*, Charlotte Pomeranz, 1969/1993) that illustrates disruption in the food chain, a video on habitat destruction, a *Newsweek* article on malaria, and an expository text on peregrine falcons. These anchoring events (CTGV, 1992) introduced the students to common knowledge via multiple genre to serve as a common source of reference.

Jigsaw activity then follows. Jigsaw in its many forms makes sense only if subgroup members need to listen and learn from representatives of the other subgroups. Unless they do so, they have no chance of understanding the entire unit or of performing the consequential task. Our adaptation of Jigsaw differs somewhat from the version commonly used in schools, where teachers typically assign responsibility to subunits arbitrarily. One popular variant of Jigsaw is that students are given a long passage about, for example, Benjamin Franklin. The passage is cut into five or so sections and each group learns one section in preparation for a test. They then share their knowledge with others via Jigsaw. A Jigsaw activity such as this could take as little as a day. Even when students are required to do research, it is often of limited duration. Thus, FCL follows the spirit of Jigsaw, but differs in two important ways: The students, to a certain extent, choose their research topics (see A. L. Brown & Campione, 1994), and research is long term. So in our adaptation, we have given certain degrees of freedom to groups in their choice of topics and extended the time span of research to 8–10 weeks or so (ideally, three units/year). In our work, we distinguish between two main types of Jigsaw: true Jigsaws and purpose-directed Jigsaws.

A True Jigsaw.   In this situation, learners need to understand all subtopics to understand the whole. The nearest example of a true Jigsaw that we have used is shown in the left-hand side of Table 11.4, Teacher A. In order to understand food webs and chains, you need all five pieces: photosynthesis, energy exchange, competition, consumers, and decomposition. True Jigsaws are difficult to design because they demand that each subunit be independently coherent, so that a group can conduct research on it. At the same time, each subunit combines with others to cohere at a higher level of meaning. We doubt that such jigsaws would often occur spontaneously, leading to the compromise we have adopted, which we call the purpose-directed Jigsaw.

Purpose-Directed Jigsaw.   Here the pieces of the puzzle are all needed before a Jigsaw group (one composed of a member of each of the research groups) can complete its consequential task. As we have already discussed,

TABLE 11.4

Food Chains and Webs: Seventh Grade
Two Iterations

Teacher A		Teacher B
True Jigsaw		Purpose-Driven Jigsaw
	Subtopics	
• photosynthesis		• rain forest
• energy exchange		• grasslands
• competition		• oceans
• consumers		• fresh water
• decomposition		• desert
	Consequential Task	
Understand Food Webs by combining 5 subtopics		Design a Space Station involving all habitats

the task can be as traditional as taking a test or it could be the less traditional design task used in the second grade described earlier, that of designing an animal of the future. Although this second-grade activity is not a true Jigsaw—one can understand a great deal about animal communication without considering any of the other topics—it becomes a Jigsaw because of the task set. The Jigsaw groups must design an animal of the future that incorporates a "solution" to each of the six problems (components of the task set): protection from the elements, communication, reproduction, and so forth. Jigsaw groups need to share to complete the design task.

True and Purpose-Driven Jigsaws: A Contrast. In Table 11.4, we show how two seventh-grade teachers chose to make jigsaws out of subunits for the topic of food chains and webs. Whereas second graders grappled with this topic at a rudimentary level, by seventh grade we require that students deal with a greater depth of biological complexity. For example, at this age they need to know about photosynthesis.

Teacher A divided the topic into subunits that are more like a true Jigsaw. One cannot really understand food webs without an understanding of photosynthesis, decomposition, and energy exchange. In contrast, Teacher B decided to look at food webs as they are embedded in a variety of habitats. All groups looked at photosynthesis, decomposition, and so on, as they play out in a particular habitat: rain forest, grasslands, oceans, and so forth. Whereas in Teacher A's class groups need to share in order to understand the whole, a true Jigsaw, in Teacher B's class, there is no reason why the rain-forest people need to talk to the grasslands people unless there is a consequential task to pull them together. In this particular class the consequential task was to design a space station, or biosphere, that incorporated aspects of all five habitats.

Supporting Diversity

The selection of a knowledge unit should support diversity, that is, it should afford students with multiple talents, or intelligences if you will (Gardner, 1983), a way into peripheral or full participation (Lave & Wenger, 1991). One obvious way to do this is to provide material that ranges widely in the degree of literacy skills needed for their access. For this reason, we provide materials that demand little reading, from children's books and magazines (*Ranger Rick, Junior National Geographic*) all the way up to college textbooks, field guides, *National Geographic*, and encyclopedias. Most students can find some text that they can read. Similarly, we provide non-textual materials (videos, CD-ROMs, illustrations). Students who need such help are encouraged to dictate their summaries and questions concerning read or viewed materials. We provide help in critical viewing just as we do in critical reading; it is perfectly possible for a video, just as much as a text, to be the subject of RT or RS. From its inception, FCL has used qualified special education teachers to smooth mainstreamed children's inclusion into these classrooms (Campione, Rutherford, Gordon, Walker, & A. L. Brown, 1994).

Within the FCL community, students major in certain aspects of the knowledge domain. Subcultures of expertise develop: Varieties of expertise are recognized by the pattern of help-seeking and the roles students assume in small- and whole-class discussions. In these discussions, the class defers to expert children in both verbal and nonverbal ways. Status in discussions does not reside "in" the individual child, however, as in the case of established leaders and followers but is a transient phenomenon that depends on a child's perceived expertise within the domain of discourse. As the domain of discourse changes, so too do the students receiving deferential treatment (A. L. Brown et al., 1993).

It is very much our intention to increase diversity in this way. Traditional school practices have aimed at just the opposite, decreasing diversity, a traditional practice based on several assumptions: There exist prototypical, normal students who, at a certain age, can do a certain amount of work, or grasp a certain amount of material, in the same amount of time (Becker, 1972). Now these are strong assumptions! They must serve a powerful administrative function (Cuban, 1984; Tyack & Tobin, 1994), for there is little that we know about learning and development that would support them. Although we aim at conformity on the basics—everyone must read, write, compute, and so forth—we also aim at increasing diversity of expertise and interests so that members of the community can benefit from the increasing richness of knowledge available. The essence of teamwork is sharing varieties of expertise. Teams composed of members with homogeneous ideas and skills are denied access to such diversity.

Learning and teaching in FCL depend heavily on creating, sustaining, and expanding a community of distributed expertise. Members of the community are critically dependent on each other. This interdependence promotes an atmosphere of joint responsibility, mutual respect, and a sense of personal and group identity. With responsibility and the acceptance of legitimate differences (Heath, 1991) comes respect, respect between students, between students and school staff, and among all members of the extended community including experts available by electronic mail. Students' questions are taken seriously. Experts, be they children or adults, do not always know the answers: Known-answer question-and-answering games (Heath, 1983; Mehan, 1979) have no home in this environment. Respect is earned by responsible participation in a genuine knowledge-building community (Scardamalia & Bereiter, 1991).

SYSTEMS ALL THE WAY DOWN

The essential point that we have reiterated throughout this chapter is that we conceive of FCL as a system of purposeful activities. There is a purpose for every activity, and nothing exists without a purpose. All members of the community—students, teachers, parents, and researchers alike—should be aware of this.

Furthermore, it is not the case that FCL can be adopted piecemeal, that favorite participant structures can be mixed and matched willy-nilly. The Chinese menu approach, one from Group A, one from Group B, will result in a variety of surface procedures being adhered to, but the overall mission will be missed. If the system is not in place, it will not be FCL.

Many schools (and researchers) now share a common language of reform, and it is not uncommon for a school district to claim to have implemented many of the surface rituals of FCL. Typically, however, their approach is the one illustrated in Fig. 11.3.

They may have adopted RT, Jigsaw, process writing, and long-term projects; but these are practiced as isolated activities that do not feed into each other in systemic ways. In contrast an FCL selection of activities would look more like Fig. 11.4. Even though only a subset of participant structures

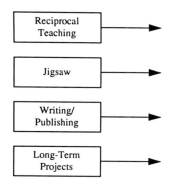

FIG. 11.3. Community of learners: A surface interpretation.

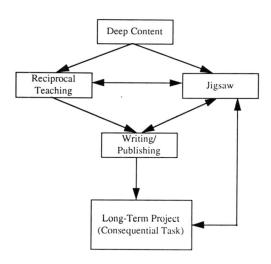

FIG. 11.4. Community of learners: A systems interpretation.

have been chosen, they are systemically aligned. Furthermore, looking beyond the particular activity structures to the simple system shown in Fig. 11.1,
we see that the selection of activities in Fig. 11.4 but not Fig. 11.3 always
supports the research–share–perform cycle that is the backbone of FCL.

The simple FCL system—research, share, consequential act—can be
maintained and implemented in many different ways. FCL is based, not on
a set of prescriptions, but rather on sets of principles having to do with the
learning environment, the content being studied, the forms of assessment,
and so forth. The various activities that were incorporated into early FCL
classrooms were chosen to serve particular functions and to support the
systemic nature of the intervention. Those activities can be modified,
dropped, or replaced by others, but only if the system itself remains intact.

For example, RT requires that students discuss complex passages, collaborate, and share their individual expertise and perspectives on a particular text. No doubt there exist other reading comprehension programs that
could support these functions. The question would be: If one replaces RT
with another activity, how does it affect the system? What perturbation in
the system might the substitute set in motion? What functions might be
lost? The emphasis is on functionality, philosophy, and principles, not on
procedures.

RT also forms a basis for the introduction of Jigsaw activities, providing a structure for the discussions that take place in that format; that is, the RT strategies transfer well to Jigsaw and help students as they begin teaching others. Would a different reading procedure perform this function at all, as well, or perhaps better than RT? Older or more experienced students may profit if we replace RT with another activity, such as RS. Again, the question is, does it serve the same function while at the same time being more in keeping with the needs of the older student population?

Jigsaw has consistently played a major role in FCL because it is an excellent way of distributing expertise. But Jigsaw can play this function only if the content that students are working on supports it. The structure of the larger units is of central importance. If the content is not compelling, not based on big ideas and deep principles, there will be little to talk about. If the research groups and their subtopics are not well chosen, there will be no reason for the different research groups to talk to each other. Similarly, if it is not a true Jigsaw or there is no consequential task that taps all students' understanding of each of the subtopics, the motivation to engage in Jigsaw and cross-talk activities will be reduced. Hence, the inclusion of well-chosen, long-term projects (design an animal) to support the system. These are not randomly selected "cute" projects but an essential part of the system of activity.

In FCL students are required to read, listen to, and view a variety of artifacts in order to do their research. These activities are unified and given purpose by the research and reporting requirements of FCL. The conclusions derived from research activities form the basis for writing activities, which in turn play a central role in teaching.

The activities of FCL are mutually reinforcing and supportive of each other. Each has a clear function within the classroom. It is quite possible, indeed extraordinarily easy, to adopt many, maybe all, of the constitutive FCL activities in a classroom and still not have what we would identify as an FCL classroom. Reciprocal teaching could be a major part of the class' reading program; Jigsaw activities could take place as a form of collaborative learning but without deep and enduring content issues; guided writing could be the approach of choice but the writing not related to any major content; and some time could be spent on long-term projects. But if they are not tied together, if the functions they are to play are not mutually supportive, the synergy that is expected from the systemic arrangement will be lost, leaving simply a set of parallel rather than interacting activities.

PRINCIPLES OF LEARNING

In this section we summarize the key principles of learning that have resulted in the invention of FCL. The key principles are shown in Table 11.5. Each time we list the key principles, there is a change in emphasis (A. L. Brown, 1994; A. L. Brown & Campione, 1994), but there is a level of constancy in the key elements of the list.

Systems and Cycles

As emphasized throughout this chapter, FCL consists of a system of activities that occurs in cycles of research–share–perform activities. FCL has relied on a set of repetitive participant structures to support the simple cycle (RT, Jigsaw, cross-talk, research/writing, design tasks, and others). All or any of these in principle can be replaced, as long as the simple cycle is maintained. Across reinventions of FCL there should be constancy at the level of deep structure; variability is permitted at the level of surface rituals as long as the variations are constrained by the first principles of learning that are constitutive of FCL.

A Metacognitive Environment

FCL grew out of our previous work on active, strategic learning, under the control of learners who have reflective access to their own repertoire of learning strategies (A. L. Brown, 1975, 1978, 1992, 1994; A. L. Brown, Bransford, Ferrara, & Campione, 1983). It is not surprising, therefore, that FCL is self-consciously and intentionally a metacognitive environment in which effort after meaning (Bartlett, 1932), comprehension monitoring, and an atmosphere of wondering and querying knowledge form part of reflective learning practices.

The Centrality of Discourse

Our classrooms are intentionally designed to give place to multiple voices in Bakhtin's (Holquist & Emerson, 1981) sense of voice as the speaking personality and the speaking consciousness. A major tenet of Bakhtin's (1986) creed was that "any true understanding is dialogic in nature."

Life in FCL classrooms involves negotiation and definition of ideas, terms, and concepts (O'Connor, 1991), so that something such as a common voice (Wertsch, 1991) and a common knowledge base (Edwards & Mercer,

TABLE 11.5
Principles of Learning to Support FCL

(1) Systems and Cycles
- Seasonal cycles of Research–Share–Perform activities
- Supported by repetitive participant structures
- Participant structures can be replaced if and only if the replacement serves the simple RSP system
- Constancy at level of deep structure, variability at level of surface ritual
- All activities for a purpose, a purpose for all activities

(2) Metacognitive Environment, Reflective Environment
- Active, strategic nature of learning
- Self-regulation and other-regulation for common good
- Autocriticism, comprehension monitoring
- Effort after meaning, search for understanding
- Atmosphere of wondering, querying, worrying knowledge
- Reflective practices

(3) Discourse
- Dialogic base
- Shared discourse, common knowledge
- Seeding, migration and appropriation of ideas
- Mutual appropriation
- An interpretive community

(4) Deep Content Knowledge
- Developmental sensitivity
- Intellectually honest and demanding
- Developmental corridors from children's intuitive knowledge to deep principles of a discipline of inquiry
- Intermediate goals and levels of abstraction
- Support, sharing
- Enriched by diversity

(5) Distributed Expertise
- Sharing for a purpose
- Collaboration not just nice but necessary
- Major, identity, and respect
- Multiple ways in, multiple intelligences
- Legitimization of differences
- Community building

(6) Instruction and Assessment
- Deliberately aligned
- Based on same theory, loosely Vygotskian
- Guided practice, guided participation
- Multiple zones of proximal development
- Transparent, authentic, and purposeful

(7) Community Features
- Community of practice
- Communities of practice with multiple overlapping roles
- Link between current practice and expert practice emphasized
- Elements of ownership and choice
- Community beyond the classroom wall

1987) emerge over time. This common voice evolves continuously via "situated negotiation and renegotiation of meaning" (Lave & Wenger, 1991). Participants in the community are free to appropriate ideas in the air and transform these ideas via personal interpretation and incorporation. Within the same classroom, participants pass in and out in multiple zones of proximal development as they appropriate ideas and ways of knowing that are ripe for harvesting. Although a common voice emerges, individuals develop ownership of separate parts of that common knowledge through a process of majoring, the intentional focusing on aspects of the system in which a learner decides to specialize. Distributed expertise is a central facet in authentic communities of scientific practice, hence the need to share knowledge among scientists via papers, conferences, and electronic mail. This distributed expertise is no less desirable for establishing a discourse community (Fish, 1980) in grade-school classrooms than it is for practicing scientists.

The core participant structures of our classrooms are essentially dialogic. Sometimes these activities are face to face in small or large group interactions; sometimes they are mediated via print or electronic mail; and at still other times they go underground and become part of the thought processes of members of the community (Vygotsky, 1978). Dialogues provide the format for novices to adopt the discourse structure, goals, values, and belief systems of scientific practice. Over time, the community of learners adopts a common voice and common knowledge base, a shared system of meaning, beliefs, and activity that is as often implicit as it is explicit.

Deep Content Knowledge

We cannot overemphasize the importance of situating FCL within the context of discovering deep conceptual disciplinary-based content knowledge. Domain-area specialists help FCL participants map developmental trajectories that unite children's intuitive theories of biological and physical causality (Carey & Gelman, 1991) with the underlying deep principles of a discipline. Intermediate goals and levels of abstraction (White, 1993) along that route need to be carefully specified. The content tackled should be rigorous, demanding, and intellectually honest (Bruner, 1963) so that there is room for depth and tenacity of inquiry. The content should be sufficiently demanding to support, indeed require, sharing. Diversity of interest and talents within the context of inquiry should enrich the knowledge base of the community as a whole.

Distributed Expertise

The notion of distributed expertise (A. L. Brown et al., 1993) is a critical feature of FCL. Ideas and concepts migrate throughout the community via mutual appropriation and negotiation. Some ideas and ways of knowing become part of common knowledge. Other forms of knowledge and knowing remain the special reserve of those who choose to major in a particular form of expertise. Expertise of one form or another is spread throughout the community at various levels of depth and personal investment. The idea that all children of a certain age in the same grade should acquire the same body of knowledge at the same time, an essential assumption underlying traditional schooling (Tyack & Tobin, 1994), is one of the reasons that contemporary school activities are to a large part inauthentic. Distribution expertise serves to legitimize differences (Heath, 1991), which in turn conveys identity and respect.

Instruction and Assessment

The theory of instruction and assessment that we have embodied within FCL has a long history in our projects dating back to the late 1970s and early 1980s when we were developing instructional procedures (A. L. Brown, Campione, & Day, 1981; Palincsar & A. L. Brown, 1984) and dynamic assessment approaches (A. L. Brown & French, 1979; Campione & A. L. Brown, 1987, 1990; Campione, 1989) grounded in our understanding of Vygotskian theory. We take it as given that learners develop at different rates and, therefore, are ripe at any time for new learning more readily in some areas than others. We favor guided practice and guided participation for both assessment and instruction (see Table 11.2), which are deliberately aligned (Campione, 1989).

Following Frederiksen and Collins (1989), we also aim to make assessment as transparent and as authentic as possible, fully informing students of the purpose of assessment and ceding to them, when possible, a portion of responsibility for their own evaluation.

Community of Practice

And finally, an overarching theme of FCL is that a community of research practice emerges, where overlapping roles create synergy and energy. There is a sense of ownership of the project and choice in its direction: Through their participation in increasingly more mature forums of scholarly research, students are enculturated into the community practice of scholars. These classrooms encourage the development of a community of discourse pervaded by knowledge seeking and inquiry processes. Links between the community practices of the students, teachers, and researchers are emphasized, and a sense of community with shared values emerges. This community extends beyond the classroom walls via cross-age teaching and electronic mail links to peers, apprentices (younger children), and experts, in ever widening circles of expertise and understanding.

CONCLUSION

We have noted that over the course of the century, there have been major changes in both the aims and goals of education and the nature of theories of learning. Those changes have been parallel in many ways. Behaviorist theories of learning emphasized the formation of simple associations and laws of learning of considerable generality; these dovetailed nicely with an educational emphasis on the acquisition of basic skills and a focus on sequencing instruction from "simple" to "more complex" forms of behavior. The subsequent emergence of cognitive theories of learning, with their emphasis on understanding within domains also dovetails nicely with the elevated goals of education, themselves stressing higher forms of literacy and in-depth understanding of content area rules and principles.

This convergence between theory and practice may be more a matter of rhetoric than reality, however. Although the rhetoric and vocabulary of educational reform efforts have changed noticeably over the century, changes in classroom practice appear to lag behind.

We see the current schism as existing in good part because the changes in classroom practice needed to incorporate the new theoretical perspectives are much more difficult to implement than are those that embody behaviorist principles (A. L. Brown, 1994). In the behaviorist period, the focus was on procedures that teachers could employ: drill and practice on targeted subskills, mastery learning, errorless learning, and so forth, with a minimal emphasis on understanding. Procedures devised in one setting, for example, by curriculum designers, could be implemented directly in classrooms in ways that reflected closely the designers' goals.

In contrast, with an increased emphasis on understanding, and the processes whereby understanding is developed, the problem is considerably more complex. The emphasis is on teaching for understanding, and communication of theoretical principles to new teachers so that the philosophy that is maintained demands a more subtle kind of dialogue. The core of our argument is that the application of procedures developed in one setting do not easily transfer to others. Theoretically-based procedures (e.g., reciprocal teaching) are designed on the basis of sets of learning principles, and it is these principles that need to be understood if the procedures are to serve their original function. Further, when a particular set of procedures is chosen, it is necessary to consider not only the principles on which each is based, but also to consider the systemic nature of the package: Do the various procedures complement and support each other, or do they actually clash in some ways? Thus, where the application of procedures was sufficient to mount behaviorist programs, the implementation of current cognitive theories requires, in addition, an analysis of the principles on which the procedures are based, and an analysis of the larger system in which the principle-based procedures coexist. Our main goal in this chapter was to elaborate these concerns with procedures, principles, and systems and consider them in the context of the FCL program.

ACKNOWLEDGMENTS

This research was supported by grants from the Andrew W. Mellon, James S. McDonnell, and Spencer Foundations, and support from the Evelyn Lois Corey Research Fund.

REFERENCES

Aronson, E. (1978). *The jigsaw classroom*. Beverly Hills, CA: Sage.

Bakhtin, M. M. (1986). *Speech genres and other late essays* (V. W. McGee, Trans.). Austin, TX: University of Texas Press.

Bartlett, F. C. (1932). *Remembering: A study in experimental and social psychology*. Cambridge, England: Cambridge University Press.

Bash, B. (1989). *The tree of life: The life of the African baobab*. San Francisco: Sierra Club Books, Little Brown Company.

Becker, H. (1972). A school is a lousy place to learn anything in. *American Behavioral Scientist, 16*, 85–105.

Binet, A. (1909). *Les idees modernes sur les infants*. Paris: Ernest Flammarion.

Brown, A. L. (1975). The development of memory: Knowing, knowing about knowing, and knowing how to know. In H. W. Reese (Ed.), *Advances in child development and behavior* (Vol. 10, pp. 103–152). New York: Academic Press.

Brown, A. L. (1978). Knowing when, where, and how to remember: A problem of metacognition. In R. Glaser (Ed.), *Advances in instructional psychology* (Vol. 1, pp. 77–165). Hillsdale, NJ: Lawrence Erlbaum Associates.

Brown, A. L. (1992). Design experiments: Theoretical and methodological challenges in creating complex interventions in classroom settings. *The Journal of the Learning Sciences, 2*(2), 141–178.

Brown, A. L. (1994). The advancement of learning. Presidential Address, American Educational Research Association, 1994. *Educational Researcher, 23*(8), 4–12.

Brown, A. L., Ash, D., Rutherford, M., Nakagawa, K., Gordon, A., & Campione, J. C. (1993). Distributed expertise in the classroom. In G. Salomon (Ed.), *Distributed cognitions: Psychological and educational considerations* (pp. 188–228). New York: Cambridge University Press.

Brown, A. L., Bransford, J. D., Ferrara, R. A., & Campione, J. C. (1983). Learning, remembering, and understanding. In J. H. Flavell & E. M. Markman (Eds.), *Handbook of child psychology* (4th ed.). *Cognitive development* (Vol. 3, pp. 77–166). New York: Wiley.

Brown, A. L., & Campione, J. C. (1990). Communities of learning and thinking, or A context by any other name. *Human Development, 21,* 108–125.

Brown, A. L., & Campione, J. C. (1994). Guided discovery in a community of learners. In K. McGilly (Ed.), *Classroom lessons: Integrating cognitive theory and classroom practice* (pp. 229–270). Cambridge, MA: Bradford Books, MIT Press.

Brown, A. L., Campione, J. C., & Day, J. D. (1981). Learning to learn: On training students to learn from texts. *Educational Researcher, 10*(2), 14–21.

Brown, A. L., Campione, J. C., Webber, L. S., & McGilly, K. (1992). Interactive learning environments—a new look at assessment and instruction. In B. R. Gifford & M. C. O'Connor (Eds.), *Changing assessments: Alternative views of aptitude, achievement and instruction* (pp. 121–211). Boston: Kluwer Academic Publishers.

Brown, A. L., Ellery, S., & Campione, J. C. (in press). Creating zones of proximal development electronically. In J. G. Greeno & S. Goldman (Eds.), *Thinking practices: A symposium in mathematics and science education.* Mahwah, NJ: Lawrence Erlbaum Associates.

Brown, A. L., & French, L. A. (1979). The zone of potential development: Implications for intelligence testing in the year 2000. *Intelligence, 3,* 253–271.

Brown, A. L., Metz, K. E., & Campione, J. C. (in press). Social interaction and individual understanding in a community of learners: The influence of Piaget and Vygotsky. In J. Vonèche (Ed.), *The social genesis of thought: Piaget and Vygotsky.* Mahwah, NJ: Lawrence Erlbaum Associates. [To be published simultaneously in *Cahiers de la Fondation.* Geneva, Switzerland: Archives Jean Piaget.]

Brown, A. L., & Palincsar, A. S. (1989). Guided, cooperative learning and individual knowledge acquisition. In L. B. Resnick (Ed.), *Knowing, learning, and instruction: Essays in honor of Robert Glaser* (pp. 393–451). Hillsdale, NJ: Lawrence Erlbaum Associates.

Brown, J. S., Collins, A., & Duguid, P. (1989). Situated cognition and the culture of learning. *Educational Researcher, 18,* 32–42.

Bruner, J. S. (1963). *The process of education.* Cambridge, MA: Harvard University Press.

Bruner, J. S. (1969). *On knowing: Essays for the left hand.* Cambridge, MA: Harvard University Press.

Bruner, J. S. (1972). Toward a sense of community. [Review of *Children teach children* by A. Gartner, M. Kohler, & F. Reissman.] *Saturday Review, 55* (15 January), 62–63.

Campione, J. C. (1989). Assisted assessment: A taxonomy of approaches and an outline of strengths and weaknesses. *Journal of Learning Disabilities, 22,* 151–165.

Campione, J. C., & Brown, A. L. (1987). Linking dynamic assessment with school achievement. In C. S. Lidz (Ed.), *Dynamic assessment* (pp. 82–115). New York: Guilford.

Campione, J. C., & Brown, A. L. (1990). Guided learning and transfer: Implications for approaches to assessment. In N. Frederiksen, R. Glaser, A. Lesgold, & M. Shafto (Eds.), *Diagnostic monitoring of skill and knowledge acquisition* (pp. 141–172). Hillsdale, NJ: Lawrence Erlbaum Associates.

Campione, J. C., Brown, A. L., & Jay, M. (1992). Computers in a community of learners. In E. DeCorte, M. Linn, H. Mandl, & L. Verschaffel (Eds.), *Computer-based learning environments and problem solving* (NATO ASI Series F: Computer and Systems Science, 84, pp. 163–192). Berlin: Springer-Verlag.

Campione, J. C., Rutherford, M., Gordon, A., Walker, J., & Brown, A. L. (1994). Now I'm a *real* boy: Zones of proximal development for those at risk. In N. C. Jordan & J. Goldsmith-Phillips (Eds.), *Learning disabilities: New directions for asssessment and intervention* (pp. 245–274). Needham Heights, MA: Allyn and Bacon.

Campione, J. C., Shapiro, A. M., & Brown, A. L. (1995). Forms of transfer in a community of learners: Flexible learning and understanding. In A. McKeough, J. Lupart, & A. Marini (Eds.), *Teaching for transfer: Fostering generalization in learning* (pp. 35–68). Mahwah, NJ: Lawrence Erlbaum Associates.

Carey, S. (1985). *Conceptual change in childhood.* Cambridge, MA: Bradford Books, MIT Press.

Carey, S., & Gelman, R. (1991). *The epigenesis of mind.* Hillsdale, NJ: Lawrence Erlbaum Associates.

Cognition and Technology Group at Vanderbilt. (1992). The Jasper series as an example of anchored instruction: Theory, program description, and assessment data. *Educational Psychologist, 27,* 291–315.

Collins, A., & Stevens, A. L. (1982). Goals and strategies of inquiry teachers. In R. Glaser (Ed.), *Advances in instructional psychology* (Vol. 2, pp. 65–119). Hillsdale, NJ: Lawrence Erlbaum Associates.

Cuban, L. (1984). *How teachers taught: Constancy and change in American classrooms, 1890–1980.* New York: Longman.

diSessa, A., & Minstrell, J. (in press). Benchmark lessons. In J. G. Greeno & S. Goldman (Eds.), *Thinking practices: A symposium in mathematics and science education.* Mahwah, NJ: Lawrence Erlbaum Associates.

Edwards, P., & Mercer, N. (1987). *Common knowledge.* London: Open University Press.

Fish, S. (1980). *Is there a text in this class? The authority of interpretive communities.* Cambridge, MA: Harvard University Press.

Frederiksen, J., & Collins, A. (1989). A systems approach to educational testing. *Educational Researcher, 27,* 27–32.

Gardner, H. (1983). *Frames of mind: The theory of multiple intelligences.* New York: Basic Books.

Gelman, R., & Baillargeon, R. (1983). A review of some Piagetian concepts. In J. H. Flavell & E. M. Markman (Eds.), *Handbook of child psychology* (4th ed.). *Cognitive development* (Vol. 3, pp. 167–230). New York: Wiley.

Gelman, S. A., & Markman, E. M. (1986). Categories and induction in young children. *Cognition, 23,* 183–209.

Hatano, G., & Inagaki, K. (1987). Everyday biology and school biology: How do they interact? *The Newsletter of the Laboratory of Comparative Human Cognition, 9,* 120–128.

Heath, S. B. (1983). *Ways with words.* Cambridge, England: Cambridge University Press.

Heath, S. B. (1991). "It's about winning!" The language of knowledge in baseball. In L. B. Resnick, J. M. Levine, & S. D. Teasley (Eds.), *Perspectives on socially shared cognition* (pp. 101–126). Washington, DC: American Psychological Association.

Heath, S. B., & Mangiola, L. (1991). *Children of promise: Literate activity in linguistically and culturally diverse classrooms.* Washington, DC: National Education Association.

Heath, S. B., & McLaughlin, M. W. (1994). Learning for anything every day. *Journal of Curriculum Studies, 26*(5), 471–489.

Holquist, M., & Emerson, C. (1981). In M. Holquist (Ed.), *Glossary for the dialogic imagination: Four essays by M. M. Bakhtin.* (M. Holquist & C. Emerson, Trans.). Austin, TX: University of Texas Press.

Keil, F. C. (1992). The origins of an autonomous biology. In M. R. Gunnan & M. Maratsos (Eds.), *Minnesota Symposium on Child Psychology: Modularity and constraints on language and cognition* (pp. 103–137). Hillsdale, NJ: Lawrence Erlbaum Associates.

Lave, J., & Wenger, E. (1991). *Situated learning: Legitimate peripheral participation.* New York: Cambridge University Press.

McLaughlin, M. W., Irby, M. A., & Langman, J. (1994). *Urban sanctuaries: Neighborhood organizations in the lives and futures of inner-city youth.* San Francisco, CA: Jossey-Bass.

Mehan, H. (1979). *Learning lessons: Social organization in the classroom.* Cambridge, MA: Harvard University Press.

Nakagawa, K., Brown, A. L., Kennedy, S., Walker, J., & Felgenhauer, S. (1994, April). *Children as resources in a community of learners.* Paper presented at the meeting of the American Educational Research Association, New Orleans, LA.

O'Connor, M. C. (1991). *Negotiated defining: Speech activities and mathematical literacies.* Unpublished manuscript, Boston University.

Palincsar, A. S., & Brown, A. L. (1984). Reciprocal teaching of comprehension-fostering and monitoring activities. *Cognition and Instruction, 1*(2), 117–175.

Pomeranz, C. (1993). *The day they parachuted cats on Borneo.* LaSalle, IL: Open Court Publishing Co. (Original work published 1969)

Resnick, L. B., & Resnick, D. P. (1992). Assessing the thinking curriculum: New tools for educational reform. In B. R. Gifford & M. C. O'Connor (Eds.), *Future assessment: Changing views of aptitude, achievement and instruction* (pp. 37–75). Boston: Academic Press.

Scardamalia, M., & Bereiter, C. (1991). Higher levels of agency for children in knowledge building: A challenge for the design of new knowledge media. *The Journal of the Learning Sciences, 1*, 37–68.

Scardamalia, M., Bereiter, C., & Fillion, B. (1981). *Writing for results: A sourcebook of consequential composition activities.* Toronto: OISE Press.

Shulman, L. S. (1986). Those who understand teach: Knowledge growth in teaching. *Educational Researcher, 15*(2), 4–14.

Stone, C. A., & Wertsch, J. V. (1984). A social interactional analysis of learning disabilities remediation. *Journal of Learning Disabilities, 17*, 194–199.

Toulmin, S. (1958). *The uses of argument.* Cambridge, England: Cambridge University Press.

Tyack, D., & Tobin, W. (1994). The "grammar" of schooling: Why is it so hard to change? *American Educational Research Journal, 31*, 453–479.

Vygotsky, L. S. (1978). *Mind in society: The development of higher psychological processes* (M. Cole, V. John-Steiner, S. Scribner, & E. Souberman, Eds. and Trans.). Cambridge, MA: Harvard University Press.

Wellman, H. M., & Gelman, S. (1988). Children's understanding of the non-obvious. In R. J. Sternberg (Ed.), *Advances in the psychology of human intelligence* (Vol. 4, pp. 99–135). Hillsdale, NJ: Lawrence Erlbaum Associates.

Wertsch, J. V. (1991). *Voices in the mind.* Cambridge, England: Cambridge University Press.

White, B. Y. (1993). ThinkerTools: Causal models, conceptual change, and science education. *Cognition and Instruction, 10*, 1–100.

Part III

CHANGING ENVIRONMENTS FOR EDUCATION

The final section, Changing Environments for Education, closes the volume with two chapters that take the entire school as the unit of analysis. These chapters take a broad and evaluative view of school reform, aiming for a review of our current knowledge about what practices and principles are most likely to result in successful school change, as well as what we know about the likely pitfalls.

In chapter 12, "Accelerated Schools After Eight Years," Levin addresses these questions by overviewing an educational reform project for at-risk students. The Accelerated Schools project aims to accelerate the learning of at-risk students by bringing them into the educational mainstream in a specified time period. Seeking to close the developmental gap in elementary school, the project relies on a language-based curriculum and a learning approach that emphasizes student discovery, peer tutoring, and cooperative learning. Spearheaded by Stanford University in 1987, The Accelerated Schools project began with two elementary schools and has grown to more than 300 elementary and middle schools in 25 states. Levin describes the background, practices, and accomplishments of Accelerated Schools and outlines lessons for instructional reform.

Chapter 13 "Below the Surface of School Reform: Vision and Its Foes" summarizes McDonald's experience with Systemic School Reform in the Coalition of Essential Schools. McDonald describes what he sees as prohibitive impediments to effective change. Interestingly, he believes that these impediments are features integral to the school environment, and moreover, that they are often so taken for granted that they go unnoticed and unnamed. McDonald and his colleagues identified these impediments to reform by studying 10 public high schools over a 3-year period, all sharing a serious intention to reinvent themselves. Although the experience of these schools suggests that reform is possible, it also suggests, according to McDonald, that it is nearly impossible, regardless of rhetoric about reform.

The chapter describes seven dynamics of schooling that constrain deep change in schools and the most promising strategies for confronting these dynamics.

These two chapters summarize the experience of reform efforts that have undergone extensive dissemination. Because they distill insights that have been gathered over the long haul in many and varied sites, the principles and cautions that they suggest are worthy of close attention.

Chapter 12

ACCELERATED SCHOOLS AFTER EIGHT YEARS

Henry M. Levin
Stanford University

This chapter presents the background, practices, and some accomplishments of an educational project, the Accelerated Schools Project, that began in 1986–1987 with two elementary schools and that has now grown in 1994–1995 to more than 700 elementary and middle schools in 37 states. The Accelerated Schools Project is devoted to bringing "at-risk" students into the educational mainstream, drawing largely on existing school resources. It calls for the transformation of schools that serve at-risk children to accelerate their education by using the enrichment approach usually reserved for gifted and talented students.

The astute reader will see elements of Dewey, Freire, and Vygotsky and, perhaps, other educational theorists at the heart of Accelerated Schools. We have certainly benefited from their ideas as well as two decades of work that we have done on the theory and practice of democracy in schools and the workplace (e.g., Carnoy & Levin, 1976, 1985; Jackall & Levin, 1984; Levin, 1970, 1973). Yet, the great failure of education to meet the needs of a growing at-risk population is not principally a failure of ideas. It is a failure to change school culture to embrace new ideas, a failure of implementation (Sarason, 1990). What is original in the Accelerated Schools Project is the melding of these ideas with an effective implementation strategy that builds on the resources of communities and the strengths of existing school staff, and provides opportunities for continuing development of students, staff, and families with a parsimonious use of resources and a constructivist philosophy.

A national educational crisis looms in the U.S. because of the growth in population of a particular group of students whom we refer to as students caught in at-risk situations. Such students do not have the experiences in their homes and communities to succeed in schools, as schools are presently constituted (Levin, 1986). Schools are not neutral about the experiences that lead to success. Native-born students from middle-class families with both parents present and a standard version of the English language spoken in the home have a high likelihood of success. Students from other backgrounds are much less favored by schools, as their backgrounds and experiences deviate from what schools build on and expect. Students in at-risk situations enter schools unprepared to take advantage of the standard curriculum and fall farther and farther behind in academic achievement as measured by standardized tests. More than half do not graduate from high school, the minimum requirement for productive entry into the U.S. labor force.

Such students are drawn heavily from poverty populations, minority groups, immigrant and non-English speaking populations, and single-parent families (Natriello, McDill, & Pallas, 1990). By the mid 1980s, they comprised about one third of all students in elementary and secondary schools (Levin, 1986; Pallas, Natriello, & McDill, 1989), a proportion that continues to rise rapidly because of the substantial immigration from impoverished and rural areas of Asia and Latin America and because of high birth rates among these populations.

A consequence of the expansion of at-risk student populations will be a serious deterioration of the future labor force. As the numbers grow and these groups continue to experience low achievement and high dropout rates, a larger and larger portion of the labor force will be unprepared for available jobs. Even clerical workers, cashiers, and salespeople need basic skills in oral and written communication, computation, and reasoning, skills that are not guaranteed among the educationally disadvantaged. A 1976 U.S. government study found that although 13% of all 17-year-olds were classified as functionally illiterate, the percentage of illiterates among educationally disadvantaged populations was about 50% (National Assessment of Educational Progress, 1976). Without successful interventions to improve the plight of the educationally disadvantaged, employers and the economy will suffer lagging productivity, higher training costs, and competitive disadvantages as well as lost tax revenues (Levin, 1989). This will occur especially in those states, regions, and localities most affected by disadvantaged labor forces, but there will be a national impact as well.

These economic losses will come at a time of rising costs of public services for populations that are disadvantaged by inadequate educational attainments. More and more citizens will need to rely on public assistance for survival, and increasing numbers of undereducated teens and adults will pursue illegal activities to fill idle time and obtain the income that is not available through legal pursuits (Berlin & Sum, 1988). A further point for consideration is that economic analyses of educational investments in behalf of at-risk students suggest that the financial value of the benefits to society far exceed the social costs (Levin, 1989).

ARE WE ON THE RIGHT TRACK?

What is clear is that the U.S. is not on the right track to meet the challenges of educationally at-risk students, despite recent educational reforms for the general population (e.g., National Commission on Excellence in Education, 1983; U.S. Department of Education, 1984). These reforms have not really addressed the specific needs of educationally at-risk students. The reforms have stressed primarily the goal of raising standards at the secondary level for students in the college preparatory track, without providing additional resources or new strategies to assist at-risk students to meet these higher standards prior to entering secondary schools.

It is not surprising that the status of at-risk students has not been found to have improved by just enlisting higher standards. Any strategy for improving the educational plight of at-risk children must begin at the elementary level and must be dedicated to preparing children for doing high quality work in secondary school. Simply raising standards at the secondary level, without making it possible for at-risk students to meet the new standards, is more likely to increase their dropping out (McDill, Natriello, & Pallas, 1985). Although there has been some narrowing of the achievement gap between at-risk and other students in certain basic skill areas—presumably as a result of greater participation in preschool programs, some efforts at compensatory education, and better health and nutritional programs—the gap is still extraordinarily large and stubborn (Smith & O'Day, 1991).

How to Produce Educational Failure

At-risk students begin school with a learning gap in those areas valued by schools and mainstream economic and social institutions. The existing model of intervention assumes that they will not be able to maintain a normal instructional pace without prerequisite knowledge and learning skills. In our view this gap is due to a lack of exposure to the types of experiences that engender the knowledge and behaviors that schools expect, not an inability to develop rapidly under the right conditions (see e.g.,

Feuerstein, 1980). But, such youngsters are placed into less demanding instructional settings—either by being pulled out of their regular classrooms or by adapting the regular classroom to their "needs"—to provide remedial or compensatory educational services. This approach appears to be both rational and compassionate, but it has exactly the opposite consequences.

First, this process reduces learning expectations on the parts of both the children and the educators who are assigned to teach them, and it stigmatizes both groups with a label of inferiority. Such a stigma undermines social support for the activity, denotes a low social status to the participants, and imparts negative self-images. The combination of low social status and low expectations is tantamount to treating such students as discards who are marginal to the mainstream educational agenda. Thus, the model creates the unhealthiest of all possible conditions under which to expect significant educational progress. In contrast, an effective approach must focus on creating learning activities that are characterized by high expectations, high academic content in a meaningful context, and high status for the participants.

Second, the usual treatment of the at-risk student is not designed to bring such students up to the point where they can benefit from mainstream instruction and perform at their appropriate age levels. There exist no timetables for doing so, and there are rarely incentives or even provisions for students to move from remedial instruction into the mainstream. In fact, because students in compensatory or remedial situations are expected to progress at a slower than normal pace, a self-fulfilling prophecy is realized as they fall farther and farther behind their mainstream counterparts. The result is that once an at-risk student is relegated to remedial or compensatory interventions, that student will be expected to learn at a slower rate, and the achievement gap between advantaged and disadvantaged students will grow. A successful program must set a deadline for closing the achievement gap so that, ultimately, at-risk students will be able to benefit from mainstream instruction of a high quality.

Third, by deliberately slowing the pace of instruction to a crawl, a heavy emphasis is placed on endless repetition of material through drill-and-practice. The result is that the school experience of at-risk students lacks intrinsic vitality, omits crucial learning skills and reinforcement, and moves at a plodding pace that reinforces low expectations. It is also totally disconnected from everyday experience and applications of knowledge. Exposure to concepts, analysis, problem solving, and interesting applications is largely restricted in lieu of decoding skills in reading and arithmetic operations in the primary grades on the premise that these fundamentals must be learned before anything more challenging can be attempted. Mechanics are stressed over content. Such a joyless experience further negates the child's feelings about school and diminishes the possibility that the child will view the school as a positive environment in which learning progress can be made. An effective curriculum for so-called at-risk students must not only be faster paced and actively engage the interests of such children to enhance their motivation, but it must include concepts, analysis, problem-solving, and interesting applications, especially those grounded in the child's previous and concurrent experiences outside school.

Most compensatory educational programs do not involve parents sufficiently or draw adequately on available community resources. Parents are not viewed or used as a potentially positive influence for their childrens' learning. Furthermore, the professional staff at the school level are usually omitted from participating in the important educational decisions that they must ultimately implement. Such an omission means that teachers are expected to create success out of programs and procedures that do not necessarily reflect their professional judgments or even their understanding of the problem. These are conditions that are more likely to spur mechanical compliance in which teachers go through the motions than the dedication or enthusiasm that leads to success. The design and implementation of successful educational programs to address the needs of at-risk students will require the involvement of parents, the use of community resources, and the extensive participation of teachers and other school staff in order to succeed.

An effective approach to educating at-risk students must be characterized by expectations of high-quality educational activities and bright futures for all children; deadlines by which such children will be academically able in the richest sense; stimulating instructional programs that build on the interests, proclivities, cultures, and experiences of students; decision making, implementation, and assessment by the educational staff who will offer the program in conjunction with students and parents; and the use of all available resources including community and social service agencies and businesses. To accomplish this, the school must incorporate a comprehensive set of strategies that mutually reinforce and transform school context, organization, curriculum, and instructional strategies in a unified way rather than relying on independent and piecemeal reforms.

ACCELERATED SCHOOLS FOR AT-RISK STUDENTS

The Accelerated School Project at Stanford University was designed as an alternative to present practice by building on these concerns and the knowledge base that forwards a different set of assumptions for achieving school success for at-risk students (Edmonds, 1979; Levin, 1987a, 1987b, 1988). At its heart is the notion of doing for at-risk students what we presently attempt to do for gifted and talented students, striving to accelerate their progress rather than slowing it down by seeking to maximize talent development for all students (Feldhusen, 1992; Renzulli, 1994). The goal of the Accelerated Schools Project is to accelerate the learning of at-risk students so that they are able to accomplish high levels of academic performance by the end of elementary school. It is important to note that although this suggests the use of standardized tests to assess grade level performance, we should not be constrained to the use of such tests. Rather, we should ask what is important to know at each level to be academically able and assess children accordingly. In the longer run we expect to capitalize on the availability of new assessment instruments that are richer and more nearly valid than present, multiple-choice format, standardized tests (Office of Technology Assessment of the U.S. Congress, 1991).

Acceleration is supported by recent approaches to the definition of intelligence and giftedness (Feldhusen, 1992; Gardner & Hatch, 1990) as well as research evidence supporting accelerated programs for at-risk students. Peterson (1989) randomly assigned low-achieving seventh graders who would have normally been given remedial instruction to three different instructional settings: remedial, average, and pre-algebra for accelerated students. He found that the remedial students who had been assigned to the accelerated, pre-algebra classes showed significantly greater achievement gains in all three areas that were tested: computation, problem solving, and mathematical concepts. More recently, Knapp, Shields, and Turnbull (1992) studied practices in some 140 classrooms among 15 schools with high proportions of children from low-income families. Over a school year it was found that high content instruction designed to create meaning and understanding was more effective in increasing knowledge of advanced skills and at least as effective in providing basic skills as was the more traditional remediation and basic skill-and-drill approach.

Accelerated Schools are designed to enable at-risk students to take advantage of mainstream or accelerated middle-school or secondary-school instruction by effectively closing the developmental gap in elementary school. The approach is also expected to reduce dropouts, drug use, and teenage pregnancies by creating a strong sense of self-worth and educational accomplishment for students who now feel rejected by schools and frustrated about their lack of recognition and accomplishment. Specific dimensions of the Accelerated School are outlined in the following sections.

Organization

The entire organization of Accelerated School focuses on the goal of ensuring that students achieve at an appropriate developmental level by the time they leave elementary school. Central to the Accelerated Schools strategy is the placement of curriculum and instructional decisions in the hands of the school staff, with participation by parent and student representatives as well. Those who work most closely with children know their students best. Daily interactions mean that teachers can understand learning needs, styles, and capabilities in ways that more distant administrators, consultants, and program specialists cannot. If desired changes in student achievement are to be realized, instructional staff, in conjunction with the other participants, must have the authority and responsibility to design curriculum and instructional programs in ways that are compatible with their unique classroom perspective. Clearly this means that teachers must build capacity to make such decisions within a powerful learning framework that we view as constructivist (Brooks & Brooks, 1993; Hopfenberg et al., 1993). At the same time they must work together to make sure that there is articulation across student experiences and grade levels.

To facilitate this process, each Accelerated School has an overall steering committee and cadres of the principal, teachers, support staff, and parents, who address major school priorities. At the upper-elementary or middle-school levels, students also participate. The principal serves a central function as instructional leader in coordinating and guiding this activity and in addressing the logistical needs for translating decisions into reality. School staff work together to set out a program that is consonant with student needs and the strengths of the district and school staff. All decisions follow a disciplined process of inquiry, a method of problem-solving method that is practiced on a daily basis among all of the decision-making groups (Hopfenberg et al., 1993). Information, technical assistance, and training are provided by district personnel or external consultants serving as coaches. In this way, the reform is a "bottom-up" approach in which those who are providing the instruction make the decisions that they will implement and evaluate.

These broad features of the Accelerated School are designed to make it a total institution for accelerating the educational progress of the disadvantaged, rather than just grafting on compensatory or remedial classes to schools with a conventional agenda. The emphasis is on embracing a philosophical framework and practices for the school as a whole rather than limiting change to a particular grade, curriculum, approach to teacher training, or other limited strategy. Within this overall framework, articulated decisions are made in teacher preparation, staff development, curriculum focus, and instructional strategies that reinforce what is learned from classroom to classroom and grade-level to grade-level. Embedded within the organizational approach are three major principles:

- Unity of purpose.
- Responsibility for decisions and their consequences.
- Building on strengths.

Unity of purpose refers to the forging of a common purpose and common practices by school staff, parents, and students in behalf of all the school's children. It is a collective set of ideal goals that members of the school community would want for their own children and that children would want for themselves. Traditional schools separate children according to abilities, learning challenges, and other distinctions; staff are divided according to their narrow teaching, support, or administrative functions; and parents are usually relegated only the most marginal of roles by the school in the education of their children. Accelerated Schools require a unity of purpose around the education of all students and all members of the school community. Strict separation of either teaching or learning roles works against this unity and results in different expectations for different groups of children. Accelerated Schools formulate and work toward high expectations for all children, and children internalize these high expectations for themselves.

Decision making with responsibilities for the consequences informs decisions and makes the school responsible for their consequences. All the key participants in the school are expected to take responsibility for making informed decisions through an inquiry process that will improve the educational status of students rather than delegating that responsibility to others. Unless all of the major actors can be empowered to seek a common set of goals and influence the educational and social processes that can achieve those goals, it is unlikely that the desired improvements will take place or be sustained. It is important to note that these general ideas are consistent with those of Freire (1970) and Dewey (1966). They also draw upon the notion of collective efficacy that is found in the work of Albert Bandura (1986).

An Accelerated School builds on expanded roles for all groups to participate in and takes responsibility for the educational process and educational results. Such a process requires a shift to a school-based governance and decision approach with heavy involvement of the full school staff, parents, and students.

Building on strengths refers to using all the learning resources that students, parents, school staff, and communities can bring to the educational endeavor. In the quest to place blame for the lack of efficacy of schools in improving the education of the disadvantaged, it is easy to exaggerate weaknesses of the various participants and ignore strengths. Parents have considerable strengths in serving as positive influences for the education of their children, not the least of which are a deep love for their children and a desire for their children to succeed. Teachers are capable of insights, intuition, and teaching and organizational acumen that are lost when schools exclude teachers from participating in the decisions they must implement. Both parents and teachers are largely underutilized sources of talent in the schools.

The strengths of at-risk students are often overlooked because they are perceived as lacking the learning behaviors associated with middle-class students rather than as having unique assets that can be used to accelerate their learning (Cummins, 1987; Heath, 1983). These often include an interest and curiosity in oral and artistic expression, abilities to learn through the manipulation of appropriate learning materials, a capability for engrossment in intrinsically interesting tasks (Csikszentmihalyi, 1990), and the ability to learn to write (Graves, 1983) before attaining competence in decoding skills that are prerequisite to reading. Such strengths can be found by connecting learning to prior student experiences, student culture, and areas of student curiosity. In addition, such students can serve as enthusiastic and effective learning resources for other students through peer tutoring and cooperative learning approaches (Slavin, 1983).

School-based administrators are also underutilized by being placed in "command" roles to meet the directives and standard operating procedures of districts rather than to work creatively with parents, staff, and students. And, communities have considerable resources including youth organizations, senior citizens, businesses, and religious groups that should be viewed as major assets for the schools and the children of the community. The strengths of these participants can be viewed as a major set of resources for creating Accelerated Schools.

Curriculum and Instructional Strategies

Accelerated Schools create powerful learning situations by connecting content, instructional strategies, and learning contexts in a cohesive manner. Consistent with its emphasis on building on strengths, the Accelerated School views all children as gifted and talented in unique ways. Traditional remedial programs look for the weaknesses of the child and never search for or discover strengths. Gifted and talented programs begin with the strengths of the child and provide accelerated and enriched approaches to capitalize on those strengths. There are many different conceptions of giftedness, but less controversy over the fact that rich learning opportunities need to be constructed to build on those gifts and talents (Sternberg & Davidson, 1986). The pedagogy is not one of remediation, but acceleration that capitalizes on the child's strengths. Indeed, we argue that what works for so-called gifted and talented students works for all students by building on the child's experiences, interests, motivations, culture, and observed abilities in a multiple-intelligence framework (Gardner, 1983; Gardner & Hatch, 1990).

Each school develops the powerful learning strategies that address its dream and that build on student, staff, parent, and community strengths. This results in rather remarkable differences among schools ("Powerful Learning in Accelerated Schools," 1994), but some commonalities are observed. Major curriculum aspects include a heavily language-based approach, even in mathematics. Language use is emphasized across the curriculum, with an early introduction to writing and reading for meaning and the development of critical literacy (Allington, 1993; Graves, 1983). Interesting applications of new tools to everyday problems and events also stress the usefulness of what is being taught and learned and introduce a problem-solving orientation. Active learning approaches based on student discovery and testing of ideas represent a basis for responding to student curiosity, and for permitting students to benefit from the advantages of learning-by-doing rather than just learning-by-listening. Instructional strategies also include peer tutoring and cooperative learning.

At this point few Accelerated Schools have extended day programs because of the lack of resources. However, if resources permit, it is desirable to consider an extended-day program in which rest periods, physical activities, the arts, and a period for independent assignments or homework are provided. During this period, college students and senior citizen volunteers can work with individual students to provide learning assistance. Because many of the students are latch-key children, the extension of the school day is attractive to parents.

Family Involvement

Family involvement is necessarily a central focus of the Accelerated School. Epstein (1987) showed that research on parental and family involvement supports the important potential role that families can have in raising the educational accomplishments of their students. The Accelerated School builds on parental involvement in the school and in the home. Parents are expected to serve as partners with the school in meeting such supportive roles as ensuring that their children go to bed at a reasonable hour and attend school regularly and punctually. They are asked to set high educational expectations for their children, to talk to them regularly about the importance of school, and to take an interest in their children's activities and in the materials that the children bring home. They are expected to encourage their children to read on a daily basis and to ensure that independent assignments are addressed. They are also expected to respond to queries from the school. Parents are afforded high status and dignity by school staff with constant reference to the school–parent partnership and special events throughout the school year honoring parents.

Parents participate in the governance structure of the school through membership on task forces and the steering committee. They are also are given opportunities to interact with the school program and school staff through an "open door" policy and a parent lounge (if possible) as well as to receive training for providing active assistance to their children. Such training includes not only the skills for working with a child, but also many of the academic skills necessary to understand what the child is doing. In this respect, it may be necessary to work closely with agencies offering adult basic education to provide the parental foundation. The parental dimension can improve the capacity and effort of the child as well as increase the time devoted to academic learning and provide additional instructional resources in the home.

Evaluation

Progress is evaluated by an assessment system that monitors both school and student progress. Schools work to align their assessment practices with the goals of the Accelerated Schools process (Hopfenberg et al., 1993). They must also review their action plans and the implementation process to make sure that decisions are making their way into school practices. In addition, they must evaluate such school outcomes as levels of student and family participation and school activities. Finally, they must assess student performance to ensure that students are on appropriate learning trajectories. These evaluations emphasize the students' acquisition of higher order thinking and reasoning skills as well as basic skills in core curricular areas. Unfortunately, assessment instruments that are presently available are not always suitable for these purposes. Accordingly, this dimension must draw on major developmental efforts both at the national level and among fledgling efforts at individual Accelerated Schools and in the Accelerated Schools Project (Wiggins, 1993).

On a regular basis, the staff examine their practices, student experiences, and school climate to see if they meet the standards they would set for their own children. The overall philosophy of assessment is based on the premise that if the school is not good enough for the children of staff, it is not good enough for any child. This means that the staff must work together to create for all children in the school the types of experiences that they would desire for their own children.

DECISION MAKING IN ACCELERATED SCHOOLS

At the heart of the Accelerated School is the emphasis on site responsibility for the educational process and outcomes (Goodlad, 1984). To make this a reality, there must be an appropriate decision-structure built around the school's unity of purpose, and there must be a functional process to develop the capacity of the school to identify challenges, create an inquiry process to understand the challenges and potential solutions, and to implement and evaluate solutions (Hopfenberg et al., 1993).

Governance Structures

We have found that three levels of participation are necessary to encompass the range of issues that must be addressed in a democratic but productive way: the School as a Whole; the Cadre; and the Steering Committee.

The school as a whole (SAW) refers to the principal, teachers, teachers' aides, other instructional and noninstructional staff, and parent and student representatives. The SAW is required to approve all major decisions on curriculum, instruction, and resource allocation that have implications for the entire school. At the opposite extreme in terms of group size is the cadre. The cadre is a small group organized around a particular area of high priority for the school. Where the concern is a continuing one such as curriculum or parent participation, a cadre is formed. In the case where the concern is episodic, such as the planning of new facilities, an ad hoc committee is formed for the duration of the task. The major guideline for forming a cadre or a committee is to create as few as possible, always looking for ways to combine related responsibilities and to dissolve entities that are no longer needed so as to avoid an overburden on staff.

The cadres are the groups that do most of the analytic and preparatory work such as defining specific problems that the school faces and searching for and implementing solutions. Before implementation begins, the recommendations of task and policy committees must be approved by the Steering Committee, and in some cases the SAW. The cadres build on the camaraderie, ease of communication, and motivations associated with small teams working together on a regular basis and building expertise through sustained exploration and investigation.

The Steering Committee consists of the principal and representative teachers, aides, other school staff, and parents. The purpose of the Steering Committee is to monitor the progress of the cadres and ad hoc committees, and to develop a set of recommendations for consideration by the school as a whole. Steering committee members include representatives of each of the cadres in order to ensure that the work of the cadres is coordinated at the level of the school. Cadres are expected to meet on a weekly basis, the steering committee on a biweekly basis, and the school as a whole on a quarterly basis, or as needed. Meetings of all entities require a public display of agendas at least 24 hours in advance and minutes of meetings within 48 hours following the meeting.

Clearly, the principal in the school has a different role than in a traditional school. The principal is responsible for coordinating and facilitating the activities of the decision-making bodies as well as for obtaining the logistical support that is necessary in such areas as information, staff development, assessment, implementation, and instructional resources. A good principal in the context of the Accelerated School is one who is an active listener and participant, who can identify and cultivate talents among staff, who can keep the school focused on its mission, who can work effectively with parents and community, who is dedicated to the students and their success, who can motivate the various actors, who can marshal the resources that are necessary, and who is the keeper of the dream. In the last role, the principal is the person who must always remind participants of the dream especially during periods of temporary disappointments or setbacks.

Accelerated Schools require that school districts play a greater service role for individual schools than they normally do (Levin, 1993). Instead of serving as regulators of schools with rules, mandates, and policies to ensure compliance of school activities with some central goals, the school district must provide support services to help the Accelerated School succeed at its mission. Central office staff assist the cadres and steering committee in identifying challenges, obtaining information on alternatives, implementation, staff development, and evaluation. They must also assist the schools to work with parents and to help families sponsor activities in the home that support the educational progress of their children.

Although most schools for at-risk students need considerable additional resources (Levin, 1989), the transformation to an Accelerated School is one of qualitative change within available resources. A major resource need is that of providing adequate release time of staff for meetings, staff development, discussion, reflection, planning, and exploration of alternatives. Most existing Accelerated Schools have been successful in using various school district resources and changes in school organization to accommodate the time requirements. In addition, expertise is needed from trained personnel in the district central office or trained consultants to assist the school in building its capacity to accelerate the education of its students. Most Accelerated Schools use their available staff development resources to accommodate these needs. The Accelerated School Project has a training program for such coaches and mentors their progress at the school site.

BUILDING SCHOOL CAPACITY

Existing schools can be transformed structurally through devolution of decision making to school sites, but they will not function as Accelerated Schools without building the capacity of the schools to establish a unity of purpose, to make responsible decisions, and to build on strengths. School staff have not been trained to function in this way, and such practices are in conflict with those of traditional schools (Keith & Girling, 1990). Much of the capability to become an Accelerated School comes directly from exposure to a new set of values and practices that is followed up by daily reinforcement through learning-by-doing. As school staff and community work at it, they become experts at the process. The goal is nothing less than the internal transformation of school culture (Finnan, 1992, 1994). But, in order to get the process started, there are a number of steps that must be taken.

Although we have used different training models, we have concluded that one is superior ("Training for Expansion of Accelerated Schools," 1994). The entire school (including all staff, parent representatives, and student representatives) participates in training. Between training sessions the school undertakes developmental tasks and practices a set of empowering skills in making decisions in areas of concern to the school. The overall training approach is based on a constructivist model in which it is assumed that humans learn most effectively when they actively construct their own understanding of phenomena rather than being passive recipients of someone else's understanding ("Constructivism and the Accelerated Schools Model," 1994). The training is built around a range of interactive endeavors in which groups reflect on a range of issues and respond by creating activities in which they must introduce the various dimensions of the Accelerated School process to students or to parents. Coaches are assigned to schools to provide both training and follow-up in terms of observations, trouble-shooting, and continuing support. Coaches learn to teach through constructivist activities as well as to provide guidance through questioning rather than criticisms and directives.

Embedded in all the training and school activities are the three principles: unity of purpose, empowerment with responsibility for the consequences, and building on strengths. These are not taught separately to school staff but are embedded in the discussions and school practices that are part of the Accelerated School process. Specific values such as risk taking, community, participation, experimentation, equity, and the school as center of expertise are also embedded in the premises and activities of Accelerated Schools training and practices.

Because much of the work at school sites is done in groups, it is usually necessary to provide some training in group process and decision making in a team context. Rarely do principals, teachers, and school staff have this experience. Meetings in traditional schools tend to be highly structured and run in a routine and often authoritarian fashion. Teachers, in particular, consider meetings a waste of time. School staff rarely view meetings as having the potential to be productive and to accomplish major goals in behalf of the school. Accordingly, school staff need experience in working together with special attention to group process and participation, sharing of information, and working toward decisions. In addition, they need exposure to inquiry-oriented processes that help to identify and define challenges, to look for alternative solutions, and to implement those solutions.

These needs can be met through special training in these areas. In addition, involvement in the Accelerated Schools process itself is an important part of capacity building. This process is initiated in four steps (see the more extensive descriptions in Hopfenberg et al., 1993). At the first phase, the school is asked to establish a rich font of base line information on itself. All school staff and parent and student representatives participate in taking stock of the school. They form teams to explore all the dimensions of the school for presentation and discussion with the entire school community. Typically, the inventory of base line data comprises a history of the school; data on students, staff, and school facilities; information on the community and cultures of the parents; particular strengths of the school; data on attendance, test scores, and other measures of student performance; and the major challenges faced by the school. Some of this information will be quantitative, although much of it will be descriptive. The purpose of this exercise is to begin the Accelerated Schools process through self-examination and the preparation of a written record of its status at the beginning to compare later with progress. The process of collecting, reporting, and discussing the base line information is done over several weeks and begins to build the research capacity of school staff.

The second part of the initial process is to establish a vision for the school that will be the focus of change. In a series of meetings of both the school as a whole and smaller components of staff, the participants focus on describing the characteristics of a school that will work for students, staff, and community. Central to this activity is the process of designing a dream school, the one that they would want for their own children. Because the Accelerated School transitional process is expected to take about 6 years, that is the time period for which the participants project a new vision of their school. Out of this process emerges a vision for the future that will be the focus of Accelerated School implementation. This phase requires considerable reflection, discussion, and decision making. It also draws heavily on the dreams of students and parents, whose views are sought through discussions, essays, poetry, and the fine arts. The vision process enhances abilities of the constituencies to work together to create a common dream that will become their destiny.

The third phase involves the comparison of the vision with the base line report. Clearly, there will be a large gap in almost every aspect between the vision and the existing situation. School staff are asked to work on setting out all the things that must be done in order to move from the present situation to the future vision. Usually they amass a very large number of changes that must be made, often 40–50 major alterations.

The fourth step takes the list of what needs to be accomplished and clusters it around central themes. From these the school selects a small number of initial priorities that will become the immediate focus of the school. No organization can work effectively on more than three or four major priorities at a time. The task facing the staff is to select those three or four priorities. This exercise can generate a very animated set of discussions that get to the heart of staff concerns. The dynamics of the discourse are themselves useful because they engage the staff in the realization that they are responsible for change and for choosing those areas where they must begin. The agreement on priorities is followed by the establishment of the first cadres—the small groups that will work on these priorities—and assignment of staff to each group, usually through self-selection. The final stage is that of deciding how to construct the steering committee and its functions.

At this point the school is ready to adopt the full Accelerated process. This process must be gradually embraced by school staff, students, and parents and practiced in an exemplary way by the principal, the cadres and steering committees, and the school district liaison personnel, as well as by building the capacity of staff to work through a systematic inquiry process. For example, cadres need training in how to take an overall challenge, such as poor mathematics performance of students, and refine the focus to understand the specific concerns. They must be able to translate concerns into specific hypotheses for further exploration. Once they narrow the problem to a specific cause or causes, they need to seek out alternatives for addressing it. Finally, they need to choose a solution or strategy, implement it, and evaluate the results. In this respect, it is necessary to provide training and guidance to all school participants on problem solving and implementation of decisions. The Accelerated Schools Project has established an inquiry process that has been especially designed and tailored to meet the needs of a school that embraces its philosophy and practices (Hopfenberg et al., 1993). Such capacity building is an ongoing activity, particularly during the first year where formal training is followed by daily practice and assessment.

A constant theme in all school activities is the emphasis on creating powerful learning situations based on a constructivist approach (Hopfenberg et al., 1993; "Powerful Learning in Accelerated Schools," 1994). Such learning situations must be connected with the strengths of students, parents, and school staff, and the vision of the school. Piecemeal approaches to improving the learning situation, such as curriculum changes independent of instructional strategies and classroom and school organization, are proscribed. Even when all of these dimensions are brought together in high enrichment strategies, they must be linked to a living vision of what the school is trying to accomplish. This connectedness among the different components of powerful learning—strengths of students, staff, and parents, and the vision of the school—is reinforced through constant reminders and questioning strategies by the coach, principal, and colleagues.

PRESENT STATUS OF
ACCELERATED SCHOOLS

The Accelerated Schools Project at Stanford University has expanded from its original two pilot schools to more than 700 elementary and middle schools in 9 years. Most of the process developed through the expansion of the model to new schools, where new ideas could be tested collaboratively and embodied in school practices, training, and mentoring. Statewide networks have arisen in Illinois, Louisiana, Massachusetts, Missouri, North Carolina, Ohio, South Carolina, and Texas, and new state networks are forming. Over the 9-year period, we have added many new pilot schools in order to develop and test new approaches to training and the Accelerated Schools process in a collaborative endeavor with school personnel, while simultaneously providing hands-on experiences for our own staff at the National Center for the Accelerated Schools Project at Stanford. However, most of the 700 schools are at great distances from Stanford and are under the guidance of local coaches and Accelerated Schools networks.

Assessment

Assessing an endeavor such as the Accelerated Schools Project is difficult because standard assessment practices are inadequate and inappropriate for understanding the kind of change that is promoted (Ascher, 1993; Hopfenberg et al., 1993). The typical assessment instruments used by school districts are not sensitive to capturing the changes in school culture and outcomes that are unique to Accelerated Schools. For example, standardized tests of achievement are not designed to assess the higher order learning, the quality of student projects, the originality of student oral and written expression, and the artistic accomplishments and scientific thinking that are expected to be accomplished through the establishment of powerful learning situations.

Although there were more than 700 Accelerated Schools by the autumn of 1994–1995, the rapid growth in the most recent years meant that only about 150 schools had more than 2 years of experience. Attempts have been made to obtain assessment data from school sites, and several of the state networks and regional centers have sponsored evaluations of the schools with which they work. In addition, more intensive evaluations have been done of a few specific sites, including multiyear comparisons with control schools. For the last 2 years we have also been exploring the design and implementation possibilities of evaluations using randomized student assignment with the Manpower Development Research Corporation.

Enrollments in Accelerated Schools are extremely diverse, encompassing African American, Hispanic, Native American, and White students, the majority coming from poverty backgrounds. The geographical settings and levels of district support have also been diverse. Even so, there is a remarkable consistency in the results that have been obtained. Schools have documented increased attendance of both students and teachers, substantial increases in parent participation, higher achievement scores, waiting lists for enrollments, and so on (e.g., see the summaries in Wong, 1994, and English, 1992).

Substantial increases in student achievement have been documented for schools in places as diverse as California, Illinois, Massachusetts, Missouri, South Carolina, and Texas. They have been found for both elementary and middle schools. Even more important from our perspective is the dramatic increase that we have seen in the amount of and quality of discourse and written work and the proliferation of rich and engaging activities and progress. Finally, there is evidence of reduced grade repetition and special educational placements, resulting in the saving of considerable costs to school funding sources.

Studies comparing Accelerated Schools with matched controls have shown strong effects. At a school in Texas composed primarily of minority students drawn from poverty families, fifth graders were 1-1/2 years behind their grade level in student achievement on SRA in 1988 and below the scores of the control school (McCarthy & Still, 1993). Three years later the fifth graders were performing slightly above grade level in overall achievement and 1 year above grade level in mathematics. The achievement scores of the matched control school declined over the period. A matched design examining not only multiyear changes in achievement, but also changes in teacher and student attitudes, found similar patterns of comparative growth (Knight & Stallings, 1995). A third comparative study of an Accelerated School in Sacramento, California also replicated the achievement results (Chasin & Levin, 1995).

Most importantly, these schools have not had any substantial change in their funding, student composition, or staff. However, a caution is in order here. Even operating at high levels of efficiency, many schools have major needs that cannot be addressed because of inadequate funding (Kozol, 1991). For example, large numbers of schools serving high concentrations of at-risk students lack sufficient libraries and resource centers with adequate staffing to engage students in independent research and projects. Class sizes of 30 or more students with different language backgrounds, abilities, and learning needs preclude much of the individual attention that some students require to achieve acceleration. Emotional needs of students that derive from unsettled home and living situations are unattended to and represent obstacles to learning because of a dearth of counselors and psychologists. Programs to increase parenting effectiveness and participation are limited by the lack of personnel who are assigned to carry out these responsibilities. School facilities are often overcrowded, inappropriate to the flexibility required of accelerated practices, and poorly maintained. All of these require adequate funding for schools as a condition to securing the necessary conditions for educational equity, and no increase in efficiency can fully compensate for their absence (Levin, 1994).

NEW DEVELOPMENTS

We have tried to use the lessons that we learned over the first years to improve the process of initiating and supporting Accelerated Schools, to develop an effective program of training and capacity building, to work more closely with school districts to make them more hospitable to Accelerated Schools, to assist schools to find ways of obtaining more planning time, and to build on the enormous talents of both school staffs and parents. These lessons have also sparked three new initiatives.

We found that the possibilities for an expanded Accelerated School movement will require a national network of centers with the capacity to collaborate with schools in their own geographical areas. The movement will necessarily be limited if it is connected only to a single center at Stanford. We have established the first eight of a larger number of university-based satellite centers. Each satellite has been initiated at a local university that is an important source for training administrators and teachers, a state department of education, or, in one case, a school district.

The satellite centers are expected to play major leadership roles in their areas in launching Accelerated Schools as well as in providing technical assistance to such schools. These centers have established pilot Accelerated Schools that are a basis for providing hands-on experiences for their staffs as well as for placing student teaching and administrative interns. In several cases they have expanded to state-wide networks with considerable numbers of schools. And some have begun to cotrain coaches with the National Center for Accelerated Schools and to mentor such coaches. It is hoped that such schools will provide a laboratory for transforming both teacher and administrative training as well as creating local models of Accelerated School success that can be replicated.

Second, we recognized that we need to set national training standards that must be met by the staff of satellite centers and Accelerated Schools. Accordingly, we have established an eight day training workshop for coaches that uses a constructivist approach to impart the knowledge and some of the skills required for establishing Accelerated Schools. This workshop emphasizes an understanding of accelerated practices which will be implemented at school sites following the training. The immediate adoption of these practices by the school following the workshop is needed to reinforce what has been learned. During the first year of coaching, the National Center for Accelerated Schools at Stanford maintains regular contact with coaches through telephone calls, exchange of materials, and periodic mentoring visits to coaches and school sites. The National Center also sponsors an end-of-year retreat for coaches to reflect on and discuss their experiences and share with them new ideas. We are attempting to ensure that all schools have accessibility to trained coaches who can provide follow-up and guidance at the school site. This training is augmented by training workshops and retreats for principals of Accelerated Schools.

Third, we have established research, evaluation, and publications programs to support Accelerated Schools. Present research is devoted to studying the behaviors of effective principals in Accelerated Schools, exploring changes in classroom dynamics in Accelerated Schools and particularly the movement toward constructivist and powerful learning, and the design and establishment of district change models for the support of Accelerated Schools. A range of evaluation activities have been undertaken, both internally and in collaboration with external evaluators. Among the publications are a quarterly *Accelerated Schools Newsletter* devoted to case studies and different dimensions of Accelerated Schools and a commercially available *Resource Guide on Accelerated Schools* (Hopfenberg et al., 1993) that is designed to provide an overall reference source for the model and process.

Finally, the Accelerated Schools Project is a project that is constantly dedicated to its own qualitative growth in terms of understanding processes of school change, school improvement, accelerated learning, assessment, and other central dimensions of Accelerated Schools. At this juncture, having completed the 8th year of a 30-year duration, it is engaged in a concerted effort to plan its own future through a Strategic Initiative funded by the Danforth Foundation. In doing so it is following a democratic process similar to that pursued by Accelerated Schools in taking stock, establishing 5- and 10-year visions, setting out new priorities, and exploring them using the same inquiry method employed by Accelerated Schools. A particular priority will be the joining together of trainers, coaches, researchers, schools, districts, and state networks into a social movement that can join with other educational reformers to create conditions of healthy development for all children, with special attention to those in at-risk situations.

ACKNOWLEDGMENTS

This chapter represents a revision of a paper presented at the conference on "The Contributions of Instructional Innovation to Understanding

Learning" at the Learning Research and Development Center, University of Pittsburgh, November 5–7, 1992. The author wishes to thank his colleagues Ilse Brunner, Beth Keller, Wendy Hopfenberg, Pilar Soler, and Pia Wong at the National Center for the Accelerated Schools Project for their support and important contributions. The author is the David Jacks Professor of Higher Education and Economics, Stanford University, CERAS 109, Stanford, CA 94305.

REFERENCES

Ascher, C. (1993). *Changing schools for urban students: The school development program, Accelerated Schools, and success for all*. New York: ERIC Clearinghouse on Urban Education, Institute for Urban and Minority Education, Teachers College, Columbia University.

Allington, R. (1993). *Reducing the risk: Integrated language arts in restructured elementary schools*. Albany, NY: National Research Center on Literature Teaching and Learning.

Bandura, A. (1986). *Social foundations of thought and action: A social cognitive theory*. Englewood Cliffs, NJ: Prentice-Hall.

Berlin, G., & Sum, A. (1988). *Toward a more perfect union: Basic skills, poor families and our economic future* (Occasional Paper 3). New York: Ford Foundation.

Brooks, J. G., & Brooks, M. G. (1993). *The case for constructivist classrooms*. Alexandria, VA: Association for Supervision and Curriculum Development.

Carnoy, M., & Levin, H. M. (1976). *The limits of educational reform*. New York: David McKay and Co.

Carnoy, M., & Levin, H. M. (1985). *Schooling and work in the democratic state*. Stanford, CA: Stanford University Press.

Chasin, G., & Levin, H. M. (1995). Thomas Edison accelerated elementary school. In J. Oakes & K. Hunter Quartz (Eds.), *Creating new educational communities, schools, and classrooms where all children can be smart* (pp. 130–146). Chicago, IL: University of Chicago Press.

Constructivism and the Accelerated Schools Model. (1994). *Accelerated Schools. A Publication of the Accelerated Schools Project, 3*(2), 10–15.

Csikszentmihalyi, M. (1990). *Flow: The psychology of optimal experience*. New York: Harper & Row.

Cummins, J. (1987). Empowering minority students. *Harvard Educational Review, 56*, 18–36.

Dewey, J. (1966). *Democracy and education*. New York: The Free Press.

Edmonds, R. (1979). Effective schools for the urban poor. *Educational Leadership, 37*(1), 15–24.

English, R. A. (1992). *Accelerated Schools report*. Columbia, MO: University of Missouri, Department of Educational and Counseling Psychology.

Epstein, J. L. (1987). Parent involvement: What research says to administrators. *Education and Urban Society, 19*(2), 119–136.

Feldhusen, J. F. (1992). *Talent identification and development in education (TIDE)*. Sarasota, FL: Center for Creative Learning.

Feuerstein, R. (1980). *Instrumental enrichment*. Baltimore, MD: University Park Press.

Finnan, C. (1992). *Becoming an accelerated middle school: Initiating school culture change*. Stanford, CA: Stanford University, National Center on Accelerated Schools.

Finnan, C. (1994). Studying an Accelerated School. In G. Spindler & L. Spindler (Eds.), *Pathways to cultural awareness: Cultural therapy with teachers and students* (pp. 93–129). Thousand Oaks, CA: Corwin Press.

Freire, P. (1970). *Pedagogy of the oppressed.* New York: Herder & Herder.

Gardner, H. (1983). *Frames of mind: The theory of multiple intelligences.* New York: Basic Books.

Gardner, H., & Hatch, T. (1990). Multiple intelligences go to school: Educational implications of multiple intelligences. *Educational Researcher, 19,* 4–10.

Goodlad, J. I. (1984). *A place called school.* New York: McGraw Hill.

Graves, D. H. (1983). *Writing.* Exeter, NH: Heinemann Educational Books.

Heath, S. B. (1983). *Ways with words.* New York: Cambridge University Press.

Hopfenberg, W., Levin, H. M., Chase, C., Christensen, S. G., Morre, M., Soler, P., Brunner, I., Keller, B., & Rodriguez, G. (1993). *Resource guide on the Accelerated School.* San Francisco: Jossey-Bass.

Jackall, R., & Levin, H. M. (Eds.). (1984). *Worker cooperatives in America.* Berkeley: University of California Press.

Keith, S., & Girling, R. H. (1990). *Education: Management and participation.* Boston: Allyn & Bacon.

Knapp, M. S., Shields, P. M., & Turnbull, B. J. (1992). *Study of academic instruction for disadvantaged students: Academic challenge for the children of poverty* (Vols. 1 & 2). Washington, DC: U. S. Department of Education.

Knight, S., & Stallings, J. (1995). The implementation of the Accelerated School model in an urban elementary school. In R. Allington & S. Walmsley (Eds.), *No quick fix: Rethinking literacy programs in American elementary schools.* (pp. 236–252). New York: Teachers College Press.

Kozol, J. (1991). *Savage inequalities.* New York: Crown Publications.

Levin, H. M. (1970). *Community control of schools.* Washington, DC: The Brookings Institution.

Levin, H. M. (1973). Educational reform and social change. *Journal of Applied Behavioral Science, 10*(3), 304–320.

Levin, H. M. (1986). *Educational reform for disadvantaged students: An emerging crisis.* West Haven, CT: NEA Professional Library.

Levin, H. M. (1987a). Accelerating schools for disadvantaged students. *Educational Leadership, 44*(6), 19–21.

Levin, H. M. (1987b). New schools for the disadvantaged. *Teacher Education Quarterly, 14*(4), 60–83.

Levin, H. M. (1988). Accelerating elementary education for disadvantaged students. In Council of Chief State School Officers (Eds.), *School success for students at risk* (pp. 209–226). Orlando, FL: Harcourt Brace Jovanovich.

Levin, H. M. (1989). Financing the education of at-risk students. *Educational Evaluation and Policy Analysis, 11*(1), 47–60.

Levin, H. M. (1993). Building school capacity for effective teacher empowerment. In S. B. Bacharach & R. T. Ogawa (Eds.), *Advances in research and theories of school management and educational policy* (Vol. 2, pp. 187–216). Greenwich, CT: JAI.

Levin, H. M. (1994). The necessary and sufficient conditions for achieving educational equity. In R. Berne & L. O. Picus (Eds.), *Outcome equity in education* (pp. 167–190). Thousand Oaks, CA: Corwin Press.

McCarthy, J., & Still, S. (1993). Hollibrook accelerated elementary school. In J.Murphy & P. Hallinger (Eds.), *Restructuring schools: Learning from ongoing efforts* (pp. 63–83). Monterey Park, CA: Corwin Press.

McDill, E. L., Natriello, G., & Pallas, A. (1985). Raising standards and retaining students: The impact of the reform recommendations on potential dropouts. *Review of Educational Research, 55*(4), 415–434.

National Assessment of Educational Progress. (1976). *Functional literacy and basic reading performance.* Washington, DC: U.S. Office of Education, Department of Health, Education and Welfare.

National Commission on Excellence in Education. (1983). *A nation at risk: The imperative for educational reform.* Washington, DC: U.S. Department of Education.

Natriello, G., McDill, E. M., & Pallas, A. M. (1990). *Schooling disadvantaged children: racing against catastrophe.* New York: Teachers College Press.

Office of Technology Assessment of the U.S. Congress. (1991). *Testing in American schools.* Washington, DC: U.S. Government Printing Office.

Pallas, A. M., Natriello, G., & McDill, E. M. (1989). The changing nature of the disadvantaged population: Current dimensions and future trends. *Educational Researcher, 18*(5), 16–22.

Peterson, J. M. (1989). Remediation is no remedy. *Educational Leadership, 46*(6), 24–25.

Powerful Learning in Accelerated Schools. (1994). *Accelerated Schools. A Publication of the Accelerated Schools Project, 3*(3), 1, 11–18.

Renzulli, J. S. (1994). *Schools for talent development: A practical plan for total school improvement.* Mansfield Center, CT: Creative Learning Press.

Sarason, S. B. (1990). *The predictable failure of educational reform.* San Francisco: Jossey-Bass.

Slavin, R. (1983). *Cooperative learning.* New York: Longman.

Smith, M. S., & O'Day, J. (1991). Educational equality: 1966 and now. In D. A. Verstegen & J. G. Ward (Eds.), *Spheres of justice in education.* 1990 American Education Finance Association Yearbook (pp. 53–100). New York: HarperBusiness.

Sternberg, R. J., & Davidson, J. E. (Eds). (1986). *Conceptions of giftedness.* New York: Cambridge University Press.

Training for Expansion of Accelerated Schools: The Coaching Model. (1994). *Accelerated Schools. A Publication of the Accelerated Schools Project, 3*(2), 1, 15–18.

U.S. Department of Education. (1984). *The nation responds: Recent efforts to improve education.* Washington, DC: U.S. Government Printing Office.

Wiggins, G. P. (1993). *Assessing student performance.* San Francisco: Jossey-Bass.

Wong, P. (1994, December). *Accomplishments of Accelerated Schools.* Stanford, CA: Stanford University, National Center for the Accelerated Schools Project.

Chapter 13

BELOW THE SURFACE OF SCHOOL REFORM: VISION AND ITS FOES

Joseph P. McDonald
Brown University

There is a conspiracy of vision amid efforts to remake American schools for the 21st century. The conspirators include cognitive scientists who have redefined learning and teaching in terms radically at odds with the common practices of American schools (Bruer, 1993; Cohen, McLaughlin, & Talbert, 1993; Gardner, 1989, 1991; Jones & Idol, 1990; Perkins, 1992). They are well positioned to dispute the powerful influences on current school design of their predecessors in psychology—the behaviorists with their passion for mincing teaching and learning, and the early theorists of intelligence with their passion for discriminatory measurement (Gould, 1981; Resnick & Resnick, 1991; Wolf, Bixby, Glenn, & Gardner, 1991). The conspirators also include organizational theorists, drawing inspiration from change under way in some American corporations (Bolman & Deal, 1991; Fullan, 1991; Mauriel, 1989; Senge, 1990). Many of their prescriptions are animated by economic anxiety, the U.S. having a long history of associating economic anxiety with school. They suggest, now as in the Taylorist past, that what is good for the Ford Motor Company is good for the schools, and vice versa. Finally, the conspirators include principals, teachers, and university-based school reformers, who labor under the abiding influence of their century-leaping mentor, John Dewey. These men and women tend to the practical details of the vision and make it seem realizable by providing a few exemplars (Fiske, 1991; Meier, 1992, 1993; Sizer, 1992; Wood, 1992).

Fundamental to this vision is a shift in the very idea of what is supposed to happen in school. According to these reformers, the learner does not

353

simply receive knowledge but reconstructs it within a context of prior information, skills, values, and beliefs—in short, by thinking about it. The intelligence he or she brings to this thinking is different from that presumed heretofore; it is multidimensional, socially distributed, tool dependent, and abundant. These basic conceptual changes affect, in turn, the role of the teacher, who becomes less the deliverer of instruction and more a cognitive coach, working across domains as well as within them, a guide to worlds that extend beyond classrooms and beyond the teacher's own expertise. These changes also affect the organizational contexts for learning. Direct instruction in isolated, departmentalized classrooms yields to a community of learners and teachers, sharing common standards, striving for connections, staying open intellectually, cultivating and respecting diverse viewpoints (Brown, 1992). This community operates within a larger educational system based on shared accountability rather than hierarchical responsibility.

Of course, vision alone is never enough to create change. There is the chance that this new vision, much like its predecessors of the 1960s and 1930s, will float above most American schools and never come to ground. If so, the fault will likely lie in the folly that Seymour Sarason identified in his works on school reform (1971, 1990), namely, that most proponents of good educational ideas consider schools the mere nodes of a complex system rather than complex systems in their own right. Whether school reform is launched from the outside or the inside of schools, it typically follows a linear strategy. That is, the effectiveness of an intervention is presumed to be intrinsic to the intervention itself, rather than a function of whether the intervention is managed to good effect within the turbulent world of the school. This is true even of many "systemic" initiatives, which typically struggle to delineate and integrate policies bearing on the school. In the process, many end up treating the school as if its effectiveness could be turned on by a remote switch. Similarly, reform initiatives launched on the inside of schools, by principals or small groups of teachers with or without consultants, typically put too much trust in add-on programs and one-shot professional development. Finally, both outside reformers and inside reformers seem to forget that schools typically exist within fractious communities. As George Counts put it in a sarcastic reference to the systemic initiatives of his own day: The Chicago public schools have always been, and probably always will be, for better or worse, in Chicago (Counts, 1928).

But what if policymakers at all levels promoted the new vision of education just described while respecting schools as they really are? Several colleagues and I at the Coalition of Essential Schools have studied this and other related questions over the course of nearly three years by means of a close study of 10 public secondary schools.[1] The schools, in nine states, offer contrasting policy contexts and contrasting settings: four urban, five suburban, one rural. We selected them because they seemed to offer a valuable dual perspective on the problems of achieving a reform genuinely oriented to the vision just expressed. Indeed, this proved true. First, their experience suggests that such reform *is* possible, despite all difficulties; second, their experience also suggests that such reform is *nearly* impossible, contrary to all hype.

The 10 schools we studied share a serious intention to reinvent themselves. Of course, they exercise this intention within a real world full of contrary influences that especially include the following three: ambivalence on the part of some or most of the schools' clients, both parents and students; resistance by the hierarchical systems that enmesh most of the schools; and certain deep dynamics of the status quo that can snare serious reform as an undertow snares a swimmer. Of these three foes, the first, ambivalence, can be overcome only through vigorous and politically skillful community outreach, which some of the schools in our study seem capable of undertaking and others not. The second, hierarchical resistance, can be overcome only through the thoughtful redesign of state and district policies, which is underway in some of the contexts of our study, though by no means all. The third, dynamics of the status quo, may be the hardest foe of all because these dynamics generally go unnoticed and unnamed even in such schools as those in our study, and one cannot overcome what one has not yet noticed.

In what follows, I name what I take to be seven such dynamics, suggested by our data. My purpose in naming them is not to suggest a definitive list, but rather to encourage other researchers and reformers to presume the existence of some such set of deep-system dynamics and to do their own work of naming and illuminating. Although I also mention one or two promising strategies for dealing with each of the seven dynamics, again suggested by our data, I believe that most of the work of inventing such practices still lies ahead. So my second purpose is to encourage such invention, especially by the people who run schools and work in them. Finally, I have a third purpose, one that undergirds the chapter's concluding section, where I use these seven dynamics to construct a template to serve the design and evaluation of education policy.

---

[1] The study was conducted between 1991 and 1993 by the Coalition of Essential Schools, a national network of some 700 reform-minded schools. It was funded principally by grants from the IBM Corporation and the UPS Foundation. It involved observations, interviews, and document analysis and also elicited writing from teachers and administrators in the schools themselves. See for example McDonald, Smith, Turner, Finney, and Barton (1993). A second book, detailing the study's findings, is (McDonald, 1996).

SEVEN DYNAMICS CONSTRAINING
DEEP CHANGE

A Preference for Central Authority
Over Shared Leadership

One sees this not only in school but throughout the education system. There is the abundance of reform initiatives in states and at the national level that all propose to employ a larger, more centrally placed lever. Energies run toward the center at the expense of what is mistakenly seen to be the periphery, namely, actual relationships between teachers and learners. The tendency is exacerbated in times of change because only enormous leverage is perceived to be capable of shifting an enormous weight. Complicating the picture at the school level is a tacit treaty that grants too much management authority to the principal and too much curricular and standard-setting authority to isolated teachers (Johnson, 1990). Again, this tendency may ironically be strengthened in times of change because in most contexts only the principal can wield enough power to marshal the outside resources that change demands, and to face the outside threats it generates. How can the principal be strong enough on the outside without throttling the development of middle-leadership structures on the inside? The problem, of course, is that a vision of education comprising a community of learners requires such middle-leadership structures. How else, for example, can a school achieve genuinely shared standards?

Our data suggest that even the rare principal who is aware of this dilemma and who manages it successfully may nonetheless face opposition from the school's "best" teachers because the definition of best teaching may rest on a presumption of isolation wherein one sets standards that heroically exceed the norm, shutting out the world beyond one's classroom in order to focus energy exclusively on the students. From the perspective of such teaching, the vision of a schoolwide community of learners may imply an abandonment of academic freedom.

The most promising strategies we have seen in our study sample for confronting the dynamic of central authority involve accountability mechanisms requiring collaboration across classrooms and subjects. In the schools we studied, these strategies have proved more effective in achieving shared leadership than have mechanisms for shared governance. Typically, they involve performance assessment systems invented by the schools themselves, sometimes combined with "descriptive reviews" or other mechanisms to focus on the needs and experiences of students who might otherwise elude notice (Weaver, 1992). In some of the schools, these assessment systems have grown quite elaborate and seem to be driving other changes (McDonald et al., 1993).

Yet, where they operate, these systems have also tended to alienate some subset of the faculty, among them some of the most successful practitioners of isolated teaching. In some cases this alienation has led such teachers to leave the school, and in at least one case, it has provoked considerable concern among parents and students. An effective way to deal with this situation, according to our evidence, is to acknowledge the tension, share with all concerned the rationale for change, and then insist on the change despite the possible loss of good people. Of course, these tasks typically require what is called a strong principal, and, indeed, most of the schools in our study have one. Thus, shared leadership is purchased, ironically, by an exertion of central authority. That may not be problematic so long as the principal who originated the change, and cares about shared leadership, remains in the job. Our study suggests that this may not be long, however; over the course of 3 years, the principalship in 7 of our 10 schools changed hands.

An Overreliance on Group Instruction at the Expense of Individual Learning

Even space and time in school are defined in terms of groups: classrooms and class hours. Being in school typically means being unremittingly part of a crowd. Of course, one of school's necessary functions is to teach children how to be part of a crowd, and certain kinds of crowds, discussion groups and cooperative task groups, for example, are essential for particular kinds of learning. But students also need opportunities for genuinely independent inquiry and for self-directed application and synthesis of the concepts they acquire (Gardner, 1989, 1991). It is not enough to consign these experiences to homework and seatwork because they require more time and resources than homework allows for, and more space and personal freedom than seatwork permits. The writer of a recent essay excoriating the excessive controls of school acknowledges that he got an idea for the essay while opening a can of chili (Brown, 1992). If students are to function as intellectuals in school rather than as empty vessels, then students too need some opportunity to intersperse concentration and productive distraction, to open cans of chili.

We did not find much chili-cooking in the schools we studied, outside the cafeteria kitchens that is; nor, in general, did we find much of the off-task informality of behavior and decor one finds in some independent and alternative schools—or indeed in many ordinary elementary-school class-rooms. That is a pity, because in the best circumstances such environments help create a sense of intellectual community independent of the instructional schedule. Ideally, what one wants is intellectual ownership—that a high-school student might occasionally think of the study of mathematics, for example, as an interest and commitment extending beyond the time he or she must sit in the mathematics classroom or at a desk or kitchen table working on highly directed homework. This presumes that the school allots time and space for other intellectual efforts besides going to class—for example, self-directed study and work in libraries, labs, or at computer work stations. By and large, the schools in our study did not handle this challenge very well.

Nonetheless, we found among them other promising practices relevant to dealing with this second dynamic. Several schools had collapsed the instructional schedule into large blocks of time managed by small teams of teachers, wherein students enjoyed greater opportunity to do more than sit attentively at small desks. Some of the schools also encouraged and even required community-based learning such as community service requirements and internships, allotting time and other resources to such experiences. Finally, most of the schools in our study encouraged project-based learning, which is undergoing a resurgence as well in other innovative schools (Olson, 1993). Some of the project work we saw happened within courses, but in a particularly encouraging development, some happened outside, too. In several cases, projects fulfill graduation requirements that exist on top of Carnegie-unit requirements. In another case, projects afford students the opportunity to gain honors-level distinction for courses, even though the project work itself happens entirely outside the courses' purview. In all cases, the project work in these schools has tended to foster teaching relationships and learning formats different from norms of classroom-based teaching and learning. In a few places it has also led to the introduction of new units of time and space: project and tutorial periods, offices for teachers, project rooms where resources for learning are generalized and students establish their own work priorities and routines.

The Habit of Maintaining Custody
of Students Through Close Supervision

The custodial imperative is strong in practice if not in law: Schools must hold students in custody while they teach them. The imperative is derived from reasonable concerns for safety and sensible awareness of the role that good direction plays in learning. Yet it is often entangled with compulsive attitudes about human behavior and with misconceptions about how people learn. Thus the close supervision of life in many schools—over studying, playing, eating, going to the bathroom, and especially working, thinking, and expressing oneself—ends up hobbling rather than enhancing learning. Indeed, it often proves counterproductive even in maintaining custody because many children held too tightly overall continuously look for places to spring loose. Finally, it impedes the growth of a learning culture by suppressing two of the most important tools of intellectual growth, namely curiosity and conflict. In the interest of maintaining custody, schools func-tion in myriad ways to prevent the kind of straying from task that is curiosity's currency and to prevent as well the expression and exploration of disagreement. So a school's people are packed safely into their respective places: the student seated silently at a little desk, the teacher standing behind a big desk, the principal shuffling papers at a still bigger desk, and the assistant principal conducting "hall sweeps" with a walkie-talkie. In such circumstances, some simple and necessary rituals of a learning culture—for example, regular and spirited faculty meetings, school convocations, and forays into the outside world—may be viewed as threats to the custodial status quo. Any more radical departures from the norm may be seen as utterly impossible. Open, hour-long lunches? Inconceivable.

The project-based learning experiences mentioned earlier in association with the second dynamic lend themselves to resisting the third dynamic too. Especially powerful are opportunities to pursue a project outside school walls during school hours. Indeed, any community-based learning experiences are helpful in promoting the idea that schools can teach indirectly as well as directly, and that mechanisms can be invented to keep students safe and productive even in the most difficult environments. Helpful in another way are the advisory and governance systems we saw in a few of our study's schools designed to foster personal responsibility and a sense of community. These include daily or weekly small-group meetings to discuss students' academic progress and problems and monthly schoolwide "town meetings" to discuss school issues and foster community building.

The Tendency to Turn Inward and to Discount Outside Perspectives

This tendency is expressed in various and even conflicting ways. There is disdain for parents and also fear of them. They are openly welcomed, but as guests, not "family." Parent involvement is secretly depicted negatively by many teachers, even as reformers are clamoring for new and better programs to support it. Similarly, businesses are invited to "adopt" schools but find themselves frozen out of any influence on the adopted school's operations. As for researchers, there is a persistent perception among school people that researchers are hopelessly out of touch with the realities of schooling, though schools also exhibit a tendency to inflate the value of research findings. This paradox is a derivative of the quest for nostrums, much encouraged by the cottage industries of school improvement and in-service professional development, and ultimately self-sealing. "We tried that already" is the chant of an enterprise prone to frequent and superficial innovation, one accustomed to the translation of radical ideas into shopworn practice. Finally, in still another manifestation of this dynamic, there is a perilously shortsighted tendency to discount the importance of education policy, particularly at the state or national level. This is part of the closed-door syndrome, the confidence that nearly every teacher carries within that if worse comes to worst, he or she can always close the door and do whatever he or she pleases inside the classroom. Of course, the reliance on this safety valve is a powerful disincentive to build genuine collegiality, to maintain common standards, to engage in team teaching, and to otherwise participate in the construction of the vision outlined at the beginning of this chapter.

Among the 10 study schools, we have seen a number of promising strategies aimed at undoing the various dimensions of this dynamic. One involves attempts to ensure that a significant number of people who work in a school live in the community that supports the school and are in other respects connected with that community. Once again, community-based learning experiences are powerful here too, insofar as they dispute the idea of the school as a self-reliant institution. Effective too are efforts to link the inside and the outside of schools through telecommunications, though these are in a very early stage of development in our study's schools.

One promising strategy we have observed is counterintuitive. It involves a reconceptualization of the school's relationship to outside expertise. Conventionally, schools receive new knowledge about curriculum, methods of instruction, and so on, from intermediate agencies who provide policy interventions, textbook changes, technical assistance, and in-servicing. By contrast, all 10 schools in our study are relatively experienced in inventing their own knowledge about these things. They are members of a network, the Coalition of Essential Schools, a network that is increasingly led by people who work in schools, one that increasingly generates its own cross-school consulting expertise. One result is that a significant proportion of the study's schools seem in charge of their own professional development in a way that is quite rare. That is not to say that the schools regard themselves as self-sufficient. In fact, we have observed a contrary effect in these schools, which is why I say that this strategy is counterintuitive. Because these schools feel more confident in assessing their own needs and more aware of their own capacity to address them, they are also more deliberate about soliciting outside consultation when that is appropriate. Indeed, this is the key difference: These schools hire consultants rather than in-service providers. That is, they contract with expertise they can draw upon as needed over time, rather than with one-shot expertise capable at best of providing one jolt of insight on an in-service afternoon. In an exceedingly promising development, there are even signs that one or two of the schools we studied are having an impact on state policy by demanding that it align with the schools' innovations.

The Assumption That the
School's Essential Function Is Meritocratic

Much of what is demanded by economic circumstances, specified by new conceptions of intelligence and learning, and suggested by new views of an optimally functioning organization, run counter to the idea of the school as a sorting machine, but the idea is deeply ingrained in practice and easily survives rhetorical assault. "All students will achieve at high levels," says the school, in accordance with the state's new goals, but in the hearts of principals, teachers, and parents, conditions are added: ". . . in proportion to their abilities, within the traditional hierarchy of achievement, consistent with their family background, given their probable career paths, and so forth." As in all winnowing organizations, an individual's worth is defined by very narrow criteria: one's grade point average, one's willingness to bake cookies for the senior bake sale, one's capacity for speaking and thinking like the majority or elite group. Even in some of the socioeconomically most homogeneous communities in the U.S., schools act as if their function were to manufacture status differences. Undergirding this phenomenon is the widespread attachment to a theory of intelligence as a unitary and easily measurable gift from the gene pool.

Taken as a whole, the schools in our study would seem to be less meritocratic in their orientation than most secondary schools in the U.S., and some of them astonishingly so. Yet, buffeted by parental fears and expectations, most also harbor meritocratic practices. In this respect, they mirror the views of most Americans whose own experience in schools and in the economy seems to belie the idea that all people really can be taught to use their minds well.

The most promising practice in confronting this dynamic that we have seen involves more than the simple substitution of heterogeneous classes for tracked ones. That can lead easily to parental backlash, despite all assurances of research findings on the value of heterogeneity; indeed, this has happened in one of our study's schools. A better strategy is to strive for an optimal balance between heterogeneity and differentiation. So the school emphasizes the value of diverse perspectives, intelligences, and skills, and it highlights methods such as seminar-based learning, problem-based learning, and cooperative learning. It also acknowledges that students differ in all kinds of ways, and especially in ways that do not show up on intelligence tests and do not cut across the entire spectrum of human capacity. It highlights methods such as individual project work or intense instructional environments as in advanced foreign language or advanced computer science. The goal here is to reconstitute the school as a community of equal intellectual strivers, all of whom pursue some areas of specialization.

The Tendency to Define Teaching as a Narrative Activity

In this image of their work, teachers, like novelists, construct narrative bridges across the incomprehensibility of experience viewed close up. They build these narratives with material supplied by scholarship they have encountered, curriculum frameworks from various sources, the stories they, too, were taught, and, of course, textbooks. They invest themselves in these stories and believe in the transformative power of them (McDonald, 1992). For their part, learners yield themselves to the power of the stories, though it is presumed that, like good readers, they eventually turn a critical eye. Yet the turn of this critical eye, the opportunity to reconstruct what has been delivered, is often expected to happen, if indeed at all, in the student's own time and space, outside the teacher's purview. That's for homework, for private study in preparation for the unit test, for college. The result is a phenomenon much in evidence in today's schools: "But I taught him," the teacher says. "It's not my problem if he didn't learn."

The new vision for teaching outlined at the start of this chapter needs a different metaphor than that of teaching as narrative. Cognitive scientists, among others, suggest *scaffolding* as a substitute, or *coaching* (Paris & Winograd, 1990; Sizer, 1984, 1992). In both cases, the new metaphor suggests that what matters after all is what the student constructs, not what the teacher intends. Both metaphors also imply an enormous shift in the strategies of schoolkeeping as well as teaching. Teachers now teach like storytellers partly because the setup of most schools suggests that they do. This involves some of the features discussed previously—the reliance on large-group instruction, the custodial role of teachers, the centripetal habit of school that makes the teacher as powerful within a single room as the principal is powerful in his or her domain and the superintendent in his or hers. It also involves the idea of curriculum as something parceled out and covered, the didactically oriented furnishings of most classrooms and the loneliness of teaching.

Addressing this dynamic in our study's schools has often involved the assiduous cultivation of alternative norms. One school has devoted years of work and training to seminar-based teaching. Others are nearly as devoted to other nondidactic methods such as cooperative learning and project-based learning. Yet in all these schools, the narrative grip has been weakened rather than broken. The effect seems strongest, though, where the cultivation of other methods has been combined with the adoption of longer teaching blocks and some team teaching. It is harder to be a storyteller for 2 hours straight than it is for 45 minutes at a time. It is harder to tell joint stories than to tell one's own. In fact, it may be that to plan together in any extended way, teachers must come to terms with the fact that human beings, whether in a collegial relationship or a pedagogical one, do not communicate directly, but always through transformative media and always on the basis of a mutual construction of meaning conditioned by values.

The Tendency to Privilege Teacher Performance
Over Student Performance

This dynamic derives from the previous two tendencies, but it is anchored also in a well-meaning conspiracy to encourage students and to preserve teachers' self-esteem. So the exhibition of student performance is reserved typically for only the best and most finished work: the papers that get tacked to the bulletin board, the speeches delivered at the assembly, the project that makes it to the science fair. Lost amid this conspiracy are opportunities for students to struggle openly with difficult tasks among multiple coaches and the varied perspectives of other strugglers, for them to grasp thereby that minds construct their own understandings, and for them to tolerate thereby the fact that failure is an essential ingredient in the pursuit of intellectual achievement.

In a book by Jackson, Boostrom, and Hansen (1993), the researchers ponder in one passage the significance of the fact that, in a wall display, one teacher has hung a boy's crudely drawn map of Sierra Leone amid his classmates' more carefully drawn maps of other African countries. Does it mean, they wonder, that the teacher does not see or value the difference? Their question is appropriate, because that may be in fact the case, but the question also illustrates the problem here. In fact, teachers cannot teach for understanding by encouraging and permitting the exhibition of impressive performance only. In an important sense, understanding *is* performance (Gardner, Perkins, & Perrone, 1992), or, at least, one cannot work on it, either as teacher or student, in any other mode. Student performance must come out from the margins of school. Getting it out will not be easy, however. Ironically, the current infatuation with performance-based assessment may hurt rather than help because it implicitly fosters a judgmental climate, and suspicions of a judgmental climate are exactly what keeps performance marginalized. The teacher and sometimes the student fears that someone else, on seeing unimpressive performance, may secretly think, "So, *this* is supposed to be good!" The solution, of course, is the cultivation of a performance-based culture for learning and teaching, one within which assessment plays a role. Trying to get there by overemphasizing that role, however, may prove counterproductive.

On the other hand, a number of the schools in our study use performance assessment to good effect in addressing this dynamic (McDonald et al., 1993). The difference may be that they control the terms of its use rather than suffer its imposition. Most of the schools call these performance assessments *exhibitions*, the term favored by the Coalition of Essential Schools. Three of the schools have even preserved some of the term's 18th-century connotation through their use of Exhibition Days, occasions when the school invites outsiders to come inside to observe and evaluate actual student performance (McDonald, 1993). The point is to accustom these visiting stakeholders, as well as the school's own teachers and students, to a face-to-face accountability grounded in the real understandings of actual people.

A TEMPLATE FOR POLICY

These dynamics are not elements in a deterministic scheme to thwart all attempts at genuine school reform in the U.S. Nor am I at all pessimistic about the ultimate chances of such reform. I simply believe those chances rest, among other things like luck, pluck, and the imagination of school leaders, on the willingness of all reformers to acknowledge the real features of the environment they address.

If I am right in assuming that the dynamics we discerned in our small sample of high schools are integral features of this environment, then they must be confronted and resolved. In particular, any policy that aims to promote the vision of schooling outlined at the start of this chapter must be constructed with the dynamics in mind. To serve this purpose, I propose a template, a simple list of questions to superimpose on some real or imagined policy implementation, seven questions, each tied to a dynamic:

1. How is this policy likely to affect the balance between central and shared leadership in schools?
2. Will the policy enhance or disturb the overreliance of school on grouping?
3. How will the policy affect schools' custodial instincts?
4. Does the policy account for the schools' usual avoidance of outside perspectives?
5. How does the policy square with the meritocratic assumptions?
6. Does the policy take account of teachers' typical reliance on a narrative style of teaching?
7. Where does the policy stand with respect to the relative importance attached to teacher performance and student performance in school?

Of course, the purpose of such questions is not to serve the construction of some universal school reform policy, one capable in a single swipe of neutralizing all seven dynamics. It is merely to help the reformer anticipate the likely pattern of environmental backlash reform will generate, and to offer valuable counsel: "Better make a frontal assault here. Go easy there and you'll just get a minor but tolerable skirmish." Of course, some dynamics will always appear more salient than others in a particular case, but sometimes the low-lying ones need just as much attention.

Let us try out the template on a real policy, one described recently in an *Education Week* article headlined, "Mass. Leads Mounting Charge Against Ability Grouping" (Schmidt, 1993).[2] The military rhetoric of the headline notwithstanding, the Massachusetts policy described here, although forthright, is also sensibly circumscribed. It aims to discourage the grouping of students by perceived ability through the award or denial of state funds earmarked for dropout prevention and remedial education, but it focuses nearly exclusively on middle schools. According to statistics cited in the article, it is enjoying some success to date. Can the template suggest why this may be so, and what obstacles may lie ahead?

---

[2]The analysis that follows is based exclusively on the *Education Week* report and is meant to be merely illustrative.

The policy has certainly stirred Dynamic 5: the assumption that the purpose of school is meritocratic, which appears to be the most salient in this application of the template. There is some evidence in the article to suggest, however, that the policy avoids direct confrontation with the theory of intelligence that undergirds this dynamic. By encouraging "heterogeneous grouping," for example, the policy may appear implicitly to endorse the validity of what are undoubtedly crudely conceived status differences: One student has *this* much ability, although another has *that* much more, yet they may profitably learn together in the same group. Meanwhile, the policy seems to acquiesce to Dynamic 2: the focus on *grouping* as the basic organizational principle of teaching. It makes the pragmatic argument that mixed groups offer a better deal to the least "bright" students in terms of "reaching their full potential," as well as to the state in terms of its interest in preventing dropouts. The policy is working well at the middle-school level, but it is probably headed for trouble in the bastion of meritocracy, the high school. It might fare better there, however, if its basic argument were revised to something such as the following. "Current grouping practices are based on crude and invalid measures. As such, they severely constrain all individual learners' opportunities to excel. What is needed is less grouping overall, with more opportunity for students to follow a relatively independent course, with most remaining large groups designed to provide the benefits of diverse perspectives." Of course, were the state to direct the policy in the way I suggest, it would likely stir up three other dynamics: (a) Dynamic 3: How will schools maintain custody if not by means of grouping? (b) Dynamic 6: How can teachers actually teach to diverse groups without aiming at the middle and losing their audience at the extremes? and (c) Dynamic 7: What will students do in school if they are not always sitting at attention in groups? Yet, these may be the most important dynamics to stir up. They may be the ones that especially block efforts to de-track schools. A de-tracking policy that does not stir them up may risk doing nothing much of lasting value.

Of course, whenever a state does any kind of stirring, it risks the wrath of Dynamic 4: The school may close its doors to the meddling world outside. What does the Massachusetts policy do to prevent this? Well, it smartly eschews mandate because, as the article reveals, it would first have to seek authority to mandate in this area. It works instead with the carrot and stick of funding awards and denials and also with the bully pulpit. The state's lead person on the issue is clearly conversant with the research in the area and seems savvy as well in how to use it to affect the climate of opinion. For example, references in the article suggest that he has cultivated the support of the state's child advocacy groups, and perhaps also of the teacher education establishment. There is no suggestion, however, that he is at work on the most difficult constituency of all: parents.

In the matter of the policy's impact on Dynamic 1, the centripetal tendency in leadership, the record is mixed. After all, this is a state-level policy, albeit a restrained one, and only the federal government is more remote from where the real action is. But as the article points out, a federal court is currently hearing a complaint by the NAACP against tracking in the Amherst-Pelham (Massachusetts) school district. The combination of a little muscle from the state plus the threat of a lot of muscle from a federal court has induced centripetal tendencies as well at the school level. The article quotes a couple of principals who are clearly "mounting" their own "charge" for heterogeneous grouping, perhaps making it the defining issue of their principalships; it also quotes one principal, from the Amherst-Pelham district, who has obviously staked out a spirited position for himself on the other side of an issue that is portrayed throughout the article, and perhaps implicitly by the policy, as two-sided. Of course, certain elements of this issue, those involving equity, are perhaps best viewed as two-sided: Either schools treat all their students equitably or they do not. Other elements are best considered multifaceted: Over the entire course of schooling, what is the optimal balance among independent learning and group learning, between small groups and large groups, between common perspectives and diverse perspectives, between task-oriented groups and process-oriented groups?

Is the template useful in this case? Perhaps only the Massachusetts policy makers can say for certain, because they must apply it to a much more complex environment than a single article in *Education Week* can possibly convey. If this template can make even a small contribution toward one state's efforts to implement the vision sketched at the start of this article, however, and if it can help avoid even one impolitic move that might make matters worse for Massachusetts children, then I would say that it is useful indeed.

REFERENCES

Bolman, L. G., & Deal, T. E. (1991). *Reframing organizations.* San Francisco: Jossey-Bass.

Brown, C. (1992, September 16). Stolen learning. *Education Week*, p. 27.

Bruer, J. T. (1993). *Schools for thought: A science of learning in the classroom.* Cambridge, MA: MIT Press.

Cohen, D., McLaughlin, M., & Talbert, J. (1993). *Teaching for understanding: Challenges for practice, research, and policy.* San Francisco: Jossey-Bass.

Counts, G. S. (1928). *School and society in Chicago.* New York: Harcourt, Brace & Jovanovich.

Fiske, E. B. (1991). *Smart schools, smart kids.* New York: Simon & Schuster.

Fullan, M. G. (1991). *The new meaning of educational change*. New York: Teachers College Press.

Gardner, H. (1989). *To open minds*. New York: Basic Books.

Gardner, H. (1991). *The unschooled mind*. New York: Basic Books.

Gardner, H., Perkins, D., & Perrone, V. (1992). *Teaching for understanding project*. (Interim report to the Spencer Foundation, Harvard Graduate School of Education.) Boston, MA: Harvard University.

Gould, S. J. (1981). *The mismeasure of man*. New York: Norton.

Jackson, P. W., Boostrom, R. E., & Hansen, D. T. (1993). *The moral life of schools*. San Francisco: Jossey-Bass.

Johnson, S. M. (1990). *Teachers at work*. New York: Basic.

Jones, B. F., & Idol, L. (1990). *Dimensions of thinking and cognitive instruction*. Hillsdale, NJ: Lawrence Erlbaum Associates.

Mauriel, J. J. (1989). *Strategic leadership for schools*. San Francisco: Jossey-Bass.

McDonald, J. P. (1992). *Teaching: Making sense of an uncertain craft*. New York: Teachers College Press.

McDonald, J. P. (1993). Three pictures of an exhibition: Warm, cool, and hard. *Phi Delta Kappan, 74*, 480–485.

McDonald, J. P. (1996). *Redesigning school*. San Francisco: Jossey-Bass.

McDonald, J. P., Smith, S., Turner, D., Finney, M., & Barton, E. (1993). *Graduation by exhibition: Assessing genuine achievement*. Alexandria, VA: Association for Supervision and Curriculum Development.

Meier, D. (1992). Reinventing teaching. *Teachers College Record, 93*(4), 594–609.

Meier, D. (1993). Transforming schools into powerful communities. *Teachers College Record, 94*(3), 354–358.

Olson, L. (1993, February 17). Progressive-era concept now breaks mold: NASDC schools explore "project learning." *Education Week*, pp. 6–7.

Paris, S. G., & Winograd, P. (1990). How metacognition can promote academic learning and instruction. In B. F. Jones & L. Idol (Eds.), *Dimensions of thinking and cognitive instruction* (pp. 15–51). Hillsdale, NJ: Lawrence Erlbaum Associates.

Perkins, D. (1992). *Smart schools: From training memories to educating minds*. New York: Free Press.

Resnick, L. B. & Resnick, D. P. (1991). Assessing the thinking curriculum: New tools for educational reform. In B. R. Gifford & M. C. O'Connor (Eds.), *Changing assessments: Alternative views of aptitude, achievement and instruction*. (pp. 37–75). Boston: Kluwer.

Sarason, S. (1971). *The culture of the school and the problem of change*. Boston: Allyn-Bacon.

Sarason, S. (1990). *The predictable failure of educational reform*. San Francisco: Jossey-Bass.

Schmidt, P. (1993, January 13). Mass. leads mounting charge against ability grouping. *Education Week*, pp. 1, 22, 24.

Senge, P. M. (1990). *The fifth discipline*. New York: Doubleday.

Sizer, T. R. (1984). *Horace's compromise: The dilemma of the American high school*. Boston: Houghton Mifflin.

Sizer, T. R. (1992). *Horace's school*. Boston: Houghton Mifflin.

Weaver, A. (Ed.). (1992). *Exploring values and standards: Implications for assessment*. New York: Teachers College, Columbia University, National Center for Restructuring Education, Schools, and Teaching.

Wolf, D., Bixby, J., Glenn, J., III, & Gardner, H. (1991). To use their minds well: Investigating new forms of student assessment. In G. Grant (Ed.), *Review of Research in Education* (Vol. 17, pp. 31–74). Washington, DC: American Educational Research Association.

Wood, G. H. (1992). *Schools that work*. New York: Dutton.

AUTHOR INDEX

SUBJECT INDEX